The Middle Ages in Texts and Texture

In memory of
Professor Robert Brentano (1926–2002)

Contents

Foreword

This is a book like no other. It resonates with the imagination of a teacher-scholar who never forgot what it was like to be a student. It is made for the bright and bewildered (of all ages) who, like Robert Brentano, are prepared to see how the original sources of medieval history are not so much answers as they are questions, questions quite as challenging to teachers as to students. With the help in this book of some who have lived and wrestled with these sources intensively, such readers may learn how to question the past and may well discover why all of us who look back need to question the evidence and its creators alike.

What the authors of this book have achieved is not simply the commemoration of a revered teacher; this is neither *Festschrift* nor memorial. It is a living testimonial *sui generis* to a way of engaging with history that is remembered, to be sure, but that is compelling in its actuality. The memory of Robert Brentano in the classroom, text in one hand, gestural imagination in the other, challenging students with his incomparable enthusiasm— yes, that is here, indeed, and who could wish it otherwise? This volume originated in a rarely successful day of sessions in honor of Professor Brentano, and in his presence, at the International Congress on Medieval Studies in Kalamazoo, Michigan, in May 2002. The authors showed there how *their* teaching, from the close reading of texts, carries on a singular and exemplary way of getting at the truths and beauties of medieval history.

Those panels at Kalamazoo were the most intellectually exciting events I have ever encountered in a scholarly conference. Something of that excitement quivers still in the pages of this book. But turning such an occasion into a book cannot have been easy. To their credit, the authors have not attempted to replicate their presentations, an experience that surely defies cross-generic imitation. Rather they have sought in their own ways to translate an exemplary pedagogy into a durably useful form for the benefit of students and teachers. And such "translation" illustrates a further point. The strength of the Brentano pedagogy lies in its humane openness to each and every style of teaching. That is why, if the text-in-hand method flickers in this book, it flickers like an eternal flame. How do we make sense of a great yet distant civilization through its artifacts? Here are the well-pondered approaches of experienced teachers who have tried.

Thomas N. Bisson,
Emeritus Henry Charles Lea Professor of Medieval History,
Harvard University

Acknowledgements

This volume was inspired by the teaching of Professor Robert Brentano. It is also dedicated to his memory. Professor Brentano died suddenly at the age of 76 during the fall semester of 2002. He was teaching that term at the University of California at Berkeley, where he had served on the faculty in the Department of History for more than fifty years. During his tenure there, he taught regularly his survey of the Middle Ages, a lower-division course that typically attracted more than 200 students from across the university. Some took the course because it satisfied breadth requirements or a requirement within the history major. Some took it out of a romantic sense for the Middle Ages. And at least a handful of students I taught as a teaching assistant in the early 1990s took the class because previous generations in their family had taken his courses — one engineering student told me that three of his four grandparents had taken courses from Professor Brentano and that both of his parents had taken his survey course. Whatever their reasons for signing up, all students were treated to a demanding and engaging experience perhaps unlike most others they would have during their undergraduate years at Berkeley. I know that this was true not only for me, when I took the course in 1986 as a sophomore, but also for several of the contributors to this volume who first encountered the medieval world in this survey course or first taught the period as his teaching assistants. We now teach our own courses, which in one way or another derive from that course. The experience of teaching with Professor Brentano has therefore shaped the perspective of each of the authors whose essays appear in this book. And I know that they join me in acknowledging our profound debt to this wonderful man who has touched all of our lives. We would also like to thank Carroll Brentano and her family for sharing him with us over the years.

As I conceived and developed this project, I sought counsel from count-less colleagues and friends to whom I am grateful. There are too many to name here, but I must thank, in particular, Courtney Booker, Scott Bruce, Maryanne Kowaleski, Paul Lerner, Anne Lester, Victoria Morse, Bill North, Clementine Oliver, Ramzi Rouighi, Jay Rubenstein, and Terry Seip for the support and suggestions they provided at various stages of this project. Likewise, I am indebted to the two (once-anonymous) readers solicited by Columbia University Press, Thomas Bisson and Adam Kosto, who read the manuscript carefully and offered suggestions and critique that were tremendously helpful when, ultimately, I prepared the manuscript for pro-duction at the University of Toronto Press. The transition from one press, to the other was facilitated by Christine Mortlock and Wendy Lochner of Columbia University Press who were remarkably supportive of the project even after it became apparent that it was not a good fit for their press — Christine, in particular, did everything she could to make the transition to the University of Toronto Press as quick and smooth as possible.

My experience with UTP has been extraordinary at every level. The History Editor, Natalie Fingerhut, was enthusiastic about the project from the first and has accelerated its long-delayed publication. It has truly been a pleasure to work with her and to see how smoothly she, Beate Schwirtlich, Anna Del Col, freelancer Ashley Rayner, and the rest of the editorial staff at UTP have moved this project through production. I sim-ply can't imagine a more effective production team. That team also includes Betsy Struthers, who copy-edited the volume and has thus spared readers countless infelicities to which I would have otherwise subjected them, and Joan Eadie, who created the index that will, I expect, be put to good use. I am likewise grateful to Ashley Dotterweich, an excellent stu-dent at the University of Southern California, who helped me to prepare the manuscript for submission to the press.

I am fortunate to have drawn not merely on the skills of these generous and talented people, but also on the financial support of several institu-tions. At the beginning, this project was conceived and developed while I was supported by a fellowship from the Mellon Foundation to be a mem-ber of the School of Historical Studies at the Institute for Advanced Study in Princeton. As the project nears completion, the Department of History at the University of California, Berkeley, generously provided a subvention to offset the production costs of the volume inspired by and dedicated to one of its greatest figures. So, too, has the College and the Department of

History at the University of Southern California, and to both I owe a debt of gratitude. I also wish to thank Italica Press and Ronald Musto for permission to use his map of fourteenth-century Rome in Chapter 24 and the University of Toronto Press for permission to quote at length from Paul Edward Dutton's *Charlemagne's Courtier* in Chapter 9.

My debt is of course greatest to my colleagues who have contributed to this volume. I appreciate profoundly the patience they've demonstrated since the spring of 2002 when we gathered together with Professor Brentano at the International Medieval Congress in Kalamazoo for a day-long series of presentations and discussions about some of the texts he used in his survey course. Some of their essays were already ready for publication at that time, but it has taken a long time — too long a time! — for their essays and this volume to make their way to print.

Finally, I'd like to thank my wife Vickie and my son Dimitri for their patience and support especially as this project drew to a close. The former still recalls with fondness the sparkle in Professor Brentano's eyes when she first met him more than 20 years ago. Unfortunately, the latter never had a chance to meet him — he was born a mere six months after his death. I hope that Dimitri and his generation of students will see that sparkle reflected in the following pages and appreciate this volume, among other things, as a celebration of the man who meant so much to me, to the contributors to this volume, and to the countless students, teachers, and colleagues he inspired over the years.

Jason Glenn
Los Angeles, CA
31 January 2011

A Note on References

Each of the essays in this volume is followed by a very brief bibliographic note. These notes are not meant to be comprehensive or complete. Limitations of space do not permit it. Nor does the genre of the volume require it, for these essays are more akin to lectures offered to students in the classroom or narratives developed in textbooks; in both cases, scholars draw on their years of research and learning to share with others, but they don't cite at each turn the particular work from which the points they make are drawn. The authors of these essays do, however, identify and give full bibliographic references for the primary sources on which their essays are based, and they refer readers to some scholarship, almost exclusively in English, from which they draw or which they think readers will find useful for further study or bibliographic orientation. In addition to these fully referenced materials, some authors also acknowledge by name scholars whose work they have used in their essay, that is, scholars whose works would typically be cited in footnotes of more formal academic writing. These abbreviated acknowledgements aim to underscore for readers that the essays, like all intellectual undertakings, represent the fruits of many scholars' labors.

References to primary texts within the essays themselves are parenthetical. They are as spare as possible so as to minimize the distraction to the reader. In essays where multiple texts are discussed, short and abbreviated titles are used to refer to the titles of the works under consideration. No such titles are used where context permits the reader to identify the text easily. Nor are they used in essays that cite only a single text.

Because many of the texts discussed in these essays are available in numerous translations, whenever possible parenthetical citations refer to the most generic divisions of the texts—i.e., books and chapter divisions, laisses (stanzas) or lines in poetry, etc. Otherwise, references to page numbers of particular translations are used. The use of page numbers and, for that matter, any exceptions or other idiosyncrasies of citation within particular essays are noted in the corresponding bibliographic notes.

Finally, given the nature of the volume and limitations in space, footnotes have been kept to an absolute minimum. They have been used principally for references to primary source material not otherwise featured in the essays. On rare occasions they have been used for essential references to scholarship.

Introduction

Jason Glenn

Introductory and survey history courses are often taught in a way described as "little steps for little feet." That means you start slowly into history and only gradually discover that history is difficult, complex, disturbing, and uncertain. This course is the opposite of the "little feet" approach. It means to pick you up off your feet and hit your head against the wall with the very first source. You will find from the beginning how difficult and complex history is, how difficult and complex a source can be. You will know from the first that the pleasures of history are always connected with complexity and difficulty…. [History] is extremely difficult, and extremely rewarding. History is also instructive…. Although history doesn't teach you morality, it does teach you to look at the complexity of issues. There are no simple problems in history. They are all difficult, and they are difficult in exactly the way that political and moral problems are today. The people with whom we are dealing are — or we would not bother to study them — real people who bleed and die, kill and are killed in the same way as us. If it works, history teaches you to think that people in distant and different places are as real as we are.[1]

— *Robert Brentano*

This book aims to introduce readers to the history of Europe in the Middle Ages. As such, it is intended principally for student use in courses at the college level, particularly — but not exclusively — introductory courses.

---

[1] This quotation comes from a lecture delivered by Professor Robert Brentano to students at the University of California, Berkeley, in History 4b ("Western Civilization: The Middle Ages") on 27 August 1986. The lecture was transcribed and made available to students by the Black Lightning Lecture Notes service at the A.S.U.C. Store of the University of California, Berkeley.

But it is not a textbook. There is no overarching narrative, no systematic attempt to offer a coherent overview of the period. In this age of information, such overviews and narratives are readily available elsewhere. Besides, in my estimation—informed as it is by the teaching of Robert Brentano—they don't make for the best introductions. In efforts to make the past comprehensible, they too often smooth over and simplify the complexity of the human experience. The genre of the textbook requires it. Yet, if we assume, as I think we must, that those people who lived in the Middle Ages were "as real as we are," then before we revert to generalizations about the period or, worse, accept such generalizations offered to us in textbooks, we need to meet at least some of these people, to see what mattered to them, and to trouble over why. In short, we need to develop a sense for the texture of the medieval world. And to do so, we must study the texts produced in it and struggle with the difficulties they present.

The essays in this volume do precisely this. Each focuses on one text or on a few related texts. Some offer close readings that aim to bring the reader into the concerns and world of a single author. Others develop broader themes raised by individual texts or through a comparison of materials within a genre. Indeed, there is no single template or model to which the contributors were asked to conform. Nevertheless, their contributions cohere in spirit.

Each of the essays provides basic information about the texts, their authors, and the larger settings in which they were written. In their interpretive approaches, the authors of these essays explore a range of historical problems, issues, and themes so that readers may see more clearly how, from primary texts, we can glimpse central developments and changes in medieval society, how to cull evidence from such texts, and how to use those texts and the opportunities they present to reflect on the norms and institutions of the period. But this volume does not aspire to—nor could a collection of this sort achieve—any sort of summary knowledge. It can only offer a finite number of points of entry into the medieval world and invite readers to explore it with a depth that most other introductory works do not and cannot. For those who are interested in the complexities of the past, this is a tradeoff worth making.

The texts discussed in these essays—and arranged in chronological order—span the period from the end of the fourth century to the turn of the fifteenth, and they range geographically across Europe and the Mediterranean, from Iberia in the west to the Bosporus in the east and from north Africa to the northern reaches of Britain. Many—indeed, most—of these texts are well-known classics from the Middle Ages and are commonly used in courses on medieval Europe or Western civilization. And they come from a wide range of genres. But the histories, chronicles, biographies, autobiographies, hagiography, legal texts, travelogues, and literature discussed in these essays are all exceptional works written by exceptional people. In other words, in a society of low literacy rates we have, for the most part, narrative and literary texts produced by a social and cultural elite. As such, we have only a partial view into this society.

This introduction to the Middle Ages is, then, just that, an introduction to—a start, a point of departure for the exploration of—the period and the texts produced in it. But it also introduces readers to a number of ways we can think about those texts and the world in which they were created. For those who never pursue further study of the period, it should provide a sense for the texture of the medieval world and what it means to study it—that is, how to do history rather than to learn it. Those who do wish to explore this world further, however, will find themselves well-prepared to encounter other sources and types of evidence that will permit them to develop an ever richer and more nuanced sense for the period. In short, *The Middle Ages in Texts and Texture* can stand on its own as an introduction to medieval Europe and as an invitation to study the texts it has left behind.

This volume cannot, however—and would never hope to—replace the dynamic exchange between instructor and student or, for that matter, between student and text. Quite the contrary. It is inspired by such exchanges and the excitement that they offer. But it is a very different matter to write about texts than to engage in classroom discussion about them, for the dynamism and flow of such exchanges, interactions, and collaborative exploration generate a type of spontaneity that cannot truly be captured in the written genre. Nevertheless, individually and collectively, these essays aim to capture the essence of what the experience of working with our texts in the classroom can offer. And it is my hope that these essays, and the volume as a whole, can contribute to and stimulate further classroom discussions of both the texts discussed herein and others read with them. Because each of the essays is self-contained and requires no previous knowledge, each can be read with or without the particular texts discussed. But this book is perhaps best used—and this should come as no surprise— in conjunction with readings in primary texts and documents of all sorts. Whether as a complement to lectures an instructor might offer or even alongside a textbook of the more traditional sort, it will serve as a powerful reminder that our texts do not merely illustrate the larger points offered in those lectures or textbooks. They also present myriad and exciting opportunities for the exploration of the medieval world and for encounters with "people as real as we are" who inhabited and shaped it.

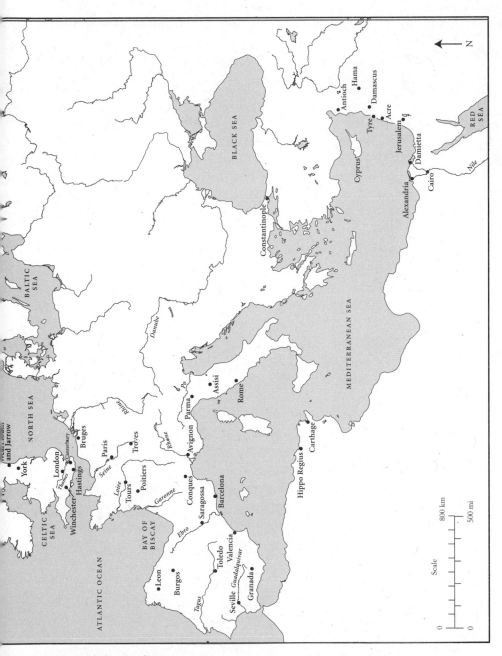

Europe and the Mediterranean.

ONE

Hearing Voices in Late Antiquity
An Aural Approach to Augustine's *Confessions*

William North

When Aurelius Augustinus was born in 354, the Roman Empire had been officially Christian for little more than a generation. The Council of Nicaea (325), which sought to settle a number of practical and theological differences among Christians, and the death of Emperor Constantine the Great (337), who had famously converted to Christianity and convened the council, were recent memories for his parents. Indeed, the ongoing theological strife among Christians throughout his youth — whether between Arians and Catholics, who could not agree over the nature of the Trinity, or the more local conflict between Catholics and Donatists about how to deal with Christians who had renounced their faith during the great persecutions under Constantine's predecessor, Diocletian (d. 311) — made Christian doctrine seem anything but settled. Augustine's world also stubbornly, if subtly, maintained its connection to the pagan past through its calendar, communal rituals, and sacred structures that dotted town and countryside. Although Emperor Julian's (361–63) efforts to restore traditional Roman religion were cut short by his death and would not be repeated, the triumph of Christianity over paganism still seemed far from self-evident (8.5). Even at the time of his death in 430, the Roman world of Augustine continued to struggle with religious diversity, the project of conversion, and the full implications of the Christian faith for individual and society.

Augustine's own family and history reflected this complexity. While his mother Monica was a devout Catholic, his father Patricius did not convert to Christianity until late in life (9.9). Although from a Christian household (1.11), Augustine pursued an education shaped by classical notions of *paideia* with its emphasis on the mastery of Latin grammar and rhetoric through intensive study and imitation of pagan Latin authors like Virgil and Cicero (1.9, 1.13–18, 3.3–4). To be sure, Augustine knew elements of the Christian faith and recalled being suspicious of philosophies where the name of Jesus Christ and the Scriptures were absent (3.3). But in most other respects the world and values of his youth were those of classical pagan Rome, and he was encouraged by his parents to excel at them, for they were the guarantors of success, status, and wealth (1.9, 3.3). Social ambition, not Christianity, set the agenda for Augustine's youth.

Funded by the meager savings of his father (2.1) and aided by a local magnate who supported his studies and remained one of his trusted supporters throughout his life, the 18-year-old Augustine left Thagaste for Carthage, the provincial capital. There he found not only advanced training in rhetoric but also the woman who would be, for the next 14 years, his concubine and the mother of his son, Adeodatus (4.1). His son's birth in 373 also coincided with the beginning of Augustine's 12-year quest for wisdom that led him to become a follower of Manichaeism, then skepticism, and finally Christianity (3.4–6, 4.1, 5.2–6). Over this same period, his career as a teacher of rhetoric and an orator prospered first in Carthage, then in Rome. At age 30, he assumed the prestigious post of professor of rhetoric in Milan (5.7). With a socially advantageous marriage arranged by Monica in the offing, Augustine seemed finally to have arrived (6.3, 6.6).

Two years later, however, Augustine abandoned this hard-won position and retired with Monica, Adeodatus, his life-long friend Alypius, and several other associates to a villa called Cassiciacum to pursue a Christianized version of the philosophical life (9.2). Baptized by Bishop Ambrose of Milan in 387, he returned home to Thagaste intending to live out his life in a small community of like-minded persons (9.2). But less than three years after his return and the establishment of his monastic community in Thagaste, he was "drafted" by the aging Greek-speaking bishop of the coastal city of Hippo Regius, Valerius, and his Latin-speaking Catholic congregation to be their priest. He proved highly effective as both a preacher and teacher in Hippo and a champion of the Catholic Church in its struggles with the schismatic Donatists and heretical Manichees. Indeed,

Augustine soon came to function as *de facto* bishop of Hippo, a position made permanent by his election upon Valerius's death in 395.

Augustine's election as bishop marked a watershed in his life and thought. As bishop, his authority and obligations as a writer and preacher as well as his involvement in local politics and religious polemics all expanded dramatically. Such prominence exposed him to the critical gaze of fellow bishops and the members of the far-flung network of the Christian-Roman elite. His contemporaries pressed to know who exactly this bishop of Hippo really was (e.g., 10.3).

Augustine marked this moment of transition with a work unique not only within his own literary corpus but within all of early Christian literature. Written between 397 and 401, the *Confessions* was in part intended to satisfy friends such as the Gallic aristocrat Paulinus of Nola who, having experienced the drama of conversion themselves, eagerly sought the stories of others. Augustine's approach to his story, however, was enigmatical. For while the first ten books, as one might expect, concerned his life, the last three dealt with specific, and quite abstract, questions of theology and sacred Scripture, namely, the nature of time, memory, and creation.

This combination of the personal and the abstractly philosophical has puzzled many readers, leading some to see the two sections almost as separate works. Yet the *Confessions* were clearly not simply an effort to narrate Augustine's life *per se* but rather to track his slow movement toward Christian faith and membership in the Church. It was a conversion narrative crafted "to arouse the human intellect and affections towards Him"[1] through its carefully assembled mix of personal testimony, moral analysis, theological reflection, and prayer. At the same time, writing the *Confessions* allowed Augustine to investigate the motive forces behind the process of conversion itself. In doing so, he discovered that Christian conversion depended to an extraordinary degree on the sense of hearing: on which voices were heard, when they were heard, and what those voices said.

As he opened Book 13, the final book of his *Confessions*, Augustine declared:

> I call upon you, my God, my mercy (*Psalms* 58:18). You made me, and when I forgot you, you did not forget me; I call you into my soul which you are preparing to receive through the longing which you have inspired in it.

---

[1] Augustine, *Retractationum Libri Duo*, 2.6, translated by author from *Patologia Latina*, ed. J.P. Migne (Paris: Montrouge, 1841), vol. 32, col. 632.

> Do not desert me now that I am calling on you. Before I called to you, you
> were there before me. With mounting frequency and strength, with voices
> of many kinds, you put pressure on me so that from far off, I heard and was
> converted and called upon you as you were calling to me. (13.1)

While Augustine the bishop now called upon God constantly, his
Confessions revealed that it had not always been so. The younger Augustine
had not called upon God, and God, in turn, was silent, or so Augustine says
he thought at the time. Yet, as he completed his examination of his own
past (Books 1–9), reflected upon his present (Book 10), and pursued a
series of scripturally based meditations on the nature of memory, time,
and creation (Books 11–13), he recognized that, contrary to his impressions at the time, God had not abandoned him but had been his silent
companion and subtle guide all along. But what God had not done — and
perhaps could not have done — was to use His own voice to summon
Augustine to the Christian faith. Unlike Paul on the road to Damascus,
Augustine received no voice from heaven. Instead, God had employed
"voices of many kinds" "with mounting frequency and strength" to spur
him to turn to God, to hear the divine Word itself, and to be moved eventually to call upon God just as God had been calling to him. Augustine's
artful deployment of verbal and nominal forms of the word *vox* (voice) as
he opened Book 13 portrayed his life as a space in which diverse voices
resounded, each leading him one step closer to (or farther from) the most
important voice, God's voice, to which he had initially been almost deaf.

Largely overlooking Augustine's emphasis on the role of *voces* (voices)
in his own conversion or understanding it merely as a generic reference to
the host of influences that shaped his path, scholars have explored in depth
the influence of figures such as Monica and Bishop Ambrose. They have
carefully tracked Augustine's movement from one set of texts to another,
each contributing a particular set of ideas, resolving a particular set of
problems, or providing a key example. And for good reason. When
Augustine read Cicero's *Hortensius* as part of his adolescent rhetorical
training, he discovered quite accidentally in its pages wisdom portrayed as
a goal for one's life, and he was overwhelmed: "[This book] changed my
feelings, it changed my prayers to you, it made my desires different than
they had been" (3.3, 8.4). Later, the "Platonic books" offered him new ways
of thinking about the nature of being and matter. Each of these new ideas,
in turn, began to transform the ways in which he understood aspects of

Scripture and problems such as the nature of evil; they also led him to a different and deeper kind of introspection (7.9–10).

Why, then, did Augustine employ the term *vox* and its cognates at the beginning of the *Confessions'* final book to describe the particular means whereby God drew Augustine to Him? What did *vox* mean to Augustine and his contemporaries? Its semantic field in Latin included "a voice, sound, tone, cry, call" but extended to include all "that is uttered by the voice," that is, the act of articulation itself. Read with this definition in mind, Augustine's opening lines of Book 13 signal to the reader that, in Augustine's movement towards God, words alone had not been enough; he had needed human voices both to activate ideas and to enable their latent power to enter his being and thereby alter it. The *Confessions*, in other words, finds its unity as an aural history of conversion, an account of Augustine's movement through an evolving landscape of human voices that guided him toward God before eventually falling silent before the *vox* of God found in prayer and Scripture.

Augustine demonstrated an acute awareness of the power of the spoken word at various points in the *Confessions*. It was, for example, the most fundamental and powerful tool of instruction. As he looked back to the torments of his school years, he interrogated his very different attitudes toward learning Latin and Greek. Why was it that, despite the great similarities in the grammatical instruction and literary themes, he found his studies in Latin so much more pleasant and rewarding than those in Greek? One crucial difference lies in the fact that he had learned Latin willingly, without threats or coercion. But another is that, in contrast to the Greek learned only at school, he acquired Latin through immersion in a social world full of Latin sounds: "From my nurses caressing me, from people laughing over jokes, and from those who played games and were enjoying them.... I had learnt some words ... by listening to people talking, and they, in turn, were the audience for my thoughts" (1.14). Just as waves lapping the shores over time can reshape coastlines in dramatic ways, so, too, the ceaseless waves of sound, of spoken language, combined with gesture and physical interaction, created the complex but pleasant contours of Augustine's Latin literacy.

The exchange of the gift of voice was also an essential component of that most important of Roman relationships: friendship. Reflecting on how friendships had eased the loss of his best friend, Augustine remarked, "There were things done in their company that still more powerfully seized my mind—to talk and to laugh with them…to read well-written books together; sometimes to tell jokes and sometimes to be serious; to disagree at times but without hard feelings, just as a man does with himself; and to keep our many discussions pleasant by the very rarity of such differences; to teach things to others and to learn from them" (4.8). Talking, joking, arguing, teaching, sharing books aloud: the utterance of thoughts and feeling through the human voice is the stuff of joy and the irreplaceable glue that binds friends together in love. Voices had the power to "set our minds ablaze" and "make but one out of many" (4.8).

It is in two stories concerning his younger friend Alypius that Augustine chose to portray the full power of sound to influence the human mind for good and evil, even against the will of the hearer. Alypius had become addicted to the circus (i.e., chariot racing) while a student at Carthage and was in danger of ruining his future. One day, when Alypius was auditing one of his classes, Augustine decided to use the circus as an example to clarify a particular point (while at the same time poking fun at circus fans). "Upon hearing those words [Alypius] burst forth from that deep pit in which he had willingly plunged himself…. He shook his mind with vigorous self-control. All the filth of the circus fell from him, and he never returned there again" (6.7). In this case, it was the words of mockery and correction—Alypius had probably heard them many times before—suddenly issuing forth in the voice of a respected teacher and friend that had sliced with unexpected ease through fetters of habit that had long held him.

Augustine illustrated sound's power to penetrate a person's inner being with another story about Alypius. One day Alypius, now living in Rome, encountered some friends who compelled him to accompany them to the gladiatorial combats, a form of entertainment that Alypius had come to despise. Entering the arena, he denied any interest in such foul pleasures and vowed that, though present, he would keep his eyes studiously shut and his mind firmly directed elsewhere. Yet, Augustine lamented, "Would that he had been able to close his ears as well! For when one man fell in the combat, a mighty roar went up from the entire crowd and struck him with such force that he was overcome by curiosity…. He opened his eyes and was wounded more deeply than the man whom he desired to look at was in his body…. The shout entered into him through his ears and opened up his eyes" (6.8). Its sensory defenses breached, Alypius's mind was quickly overrun. He drank in the arena's violence; the sensory fascination of the combats took root in his mind and called him back to the arena ever more frequently. A new addiction had been born.

In these examples, Augustine showed his readers the unique power of sound to enter the human interior and bring about almost instantaneous psychological and physical change. In contrast to sight, humans have no easy way of "not hearing"; ears have no eyelids with which to staunch the flow of sensation and external influence. Through the materialization of their thought in sound, ears allow the minds of others to enter the self. This is not to say that Augustine portrays hearing as total or accurate; after all, had Alypius fully heard Augustine's lesson, he would have realized that the remark was not directed at him. But, Augustine argues, whatever is heard has a special quality that enables it to bypass mental defenses and to implant itself in the mind in what is often an unusually compelling way.

Whose then were the "voices of many kinds" that had entered Augustine's mind, calling him back "from far away" and teaching him to hear God's voice and to know thereby to call upon Him? Read with this question in mind — and it is well to remember that Augustine himself urged the reader to ask it — the *Confessions* become a chronicle of Augustine's changing circle of interlocutors, each preparing him in some way to enter into conversation with the ultimate interlocutor, God. This perspective places in a new light such familiar aural elements of the text as Augustine's attention to Ambrose the rhetor and the voice in the Milanese garden crying out, "Take and read, take and read," which precipitates Augustine's full conversion to Christianity. Finally, it offers a way of integrating the two sections of the *Confessions* (Books 1–9 and 11–13) that preserves the distinctiveness of each even as it demonstrates their organic connections.

The influential human voices used by God to correct Augustine and to call him to hear the divine voice were many and various. A quick study and keen intellect, Augustine became one of the foremost proponents of Manichaeism. Yet after being a "hearer" for almost nine years, he had begun to find their doctrines increasingly problematic as his own knowledge grew. He was urged to await the coming of a special voice, that of Faustus, who would be able to resolve all his questions and doubts. Yet when Faustus did come to Carthage, Augustine found that, although an eloquent, affable, and modest man, he was incapable of resolving his questions and doubts. Through this direct encounter with the living voice of the master Manichee in dialogue — with its open-endedness, the possibility for probing questions, and the ability to assess doctrine through not only words but tone and deportment — Augustine was able finally to put to rest the possibility that Manichaean doctrine was true but simply beyond his reach (5.3–5).

Augustine's conversations with the doctor Vindicianus, in contrast, shifted other ideas. As he remarked: "I became better acquainted with him and attended assiduously and earnestly to his words, which were both pleasant and serious in the liveliness of his opinions though without rhetorical adornment"(4.3). Learning of Augustine's interest in astrology, the pagan Vindicianus urged him not to waste his time on it, arguing this point through his own kind of confession. Long before, he confessed, he, too, had pursued astrology not as an avocation but as a career. Yet, after finding its doctrines completely false, he turned instead to the real science of medicine, lest he make a living through deception. Although it did not immediately dissuade Augustine from his interest in astrology, the voice of Vindicianus, like a sharp stylus, "drew the outlines upon my memory of what I later investigated for myself" (4.3).

Augustine's move to Milan at the age of 30 to take up a professorship in rhetoric led him to encounter a variety of voices that gave new energy and direction to his drift toward Christianity. Of these, the most important was that of Bishop Ambrose of Milan, whose significance to him Augustine summed up with eloquent brevity: "I came to Milan and to Ambrose...a man famed throughout the world as one of its very best men and your devout worshiper.... All unknowing, I was led to him by you [God] so that through him I might be led, while fully knowing it, to you" (5.13). Initially, Augustine's interest in Ambrose's voice was purely professional; he joined the bishop's audience not to learn the substance of his speaking but to observe its style and perhaps to learn trade secrets. Yet, as Augustine later recalled, he recognized that "with the words, which I loved, there also entered into my mind the things themselves, to which I was indifferent.... And when I opened my heart to receive the eloquence with which he spoke, there likewise entered, although only by degrees, the truths that he spoke" (v.14). Like a Trojan horse, Ambrose's words entered the citadel of Augustine's mind in one guise—classical eloquence—but, once inside, out jumped a host of new ideas and ways of thinking that gradually won over Augustine's thought.

Although Augustine never seems to have obtained the long, private conversation with Ambrose that he so often sought at this time, it is clear that he was growing acutely sensitive to the powerful affective role of sound within the Christian Church. He describes the sweet sound of the bishop's voice, evaluates its rhetorical style (5.13), and imagines it as almost never at rest (6.3). Likewise, he notes that it was during a siege of his church by imperially backed Arian forces that Ambrose introduced the eastern practice of singing hymns and canticles, for this musical secret weapon would ensure "that the people would not become weak through the tedium and sorrow" (9.7). Augustine later would bear first-hand witness to the power of the music-filled basilica to move the Christian heart when he, recounting his baptism, recalled: "How greatly did I weep during hymns and canticles, keenly affected by the voices of your sweet-singing Church! Those voices flowed into my ears, and your truth was distilled into my heart" (9.6; see also 10.33).

During his stay in Milan, Augustine heard other important voices. From Simplicianus, Ambrose's spiritual father and successor as bishop, Augustine heard the story of how Victorinus, the renowned philosopher and rhetor, overcame his reticence about his Christian convictions to declare his affiliation publicly (8.2). By recounting the asceticism of the Egyptian desert father Antony and the powerful effect of this text on several imperial servants of reading this saint's life, the voice of a North African friend confronted Augustine with the confused and distorted image of his own inner being: "Ponticianus told us this story, and as he spoke, you, O Lord, turned me back upon myself. You took me from behind my own back, where I had placed myself because I did not want to look upon myself. You stood me face to face with myself, so that I might see how foul I was, how deformed and defiled, how covered with stains and sores…. If I tried to turn my gaze from myself, he still went on with the story that he was telling, and once again you placed me in front of myself" (8.7). Just as, years before, Augustine's passing reference to the circus had shattered Alypius's self-delusion and helped to liberate him from the games, so now Ponticianus's stories of ascetic renunciation entered Augustine's mind and forced him to recognize the true origins of his reluctance to convert: not uncertainty but simply vanity and lust.

Driven into the garden by one voice, his tormented mind eventually found its peace in another: "And, lo, I heard from a nearby house a voice like that of a boy or girl, I know not which, chanting and repeating over and over, 'Take and read. Take and read.' Instantly, with altered countenance, I began to think most intently whether children made use of any such chant in some kind of game but could not recall hearing it anywhere. I checked the flow of my tears and got up, for I interpreted this solely as a command given to me by God to open the book and read the first chapter I should come upon"(8.12). Guided by this mysterious child's voice,

Augustine read a passage in Paul's letter to the Romans—which he had clearly read many times before—with new and believing eyes. No longer mere words on a page, he now recognized these words as the voice of God.

Over the course of his early life, and especially in the years immediately before his conversion in 387, a diverse range of stories, ideas, ways of thinking, and models for life had found their way into Augustine's mind through voice and sound. Yet each of these voices—even that of Ambrose—was only a brief or sporadic presence (though the memories of them endured). One voice, however, accompanied Augustine throughout his life until he was safely within the Church: Monica's. Although its full effects upon her son may only be imagined, the presence of Monica's voice in his world exercised a potent and memorable force in his evolution.

When he returned from Carthage as a young Manichee confident in his new doctrine, his mother had vehemently opposed him. Reassured in a vivid dream that her errant son would eventually stand where she stood, Monica revealed this to Augustine. As he later recalled the scene, he initially argued that it meant that he was in the right and that she would convert to Manichaeism. Her response was swift and unhesitating: "No.... It was not said to me: 'Where he is, there also are you,' but 'Where you are, there also is he.' I confess to you, Lord, that my memory of this, as best I can recall it, and I often spoke of it, is that I was more disturbed by your answer to me through my mother—for she was not disturbed by the likely seeming falsity of my interpretation and quickly saw what was to be seen, which I certainly did not see before she spoke—than by the dream itself" (3.11). Uttered with total certainty by a person whom Augustine loved and respected (but perhaps thought of as his intellectual inferior), Monica's spontaneous dream interpretation broke through Augustine's self-satisfaction and exposed the possibility of his own error.

In her youth, Monica, too, had experienced the piercing quality of human utterance and its capacity to alter habit and outlook, and she seems to have spoken to Augustine of the converting power of *vox*. As a young girl, she was often sent to draw wine from the cellar. Curious, she initially tasted the wine for fun but came to drink more and more until "she had fallen into the habit of greedily drinking her little cups almost full up with wine." From this perilous path she was rescued not by parents or teacher but by a servant's harsh voice:

> My God, what did you do at that time?... Was it not that you brought out
> of another soul a hard and sharp reproach, like a surgeon's knife out of

your secret stores, and by one stroke you cut away all that foul matter? A maidservant with whom she used to go down to the cellar, quarreled with her little mistress, the two being all alone, as it so happened. She threw this fault at her with most bitter insults, and called her a drinker. Wounded through and through by this taunt, she beheld her own foul state, and immediately condemned it and cast it off. (9.9)

By disparaging Monica's drinking habits aloud, the maidservant's voice shattered Monica's deceptive self-image and forced her to recognize that she was quickly becoming something that she did not want to be.

The most important role that Monica's voice played in Augustine's life, however, was as a model of the kind of constant dialogue with God that he himself came to desire. In contrast to the young Augustine, who seems aware only of earthly interlocutors, his mother is seen both to hear and be heard by God. Through dreams and visions such as the one mentioned above, God speaks directly to her; indeed, she would claim "that she could distinguish by some sort of savor, which she could not explain in words, the difference between [God's] revelations and her own dreaming soul" (6.13). Monica, in other words, knew the sound of God's voice when she heard it. And God knew the sound of Monica's, for she constantly spoke to Him in prayer using her words and tears. Indeed, as the *Confessions* unfolded, Augustine reflected again and again on the way in which his mother's prayers had or had not been answered at any given time according to God's will; what was never questioned, however, was that God was listening.

Although a chorus of voices had brought him to accept the Christian faith and to devote his life to the Church, the Augustine of the *Confessions* recognized that these earthly voices, too, must grow silent. Speaking with his mother just days before her death in Ostia, he recalled their shared vision of the true end of Christian life:

The tumult of the flesh shall fall silent, silent the images of earth, and of the waters, and of the air; silent the heavens, silent for him the very soul itself, and he shall pass beyond himself by not thinking upon himself; silent his dreams and all imagined appearances, and every tongue, and every signal and if all things that come to be through change should become wholly silent to him ... God alone will speak, not through such things but through himself, so that we hear his Word, uttered not by a tongue of flesh, nor by an angel's voice ... but by himself whom we love in these things, himself whom we hear without their aid. (9.10)

To hear only God's voice in an otherwise perfect silence, to receive his Word with ineffable immediacy and clarity, was thus the mystical end of all Christians. Such a perfect and unmediated dialogue with God was impossible in this world, however. How then could the dialogue between human and God be maintained? For Augustine, the answer lay in constant meditation upon sacred Scripture. Amid the forest of its words, the diligent explorer would come to hear the *vox Dei* (voice of God). Had not Ambrose escaped the tumults of his life as bishop in such silent study of Scripture? "When he read his eyes moved down the pages and his heart sought out their meaning, while his voice and tongue remained silent" (6.3).

Seen from this perspective, the strongly exegetical and philosophical books (11–13) of the *Confessions* represent not a radical departure from the more biographical journey detailed in earlier books but its natural culmination. We still see an Augustine who continues to seek the voice of God but now through constant reflection on the Word of God itself and through prayer, entreaty, and praise. In these books, no other voices are needed. Augustine used Books 9–13 of his *Confessions* to offer a glimpse of that ultimate conversation — amid utter silence — that all Christians should strive to have with God.

In highlighting the role of diverse human *voces* in his own journey to hear the *vox* of the Christian God, Augustine offered at the outset of Book 13 a crucial clue to the ultimate significance of the *Confessions:* they described and explored the complex and dramatic beginning of the conversation between a Christian and his God and the shape of that dialogue once it was underway.

At the same time, Augustine's sustained analysis of the role of voices — and by implication the individuals, groups, and communities from which these voices arose — in his own movement toward the faith made clear to readers that Christian conversion was not merely a matter of presenting a set of texts or doctrines. It was a process that depended on patterns of sociability, amalgamations of personal charisma and ideas, and the embodiment of ideas and ideals in material forms such as sound that enabled them to penetrate an individual's inner being. Real conversions, in other words, depended on people hearing the right things from the right people at the right time, on being part of certain circles and not others, and on hearing and experiencing the same message in many different ways. Conversion in Late Antiquity, in other words, was not just a matter of faith but, inevitably, of community.

Bibliographic Note

Translations of the *Confessions* abound. For this essay I have used that by Henry Chadwick (Oxford: Oxford University Press, 1991). For a comprehensive commentary on the text see the Latin edition: Augustine, *Confessions*, ed. J.J. O'Donnell, 3 vols. (New York: Oxford University Press, 1992). Possidius, *Life of Saint Augustine*, trans. Sister Mary Mueller and Roy DeFerrari (Washington, DC: Catholic University of America Press, 1952), 71–124, offers a fascinating account of Augustine's life by a younger contemporary and is rich in detail about the North African milieu.

Excellent studies that place the *Confessions* within the larger context of Augustine's life and world are Peter Brown, *Augustine of Hippo: A Biography* (Berkeley: University of California Press, 1967), a new edition of which was also published by the same press in 2000; J.J. O'Donnell, *Augustine: A New Biography* (New York: Harper Collins, 2005); and Henry Chadwick, *Augustine of Hippo: A Life* (New York: Oxford University Press USA, 2010). F. Van der Meer, *Augustine the Bishop: Church and Society at the Dawn of the Middle Ages*, trans. B. Battershaw and G. Lamb (New York: Harper Torchbooks, 1961), remains an outstanding analysis of Augustine's day-to-day activities as bishop in Roman North Africa. On Augustine's conversion and its relationship to his Manichaeism, see Jason D. BeDuhn, *Augustine's Manichaean Dilemma*, Vol. 1: *Conversion and Apostasy, 373–388 C.E.* (Philadelphia: University of Pennsylvania Press 2009). For his theology, see Carol Harrison, *Rethinking Augustine's Early Theology: An Argument for Continuity* (New York: Oxford University Press USA, 2008).

Confessor Saints and
The Origins of Monasticism
The *Lives* of Saints Antony
and Martin

John M. McCulloh

Hagiography — that is, writing about saints — was one of the most common forms of narrative literature in the European Middle Ages. The earliest Christian saints were martyrs, executed for their faith during the Roman persecutions of the second and third centuries. Other Christians recorded these heroic deaths in works known as "passions," a term that derives from the Latin word for suffering. After the persecutions came to an end in the early fourth century, the heroes of the faith came to include not only martyrs but also those known as "confessors," who witnessed to their Christianity by living lives of extraordinary holiness. In this case the individual's reputation for sanctity rested on the conduct of an entire life, and recording this idealized existence demanded a new and ultimately very popular form of hagiography, the saint's "life" or *vita*. The lives of Antony of Egypt (c. 251–356) and Martin of Tours (c. 335–97) were early examples of this form, and they established patterns for depicting sanctity that influenced writers throughout the medieval period.

The passions and lives of the saints served to preserve the local memory of these holy people and also to convey information about them to Christians elsewhere. That some saints, such as Antony and Martin, who lived before the development of papal canonization, gradually came to be known and venerated throughout Christendom often depended on the existence of a hagiographic record of this sort.

These two lives also publicized monasticism, a form of religious life that was rapidly gaining popularity among Christians in the later Roman Empire. Indeed, Antony is generally regarded as the father of Christian monasticism, and Martin was among the first to adopt a monastic life in the western half of the empire. The monastic ideal involves withdrawal from normal human associations and activities to live an ascetic existence focused on spiritual pursuits. Even in the early Church, some Christians lived lives of rigorous self-denial within their communities. Then, in the later third and fourth centuries, large numbers of Christians, mostly men, withdrew from society to live at first as individual hermits and soon in small communities on the fringes of civilization and even beyond. This movement began in Egypt and Palestine where would-be monks could find solitude in the desert.

A fundamental conception underlying Christian monasticism is the belief that all people are sinful, that they are separated from God as a result of the disobedience of Adam and Eve. The goal of the monastic life is to bridge the chasm that separates human beings from their creator. Thus, monks sought to obtain salvation by forgoing the pleasures of life in the world (such as social contacts, sexual relations, and physical comfort) and to some extent even the necessities of life itself (food and sleep) in order to devote their time instead to labor, prayer, and meditation. Those who were most successful in this effort came to be recognized as "friends of God," whose close relationship with the divinity was attested by their power to perform miracles.

Christians had ample precedents for seeing a monastic-style life as particularly holy. Many of the Old Testament prophets had spent substantial time in the wilderness, and John the Baptist dwelt there as well. After his baptism, Jesus himself went into the wilderness, where he fasted for 40 days and was tempted by the devil. Yet, in spite of these early examples, the Christian call to the desert developed only several centuries later. Saint Jerome (c. 342–420), who translated the Hebrew and Greek Bible into Latin and lived the ascetic life in both Italy and Palestine, declared that the earliest monks were refugees from the Roman persecutions. That may have been true in some cases, but the literary image of the monastic founders recorded in their lives suggests that most of them would have accepted martyrdom rather than flee. Moreover, the persecutions were intermittent rather than constant, and the Church was largely at peace between the mid-third century and the beginning of the so-called Great

Persecution. Decreed in 304 by the emperor Diocletian (284–305), this persecution formally lasted until 312; in 313 Constantine (306–37), the first Christian emperor, extended official toleration to the Christians. The intensity of Diocletian's anti-Christian offensive varied greatly from time to time and place to place, but the number of its victims was large. It was also the last major persecution, and many who died were commemorated for their courage by the survivors.

Some monks, including Antony, withdrew from society even before the Great Persecution, and his biographer describes how he encouraged other Christians who suffered and courted martyrdom (*LA* 37). Nonetheless, the great surge of enthusiasm for the monastic life came as the persecutions wound down. On this basis, many historians argue that monasticism as a popular movement began as a reaction against the institutional Church of the time. The third century was an age of substantial change in the Church. The earliest Christians had expected the world to end quickly and had devoted most of their efforts to preparing for that event. As time passed, however, the threat seemed to be less pressing, and Christians began to concern themselves with more mundane affairs such as developing ecclesiastical organization and defining Christian beliefs. In short, the Church began to come to terms with its political, social, and intellectual environment. With the conversion of Constantine to Christianity in the early fourth century, this trend intensified. The Roman emperor patronized the Church and became directly involved in its affairs. Christianity became fashionable, and as the Church grew, its fervor cooled. But some Christians did not wish to come to terms with the world. Among the heroes of the rigorous religious life, Antony and Martin attained extraordinary fame, and they owed their reputations primarily to their hagiographers.

Athanasius, author of the life of Antony, was bishop of Alexandria from 328 until his death in 373. Located in Egypt, Alexandria had long been the chief city of the Roman East. Historically a hub of Hellenistic Greek and Jewish scholarship, it early became a center of Christian intellectual activity as well. One of the products of its schools was Arianism, a view of the nature of the Christian Trinity that split the Church and attracted the support of Emperor Constantine and his immediate successors. As a leading opponent of Arianism, Athanasius was expelled from his bishopric on several occasions, and his *Life of Antony* was most likely a product of one of those periods of exile. Athanasius wrote the *Life* in Greek, and it spread rapidly in both the original language and translations. Among these, a Latin version by Evagrius of Antioch — I cite a translation of his text throughout this chapter — made Antony a widely admired model of asceticism in the West.

Even more influential in that region was the *Life of Martin*. Its author, Sulpicius Severus, was born around 360 in Aquitaine, the southwest of modern France. His family was wealthy, and Sulpicius embarked upon a promising career as a lawyer. Following the early death of his wife, however, he began to reassess his priorities. Through a personal contact he learned about Martin and decided to write an account of the holy bishop's life. He traveled to Tours to talk to and observe his subject, and he supplemented his personal investigations with literary material borrowed from various sources, including Athanasius's *Life of Antony*. Sulpicius finished his work and began to circulate it shortly before Martin died in 397, but it did not meet with universal approval. In particular, critics challenged his depiction of Martin as a miracle worker, and after Martin's passing Sulpicius composed several additional works in which he undertook to defend his claims by citing more miracles and naming witnesses.

Athanasius reports that Antony was the son of well-to-do Christian parents in an Egyptian farming community and that he was about 20 years of age when his father and mother died. Shortly thereafter, while attending church, he was moved by the passage from Matthew's gospel (19.21–22) in which Jesus declares that those who wish to be perfect should sell their possessions, give the proceeds to the poor, and follow him. Antony disposed of his goods and began to live at the boundary between the cultivated fields along the Nile and the Egyptian desert, where he devoted much time to prayer and to learning from more experienced hermits how to live the holy life. He suffered many temptations and resisted them with rigorous self-denial through fasting and prayer, often at the expense of sleep. When he moved farther from his home to live among some nearby tombs, his sufferings continued until, Athanasius says, Jesus came to comfort him, and the demons disappeared. Antony then sought greater solitude, entered the desert, and walled himself into an abandoned fort to avoid human contact. Yet, in spite of his efforts, people came. Some sought his assistance for cures or exorcisms; others tried to imitate his example and established cells around his hermitage. These disciples learned their vocation through long association with the master, but Athanasius rhetorically compresses this apprenticeship and has the saint present the fruits of his experience in a single extended lecture on the ascetic life. Despite his efforts to withdraw further from human contact by setting up a new hermitage away from the press of visitors, worldly business drew him back periodically to his earlier residence, where he helped many people who sought his aid by casting out demons, curing illness, and revealing future or distant events. He denounced heresies, successfully defended Christianity against the attacks of pagan philosophers, and even corresponded with Emperor Constantine and his sons. Finally, at age 105, when God revealed his approaching end, Antony withdrew to his more remote hermitage to die.

Like Antony, Martin was drawn to the monastic life, but he arrived there by a different route. Sulpicius Severus recounts that Martin, born of pagan parents in Pannonia (modern Hungary) and reared in Italy, became a catechumen over his parents' objections at age ten. When he soon began to contemplate a monastic life, his father took advantage of an imperial decree requiring the sons of veterans to enter military service and had Martin arrested and enrolled in the army at age 15. Even as a soldier Martin practiced Christian virtues: he was particularly generous to the poor and famously cut his cloak to share it with a freezing beggar who, we learn, was actually Jesus. Following his baptism and release from the army at age 18, Martin visited Bishop Hilary of Poitiers. He then left Gaul for home, where he persuaded his mother and many others to become Christian—although his father remained pagan. After some time in Italy, where he suffered persecution, he returned to Gaul, where his reputation for holiness led to his election as bishop of Tours. In that position, Martin continued to follow the monastic life. He first lived in a cell next to his cathedral, but, besieged by visitors, he moved a short distance outside the city. There he dwelt in his own cell surrounded by some 80 followers who occupied individual cells but came together for communal meals and prayer. Of Martin's work as bishop, Sulpicius tells us very little. His account of that period focuses on the saint's miracles that supported his efforts to convert the remaining pagans of his diocese. The most frequent miracles, however, were cures. Sulpicius concludes with a summary of Martin's astounding virtues and a final stab at the saint's critics who, he says, were mostly bishops.

Hagiographers write to convince readers that their subjects possess recognized qualities of sainthood. As a result, saints' lives are filled with stock situations and even standard phrases that reveal the hero's holiness. Athanasius and Sulpicius were among the founders of the genre, and their widely read works played a prominent role in establishing its conventions. All lives are not alike, however. Their contents vary somewhat according to the particulars of the life of the saint and, likewise, the particular circumstances surrounding their composition. This chapter will examine first those features of these two works that are common to saints' lives in general and, especially, to those of monks and then turn to those elements that illuminate the late antique world of Antony and Martin.

Each author prefaces his life by stating why he has undertaken his task. Athanasius claims that he is responding to a request, and Sulpicius declares that Martin's life is so edifying that he cannot remain silent. In an accompanying letter to his brother, Sulpicius adds that he is unequal to the task imposed upon him. Both authors also indicate that they have described the saint so that others may imitate his holy example. Finally, each concludes his preface with reference to the sources of his information, aimed to assure the audience of the factual basis of the text. These features appear frequently in the prologues to hagiographical works and other medieval texts as well. Expressions of humility such as that of Sulpicius are particularly common and often appear more conventional than sincere.

The biographies then begin with a few words about the saint's family and move on to brief accounts of the saint's youth (*LA* 1; *LM* 2.1). In both cases the children reveal maturity beyond their years. Martin shows adult judgment in his acceptance of Christianity, even against the will of his parents, and in his early desire for the monastic life (*LM* 2.3–4). Antony's case is more typical of saints' lives, as Athanasius says that young Antony avoided childish activities, including learning to read and write (*LA* 1). Antony may in fact have been quite learned, but the life projects a different image. Athanasius's hero lacked book learning but possessed what hagiographers often call "simplicity," an openness to receiving divine knowledge and an artless manner of presenting it. Sulpicius likewise praises the knowledge and insight of his uneducated saint (*LM* 25.6–8).

Whatever their formal instruction, both Antony and Martin had to learn the ascetic life, and just as their lives provided examples for future imitators, so each of them patterned his own life on earlier models. When Antony first abandoned the world and undertook to live at the fringe of

Egyptian society, he sought to emulate an old man who had followed the solitary life for many years. He also visited others with holy reputations, talking to them and imitating their best qualities (*LA* 3–4). When he moved to the tombs, however, he found his inspiration in the Bible. He took as his model the life of the prophet Elijah, whose example he probably also had in mind later when he became the first monk to move into the desert itself (*LA* 8, 11). Athanasius thus emphasizes that a key to living a truly holy life lay in imitating people who had already achieved that goal.

According to Sulpicius, Martin desired "the desert" from the beginning (*LA* 2.4), and that mode of expression suggests the degree to which the model of Antony and other desert-dwelling holy men had become a standard for ascetic practice. For Martin in western Europe, the desert was not a waterless, sandy waste; it was a way of life. Thus, Sulpicius says in effect that, even as a youth, Martin longed for a solitary monastic existence. Life in the desert, whether literal or metaphorical, was a struggle. This conception finds expression in the military terminology that many monastic writers employ. Athanasius calls Antony a "soldier of Christ" (*LA* 6), and Sulpicius declares in his prologue that Martin's life will inspire its audience to "heavenly military service" (*LM* 1.6). In a very real way, the desert monk's struggle was a struggle against himself, an effort not only to separate himself from the world in a physical sense but to overcome the desire and longing for life in the world. The goal was to return to God, to bridge the chasm created by the sin of Adam and Eve, and to re-establish the relationship that had existed between God and humanity at the time of creation.

The battles of Antony and Martin — and by extension other desert monks — against the devil and his army of demons suggest a parallel to Jesus's experience in the wilderness, for Satan appeared to him there and tempted him (*Matt.* 4.1–11; *Luke* 4.1–13). Demons threatened all Christians, but they were particularly eager to challenge monks because of the monks' moral superiority. In some cases the attacks were essentially mental. Athanasius declares that Antony struggled with thoughts of his former possessions and his family, as well as with sexual longings, because the devil placed these temptations in his mind (*LA* 4–5). But evil also manifested itself in intensely physical ways. The *Life of Antony* describes numerous encounters with the devil and demons who appeared in various forms, including a seductive woman, but they were physically most threatening when they came as wild beasts and set upon him, inflicting painful wounds (*LA* 5, 8–10). The saint declared that, if God had given them power over him, they should proceed to devour him, but when thus challenged in the name of God, they slunk away. Sulpicius states that the devil sometimes adopted the likeness of a pagan god or goddess, but he notes that Martin could recognize his foe regardless of the devil's disguise (*LM* 21.1, 22.1). Even more terrifying than the devil's physical threats were the psychological deceptions by which he might lead a monk astray. Antony warns his followers that demons appear in the guise of ascetics offering instruction on how monks can please God. They encourage monks to exceed their physical limits, to stay awake to pray, and to continue fasting when they cannot survive without sleep or nourishment (*LA* 25). Sulpicius tells a related story in which the devil appeared to Martin wearing royal robes and claiming to be Christ (*LM* 24). It was in the face of such deceptions, physical challenges, and mental temptations that the desert monks of Late Antiquity overcame desire. The signs that they had successfully done so, that their lives and virtue had found favor with God, often took the form of miracles, for the supernatural events that occurred in the presence of a holy person or as a result of that person's intercession were evidence of spiritual power.

The many dreams, visions, and supernatural events in these texts speak to the ways that these authors and, more generally, their intended audiences in the fourth century believed that the world is filled with spiritual beings, both good and evil, who are capable of appearing to humans and producing paranormal events. Perhaps even more important, these two lives reveal the difficulty people faced in distinguishing between true visions and miracles on the one hand and diabolical deceptions on the other. The hagiographers see the ability to make such distinctions as evidence of sanctity.

The supernatural events most frequent in the lives of Antony and Martin were cures of various sorts, just as most of the miracles attributed to Jesus were acts of healing. In particular, a number of the cures concern the casting out of demons — exorcism — as demonic possession seems to have been a widespread ailment in the ancient and medieval world. Indeed, families and friends brought the possessed to the holy men for help since they were thought to have power over evil (*LA* 57, 63–64; *LM* 17). In Martin's case, the evidence of his spiritual power extended beyond even exorcism, for he was credited with the ultimate in miracles — the raising of the dead (*LM* 7–8). Tales of successful intercession of this sort enhanced their reputations, but as both lives attest, such renown would bring more visitors whose presence made the solitary life impossible. Antony responded by withdrawing step-by-step ever deeper into the desert as his fame as a holy man and worker of miracles grew, and Bishop Martin abandoned his episcopal residence to establish a cell outside the city (*LA* 49, *LM* 10.3).

Despite such efforts to escape from mundane affairs, according to their biographers both men were involved in relationships between groups with differing, and sometimes conflicting, interests. During the lives of Antony and Martin, the Roman populace underwent a gradual process of Christianization. Yet in spite of the boost that Constantine's conversion gave to the movement, at the time of Martin's death at the end of the fourth century many people in the empire still followed their traditional religions. Furthermore, the Christians differed among themselves, often violently, on matters of belief. Our authors were themselves concerned with the relationship between representatives of the dominant Christian Church and those whose beliefs differed from the official doctrine on the one hand, and with the relationship between religious and civil authority on the other. It is therefore unsurprising that their heroes also dealt with such matters in their lives.

Athanasius presents several examples of Antony dealing with pre-Christian beliefs in his debates with philosophers (*LA* 72–80). According to Athanasius, Antony lacked formal education and required an interpreter to conduct conversations with Greek-speaking scholars. Nevertheless, these intellectuals, full of worldly wisdom, came to the desert to challenge his beliefs, and the monk employed both spiritual wisdom and miracles to confound them. Martin's efforts to spread Christianity also benefited from miracles, but the wonders Sulpicius describes served to protect the saint from resistance to his missionizing. Even so, Sulpicius insists that these displays were rarely necessary and that the pagans were usually so moved by Martin's teaching that they tore down their own temples (*LM* 13–15). Thus, both persuasion and coercion played a role in Christianity's ultimate victory over the traditional religions of the Roman Empire, but Christians employed the same weapons against one another.

Since the early days of their religion, Christians accepted the Bible as the ultimate source of information about God's plan for the salvation of humankind, and since the second half of the fourth century, they have been in substantial agreement about its contents. On the other hand, there have always been disagreements about its interpretation. The vehemence of these arguments reflects the conviction that faith is essential to salvation, but misplaced faith leads to damnation. People who believe false doctrine forfeit their chance of salvation, and those who preach false doctrine endanger others. In religious terminology, correct belief is labeled "orthodox," and incorrect belief is "heretical." In doctrinal conflicts, however, both sides consider their own beliefs to be orthodox, and each sees the other's teaching as heretical.

The most bitterly fought doctrinal struggle in the age of Antony and Martin was over the teaching known as Arianism. Despite disagreements over details, early Christians came to regard their God as a trinity, a single deity comprising three persons — Father, Son, and Holy Spirit — but the relationship among the three remained a source of contention. Early in the fourth century, Arius (c. 250–c. 336), a scholar and priest of Alexandria, taught that the Father had created the Son, and the Son was therefore subordinate. Arius's doctrine led to a very divisive and public dispute with supporters of equality among the three persons of the Trinity. The so-called "Arian controversy" became so acrimonious that in 325 Emperor Constantine summoned a council to meet in Nicaea to resolve the issue. Including several hundred bishops from the eastern part of the empire and a handful from the west, this meeting constituted the first ecumenical, or universal, council of the Christian Church. Thanks largely to the efforts of Athanasius of Alexandria — the very Athanasius who later wrote the life of Antony — the delegates condemned Arius's teaching and declared the equality of the Father and the Son. But condemning Arianism did not eliminate it. Within a few years, Constantine himself began to favor the Arian version of Christianity, and after his death in 337 his son Constantius emerged as a forceful advocate of the doctrine.

Given the prominence of Athanasius in the controversy, it is not surprising that his life of Antony bears witness to it. He reports, for instance, that the Arians claimed Antony as a supporter of their faith, but the indignant hermit returned from the wilderness to Alexandria to condemn their doctrine. Athanasius's summary of the monk's speech corresponds precisely to his own view of orthodoxy (*LA* 69). Sulpicius's Martin takes no such polemical position, but Martin must have been introduced to the Arian controversy through his association with one of its most ardent opponents in Gaul, Bishop Hilary of Poitiers. Later, as he returned from visiting his parents in Pannonia, Martin suffered physical violence for speaking out against the rival doctrine, and he was subjected to persecution by the Arian bishop of Milan (*LM* 6.4).

Just as these texts reveal traces of the doctrinal struggles that marked the world in which they were written, they also offer insight into the normally cooperative but often contentious relationship between worldly and spiritual power in the fourth century. Athanasius reports, for example, that Constantine and his sons wrote numerous letters to the hermit (*LA* 81). He tells this story to illustrate Antony's exalted status as a holy man, but the emperors surely wrote because association with such a friend of God represented good public relations. Indeed, in pre-Christian Rome, the emperors had sought to maintain the good will of the gods for the benefit of the state, and after their conversion, as this passage suggests, they expected the same patronage from their new deity, the Christian God. Sulpicius presents a more pointed example of the superiority of spiritual over worldly values in his description of Martin's interactions with the emperor Maximus. In contrast to the other bishops who sought the ruler's favor, Martin repeatedly refused his invitations to dinner. Then, when Martin finally did accept, Maximus sought to show he had gained favor with the soldier of Christ by having his guest pass him the cup in a drinking ceremony, but after he had taken a drink the bishop humbled the emperor by handing it to a priest instead (*LM* 20).

Today when someone labels a contemporary work "hagiography," the connotation is normally negative. It is applied most frequently to unrealistically positive portraits such as the "authorized" biographies of celebrities or the campaign biographies that laud candidates for public office. Keeping this modern meaning in mind can help us assess the works of Athanasius and Sulpicius — and medieval hagiographers whose work they informed — by suggesting questions to consider. Are the saints depicted in these lives simply too good to be true? Are the lives promotional literature, and, if so, what do they promote? Could the saints possibly serve as models of behavior or commitment for other Christians? If the saints represent an ideal, whose ideal is it? What functions do the saints perform in their societies? Do all saints act alike? Do they have any individuality? Is the idea of what constitutes a holy life fixed, or does it change over time? Finally, are there any characteristics that distinguish saints' lives from other biographical and historical writings of the Middle Ages? Contemplating such questions can help us understand both the authors and the audiences of saints' lives in the fourth century and throughout the medieval period. Asking such questions will also permit us to use these unfamiliar and often formulaic sources to gain deeper insight into the worlds in which and for which they were written.

Bibliographic Note

Athanasius's *Life of Antony* (*LA*) and Sulpicius Severus's *Life of Martin* (*LM*) are available in numerous English translations. David Brakke has translated most of what is now considered the best version of the original Greek text of the former in *Medieval Hagiography: An Anthology,* ed. Thomas Head (New York: Garland, 2000), 1–30. A translation of Evagrius's Latin version of the *Life of Antony,* the *Life of Martin,* and Gregory the Great's *Life of Benedict of Nursia* (discussed in Chapter 7 of this volume) all appear in a convenient collection: *Early Christian Lives,* ed. Carolinne White (London: Penguin Books, 1998). A recent study of Athanasius's depiction of Antony is David Brakke, *Athanasius and Asceticism* (Baltimore: Johns Hopkins University Press, 1998). The fundamental work on the life of Martin is Clare Stancliffe, *Saint Martin and His Hagiographer* (Oxford: Oxford University Press, 1983). The first chapter of C.H. Lawrence, *Medieval Monasticism,* 3rd ed. (New York: Longman, 2001) offers a succinct introduction to the origins of the movement. On special topics discussed in this essay, see Peter Brown, *The Body and Society: Men, Women, and Sexual Renunciation in Early Christianity* (New York: Columbia University Press, 1988), 213–40; Caroline Walker Bynum, *Holy Feast and Holy Fast: The Religious Significance of Food to Medieval Women* (Berkeley: University of California Press, 1987), 33–47; and Jeffrey Burton Russell, *Satan: The Early Christian Tradition* (Ithaca: Cornell University Press, 1981), 149–85. Although it deals with a somewhat later period, the classic work on the multiple roles of saintly individuals in human society is Peter Brown, "The Rise and Function of the Holy Man in Late Antiquity," *Journal of Roman Studies* 61 (1971): 80–101.

THREE

The Barbarian Ethos
The *Germania, Beowulf,* and the *Life of Saint Boniface*

Judith Beall[1]

C hristianity became a legal religion in the Roman Empire in the early fourth century and then spread rapidly into western Europe and Britain. Nevertheless, even in the seventh century much of Europe was still pagan. The great cathedrals of Germany, Scandinavia, Russia, and points in between were yet to be built. Missionaries and new converts in those regions sought to convince their neighbors, on the basis of familiar cultural concepts, of the truth of the Christian faith. But how would a "barbarian" culture recognize its own values in an alien religion? We can see an example of this kind of cultural translation when we compare three diverse historical texts: Tacitus's *Germania,* the Anglo-Saxon poem *Beowulf,* and Willibald's *Life of Saint Boniface.*

Tacitus completed the *Germania* in 98 AD. At that time, the Roman Empire was at its height, and Roman legions were well on the way to Romanizing Gaul. They founded cities in which Latin was spoken. They built temples, roads, baths, and amphitheaters. And trade flourished. Slaves and hides, for example, were exported to Rome, and luxury goods flowed back into Gaul. The Romans also introduced into the province new military tactics, a sophisticated public administration, and taxation. In the process, however, they came into conflict with barbarian peoples from

---

[1] This article is dedicated to Fr. Boniface Hicks, O.S.B., and Fr. Maurus Mount, O.S.B., in honor of their solemn vows at Saint Vincent Archabbey, Latrobe, Pennsylvania.

across the Rhine in the province of Germania, peoples who were determined to enter Gaul themselves. Along the frontier between Roman Gaul and these encroaching tribes, the Romans built a series of forts. The commanders and young officers stationed there were, we believe, the source of much of the information that Tacitus relates in his *Germania*; he may also have relied on the work of other notable historians.

The barbarian peoples about whom Tacitus wrote were part of a larger westward migration involving the Franks, Goths, Alemanni, and other tribes. While they brought their own cultures, laws, and values into Roman lands, they gradually (and often reluctantly) adopted many Roman practices and frequently ended up as members of the Roman army. In the fifth century, barbarian tribes moved in large numbers from Germania into Britain. They came principally from two powerful tribes, the Saxons and the Angles, from which we get the familiar term "Anglo-Saxon." Literary and archaeological evidence indicates that the Angles came from the southern part of the Danish peninsula and the Saxons from what is now northern Germany. Thus, it is not surprising that the poem *Beowulf,* the lengthiest surviving poem in the Anglo-Saxon language, takes place in Sweden and Denmark. Of this poem we have only one early manuscript, made in the eleventh century. At the moment, there is no consensus among scholars about the date of *Beowulf*'s composition. At one time it was assumed to have been composed in the eighth century, but later scholars have dated it to the tenth century. The tide now seems to be turning again, with many scholars favoring an earlier date, probably in the eighth century.

It was perhaps around the same time the poem was composed that the barbarian invaders, now Christian, returned in a sense to their roots. Born in England in 680, Saint Boniface devoted most of his adult life to the conversion of pagans and the organization of the Church in the lands of Germania, east of the Rhine. As a bishop, he was martyred at a spot near the present-day Netherlands at the age of 74. Shortly after his death, Willibald, an Anglo-Saxon priest, wrote his *vita*.

While *The Life of Saint Boniface, Beowulf,* and the *Germania* belong to different times and places, they converge in their use of certain key concepts in early barbarian culture. In the following pages, we shall consider some of these concepts, as the texts help us to see how early missionaries translated Christian values for their brethren across the Rhine. Let us begin our exploration with a consideration of treasure in the *Germania*.

———

From the perspective of the first-century Roman, the tribes and economy of Germania depended, to a certain extent, on the advantages gained from waging war: as Tacitus says, "the Germans have no taste for peace; renown is more easily won among perils, and a large body of armed retainers cannot be kept together except by means of violence and war" (14). He adds, "A German is not so easily prevailed upon to plough the land and wait patiently for harvest as to challenge a foe and earn wounds for his reward. He thinks it tame and spiritless to accumulate slowly by the sweat of his brow what can be got quickly by the loss of a little blood" (14). Even if we allow for some rhetorical exaggeration here, Tacitus presents a picture of a people who regard war as a noble occupation and whose economy is somewhat tailored to it. In such a world, the warband, its leader, and the treasure it obtains are important cultural symbols and speak to the value placed on war.

According to Tacitus, warriors were "always making demands on the generosity of the leader, asking for a coveted war-horse or a spear stained with the blood of a defeated enemy... the wherewithal for this open-handedness comes from war and plunder" (14). In other words, when the chiefs went to war, they were expected to bring back prizes, including equipment for battle. This gear was then distributed to the followers, so that the equipment needed to do battle was won in battle. Later in the text, Tacitus mentions that Germanic leaders took particular pleasure in receiving "gifts" from neighboring states (15). The nature of these gifts suggests that they were paid as tributes or bribes in compensation for plunder that was, in this case, not taken; they included "choice horses, splendid arms, metal discs, and collars" (15). States on equal terms would not have exchanged arms and horses, which could have been used against themselves, but it was important for the stronger state to increase its stock of weapons.

In Tacitus's account, then, both "plunder" and "gifts" refer to the same objects, which serve the same purpose. These were more than a fringe-benefit of conquest or a token of status; they were an essential resource for the protection of the society. In particular, they served as the means of forming and maintaining military associations of "companions" (*comites*), as Tacitus calls them—we might call them "warbands." In any event, the warband was more than a loose association of men engaged in the pursuit of plunder: it was an essential element of personal identity and social cohesion. From the leader's point of view, "Both prestige and power [for the leader] depend upon being constantly attended by a large train of picked young warriors, which is a distinction in peace and a protection in war." And it is not only in a chief's own action that the superior number and quality of his retainers brings him glory and renown: "Very often the mere reputation of such men will virtually decide the issue of war" (13). The warriors protected their leader not only by their ability to fight but also by their reputation for fighting. When they protected the chief, however, they also protected their tribe. Tacitus relates that women were known to rally failing warriors by "pleading heroically with their men, thrusting forth their bared bosoms, and making them realize the imminent prospect of enslavement" (8). Thus, the dependence of the tribe on the warband strengthened the bond between the chief and his retainers: "On the field of battle it is a disgrace to a chief to be surpassed in courage by his followers, and to the followers not to equal the courage of their chief. And to leave a battle alive after their leader has fallen means lifelong infamy and shame. To defend and protect him... are the most solemn obligations of their allegiance. The chiefs fight for victory, the followers for their chief" (14). This passage focuses on the importance of loyalty to the chief, even after he had fallen. Nevertheless, the tribe benefited from this arrangement as much as the leader, for it continued to enjoy the protection of the avenging warband, even in the absence of its leader. Consequently, it was the tribe that enforced the warriors' allegiance.

Tacitus indicates, however, that each member of the warband also had a strong bond with other members and that retainers were expected to look out for each other. He says, for instance, that the warriors "bring back the bodies of the fallen, even when a battle hangs in the balance" (6). Few actions show more clearly the warrior's respect for a fellow fighter. Each warrior had confidence, at least as Tacitus imagines it in the ideal, that other members of the band would rescue his body, treat it with respect, and return it to his family for a proper funeral. Tacitus adds, "To throw away one's shield is the supreme disgrace, and the man who has thus dishonored himself is disbarred from attendance at sacrifice [religious ceremonies] or assembly [government]. Many such survivors from the battlefield have ended their shame by hanging themselves" (6). Like their loyalty, the camaraderie of the warriors was enforced by social stigma, because so much was at stake. Germanic peoples fought, according to Tacitus, in a battle-line of "wedge-shaped formations." They had long shields, and each man overlapped his shield with the men on either side to form a shield-wall. If a single warrior threw away his shield, the men on either side (and possibly the whole formation) would be placed in jeopardy (6). It follows that a warrior who put at risk the rest of the warband, and consequently his people, deserved the terrible consequences of his action.

Thus, the warband can be understood as a group of companions bound to one another and to their leader in a voluntary but enduring relationship that often extended beyond traditional ties of kinship. These men had a solemn obligation to protect one another and their leader; the leader, for his part, had a reciprocal obligation to his men, since he was chosen for his courage and expected to "press forward in the front of the ranks," lest he be outdone in valor (7). The burden of military command, then, was to earn and maintain the confidence of one's followers, first through the distribution of treasure and then by the example of one's courage. Ultimately, however, it was the whole tribe that benefited from, and thus enforced, the obligations of the warband; both treasure and honor existed for the sake of the community. Tacitus, from an outsider's perspective, is able to glimpse the logic of the warband. He may thereby tell us as much about the Romans themselves — his interests and agendas as a Roman author writing for a Roman audience are accessible to the discerning reader — as he does about the barbarians of whom he had heard. Nevertheless, his picture shares much with an insider's perspective of the sort we see in *Beowulf*, to which we now turn.

Beowulf tells the story of a Swedish hero, the son of the king of the Geats. The main figure, Beowulf, goes to help the Danish king and his warband, who are feuding, unsuccessfully, with a monster from the swamps named Grendel. He kills both Grendel and Grendel's mother, receives thanks and rewards from the Danes, and returns to his home in Sweden. Eventually, Beowulf becomes king, but when a dragon attacks his people, he dies while fighting it to defend them. So ends the saga that reprises many of the themes present in the *Germania*, albeit in a language and with an outlook that are distinctly non-Roman. Its prologue explicitly connects the motifs of treasure, the loyal warband, and the courageous leader to the welfare of the people. "With splendid gifts (*feoh-gift* for loyalty) from his father's store," a young man should "win loyal companions (*gesith*) who will stand by him in old age and serve the people when war comes" (20-25). In other words, a leader used his inherited gifts to acquire the warband with which he protected himself and his people. The poem thus appears to be in step with the *Germania*, but *Beowulf* also allows us to look more closely at the special character assumed by these gifts. Unlike Tacitus's treatise, which uses slippery and inexact vocabulary, *Beowulf* is rich in passages that illuminate the concept of treasure (*hord*, from which we get the modern "hoard") as a force of its own.

One of the most instructive passages occurs in the second half of the poem, beginning at line 2210. Long ago, we are told, an ancient people hid their *hord* in a barrow or grave-mound. The treasure consisted of jeweled vessels, wonderful swords, helmets of hammered gold, and finely crafted armor — treasure of the sort described by Tacitus. Only one warrior of this ancient race survives; therefore, there is no one left who can use the sword, the helmet, the drinking cup, or the armor. The treasure lies useless — although not without its attractions. A great dragon finds it, and "though it does him no good" (2277), he becomes its guardian for 300 years. Eventually, a thief sneaks in and steals a jeweled cup from the dragon, who proceeds to express his displeasure by ravaging the countryside: "The invader [dragon] began to spew forth flames, burning the bright dwellings. The gleam of fire shone forth in enmity to men; the hateful air-flyer would not spare anything alive" (2312–15). So enters Beowulf's fatal adversary.

The king is motivated to face him in part because a king must protect his people: he is "the protector of the nation" (428). Nevertheless, his stated purpose in fighting is simply to gain the treasure: "Now my hand and my strong sword's edge shall fight for the hoard," for "I shall win gold by my valor" (2508–09, 2535–36). This attitude does not suggest avarice on the king's part; it is simply the expected behavior of a leader. Like the princes in Tacitus, Beowulf acquired an army through previous gifts from his own treasure: "I remember the time when, as we drank mead, we promised the lord who gave us treasure in the beer hall that we would repay him for that war gear, helmets, and hard swords, if such a need befell him" (2633–38). Unfortunately, his followers fail on this occasion to protect him, and he is mortally wounded by the dragon, who also perishes. Although he can no longer benefit personally from the dragon's treasure, Beowulf is still concerned that his people should benefit from it: "I give thanks to the Lord — to the King of glory, the eternal Ruler — for all the treasures I now gaze on; I give thanks that I could gain such for my people before my death-day. Now I have sold my old lifespan for the hoard of treasure; now you must take care of the people's needs" (2794–801). Beowulf is consoled by the idea that the dragon's treasure will benefit the people in his absence; he will not have died in vain. This, however, is not what actually happens. One of his kinsmen suggests, "Now it would be best if we hastened to look at the king there, and bring to the funeral pyre him who gave us treasure. Nor shall only a part of the treasure hoard be melted with the brave hero; that vast amount of gold, so grimly purchased, rings bought in the end with his own life: these the fire shall eat, the flames enfold" (3007–315). The treasure is consigned to the flames with Beowulf, for it is useless, "bound with a spell so that no man could touch the ring-hall (the treasure)" (3051–54). Moreover, the poet has a premonition of doom. The people now fear "evil days...much carnage, the terror of the foe, humiliation and captivity" (3151–55). Having neither leader nor treasure, they are left defenseless; Beowulf's dying hope is disappointed. What went wrong?

The key to the poem's resigned conclusion is the failure of the warband itself. When Beowulf goes to fight the dragon, "no band of noble comrades stood courageously about him: they had fled into the wood to protect their lives" (2596–99). Only his kinsman, Wiglaf, stands by him, and he later curses the faithless band: "Now the receiving of treasure and giving of swords, all the enjoyment of hereditary estate and comfort shall cease for you and your kin; every man of your clan will have to turn away, deprived of the landowners' privileges, when noblemen far and wide hear of your flight, your shameful act. Death is better to every noble warrior than life in disgrace" (2884–91). Here we are reminded of Tacitus's note on the proscription of deserters in Germania. *Beowulf*, then, portrays an instance of the breakdown of the military code. Treasure has an inherent power to activate the reciprocal loyalties of leader and warband. It acquires a sacred or magical quality (indicated here by its dragon protector) and may even be worth dying for. But if human loyalties fail, the treasure loses its power. It must be hidden or destroyed, while the people face enslavement.

While *Beowulf* may serve to idealize the portrait of a heroic warlord, the main purpose of Willibald's hagiographic *Life of Boniface* is to bear witness to an exemplary Christian life and to encourage others to emulate it. However, it also provides an insight into the way missionaries attempted to make Christian values intelligible to pagans in the lands of their ancestors. Here, we shall limit our examination (and thus our quotations) to the end of the text, that is, to the eighth chapter, in which Willibald describes the death of Saint Boniface.

The bishop had journeyed to Frisia, deep in pagan territory, to proclaim the Gospel. According to Willibald, he foresaw his approaching death. Early one morning, Boniface, surrounded by a "number of his personal followers," was camped in Frisia waiting to confirm some new converts who had recently been baptized. Instead, the group was attacked by a pagan band, "a vast number of foes, armed with spears and shields." At the moment of attack, Boniface demonstrated a "conspicuous courage" not unlike that described by Tacitus. He "called the clergy to his side, and, collecting together the relics of the saints, which he always had with him," rushed out to face the foe. Unlike Beowulf's companions, Boniface's attendants (*pueri*) "sprang from the camp to meet [his foes] and snatched up arms" to defend their leader and the clergy. In many ways, this scene and the way it unfolds remind us of the warbands and leaders of the *Germania* and *Beowulf*.

Warfare, however, is not a Christian value, nor are we dealing here with a heroic saga of pagan times but with the supreme act of Christian witness. Nevertheless, Willibald is careful to appeal to sensibilities akin to those observed by Tacitus: "It is a disgrace for a leader to be surpassed in courage by his followers" (14). Willibald goes to great lengths to deliver Boniface from this disgrace and to portray him as the ideal leader, even in death. Thus, Boniface reproved his attendants and he "forbade them to continue the conflict," for "we are told in Scripture, that we render not evil for good but to overcome evil by good." He announced that the day of their release was at hand. To the "priests and deacons and other clerics," he also spoke: "Brethren, be of stout heart, fear not them who kill the body, for they cannot slay the soul which continues to live forever…endure with steadfast mind the sudden onslaught of death, that you may be able to reign evermore with Christ." In this way Boniface encouraged both his lay attendants and fellow clerics by his own example of valor, even as he urged them to accept the crown of martyrdom as an assurance of eternal life in heaven. Thus, he saved his companions and, like the victorious leader of a warband, enabled them to share in a common victory.

Here then, we have a Christian reworking of the themes of leadership and loyalty, with the promise of ultimate safety and victory, but what about treasure? It, too, is present in Willibald's account: "The heathens seized with exultation upon the spoils of their victory (in reality the cause of their damnation) and…carried off and shared the booty; they stole the chests in which the books and relics were preserved…thinking that they had acquired a hoard of gold and silver." The pagans got drunk on wine from the ships and started killing each other for the chests. They were disappointed, however, to find not gold and silver inside, but only manuscripts. In anger, they threw these into the marshes. Willibald adds that "by the grace of God and through the prayers of the archbishop and martyr Saint Boniface, the manuscripts were discovered a long time afterwards" and were returned to Saint Boniface's monastery at Fulda, where "they are used with great advantage to the salvation of souls even at the present day." Three of these recovered manuscripts appear to be still extant — tradition identifies one of them, which was almost cut through by a sharp instrument, as the one that Boniface is said to have held above his head when he was killed. What the pagans failed to realize in tossing them aside, however, was that such books were to Boniface and his contemporaries (as they remain for us) treasures more valuable than gold; they were the implements and weapons of their ancestors, and they continued (and continue now) to provide people with the ultimate and most lasting form of protection, "the salvation of souls."

Boniface's treasure, however, was not limited to the discarded books. Willibald also mentions the presence of "holy relics," with which Boniface evidently "armed himself" when he left his tent to confront his attackers. After the massacre, the pagans threw away the books; we do not know what happened to the relics. Willibald does, however, relate that "the bodies of the holy bishop and of the other martyrs" were brought back for burial. A disagreement ensued over where they should be interred, but God intervened and the saint's body was returned to Fulda. The people of Fulda, in spite of their mourning, experienced great joy, because Boniface "would protect them and their heirs for all time to come."

Of what, then, did Boniface's treasure consist? Of the "profitable" books, to be sure, but these were not the only weapons of the Christian warrior. The relics with which he "armed" himself for his last battle were lost, but they were replaced by those of the new martyrs, particularly by the body of the great apostle, Boniface himself. Willibald's *Life*, then, is a kind of *Beowulf* in reverse. Here the deceased warrior is not buried uselessly, with a useless treasure; instead, he actually becomes the treasure, for his relics are a channel for spiritual grace to the living. He also becomes a living defender and savior of his fellow warriors — the monks and the clergy — and the Christian people of Fulda for all time to come.

We began this essay by noting the problem faced by missionaries in all times: how to appropriate existing values without losing the counter-cultural and transforming values proper to the new religion. In the early Middle Ages, Christian missionaries to Germania dealt with a formidable version of this problem: the native cultures they encountered were deeply committed to ideals of military leadership and loyalty in which "treasure" had both a practical and a symbolic role. Saint Boniface and his biographer Willibald did not negate these values; rather, they transformed them into something that their ethnic brethren would have regarded as both strange and strangely appealing. Instead of fighting, the leader displayed courage that strengthened the followers' steadfast resolve not to fight; the martyrs themselves assumed the role of treasure, to safeguard the people and lead them to glory with God in the hereafter. In this way, the barbarian ethos was reconciled with the Gospel of Peace.

Bibliographic Note

Tacitus's *Germania* is readily available (with his *Agricola*) in a translation by Harold Mattingly and S.A. Handford (Harmondsworth: Penguin Books, 1970). Constance B. Hieatt's translation of *Beowulf* in *Beowulf and Other Old English Poems* (New York: Bantam, 1983) is a good prose rendering and easy to read, and there is a fine inter-linear text in Richard M. Trask, *Beowulf and Judith: Two Heroes* (Lanham, MD: University Press of America, 1997). For the English translation of "The Life of Saint Boniface" by Willibald, see *The Anglo-Saxon Missionaries in Germany*, ed. C.H. Talbot (London: Sheed and Ward, 1981 [1954]), 25–62, which also contains several other relevant primary texts, including Alcuin's "Life of Saint Willibrord" and "The Correspondence of Saint Boniface." For additional primary source material concerning Anglo-Saxon England, see the bibliographic notes to Chapters 6 and 7, below.

In addition to studies cited there, see Peter Hunter Blair, *Introduction to Anglo-Saxon England*, 3rd ed. (Cambridge: Cambridge University Press, 2003); it has an excellent introduction and commendable bibliography by Simon Keynes. For overall information on the Anglo-Saxons, one cannot do better than *The Blackwell Encyclopedia of Anglo-Saxon England*, ed. Michael Lapidge, John Blair, Simon Keynes, and Donald Skragg (Oxford: Blackwell, 2000). For a general but intelligent discussion of the early spread of Christianity in Europe, see Ian Wood, *The Missionary Life: Saints and the Evangelization of Europe, 400–1050* (London: Longman, 2001). See also H. Mayr-Harting, *The Coming of Christianity to Anglo-Saxon England* (London: B.T. Batsford, 1972); and J.H. Clay, *In the Shadow of Death: Saint Boniface and the Conversion of Hessia, 721–54* (Turnhout: Brepols, 2011). Finally, for the spectacular archaeological find at Sutton Hoo, see M.O.H. Carver, *Sutton Hoo: Burial Ground of Kings?* (Philadelphia: University of Pennsylvania Press, 1998).

FOUR

The Written World of Gregory of Tours

Sam Collins

The *Histories* of Gregory, Bishop of Tours, can be bewildering. Clear and obvious narrative connections are few and far between in a jumble of vivid scenes of sixth-century life: kings and bishops, holy men and witches, priests and pagans, divine fire, frozen summers, and spring at midwinter. Gregory presents us with an entire world, chaotic, unpredictable, and alive with detail. He tells us that his work sets out to reproduce the confusing and confused surface of life itself: "As I continue to follow the march of history I recount for you at one and the same time, and in the muddled and confused order in which these events occurred, the holy deeds of the Saints and the way in which whole races of people were butchered. It will not, I am sure, be held unreasonable of me if I describe the blessed lives of the Saints together with the disasters of the unfortunate: for it is the course of events which demands this and not my own fantasy as a writer" (2.preface). With these words, Gregory minimizes his role as shaper of his own text just as he plays down the distance between text and experience. He sees his role as historian not as one who orders reality but as one who captures it. He announces his text as a conduit for pure experience and perception of a chaotic world, all of which can become the experience and perception of his readers. He presents his work not as a tract, not as a vehicle for advancing any specific argument, but rather as a way of seeing reality.

One of the most difficult challenges for readers of the *Histories* is to find a way through the thicket of circumstantial detail that makes up this reality. It is possible to dwell on Gregory's sense of the particular and never find a way to the structures and patterns that bind the work together. Yet, for all its detail, the world of the *Histories* is not all surface, nor is the surface the sole object of Gregory's attention. Gregory's literary creation may be compared to a carpet page from the roughly contemporary Book of Durrow, a beautifully illustrated gospel book produced in either Ireland or Northumbria in the second half of the seventh century. Up close we see individual figures and animals tangled together to the point of abstraction. Step back, however, and this detail recedes to reveal a unified pattern and structure. Gregory's project displays a similar tension between the chaotic appearance of individual events and the divine pattern and plan that he sees directing the course of history. Throughout his work Gregory strives to interpret reality, to see beyond its jagged surface to the divinely guided truth beneath. His confidence as a reader of this reality may waver, but his intention to find patterns in the life of the world does not. He presents a disordered swirl of events while arguing for an underlying reason that drives forward the history of the world.

Gregory's major work has come to be known in English as the *History of the Franks*. This is a shame. His original title, *Ten Books of Histories,* or simply *Histories,* better conveys the scope of his project, as the Franks and their history represent only one aspect of his work. We owe the misleading title to an early abbreviator, who, working shortly after Gregory's death and ignoring Gregory's curse on those who would tamper with his work (10.31), produced an abridged text by removing most of the ecclesiastical material and focusing instead on the affairs of the Frankish royal house. *History of the Franks* would indeed be an appropriate title for this much shorter work, but in the *Histories* Gregory is after something bigger: all of life is his subject.

Gregory's literary output suggests his wide interests and learning. He lists his bibliography at the end of the *Histories:* "I, Gregory, have written ten books of this *History,* seven books of *Miracles* and one on the *Lives of the Fathers.* I have composed a book of *Commentaries on the Psalms.* I also wrote a book on the *Offices of the Church* [*On Reckoning the Movement of the Stars*]" (10.31). In addition to these, we can also attribute to Gregory the preface to a collection of the masses of Sidonius Apollinaris, the fifth-century Gallo-Roman aristocrat and bishop of Clermont; an adapted translation of an account of the Seven Sleepers of Ephesus; and a short tract on the miracles of Andrew. Aside from the psalm commentary, of which only a few short fragments exist, all his literary works are extant.

While the bulk of his literary production can be attributed to the years of his episcopate (573-94), it is difficult to assign precise dates to Gregory's different works. Frequent cross-references among them help establish a relative chronology for his writings, and some dates may be gleaned for the composition of individual chapters in the various works. This chronology is complicated, however, by evidence that Gregory continually revised his work and added new material to it; he seems therefore to have worked on most of his books simultaneously over a period of many years.

Details of Gregory's ancestry and career are impressive, even if they are fragmentary. We know that he was born in the late 530s in the Auvergne, a mountainous area of what is today central France. His wealthy Gallo-Roman family could boast a senatorial pedigree and a long tradition of producing ecclesiastical office-holders. This was status of the highest order. Ancestors on both sides of Gregory's family, many of whom appear in the *Histories,* had been bishops in Gaul at a time when hereditary succession to episcopal office was common, if not expected. Gregory could claim descent on his father's side from one of the 48 martyrs of Lyon (177 AD), among the most celebrated spiritual fathers of Gaul. His mother's side of the family included two bishops commemorated as saints.

Gregory spent his early years, for which we have very little information, at the episcopal see of Clermont, held at the time by an uncle, and at Lyons where another relative and future saint seems to have been his tutor. In 573, probably in his mid-30s, he was appointed bishop of Tours by King Sigibert and his queen Brunhild, both of whom play modest roles in the *Histories.* It is telling that we know of Gregory's episcopal appointment not from Gregory himself but only through his friend, the poet and courtier Venantius Fortunatus. Gregory's silence about the circumstances of his own elevation to the see of Tours may indicate unease over the prominent role played by a king in a matter that, in Gregory's mind, should have been subject to the authority of other bishops. Whatever the circumstances of his elevation to the episcopate, Tours was an appropriate venue for the advancement of his career. Gregory's family had long been associated with the see. Of the 18 bishops of Tours before him, only five lacked any relation to his family (5.49). Gregory served as bishop of Tours until his death in 594.

These concrete details of Gregory's biography, however revealing they may be, are misleading. His literary goals do not seem to have included autobiography of any easily recognizable sort. So biographical information of this kind must be teased out of brief and oblique references scattered across his many works, a formidable task indeed. Gregory could have devoted his *Histories* to the successes of his family and their long-lived tenure in the ecclesiastical hierarchy of Gaul, but his famous family enters his work virtually unannounced. Only very careful readers will know that it is Gregory's family to which King Lothar refers as one of "the noblest and most distinguished families in the land" (4.15). In his text the significance of his family and its important connections recede; so too does Gregory himself.

Although Gregory was an eyewitness or participant in many of the episodes in the later books of the *Histories,* he is often easy to miss. He enters and exits the pages of the text quietly, never privileging moments of his own observation over scenes built solely on others' reports or his own imagination. His narrative is just as vivid and detailed for events he could not possibly have seen (3.15, 4.12) as it is for events at which he was present (5.14, 9.6). When he does appear, he presents himself as one character in a much larger panorama. Take, for example, the dramatic events surrounding the trial of his fellow-bishop, Praetextatus, a key moment in Gregory's discussion of the reign of Chilperic, the most wicked of the *Histories'* many wicked kings. Here a group of bishops gather to debate what should be done about trumped-up charges of treason brought by the king against Praetextatus. Gregory is present at the council, but inconspicuously so. His narrative opens as Praetextatus faces the combative accusations of the king before the assembled bishops. The first hint we have of Gregory's presence in this audience comes when the king withdraws, leaving the assembled bishops to debate among themselves; Gregory refers to this group as "we" (5.18).

Later, Gregory's role in the scene expands. As the deliberation wears on, he inserts a speech of his own. In it, he calls for bravery in the face of an unjust king bent on revenge. He gives us this speech because it is the act of a bishop, doing what bishops ought to do. In other words, Gregory is more interested in archetype and the moral quality of events than he is in emphasizing his own role. Here the archetype is familiar: in this moment bishops act, if only reluctantly, on behalf of the good in opposition to a king whose motivations are suspect at best. Gregory thus emphasizes the continuity of episcopal history over the particulars of the moment. Episcopal voices raised in righteous opposition to the wicked are more important to him than autobiography. It is pattern that comes to the fore, and patterns—or at least a search for patterns amid the jumbled events of daily reality—is what the *Histories* are all about.

Gregory's self-presentation is analogous to his presentation of the world around him. As he emphasizes his own role as a bishop among bishops, so in his presentation of the Frankish kings of Gaul he underscores the universal through the particular. The Franks of Gregory's day were relative newcomers to Gaul, and they ruled as a tiny minority over the much larger population of this formerly Roman province. As the scion of an aristocratic Gallo-Roman family with deep local roots, Gregory has the advantage of being an outsider in his observations of the Franks and how they rule over their new kingdom, but it is striking how little he presses this advantage. Barbarians and Romans are not categories that hold much interest for him. Nevertheless, the Frankish kings, their wives, and their rebellious children are central to the *Histories*.

As Gregory records the many misdeeds (and occasional good deeds) of the Franks, he presents their wickedness and greatness as part of a larger pattern of human kingship and history. He tells us a good deal about the myths and expectations surrounding Frankish royalty: Clovis divides the spoils of war (2.27); his father Chloderic's virility provides a messy origin story (2.12); his queen Clotild faces a terrible set of choices for two young princes (3.18). While such lovingly crafted episodes add life to the narrative, when Gregory analyzes the bigger issue of royal success and royal failure, his vision encompasses more than the Frankish kings of Gaul. From the start of his work he assesses the kings of his day in universal terms: Cain and Abel are flagships for the *Histories* (1.2–3). Rather than original sin in the Garden of Eden, Gregory presents the fratricide of Cain as the crime that plunges mankind into wickedness forever. Cain's murder of his brother is the sin that dominates the landscape of Gregory's Gaul and that preoccupies Clovis and his descendants (1.2–3, 2.42, 5.preface). Gregory's kings are prone to wickedness not because they are Franks but because they are subject to the primal sin that deformed human society from the beginning. Gaul suffers from unending civil wars brought about not by the barbarity of the Franks but by this sin endemic to mankind.

The figure of Clovis (whose name means "Glorious Warrior") looms over the later kings of the *Histories,* and Gregory's narrative technique is on full display in recounting his deeds. These stories have the quality of legend, especially when read next to the disorderly later generations of the *Histories.* The figure of Clovis that emerges in these episodes, however, is

no unambiguous champion from an heroic past. He is intriguingly contradictory, both the model of murderous political efficiency and the recipient
of effusive praise (2.40, 2.42, 5.preface). In his combination of cunning
wickedness and divinely guided greatness, his character shows a pattern
integral to the *Histories*' presentation of the possibilities and limitations of
royal power. For Gregory, Clovis's greatest deed is his renunciation of his
ancestors' paganism and his conversion to Catholic Christianity. In this
context he calls Clovis the "new Constantine" and depicts his battlefield
conversion in a decidedly Constantinian light (2.30–31). This praise is,
however, more ambivalent than it first sounds. Gregory has already introduced us to Constantine, but his description little resembles the great
Christian emperor familiar to readers of Eusebius. Gregory mentions
Constantine's conversion almost in passing while he attempts to provide a
secure date for the birth of Martin, a far more important and certain figure in his universe (1.36). Beyond Constantine's conversion to the true
faith, Gregory quickly summarizes the emperor's other achievements: "In
the twentieth year of his reign Constantine killed his son Crispius with
poison and his wife Fausta in a hot bath, because they had planned to remove
him from the throne by treason" (1.36). Gregory thus mixes Constantine's
virtues (his conversion) with his faults (the murders of his wife and son).
Compare this to Gregory's Clovis and his lengthy list of virtues: Clovis listens to bishops and believes what he should; he wages war against those
who do not, and in his rough way he brings peace and stability to Gaul
(2.31, 2.37, 5.preface). At the same time Gregory shows us that Clovis buys
this stability with a series of treacherous murders of family members and
other rivals (2.40, 2.42). While the Clovis who "walks before God with an
upright heart" (2.40) is difficult to reconcile with the Clovis who has run
out of family members to murder (2.42), it is from these contradictions
that we begin to discern the texture of Gregory's political expectations.

The most iconic scene in all the *Histories* nicely encapsulates Gregory's
political vision. In the twenty-seventh chapter of the second book,
Gregory records Clovis's first act as king: the defeat of a confederation of
enemies at Soissons. Gregory's scene and the conquering warband bring to
mind the barbarians of Tacitus. When the time came for the Franks to
divide the spoils of war among themselves, the bishop of Soissons begged
Clovis to return sacred vessels stolen in the battle. Although not yet a
Christian convert, Clovis complied with the bishop's wishes. As the army
set about to divvy up the treasure, the king asked for the bishop's silver

ewer, probably a eucharistic vessel, over and above his rightful portion of the loot. Gregory describes the Frankish warband, always an egalitarian institution, bristling at Clovis's claim to more than his fair share. One of their number stepped forward, Gregory tells us, "a feckless fellow, greedy and prompt to anger...raised his battle-axe and struck the ewer"; the bishop's sacred vessel fell to the ground cut in two. Gregory imagines Clovis's thoughts: "The king hid his chagrin under a pretense of long-suffering patience. He took the vessel and handed it over to the envoy of the church; but in his heart he resented what had happened." Several months later, in the spring, as he inspected his troops on the parade ground, Clovis had his revenge. When he came to the man who had destroyed the bishop's ewer, Clovis upbraided the state of his equipment and threw his axe to the ground. "As the soldier bent forward to pick up his weapon, King Clovis raised his own battle-axe in the air and split his skull with it. 'That is what you did to my ewer in Soissons'" (2.27).

Deference to bishops and brutality to everyone else define Gregory's account of the reign of Clovis. His Clovis, like all the kings of the *Histories*, is never far from murder. Unlike many of the kings of the *Histories*, however, Gregory's Clovis uses violence to make Gaul safe for the bishops and the churches they govern; for this, Gregory celebrates him.

The *Histories* then are not in any sense a national history; they do not require a heroic trajectory tied to the fate of the Frankish kings. Nor do they tell the story of how the Frankish kings became good, but rather how, sometimes with the help of kings and sometimes without, the Catholic Church in Gaul grows and prospers. We wait in vain for Gregory to come forward with a model Christian king of the kind Einhard would make of Charlemagne more than two centuries later. Even the Edwin of Bede's *Ecclesiastical History* (see below, Chapter 8), parallel to Clovis in many ways, is a cleaner figure, an unambiguously Christian king on whose goodness the fate of Christianity in his kingdom depends (2.9–20). Bede has faith in the power of kings to do the work necessary for a Christian world. Gregory's assessment of the place of kings in human society is more skeptical; the goodness of kings is inevitably compromised, and their potential for wickedness must not be underestimated.

Wicked kings come in many varieties and degrees in the *Histories*, but none is so wicked as Chilperic, who dominates the narrative in Books 5 and 6. Gregory singles out "the Nero and Herod of our time" for the most extensive treatment of royal misbehavior anywhere in the *Histories* (6.46).

Chilperic displays a rich assembly of those sins that plagued Clovis and his sons; the Chilperic episodes are steeped in fratricidal warfare and indiscriminate murder. But Gregory's attention lingers on Chilperic for more than just these most royal of sins. Chilperic fails where Clovis, for all his faults, succeeded. While Gregory's picture of Clovis was tempered by his timely conversion, his respect for the saints (particularly Martin), and his deference to the opinions of his bishops, Chilperic has none of these qualities to recommend him. Gregory's Chilperic is defined and, according to the *Histories,* undone by his religious presumption. We see him busily engaged in the prosecution of unjust trials, first against Bishop Praetextatus (5.18) and then against Gregory himself (5.49); another bishop claims that having his diocese come under Chilperic's control is like falling from heaven into hell (6.22).

This portrait of Chilperic reaches its nadir when, in Gregory's presence, the king steers into heretical waters by publishing a decree on trinitarian doctrine (5.44). The nature of the Trinity had been the subject of many of the fiercest doctrinal struggles in the recent past, and not least in Gaul. Chilperic's confidence in his ability to arbitrate Christian doctrine and his presumption of episcopal authority dominates the scene. Gregory tells us that Chilperic had published a decree that abolished any distinction between the Father, Son, and Holy Spirit, and insisted that all in the kingdom call the Trinity simply God. The king came to his idiosyncratic view not out of ignorance but through his own reading of Scripture: "'That was how He appeared to the prophets and patriarchs,' he said, 'and that is how He was considered in the Law.'" Chilperic shows here that he is thoroughly Christianized in a way Clovis was not. He writes Christian poetry in poor imitation of a master from the past; his religious knowledge is so subtle and extensive that he can commission forged canon law when the situation demands it (5.18). This Chilperic may seem to us to be more thoroughly Christian than Clovis with his rough piety, but Chilperic's assumptions about the king's role in the religion of the kingdom earn him Gregory's scorn.

Gregory presents us with a king who assumes it is his right to set out religious doctrine for the kingdom. This conjunction of royal power and right religious belief has a long history in Europe. Roman emperors had always been ultimately responsible for the maintenance of correct religious doctrine in the empire. When Constantine gave his support to the Christian god he did not abandon this ancient relationship between the emperor and the heavens. In his account of the Council of Nicaea in the *Life of Constantine,* Eusebius presents the emperor as the guardian and enforcer of orthodoxy, a force for religious order in a divided world of quarreling bishops. Gregory's Chilperic seems to work from a similar set of assumptions about royal power, but to the opposite effect. Chilperic claims his royal decree on the Trinity trumps the authority of his bishops, and in so doing Gregory makes him look foolish. He gives us a king who bundles heresy together with disdain for the saints, the authority of church doctrine, and episcopal hierarchy. Unlike those moments of correct belief that softened and justified Clovis's otherwise bloody career, Chilperic emerges as still decidedly royal but also as the mortal enemy of right belief as maintained and handed down exclusively by an unbroken chain of bishops. In this way Gregory uncouples royal legitimacy from right doctrine, just as he gives us a world in which the progress of the Church depends only marginally on kings.

The failings of rulers, from Constantine to Chilperic, are predictable: kings may sometimes act on behalf of correct Christianity, but just as often they stand in the way of the advancement of the Church. For positive continuity in the sweep of history, Gregory looks elsewhere — to the saints, bishops, and other holy men and women who populate the pages of his work. They provide what kings cannot, an unbroken chain of right action that stretches back to the life of Christ and looks forward, beyond the end of the text, to the next world. Gregory sees this continuity around him, and he wants to underscore its presence to his readers. This kind of continuity in the fabric of history comes out in Gregory's taste for describing the essential moments in the lives of the saints as lists of miracles, just as he reduces the life of Jesus to a series of miracles (1.20). There is room for variation among miracles, but within this variation the dominant note remains that of harmony among the holy actions of the saints. This harmony is not simply a matter of literary taste; the miraculous power of the saints binds Gregory's own day with the beginning of creation.

The saints and their miracles are solid points of meaning in the otherwise turbulent course of history. In direct contrast to the sporadic, inchoate acts of goodness and wickedness performed by kings, the saints present a stable picture of the actions of the divine in the created world. In this way Gregory does more than connect contemporary history in Gaul with biblical history; he works to show that contemporary history grows smoothly out of the biblical past. He is after deeper patterns. The actions of the saints provide continual evidence for the presence of divine action in the world and of a divine plan for it. When Gregory announces in his preface to Book 1 that his purpose in writing the *Histories* is to provide comfort "for the sake of those who are losing hope as they see the end of the world coming nearer and nearer," he means to reassure his readers that God's plan still guides the course of the world. The actions of the saints in contemporary Gaul prove the presence of a divine plan steering worldly events exactly as they always have since the remote biblical past. Gregory, in this way, both describes reality and subtly interprets it. He reports the miracles of the saints and at the same time through this act of reporting emphasizes the unbroken connection of divine presence in historical time.

Just as the miracles of the saints provide evidence for God's continued action in the world, so the world itself provides Gregory with signs of the divine plan. An assiduous reader of the wonders of nature, Gregory is repeatedly confronted in his *Histories* with seemingly impossible or miraculous natural phenomena. He searches for meaning in these signs. At his most confident he reads them as if their meaning is clear. A "great beacon" in the sky and an earthquake presage the death of King Gundovald, he tells us, as if such signs must mean only this (7.11). Elsewhere, however, he is less sure; wonders of nature can mislead (9.5) or be utterly inexplicable (5.23). Whatever the limits of his interpretative powers, Gregory imagines the role of the historian as being one who looks for meaning beyond the confusing surface of events: "Just as I have done myself, so Eusebius, Severus and Jerome mingled together in their chronicles the wars waged by kings and the holy deeds of martyrs. I have composed my book in the same way, so that the onward march of the centuries and the succession of the years down to our own times may be studied in their entirety" (2.preface). On this model, history is jumbled events collected and laid out in order so that it may be studied (like portents in the sky) for its meaning. For this reason Gregory is adamant that his works be kept whole: "Nevertheless I conjure you all, Bishops of the Lord who will have charge of Tours cathedral after my unworthy self, I conjure you all…that you never permit these books to be destroyed, or to be rewritten, or to be reproduced in part only with sections omitted…. Keep them in your possession intact, with no amendments and just as I have left them to you" (10.31). The crush of detail that makes the *Histories* difficult reading thus struck Gregory as his work's essential feature. No detail is more important than another; all creation, when closely observed, points to the same truth.

Bibliographic Note

The *Histories* are widely available in Lewis Thorpe's serviceable translation, *History of the Franks* (London: Penguin Books, 1974). A.C. Murray, *Gregory of Tours* (Toronto: University of Toronto Press, 2005), translates the shortened version of the *Histories*, which limits its usefulness but is otherwise excellent. Gregory did not think of his *Histories* in isolation and neither should we. Major hagiographical works are *Life of the Fathers*, trans. Edward James (Liverpool: Liverpool University Press, 1985); *Glory of the Martyrs*, trans. Raymond Van Dam (Liverpool: Liverpool University Press, 1988); and *Glory of the Confessors*, trans. Raymond Van Dam (Liverpool: Liverpool University Press, 1988). Two further hagiographic texts are "The Miracles of the Bishop Saint Martin" and "The Suffering and Miracles of the Martyr Saint Julian," both in Raymond Van Dam, *Saints and their Miracles in Late Antique Gaul* (Princeton: Princeton University Press, 1993); and "On the Course of the Stars," in Edward Peters, *Monks, Bishops, and Pagans* (Philadelphia: University of Pennsylvania Press, 1975).

The three major interpreters of Gregory's work, on whose expertise I have relied in this chapter, are Walter Goffart, *The Narrators of Barbarian History* (Notre Dame, IN: Notre Dame University Press, 2005 [1988]); Martin Heinzelman, *Gregory of Tours* (Cambridge: Cambridge University Press, 2001); and Giselle de Nie, *Views from a Many-Windowed Tower* (Amsterdam: Editions Rodolphi, 1987). These should be supplemented with Kathleen Mitchell and Ian Wood, eds., *The World of Gregory of Tours* (Leiden: Brill, 2002).

For the *Histories'* textual problems, see Walter Goffart, "From *Historiae* to *Historia Francorum* and Back Again," in *Religion, Culture, and Society in the Early Middle Ages*, ed. T.F.X. Noble and J. Contreni (Kalamazoo: Western Michigan University Press, 1987). Older, but still essential, are Eric Auerbach, *Mimesis* (Princeton: Princeton University Press, 1946), and J.M. Wallace-Hadrill, "The Work of Gregory of Tours in Light of Recent Research," in his *The Long-Haired Kings* (Toronto: University of Toronto Press, 1982 [1962]), 49–70.

FIVE

Two Lives of Saint Radegund

Jason Glenn

On 13 August 587, Radegund, once queen of the Franks, died in the monastery she had established for a community of women three decades earlier in Poitiers, an episcopal city in the heartland of Frankish Gaul. By all accounts, she was a remarkable person who had lived a remarkable life. A Thuringian princess, she was a still a young child in 531 when the Frankish king Lothar and his brother slaughtered the royal family of the Thuringian peoples who lived to the north in what is today Germany, between the Rhine and Elbe Rivers. Lothar sent Radegund and her brother off to one of his estates where she spent seven years until he married her in 538. Although we know little about the details of their relationship, we do know that they had no children and that by 550 she had withdrawn from the king's company to a villa that he had previously provided for her not far from Poitiers. It is unclear whether her retreat from married life had anything to do with Lothar's supposed murder of her brother around 550. It is likewise difficult to determine from contemporary sources how Lothar reacted to her departure. While there is some reason to believe that he sought her return, the king appears to have consented to the separation and, ultimately, to her decision to build and enter the monastery in Poitiers. It was there that the holy Radegund lived within a monastic community from about 560 until her death.

Shortly thereafter, a friend and admirer wrote a hagiographic account of her life. Nearly 20 years later, one of the women who lived in her monastery added to that *vita* a second book, in fact, a second *vita* that complements rather than merely extends the first. Together, the works have typically been viewed as two components of the *Life of Radegund*. Saints' lives are notoriously unreliable as sources of detailed information about the lives and experiences of the saints themselves. Unlike modern biographies, they were not intended to show what made a saint unique but rather in what ways they conformed to accepted ideals of holiness. These *vitae* are no exception. Indeed, they hardly permit us to enrich the contours of Radegund's life as sketched roughly above. Nevertheless, if we leave aside questions about their historical accuracy, they do offer insight into the particular qualities the authors sought to emphasize in their efforts to preserve or, rather, to shape her memory. And when read together, they offer a glimpse into the ways these two authors—and, perhaps, by extension, their audiences—conceived holiness. They may also permit us to detect some of the ways in which the first *vita* may not—or may no longer—have served sufficiently the interests of the community for which the second was written. In other words, even if they tell us less than we might like about Radegund herself, these *vitae* teach us something about their authors and about the larger world in which they wrote.

Venantius Fortunatus, a poet who moved freely in the elite circles of the Frankish and Gallo-Roman aristocracy, met Radegund when he was in his twenties during a trip to Poitiers in the mid 560s, a few years after he had come to Gaul from Italy. He struck up a friendship with her—the two exchanged letters and poems—and ultimately wrote the first *vita* shortly after she died in 587. For it, he drew on the early Christian hagiographic tradition, most notably the works of Sulpicius Severus and Athanasius of Alexandria discussed above in Chapter 2. Venantius thus presents a Radegund whose spiritual virtues and piety place her comfortably alongside the great saints of the early medieval world. But Venantius faced two particular challenges in making use of this tradition. In the first place, unlike Martin and Antony, about whom they wrote, or most other early monastic figures, Radegund was—to state the obvious—a woman. Of those relatively few women to be held up as exemplars for their piety in the early centuries of Christianity, most were celebrated for their deaths as martyrs rather than for their ascetic practices. And those ascetic men who so impressed early Christians for their dedication to the holy life were of more common origins than Radegund. Martin, for instance, was the son of a soldier. Radegund, by contrast, was not merely born of royal blood, but she had become a queen. For Venantius, her social status and her sex posed problems he needed to address to make the case for her sanctity.

Venantius deals with Radegund's sex in the prologue, which I quote here in full.

> Our Redeemer is so richly and abundantly generous that He wins mighty victories through the female sex and, despite their frail physique (*fragiliores*), He confers glory and greatness on women through strength of mind. By faith, Christ makes them strong who were born weak (*mollites*) so that, when those who appeared to be imbeciles (*imbecilles*) are crowned with their merits by Him who made them, they garner praise for their Creator who hid heavenly treasure in earthen vessels. For Christ the king dwells with his riches in their bowels. Mortifying themselves in the world, despising earthly consort, purified of worldly contamination, trusting not in the transitory, dwelling not in error but seeking to live with God, they are united with the Redeemer's glory in Paradise. One of that company is she whose earthly life we are attempting to present to the public, though in homely style, so that the glorious memory that she, who lives with Christ, has left with us will be celebrated in this world. (1.prologue)[1]

If Venantius hoped, as he suggests, that what followed would secure the celebration of Radegund's memory, that is, that it would persuade the "public" of her exceptional holiness, then we might assume that his likely audience shared his reservations about the "female sex." For the moment, however, let us leave open the question of his public and the makeup of his intended audience. Let us simply note instead that, for him — and presumably at least some of that audience — women were more frail than men (*fragiliores*), were weak or unmanly (*mollites*), and appeared to be feeble (*imbecilles*). When infused with faith, however, they could be strong enough to escape their transitory earthly existence, achieve salvation, and live with God. In other words, a woman who dedicated herself to a Christian life of the sort exemplified by Radegund — or, at least the Radegund he would go on to present — could, like her, transcend the inherent shortcomings of her sex.

From the outset, Venantius presents us with anecdotes in which Radegund does precisely those things he signals in the prologue. As a young child in the custody of her Frankish guardians who taught her,

---

[1] Note that I have inserted parenthetical references to the Latin, which are discussed below.

among other things "suitable to her sex," to read and write, Radegund often spoke to other children about her desire to be martyred (1.2). She did likewise as an adult, "though it was not an age of persecution," by trying to burn her body (1.26). Venantius offers other examples of her abnegation of the flesh: she wore a hair shirt—a course undergarment commonly worn by ascetics for bodily mortification—and one year during Lenten season she fettered her arms and neck in iron rings bound together by heavy chains, which caused her flesh to swell and bleed (1.5, 1.25). She also branded herself with a cross made of brass and carried a basin full of burning coals to make her agony more terrible. Venantius vividly describes the hissing of her flesh and the pain she concealed: "Thus did a woman willingly suffer such bitterness for the sweetness of Christ" (1.26). In other words, as these examples attest, she mortified the flesh and sought to live with God, which were two of the ways Venantius asserts in the prologue that a woman could overcome the weaknesses of her sex and make her way to salvation.

As we saw above, Venantius suggests that a woman must also despise an earthly consort, cleanse herself of worldly contamination, and distrust the transitory. The *vita* is peppered with examples of Radegund's piety framed in this way. In particular, Venantius takes pains to explain away her earthly union to a man. He reports, for instance, that "she was more Christ's partner than her husband's companion" (1.3). And his description of her nocturnal habits suggests that she found the thought of lying with her husband distasteful. According to Venantius, she would ask to leave his side and the warmth of the bedchamber in order "to relieve nature." She would then lie prostrate in prayer by the latrine "so long that the cold pierced her through and through." She willingly suffered such "torments" to avoid "becoming cheap in the eyes of Christ." In short, and in the words of Venantius, "People said that the King had yoked himself to a *monacha* [female monk] rather than a queen" (1.5). Whether people actually said such things, Venantius wants his audience to think it an apt assessment.

As this passage suggests, it was perhaps as great a challenge for him to deal with Radegund's royalty as it was to deal with her sex. While he does assert that "the most Blessed Radegund was of the highest earthly rank" and elaborates her royal pedigree at the outset (1.2), there are remarkably few references to her royal status throughout the text. Instead, there is a noteworthy tension between the fulfilment of her queenly duties and her desire to live a holy life. This tension seems, in his presentation, irreconcilable, and he goes to great lengths to demonstrate how Radegund rejected her status and the worldly role and responsibilities that came with queen-ship. Indeed, when Lothar wanted to make her his queen, Venantius reports, "She avoided the trappings of royalty, so she would not grow great in the world but in Him to Whom she was devoted and she remained unchanged by earthly glory" (1.2). And on those few occasions when he mentions her "queenly splendor," adorned with gems, gold, and fine fab-rics "in the barbarian fashion," he notes that she left her clothes and orna-ments for the poor or to a church (1.9, 1.13). Even when she felt compelled to maintain appearances, we see that she nevertheless rejected the material comforts to which she had access. At meals, we are told, she wore a hair shirt under her royal garb (1.6). Likewise, she eschewed the earthly riches of her station by giving away tribute and thus "paid out what she received lest the burden weigh her down" (1.3). Elsewhere we read that she "acted like a servant," that "the devout lady, queen by birth and marriage, mistress of the palace, served the poor as a handmaid" (1.4). In each of these instances—which, incidentally, offer a glimpse into Frankish queenship of her day—Radegund overcomes not merely the obstacles to holiness inher-ent in her sex, but also those she faces as a person of royal blood.

Venantius thus had a particular type of sanctity in mind when he set out to demonstrate the holiness of Radegund. He offers readers a holy woman comparable to the men whose deeds inform his sense of holiness, a holiness easily recognized by the literate clerical elite of his day. This is not to suggest that he was self-consciously proposing a male model of behavior for religious women. But in efforts to demonstrate that her holi-ness transcended the limitations of her sex and social status—i.e., that she was a worthy saint—he transposed and thereby, if unwittingly, reinscribed conventional ideals of holiness, of the holy man. Indeed, her first miracle—the resuscitation of a dead girl—is "patterned after an ancient model in the tradition of the blessed Martin" (1.37), which is in turn patterned after a miracle of Christ (*Matthew* 9). Likewise, Venantius says that she emulates Saint Germain of Auxerre (d. c. 450) by grinding flour with her own hands (1.16). Thus, Venantius wrote in the idiom of the elite churchmen of his day. And not long before his death (c. 609), he became one himself, as he was made bishop of Poitiers.

———

Shortly after the death of Venantius and thus approximately two decades after Radegund had passed away, a member of the religious community she had founded wrote a second book for the *vita*, apparently at the

request of Abbess Dedimia and the whole congregation (2.prologue).
Although she is one of the few early medieval women writers we know by
name—Baudonivia—we know nothing about her apart from her work.
She claims in a prologue that she will recount, among other things, "a few
of her many miracles" not otherwise included in the work of Venantius.
But she does not merely continue his account chronologically with
posthumous miracles as we so often find in continuations of saints' *vitae*
or miracles collections. Quite the contrary, she devotes most of her attention to the deeds of Radegund while she was a member of the community
in Poitiers. Indeed, although Baudonivia may well have intended for her
book to follow and to complement that of Venantius—she refers to his
work on a number of occasions (2.prologue, 2.1, 2.8)—it is no mere continuation. It stands alone as a more or less autonomous *vita*. As we now
turn to her work, let us note that we are not concerned, here, with questions about which of the two *vitae* is more accurate. Rather, we shall be
more interested in how each of the two authors chose to demonstrate the
holiness of the saint.

Baudonivia's Radegund is not the Radegund of Venantius. To be sure,
both Radegunds are holy. And both *vitae* draw on hagiographic traditions
grounded principally in the lives of holy men. But the qualities of sanctity
in the two are not quite the same. Baudonivia's Radegund hardly mortifies
the flesh, nor is she overly conflicted about her royal status. Her creator
feels no compulsion to demonstrate that Radegund needed to overcome—
or that she did overcome—the shortcomings of her sex. Indeed, Baudonivia's
vita is more self-confident in tone than that of Venantius, which reads, at
times, as if its author protests too much in efforts to craft his ascetic saint.
Perhaps because Venantius had already done so—although, I suspect not—
Baudonivia feels no real obligation to emphasize the queen's impulses and
inclinations for a life of poverty and suffering. This is not to suggest that
her Radegund did not pursue a life of abstinence, that Baudonivia fails to
appreciate these pursuits, or that, more generally, Venantius's Radegund is
not recognizable in her presentation of the saint. But when we read the two
vitae side by side we discover that the two authors had quite different concerns and aims.

In contrast to the picture Venantius develops, Baudonivia shows us a
holy woman whose royal ties serve not merely the interests of Radegund
and her community but also those of the larger Frankish population. She
tells us very little about Radegund's life before she withdrew from the king,

but in the single episode she does present we see a strong and self-confident queen. En route to a banquet, Radegund and her retinue passed near a fane where non-Christian Franks worshipped, and she ordered it destroyed. Some Franks tried to stop her and defended the fane with swords and clubs. But Radegund, "who bore Christ in her heart, persevered unmoved" and had it burned to the ground. Before she moved on to the banquet, however, the Franks made peace with her retinue "thanks to her entreaties" and, perhaps more importantly, they became Christian: "They blessed the Lord, admiring the virtue and constancy of the queen" (2.2). In other words, rather than distance her Radegund from royal office, Baudonivia embraces it and shows how the queen used her power for good. As she says about the marriage to Lothar in passing before this episode, "For a brief while, in that union, she played the part of wife only to serve Christ more devoutly acting as a model laywoman" (2.1).

Even after she has withdrawn from the king to live a religious life — and after a more lengthy account of the process by which she withdrew (2.3–7) than we find in Venantius's *vita* — Baudonivia embraces Radegund's royal heritage and status among the Franks as well as the opportunities that they brought: "Whenever she heard of bitterness arising among [the kings], trembling, she sent such letters to one and then to the other pleading that they should not make war among themselves nor take up arms lest the land perish. And, likewise, she sent to their noble followers to give the high kings salutary counsel so that their power might work to the welfare of the people and the land.... So, through her intercession, there was peace among kings" (2.10). However celestial the holy woman's concerns may have been, Baudonivia thus also appreciates her intercession in secular matters.

Indeed, her secular connections could bear holy fruit. In a passage in which Baudonivia evokes the memory of Saint Helena (c. 250–c. 330), mother of Constantine (272–337) — "What Helena did in oriental lands, Radegund the blessed did in Gaul!" — she recounts how Radegund managed to get a relic of the True Cross for her community. "She sent letters to the most excellent King Sigebert ... asking that, for the welfare of the whole fatherland and the stability of his kingdom, he would permit her to ask the emperor for wood from the Lord's cross." Her wish was granted. She then sent off messengers east to the emperor who in turn sent to Poitiers not merely the relic, but "a congregation of saints" (2.16). It was therefore through, not despite, her royalty and worldly station that Radegund was able to undertake at least some of the good works to which Baudonivia points.

In this case and others, her intercession enhanced the physical and spiritual space of the community. Indeed, some of the miracles she performed enabled or led directly to the endowment of the monastery. Just before the account of the acquisition of the relic of the True Cross, Baudonivia recounts a miraculous healing of an "illustrious man" named Leo, who was accompanying two bishops to a synod. Leo's vision blurred during their travel, and by the time they arrived at Radegund's monastery, he could hardly see. He prostrated himself on Radegund's hair shirt in the chapel of Mary and was healed. Thereafter, "he laid the foundations for a basilica for Saint Radegund and gave a hundred *solidi* for the construction of the fabric" (2.15). Baudonivia mentions in passing that Leo had previously dedicated to the monastery his daughters "as the Lord's servants," which may in part explain some of his munificence. But she prefers to see it as the direct consequence of Radegund's holiness. In a similar way, Baudonivia tells us that Radegund "was determined, with great devotion, to collect relics of all the saints" and then explains how she was able to bring to her new monastery relics she had previously collected (2.13). She also offers an account of a miracle in which a priest, whom Radegund had sent to Jerusalem in search of more relics, invoked her name at a martyr's tomb and was thus able to break off a pinkie from the saint's body as a relic for her and the community (2.14).

The miracles of Baudonivia's Radegund generally differ from those recounted by Venantius. Venantius records numerous healing miracles performed mainly on women who had come to Radegund for this purpose (1.27–38). The point of such stories in the earlier work is simply to illustrate Radegund's intercessory power and to demonstrate her holiness and proximity to God. To be sure, Baudonivia sometimes writes with similar aims. In the final chapter of her book, for example, she notes that any invalid who drank water into which Radegund's pall had been dipped would be healed (2.28). However, it is remarkable that the social status of the people whom her Radegund heals is generally higher than those healed by Venantius's saint. And, like Leo whom we encountered above and an abbot from Burgundy (2.26), some of them are men. Radegund performs other types of miracles, too. In one case, she saves men in her service who had "death before their eyes" on a sinking ship. Given her concern for the endowment of the monastery, we should not be shocked to learn that these men were carrying a garment to the emperor in the east to thank him for the relic of the cross (2.17). I do not wish to suggest, here, that Baudonivia or her Radegund is somehow crass but rather that the miracles the latter performed tell us something meaningful about how and why the author values her saint. Through such deeds and the miracles by which she accomplished them, Baudonivia's Radegund brought glory to the monastery.

She also facilitated and exemplified for members of the community a life dedicated to prayer within its walls. Radegund's devotion to prayer and the celebration of the Divine Office is more prominent in Baudonivia's *vita* than in that of Venantius. She keeps vigil in prayer (2.13). She chants hymns and psalms (2.14). And she reads on in the Psalter even after the end of antiphons: "Her reading would continue and by day or by night it was never stopped" (2.9). One night, Baudonivia reports, "a raucous night bird, hateful to mankind, was breaking the peace from a tree in the middle of the monastery" while Radegund was chanting the office. With her blessing, one of her companions made the sign of the cross and told the bird that Radegund wanted it to leave: "Then, as if the creature had heard the words from God's own mouth, it took flight and was never seen again," so we are told, because birds and beast obeyed her just as she obeyed God (2.19). Likewise, in the passage that immediately precedes this one in the *vita*, we learn that she would regularly spend the night in prayer after the rest of "her flock" had gone to bed. During these vigils, "she would protect her monastery with the sign of the cross, and one such night as she was doing so, one of her monks [let us note that both authors refer to the women in Radegund's community as female monks (*monachae*)] saw a thousand demons standing on top of the wall in the form of goats." These demons promptly fled when Radegund raised her right hand (2.18).

Baudonivia's Radegund thus draws on her intimate connections with secular and divine powers to enrich her monastery, to maintain peace and tranquillity within the monastery's walls, and to create a suitable environment for — and to facilitate a life dedicated to — the practice of prayer. It is therefore hardly surprising to read in Baudonivia's account a sense of the profound loss that she and her community suffered upon Radegund's death. "Since it was ordained that no living person should issue out of the gates of the monastery," she recalls, "the whole flock stood on the walls while they bore the holy body with psalms beneath the walls. They lamented so loudly that their grief drowned out the psalms, rendering tears for psalms, groans for canticles, sighs for alleluias" (2.24).

Approximately two decades before Baudonivia wrote her account, Venantius's friend Bishop Gregory of Tours, discussed above in Chapter 4, was among those who moved Radegund's body from the cloister. In his *Glory of the Confessors*, written in 587 and 588 and thus shortly after her death, he describes vividly the wailing of the women on the walls above. He reports that, after the body was entombed, he returned to the monastery. The weeping abbess led him to those places where Radegund would typically read or pray. According to Gregory, she exclaimed, "Behold, we are entering her cell, but we do not find the mother who is lost! Behold this mat on which she bent her knees, wept, and prayed for the mercy of omnipotent God, but we do not see her! Behold the book in which she read, but her voice that was seasoned with a spiritual sharpness does not strike our ears! Behold the spindles on which she used to weave during her long fasts and while weeping copiously, but the beloved fingers of her holiness are not to be seen!" Her weeping and those of the others in their company was so intense, Gregory tells us that "such [a] grief overwhelmed my breast that I would not have stopped weeping if I did not realize that the blessed Radegund had departed from her convent in body but not in power" (104).

While these final words are Gregory's, they are wholly consistent with the sentiment expressed by Baudonivia. Together with her words, they suggest that Baudonivia and her fellow monks within the monastery's walls would have known Radegund — or, rather, missed her — in a way that was different from those who lived in the larger world outside. Everywhere around them, in the very fabric of their monastery and in the remains of the saints with whom they shared it — saints whom Radegund had brought into their community — they would recall her. Their Radegund had shaped not merely the physical but also the spiritual and emotional space in which they lived, through which they moved, and in which they prayed. She had been an extraordinary figure for members of the community, and her loss was real for Baudonivia even 20 years after her death. Baudonivia thus seems to speak for her community as a whole when, just before describing Radegund's passing, she declares, "However much we recall of her love, nurturing, charity, teaching, and all of her utterly holy way of life, however much we torture ourselves and grieve to seek again the great goodness, we cannot find again what we have lost. Oh most cruel fate, which falls so unhappily upon us! Oh most pious lady, may the Lord in Heaven grant that you may herd before you the sheep once gathered.

Following the steps of the Good Shepherd, may you bring your own flock to the Lord" (2.20). It is for this flock that so mourns Radegund, a community that both grieves her absence and seeks to feel her continued presence, that Baudonivia writes her *vita* as a "a public celebration" (2.prologue).

This flock may be different from the "public" Venantius imagines in his prologue. While Venantius writes in the idiom of his contemporary clerical elite, he uses a language self-consciously "homely in style," certainly plain next to some of his other works. And his references to well-known ascetics would associate Radegund with other saints in the minds of readers and listeners. In other words — and as he says in his prologue — he seeks to assure that Radegund's memory "would be celebrated in this world," that is, to establish and publicize a cult for the saint. To do so, let us recall, he tells his public from the outset that Radegund was able to overcome her sex and, if only slightly less explicitly, her royal status.

While Baudonivia and, presumably, some of her sisters could likely appreciate Venantius's literary allusions and the rhetorical devices he employed — and there is reason to believe that they were part of his public, that his *vita* was intended, among other things, to edify the members of the community — his Radegund was perhaps incomplete or insufficient. His image of the saint did not serve fully their needs or capture the essence of the matron they wished to remember. Indeed, it is not hard to imagine that the abbess and the community wanted, even needed, Baudonivia to write a new life of Radegund because they did not recognize in Venantius's *vita* the Radegund who once shared their space, whose prayers and presence still lingered in it.

Among other things, these women never forgot that Radegund was a queen. Nor could they. After all, royal blood mattered outside the monastery's walls, and in the years immediately after Radegund's death, there were women of royal status — women whom Baudonivia surely knew — within the monastery as well. Indeed, when Gregory of Tours recounts his visit to the monastery in his *Glory of the Confessors* cited above, he describes "a large crowd of nuns, about two hundred of them," standing around her bier. He notes, "According to the status of this world not only were they [descended] from senators, but some were [descended] from the royal family." Here Gregory's focus is to underscore Radegund's influence on them, as he suggests that these women left behind the material world and its trappings to follow her and pursue a holy life (104). In other words, as Gregory presents it, the monastery was populated by women of the Gallo-Roman and Frankish elite, members of families of the same social strata as the patrons of Venantius and as Gregory himself— indeed, in his *Histories,* Gregory notes that his niece held the office of pri- oress at the monastery (10.15). For all we know, Baudonivia herself may have come from such a family.

Whatever Baudonivia's background, in the years after Radegund's death, there were at least some women of royal status within the monastery who did not share the saint's spiritual devotion. Those who could remem- ber Radegund could also recall a divisive conflict that erupted a few years after she departed, a conflict over the abbatial office that nearly tore the community apart, probably shortly after Venantius had completed his *vita.* Gregory of Tours, who had to deal with the at-times violent conflict for nearly two years, offered an extensive account of it in his *Histories* (9.39–43 and 10.15–17). There, he uses Radegund as a foil to critique those women who, unlike her, could not let go the trappings of their royalty (9.39). There is no reason to assume that the monastery did not continue to be a repository for women of royal status even after the conflict sub- sided. We might therefore wonder whether Baudonivia sought to offer up to such women and the community as a whole an alternative and more appealing, attainable depiction of Radegund than had Venantius. Perhaps her Radegund was to serve as an example for how a royal woman could use her status to enhance rather than detract from the welfare and prestige of the community.

―――――――――――

However we understand Baudonivia's efforts and the differences between her Radegund and that of Venantius, we are fortunate to have the two *vitae.* Even if neither of the texts tells us all that much about Radegund per se, together they do provide a glimpse of the intellectual and religious landscape of the later sixth and early seventh century. In that landscape, we see how the hagiographic traditions used principally to demonstrate the holiness of men could be applied to a woman and what types of obstacles a hagiographer might face in his effort to establish and develop the cult of a female saint; that women, a generation later, could find that portrait of their saint in need of some touch-up; and thus that the memory of a saint could be malleable enough to be tweaked so as to address the different circumstances, concerns, and tastes of different authors and their audiences. Indeed, the two lives of Radegund provide insight into those circumstances, concerns, and tastes and, by extension, into the society in which they took shape.

Bibliographic Note

The two *vitae* of Radegund on which this essay focuses are readily available in an English translation by Jo Ann McNamara as "The Life of Radegund" in her *Sainted Women of the Dark Ages* (Durham, NC: Duke University Press, 1992), 70–105; above, I cite the text by the book and chapter divisions she uses. See other texts in the volume for additional *vitae* of early medieval women. For the larger world of Radegund, the works of Venantius and Gregory of Tours are essential. For the latter, see the bibliographic note to Chapter 4 in this volume; for the former, see *Venantius Fortunatus: Personal and Political Poems,* trans. Judith George (Liverpool: Liverpool University Press, 1995). Alexander Callander Murray's collection of primary sources in *From Roman to Merovingian Gaul: A Reader* (Toronto: University of Toronto Press, 2000) broadens our perspective on the period further.

The *vitae* have received a good deal of scholarly attention, particularly in the past 25 years, beginning with Suzanne Fonay Wemple's seminal work, *Women in Frankish Society (500–900)* (Philadelphia: University of Pennsylvania Press, 1985). I am unable to cite here all of the other studies that have informed this chapter. I do, however, wish to acknowledge the work of Brian Brennan, Bonnie Effros, Judith W. George, John Kitchen, Marie Anne Mayeski, Jo Ann McNamara, and Jane Tibbetts Schulenburg; reference to much of their work and other relevant titles can be found in the bibliography and notes in John Kitchen, *Saints' Lives and the Rhetoric of Gender: Male and Female in Merovingian Hagiography* (New York: Oxford University Press, 1998); and Marie Anne Mayeski, *Women at the Table: Three Medieval Theologians* (Collegeville, MN: Liturgical Press, 2004). See also Simon Coates's excellent essay, "Regendering Radegund? Fortunatus, Baudonivia, and the Problem of Female Sanctity in Merovingian Gaul," in *Gender and Christian Religion,* ed. R.N. Swanson (Rochester: Boydell, 1998), 37–50; and Ruth Wehlau, "Literal and Symbolic: The Language of Asceticism in Two Lives of St Radegund," *Florilegium* 19 (2002): 75–89.

The Avenging Abbot
Gregory the Great and His
Life of Saint Benedict

Carole Straw

P ope Gregory I, "the Great" (c. 540–604), is often considered the founder of the medieval papacy and, as the fourth doctor of the Latin Church, the exponent of the first truly medieval spirituality. His writings are shaped by turmoil he considered apocalyptic: Italy had little respite from wars between barbarian peoples and their equally destructive Byzantine opponents, or from the accompanying famines and cyclical plagues. The depopulated peninsula drifted toward a natural economy as commerce and trade declined. Along with city life, civic institutions waned; as communities reorganized in fortified hill towns protected by local strong men, the civilian aristocracy gave way to a new military order whose usurpations, rapacity, and violence alarmed the Church and earned its censure. In the cities, the Church assumed many functions of the old Roman state. As pope, Gregory was Rome's *de facto* governor: he secured the grain supply, repaired aqueducts, paid soldiers to defend the city, etc. As with Rome, in other declining cities bishops assumed civic responsibilities; in consequence, the Church attracted many who sought power and a lucrative career. The Church was definitely in the world; the challenge was not to be of it, and this haunted Gregory.

A talented administrator, Gregory had been urban prefect of Rome before he retired to a monastery. Duty forced him back to the world to serve as deacon and papal legate to the imperial court in Constantinople (579–85/86). Returning to Rome and his monastery, he resumed the office of deacon until his election as pope in 590. Gregory affirmed that worldly power could serve the good and that it could be exercised without jeopard-izing the soul, but only through humility and worldly detachment. He sought to lessen simony and corruption by vetting, then monitoring, his appointees carefully, when possible choosing monks rather than secular clergy for offices. With competent agents, he reorganized the landed estates of the papal patrimony, securing the papacy's economic future, per-haps his greatest achievement. Although ties with Byzantium were strained, Gregory still affirmed the pope's obedience to the emperor in temporal affairs, envisioning a Christian "commonwealth" or "republic" in which princes served priests, one quite different from the reality he knew. Byzantium might ignore Rome, but the barbarian kingdoms were a part of this com-monwealth, too. Gregory sought the help of Frankish queens Theudelinda and Brunhild in fighting simony and the Arian heresy. His connections with Princess Bertha, who became the wife of Ethelbert of Kent, were cru-cial to the conversion of the English. In 594, Gregory sent his fellow-monk Augustine to their court in Kent to begin his legendary mission.

A moral theologian, Gregory wrote many commentaries on the Old Testament that survive partly or only in fragments; that on *Ezekiel,* how-ever, is complete, as are his examination of theodicy in the famous *Morals on Job* and his *Homilies on the Gospels.* Gregory also wrote a popular hand-book for rulers that became a favorite of the English king Alfred (871–99) and four books of *Dialogues* in which he addressed diverse questions posed by his fellow-monk, Peter the Deacon, who managed the papal pat-rimony in Sicily. The *Life of Benedict* is the second book of the *Dialogues.* As in his works as a whole, here Gregory emphasizes *stabilitas* (stability) and *discretio* (discernment), virtues of social as well as personal benefit, especially in an anxious society dislocated by generations of war.

Gregory's Benedict is not particularly endearing. A resolute discipli-narian, Benedict always knows when monks sin; his omniscience is god-like. Nor does he mitigate strict judgment, lest laxity encourage further rebelliousness. Gregory's Benedict is much like the authoritarian abbot presented in *The Rule of Saint Benedict,* written some 60 years before: both works are products of the troubled sixth century, when peace, order, and prosperity were distant dreams. Monastic life, however, had not always been as harsh an ordeal before an abbot who inspired such fear and awe.

In the fourth-century *Sayings of the Desert Fathers,* the patient kindness and mercy of the abbas—the "fathers"—so often reveal their likeness to God. To forgive is indeed divine: "They said of the abba Macarius the

Great, that even as God protects all the world and bears the sins of men, so was he to the brethren as might be an earthly God, for he covered up their faults, and what things he saw or heard, it was as though he saw and heard them not" (*Sayings* 32).[1] Macarius would raise the dead to exculpate the innocent, but he refused to betray the guilty (*Sayings* 56). While the abbas cultivated self-rebuke through painful austerities, they forbore judging others. Abba Moses fled the assembly rather than judge the sins of another; Bessarion left the Church when a brother was excommunicated, saying, "I too am sinful" (*Sayings* 96). Forgiveness was reciprocal and therefore necessary: "In what moment we do cover up our brother's sins, God shall cover ours" (*Sayings* 97). With forgiveness, one dared have hope. If one could repair a torn cloak, thus sparing the garment, would not God have mercy on his own image (*Sayings* 129)? Mercy, however, did not mean laxity: these monks were always fighters, athletes in the contest for perfection. In the desert, one can find the peaceful confidence of Saint Jerome's Paul the Hermit, who died anticipating the crown of righteousness, having won the race. Witnessing his death, Antony "saw [that] Christ is Paul, and worshipped God in Paul's heart." Assimilation to divinity will never again seem so possible: "If a man willed it, in one day up till evening he might come at the measure of divinity" (*Sayings* 108).

The charism of these *Sayings* cools when institutionalized in Basil of Caesarea's *Shorter* and *Longer Rules* (c. 362) and John Cassian's *Conferences* and *Institutes* (c. 425), which later are sliced and diced by the anonymous redactor of the *Rule of the Master* (c. 480). These documents are the direct ancestors of the charmless *Rule of Saint Benedict* (c. 535), which distills generations of inward struggles and external hardships suffered as barbarian tribes took over the empire. Whatever the future, Romans were certain it was not theirs. The enormous economic and political upheavals of the times help explain the *Rule*'s emphasis on stability. It proffered a safe haven, a "school for God's service," where one would learn "to fight under the commandments of holy obedience" (*Rule* Prologue). The way to salvation lay in "patiently shar[ing] in Christ's passion" (*Rule* Prologue). The monk was to sacrifice himself in obedience as Christ sacrificed himself to the will of the Father, obedient unto death. "Self-will has its punishment, necessity its crown," the *Rule* (7.33) quotes ominously from the *Acts of the Martyrs*. In such self-abnegation, monks became successors to the martyrs.

---

[1] I thank Philip Rousseau for help in locating the passage I translate here.

The *Rule*'s fearful images of God were meant to pique obedience. God is the angered Father disinheriting his children, the dreaded Lord of worthless servants (*Rule* Prologue). But who speaks for God? For Gregory, the relationship between monk and abbot is analogous to that of Christ the Son and God the Father, particularly Christ's absolute submission to the Father's will and his own death in Gethsemane: "If it be thy will, take this cup from me" (*Luke* 22.42). Accordingly, the commands of superiors must be obeyed as if they were the command of God (*Rule* 5.4), and obedience to God is shown through obedience to superiors (*Rule* 5.15).

The abbot may be God to the monk's Christ, but the abbot must account for the souls of his monks before God and so must be certain that his monks behave. To strengthen his hand, sins are categorized (lesser and graver) and punishments defined, ranging from admonitions and enforced fasting to various degrees of excommunication and corporal punishment (*Rule* 23–25). In the *Rule*, the imitation of Christ is institutionalized: the monk must extinguish self-will in absolute obedience to the superior's command. This fundamental teaching lies at the heart of Gregory's *Life of Benedict*. It is Gregory who credits Benedict with writing a rule "famous for its discretion" — its moderation and adaptability to specific circumstances.

Gregory's *Life of Benedict* is the earliest and the chief source about Benedict. As the second book of his popular *Dialogues* (c. 594), it was translated soon into Greek. The spiritual, at times magical, reality that informs the book is characteristic of the Middle Ages. The supernatural mingles with the world of ordinary experience: visible and invisible, natural and supernatural, human and divine, carnal and spiritual are connected directly and causally as God disciplines his people with earthquakes, wars, and famine or blesses them with peace and prosperity. Supernatural, moral causes displace natural and neutral explanations. A nun has indigestion not from cabbage but because of the demon sitting on the cabbage; she neglected to sign the cabbage with the cross before eating it (*Dialogues* 1.4.7). In this sacramental spirituality, tangible signs mediate this world and the next; the core of this mediation is the sacrifice of the Mass when the heavens open, linking earth with the world beyond (4.60.3). Masses and the Eucharist have power to change the fate of a soul after death, even as the human saint intercedes with God for sinners and transmits God's messages to them, and earthly events such as a good harvest or a famine communicate God's grace or wrath. Gregory's world is alive with spiritual meaning.

Having lived as a monk, Gregory was as familiar with the ascetic monk John Cassian (c. 360–435) and the Desert Fathers as he was with Augustine of Hippo. Even as pope, he remained inwardly a monk, an ascetic worried that the temptations of worldly power would be his undoing. When he retired from secular life in 574, Gregory turned the family estates on the Caelian Hill in Rome into a monastery. While scholars do not think that this monastery followed Benedict's *Rule* (as it would be followed in its later sense), Gregory knew the *Rule* and was inspired by it, finding in its emphasis on stability a new compass charting the path of holiness.

Gregory sees Benedict's authority as god-likeness, which accounts for his power. Where Benedict's *Rule* emphasizes the monk's sacrifice of his will, Gregory's *Life* focuses on the transformation it brings. Through a sacrifice of the will in humility, Benedict rises in sanctity. He always imagines himself standing in judgment before God, and this preserves his humility (2.3.6–7). By abnegating his will, Benedict becomes "one with God" (2.15.2), "fixed in God" (2.23.1), and "uniting himself to the Lord [he] becomes one in spirit with him" (2.15.4).

Benedict is so much "the servant of God" and "the man of God" that these identities blur. Earlier in the *Dialogues* (1.9.9), Gregory calls the saint a temple of God indwelt by Him: to provoke the holy man is to anger Him who dwells within and risk His considerable vengeance. Participating in God, holy men have miraculous powers they can even pass to others, as Benedict does when allowing Maurus to save the drowning boy Placid (2.7, 2.8.9).

This transformation of the saint follows a paradoxical economy that validates hierarchical order (cf. *Moralia* 8.10.19). Before the Fall, Adam obeyed God because servants rightly submit to their masters' wills. By submitting to God, he rose ontologically. Being "united" with God, he enjoyed "stability" — an ability to resist sin — that meant he was master of his own servant, the body. But the devil tempted Adam, and he swelled with pride, desiring to follow his own will and be his own master. In reciprocal justice, the servant's rebellion against God was avenged with the rebellion of his own servant, the body. Now akin to beasts, he is subject to carnal desires; his "stability" is replaced by "mutability" — temptation, sin, and sensitivity to changes of fortune. Accordingly, the saint's humility restores hierarchical order, recovering the primordial stability Adam lost and anticipating the union with God in heaven. The lesson is clear. To rise up against authority and follow one's own will leads downward to disaster, while heaven and all goods are reached only by self-abnegation and submission to authority.

Gregory's emphasis on Benedict's supernatural qualities distances him from early monasticism. Where the *Sayings* warn of spiritual pretension — "If you see a monk levitate, catch him by the foot and throw him to the ground, for it does him no good" (*Sayings* 107) — Benedict actually has supernatural powers. This change of perspective reflects the increasing importance of the Church as an institution in the early Middle Ages, for in praising the saint, one honors less the individual than the Church he or she represents. The contest for perfection is no longer an individual quest as it was for monks of the desert, "alone into the alone" (*Sayings* 108), or with the *Rule*'s sacrifice of will in obedience to the abbot. With Gregory, the self-sacrifice demanded of the individual is inseparable from the Eucharist administered by the priests of the Church. In a later passage of the *Dialogues* (4.61.1), he explains that as Christians must offer themselves as victims when they receive the Sacrifice (i.e., the Eucharist) at the Mass, "We need to sacrifice ourselves to God in a sincere immolation of the heart whenever we offer Mass, because we who celebrate the mysteries of the Lord's passion ought to imitate what we are enacting. The Sacrifice will truly be offered to God for us when we present ourselves as Victim."

With Gregory, the sacrament of the Mass and the Church are the way to salvation. This mediation by the institution does not, however, end the need for human effort, for only when Christians offer themselves as sacrifices (*Romans* 12:1) can they "activate" the sacrifice of Christ on their behalf. Free will and grace are balanced and complementary. Christians must do what they can to return to God the gifts He has given, to repay Christ for his sacrifice, for the universe operates reciprocally as Gregory sees it.

Through humility, saints are elevated; they act more perfectly and view the universe from a new perspective. Possessing stability, Benedict is sublimely self-controlled. Augustine of Hippo would approve heartily: Benedict does not allow his attention to be scattered on worldly affairs that would carry him "outside himself." Mindful of judgment, Benedict searches his own soul continuously, keeping a close watch on his thoughts and actions; he lives "with himself" (3.5–9). He is detached, self-possessed, "above it all," as we might say; contemplation gives him the discretion to perceive the world as it really is, tiny and insignificant. With magnanimous tranquility, Benedict rises above this "little ball" of the earth and its noisome concerns.

Despite Gregory's idealization of Benedict, his *Life* is not triumphal but defensive and apologetic; it is the story of a fighter who does not always win. Benedict's authority is mocked, defied, and tried; he parries the devil's insults constantly to save face. Gregory scrambles to vindicate Benedict's authority, to convince the audience that God is on Benedict's side, despite the adversities and insults he suffers. Such chagrin mirrors Gregory's frustrations as a leader in a fluid society where the Church's authority is contested by rebellious monks, invidious clerics, lax laymen, stubborn pagans, and brutal barbarians. Power and authority are indeterminate, contingent upon unpredictable circumstances and personalities. Leaders are not always the most worthy but are those most successful in controlling resources and dominating others. Knowing this, Gregory tries to rig the scales in favor of the Church. His efficient administration (most evident in his organization of the papal estates) is the Church's answer to the brute force of regional warlords and the incompetence of the Byzantine bureaucracy and its representatives in Ravenna.

Gregory is at pains to prove that Abbot Benedict is nobody's fool and quite capable of avenging those who would mock him, chief of whom is the devil himself. The specific character of the Adversary is telling; he is the trickster who taunts Benedict. His insults may seem silly, but to Gregory and his contemporaries they are affronts to Benedict's (and God's) honor, a mockery of his authority. In his pride and hubris, the devil would overthrow just authority and supplant it with his own. Gregory's Satan is the *simulator* aping God brazenly, the deceiver disguised as an angel of light who aims to subvert the right order Benedict represents. Gregory sets obedience to a single authority against autonomy and anarchy. Benedict offers amnesty from the chaos created by those who live by their own will; the safety and security of God's protection is granted those who accept His light yoke. The devil's subversion of just order reflects an age where usurpations of the rights, privileges, and even the regalia of others are commonplace, where "savage barbarians" extort ransom from whole cities, where new men seize whatever opportunity affords. Benedict offers the remedy of stability to the tumult of this frontier mentality ruled by the sword and bribery.

Like any competitive rival, the devil is "full of envy." Ignoble and contemptible, he even tries to starve Benedict out of his remote cell in a mountain cave. (He breaks the bell that announces the arrival of his breadbasket on rope sent down the mountain by his friend Romano; cf. 2.1.5).

Mean-spirited, the devil sits on a huge rock that the monks need for building an abbey at Cassino. Work stops until Benedict prays "against the
devil," after which the rock seems "weightless" (2.9.11). When Benedict
turns the temple of Apollo into a chapel dedicated to Saint Martin, the
devil is peeved. With fire pouring from his eyes and mouth, he "complains
of the offense," and retaliates with an insulting pun on the holy man's
name, "Benedict, Maledict" (2.8.12). Gregory sees the most frightening
manifestations of evil in such confrontations with pagan idols. In these
ultimate tests of powers, Gregory demonstrates that Christianity is indeed
stronger than paganism simply because the devil is incapable of avenging
himself. Benedict does not even see the fire the monks see when a brass
idol is thrown into the kitchen. Wondering why the monks panic, he prays
that they will "bless their eyes" and see that the blaze is illusory. Exposed as
the mischief of demons, the fire vanishes (2.10).

Evil is petty and malicious, but this does not mean that good always
prevails. Gregory's world is a trial, an apocalyptic, black-and-white contest
between good and evil. Yet the devil is God's servant and it is God who
unleashes him to try Christians, even as he allowed him to smite Job
within an inch of his life. Gregory's God is as fearsome as Augustine's, and
Gregory is less convinced of mercy. The sacrament is essential if hope is to
exist, but more secure is one's own self-sacrifice. "Let us do for ourselves
during life what we hope others will do for us after death," he writes, for
"we will have no need of the Holy Sacrifice after our death if, before death,
we offer up ourselves as a sacrifice to almighty God" (4.60.1).

The struggle to secure salvation is burdensome. Safety lies in abnegation of the will to authority, but tests and challenges to Benedict's leadership are constant, be they trivial or grave. His powers are limited, and that
is the point. Insofar as he is one with God, he can know God's thoughts,
but to the degree that this union is imperfect, he is unable to grasp fully
God's designs (2.16.3–8). In the balance and cooperation of human and
divine agencies typical of Gregory's thought, he allows that Benedict is
able to do some miracles without prayer, accomplishing them immediately with his own power (albeit a gift of God); for other miracles, however, Benedict must pray because they are beyond his power (2.30.32).
(The speed with which the miracle is wrought reveals its source: supplica-
tion is time-consuming!) Nor does Benedict always get his way, even when
he prays. Visiting his sister, Scholastica, he is anxious to return to his
monastery, but she weeps abundantly, petitioning God that he stay to keep

her company. God grants her wish, sending rain abundant enough to detain Benedict. Since God is love (*1 John* 4:8), it is fitting that God favored the one who loved the most, overriding Benedict's desire to depart (2.2.33). Gregory's Benedict is holy, but still human and imperfect. Gregory's message is precisely that such boundaries and limitations exist.

In the larger cosmic conflict of good and evil, Benedict prevails as a strict enforcer, who "allowed [no one] to turn from the straight path of monastic discipline either to the right or the left" (2.3.3). That such severity stirred resentment is no surprise to Gregory, who observes pessimistically that "the wicked are envious of the holiness in others they are not striving themselves to acquire" (2.8.1). A sharp line separates the evil from the good: time and again Benedict's experiences prove that "the very life of the just is a burden to the wicked" (2.3.4; cf. *Wisd.* 2:12–20). Just as Benedict fights and speaks on God's behalf, so his rivals represent the devil. When Benedict is driven out of his monastery by the invidious priest Florentius, Gregory reflects, "Although [Benedict] moved to a different place...his enemy remained the same. In fact, the assaults he had to endure after this were all the more violent because the very Master of Evil was fighting against him in open battle" (2.8.10).

Evil looms large and must be given no quarter. Fierce discipline is necessary in a world so dubiously Christian and corruptible. Corporal discipline reveals the mingled reality of Gregory's universe where supernatural and human intersect and where carnal, worldly actions evoke inner, spiritual results. Physical discipline exorcises the demonic from human beings in ways that presume intimate connections. Chastising a fugitive monk, Benedict does not spare the rod because the blow hits the Enemy himself in order to free the sinner from the devil's dominion (2.4.3, 2.30.1). When Benedict feels the stings of lust, his remedy is to throw himself into the stinging nettles of a briar patch where the poison of temptation can pour from his wounds (2.2.2). Demons upset bodily humors, but corporal discipline (in this case, a scourging with thorns) purifies the body. The soul is connected inversely to the body so that "when the body is abased, the goal of the soul is elevated," as Gregory writes in *Moralia* (7.15.19).

Benedict's severity is indispensable and praiseworthy, but it often inspires resistance. Retreating often, Benedict never overwhelms the enemy. His victories can be slow in coming, and they are seldom spectacular. Benedict's monks are sullen when they find him "trying to curb every evil habit." They poison his wine, but when he signs the wine pitcher with the cross, it shatters "as it could not bear the sign of life." Benedict rebukes these murderous monks, but his chastisement does not heal and restore the community. Instead, he dismisses the monks and returns alone to his hermitage (2.3.3–5). Gregory justifies Benedict's retreat by citing Paul's actions in Damascus: he left to save himself for more fruitful battles later (2.3.11). "Battle" is the operative word. Recognizing his defeat, Benedict cuts his losses.

In a second instance, the jealous priest Florentius sends Benedict poisoned bread. Graciously, Benedict's pet raven saves him by carrying it away. But when Florentius sends seven dancing girls to seduce Benedict's disciples, Benedict "lets envy have its way" and again departs, taking only a few disciples with him (2.2.8). In the battle for conversion, Gregory acknowledges that the Enemy sometimes cannot be conquered. In *Moralia* 33.14.19, Gregory mentions the mosaic of black and white that God's Providence creates. In Benedict's *Life* one senses how frequently the black overshadows the white.

Few of Benedict's miracles spring from sympathy and compassion; most avenge insults or otherwise vindicate his power, like those noted above. True, he does repair the broken tray of his faithful nurse (2.1.2), recover the blade of a Goth's scythe (2.6.1–2), and send Maurus to save the boy Placid, whom he saw drowning in the lake (2.8.1–2). Yet Benedict's most breathtaking miracle—reviving the dead—turns out to be the vindication of an insult. When a sarcastic demon taunts Benedict that he is "off to work with the brethren," causing a young monk to die when a wall collapses, Benedict raises the lad, defying the devil's attempt to "mock" him (2.11.1–2).

Most of Benedict's miracles are didactic, teaching that one dare not defy him, for divine power will surely avenge him. None can escape Benedict's searching vision. He knows every infraction of the *Rule,* a fact that might make all subordinates wary of testing their superiors, who are, after all, God's representatives on earth. Benedict's remote vision allows him to monitor his monks' behavior even when they leave his presence, for he is "always present in spirit" (2.12.2). Nothing can be kept secret from him (2.20.2). He chastises monks who have eaten when away from the monastery; when they dare to lie about it, he reveals his vision of their sins, and they fall at his feet trembling with remorse (2.12.2). He rebukes Exhilaratus for his secret stash of wine, forbidding him to drink it. When Exhilaratus dares to test Benedict's admonition, a snake hiding in the flask utterly terrifies him: Benedict is avenged dramatically (2.2.18). Monks, Gregory assures us, cannot ignore Benedict's commands: he even comes to them in dreams to chastise them when they doubt his presence and fail to carry out his orders (2.22.3). Because "nothing [can] be kept secret" from Benedict (2.16.2), he discerns souls with uncanny sensitivity. He reads the spiteful heart of a discontented monk and rebukes him for his envy (2.20.2).

Like God (or an intrusive parent), Benedict is omniscient and omnipresent. For monks, if not laymen, the thought that every abbot, as God's representative, might partake of His supernatural power must have been sobering. In the broadest sense, the saint's power vindicates not only his authority but faith itself. Benedict chastises doubt, hesitancy, and uncertainty. When he produces food in a famine, he does so the day after monks have gazed in despair at their five remaining loaves, rebuking them for lacking faith that God would provide (2.21.1–2). When a niggardly cellarer refuses to give oil to the poor "to lay up riches in heaven," Benedict rebukes his disobedience by making him throw a glass of oil out of the window. It does not break. Astonished, the monk takes a leap of faith, and oil flows copiously from his cask (2.28). To quell those who complain that his monasteries should be moved for lack of water, Benedict again silences them. He prays and finds water, proving again that God provides for the faithful (2.6.23).

Gregory seems content with Benedict's understated progress. If victories are not dazzling, minor advances can be cherished. The cold-blooded Goth, King Totila, tests Benedict's gift of prophecy. Trying to deceive him, Totila sends a messenger disguised as himself. Benedict unmasks the fraud, and those who tried to mock him fall to the ground in terror. Benedict foretells Totila's demise; and Totila, if not tamed, is at least "less cruel" after Benedict's rebuke (2.14–15). Benedict can offer protection sometimes but not all the time. He prays assiduously, but he cannot prevail upon God to spare his doomed monastery; indeed, he barely persuades God to grant mercy for the lives of the monks (2.17.1–2). He does intercede with God, but his mediation on behalf of human interests is only partly successful.

Benedict's intercession for those dying in unhappy circumstances is more effective because the Eucharist is part of these miracles. Secure and indisputable power exists in the Church and its sacraments. As with other miracles, those involving the Eucharist point to transgressions of authority and remind Christians of their need for obedience. Overly attached to his parents, a young monk deserts the monastery. He dies suddenly and will not stay buried until Benedict reburies him with the Eucharist (2.24.1–3). The lesson is obvious: disobedience prevents entrance to heaven, but more important is Gregory's argument that the Church with its sacraments holds the keys to the kingdom: God imparted to men who govern the Church the power to bind and loose, to pardon those in the mortal flesh judged before the invisible tribunal (2.23.5). In another miracle, Benedict rebukes two nuns for their insults, warning he will excommunicate them if they do not curb their tongues. They die and are buried in the parish church, but they leave their graves at Communion when the deacon announces that non-communicants must leave. Again, the Eucharist is the remedy. Benedict sends an oblation to be offered at Mass to free the nuns from the threatened sentence of excommunication, and they return peacefully to their graves (2.23.3–6). Significantly, the personal charisma of Benedict is less effective than his role dispensing the Eucharist. The sacrament has perfect and indisputable power to mediate; the holy man will always remain "one with God," yet imperfectly transformed.

Benedict dies a good death, revealing the connections between heaven and earth. He foreknows his passing and dies fortified with the Eucharist. Monks see a magnificent road stretching to heaven, glittering with lights signaling that Benedict has passed that way. Miracles come from his tomb and cave, but they are not limited to contact with them, for they also come from a distance to those whose faith in God earns more merit. The very absence of the body teaches one spiritual love (2.38).

While Gregory emphasizes that Benedict participates in God's powers and that God will avenge insults to his authority, he also recognizes the limits of the saint's powers. Strategic accommodations soften Benedict's more embarrassing retreats and failures. Gregory's final message is not too different from that of Athanasius in his fourth-century *Life of Antony:* religious life is a trial, and it is open to everyone. But one must always persevere, despite temptations and frustrations. "*Age quod agis!*" Gregory writes (4.58.1): "Do what you should do," never cease striving. Progress is slow because human beings can be as dull and resistant as Benedict's monks.

To Gregory, "genuine" Christianity means the rejection of worldly corruption and true obedience to precepts taught by Christ. The Church as an institution and its sacrament become instrumental to salvation and central to Christian life in a way different from that of the past. With Gregory, the medieval Church and its cultural predominance emerge. Gregory's Saint Benedict is tied to the Mass and the mediation of the Eucharist, which is glorified. The tenuous authority of spiritual leaders, be they abbots or bishops, is now fortified by the sacrament, whose success in mediating with God cannot be doubted.

Bibliographic Note

Most of Gregory's works are available in translation. *The Book of Pastoral Rule* and select letters translated by James Barmby appear in the *Nicene and Post-Nicene Fathers,* ed. Philip Scaff and Henry Wace, 2nd series, vols. 12–13 (Oxford: J. Parker, 1898; repr. Grand Rapids: W.M. Eerdmans, 1969). The complete letters of Gregory have been translated by John R.C. Martyn in *The Letters of Gregory the Great,* 3 vols. (Toronto: Pontifical Institute, 2004). A good translation of all the *Dialogues* is *Saint Gregory the Great: Dialogues,* trans. Odo John Zimmerman (New York: Fathers of the Church, 1959). Gregory's homilies are in *Gregory the Great: Forty Gospel Homilies,* trans. Dom David Hurst (Kalamazoo, MI: Cistercian Publications, 1990); and *The Homilies of Saint Gregory the Great On the Book of the Prophet Ezechiel,* trans. Theodosia Gray (Etna, CA: Center for Traditionalist Orthodox Studies, 1990). The only translation of the *Magna Moralia* is that of the Library of the Fathers, *Morals on the Book of Job,* 4 vols. (Oxford: J.H. Parker, 1844–50).

I have cited several early texts of great importance to Gregory. *The Sayings of the Fathers* are found in Helen Waddell, *The Desert Fathers* (Ann Arbor: University of Michigan, 1966). Basil's rules are in *Ascetical Works,* trans. Sister M. Monica Wagner (Washington, DC: Catholic University of America Press, 1962). Boniface Ramsey has excellent editions of John Cassian, *The Conferences* (New York: Paulist Press, 1997) and *The Institutes* (New York: Newman Press, 2000).

The precursor to the *Rule of Benedict* is *The Rule of the Master,* trans. Luke Eberle (Kalamazoo, MI: Cistercian Publications, 1977). There are countless translations of *The Rule of Saint Benedict* readily available.

For bibliographic orientation on Gregory the Great, see Francesca Sara D'Imperio, *Gregorio Magno Bibliografia per gli Anni 1980–2003* (Florence: Sismel, 2005). Of those works in English, see Robert Markus, *Gregory the Great and his World* (Cambridge: Cambridge University Press, 1997) and Carole Straw, *Gregory the Great: Perfection in Imperfection* (Berkeley: University of California Press, 1988).

SEVEN

Crime and Punishment
Anglo-Saxon Law Codes
Kathleen Casey

The year is 602, perhaps 603, of the Christian era. An old man in Kent, a small kingdom at the southeastern edge of Britain, trolls the vast ocean of unwritten customary law. He considers a number of matches between offense and penalty, and he orders a list to be set down in his mother tongue, Old English. A new Christian, he leads off with a note about offenses against Church property and personnel, offenses calling for special sanctions. In some cases, they are as high as ninefold, elevenfold, even twelvefold the usual penalties, much heavier than any of those invoked in the next 11 rules for acts involving a king and his dependents. Had the late sixth-century bishop Gregory of Tours, astute king-watcher that he was, lived long enough to hear about the list, he might well have wondered what this petty Anglo-Saxon king was up to, this Ethelbert of Kent (560–616). A seasoned ruler in the forty-second year of his reign, the man should have known that almost any ruler's protection (*mund*) ended not much farther from home base than a horse could gallop in a day. Local custom was self-administering. What could a written list of laws accomplish when circumstances as banal as physical distance limited real authority?

Whatever or whoever compelled King Ethelbert to issue such a document in his name, Anglo-Saxon rulers over the next four centuries expanded or adapted it, with far-reaching consequences. Kings Hlothhaere (673–85) and Eadric (685–86) of Kent added a few more items to the list later in the century. In 695, according to the preamble to the Laws of King Wihtraed (690–725), a "deliberative convention of the great men" at

Berghamstyde appended another six rules concerning the Church to "the lawful customs of the Kentishmen." In the eighth and ninth centuries, West Saxon kings Ine (688–726) and Alfred (871–99) produced their versions of customary law. Then Edward the Elder (899–925), Ethelstan (925–39), and Edmund (939–46) issued ever longer and broader lists, prefaced with ever loftier language. Like all of them, Edgar (959–75) and Ethelred (979–1013, 1014–16), rulers of all England, followed Ethelbert's example and rejected Rome's elite idiom along with the influence of its alien legal system. The body of Old English texts these kings left behind remains the only vernacular expression of customary law in all of Europe.

These law lists cannot have fully covered every variation of customary law among Anglo-Saxon communities nor portray all the versions under which barbarian tribes everywhere lived, but we can assume certain similarities, and that will have to do. Using new linguistic techniques to study them — they are the subcontinent's sole surviving vernacular expression of customary law left uncorrupted by Latinate legal concepts — contemporary historians glimpse graphic images of the chaotic, unpredictable, poorly sheltered, and brutally challenging daily life endured from the sixth through the tenth centuries — images of rulers trying out new ideals and standards for a kind of law they could not imagine throwing out. Once thought changeless in an unchanging society, customary law can be seen warping and bending in the heat of hard times while kings strive and fail to imbue its ethics with the Christian ideal of redemptive justice, even as they strive and fail to shore up custom's ancient framework and purposes. Historians have faulted gifts of land to monasteries during the sixth and seventh centuries for steadily diverting wealth away from kings and tribes and thereby weakening their power to maintain order. Bede (673–735) fingered the eighth century's predatory warrior class for furthering the interests of their own families at the expense of royal and customary authority, a process halted by ninth-century Viking invasions, but the long, drawn-out resistance mounted by West Saxon kings may simply have worsened the effects of an environmental calamity hitherto barely noticed or understood.

Evidence drawn from archeological digs, the study of atmospheric residues in ice cores drilled in arctic regions, and examination of tree rings point to a massive eruption in the Javanese volcanic chain in 535 as the source of an earth-encircling cloud of dust and debris that stressed climate, flora, and fauna for many years to come. Its effects are said to have destroyed certain Asian cultures, spurred the rise of Islam, and enfeebled the ethics of once stable barbarian populations in northeastern Europe. It also brought on an outbreak of the bubonic plague, called Justinian's plague, believed to be the worst on record before 1348. First appearing in the Near East around 542 and lasting well into the seventh century, the pandemic was seemingly linked to climatic chaos. Between 535 and 555, an erratic pattern of rainfall and drought, observed anecdotally, brought floods, intense cold, destructive storms, hailstones, and incessant rain to Britain. The plague touched western British trading ports in 546 and turned back eastward, trailing disaster.

Anglo-Saxon (and subject Welsh) populations exposed to the resultant subsistence crises were more fortunate than, say, Mongolians and Avars only in that western cattle survived tough weather conditions better than eastern horses less equipped to digest inferior grasses. But a cattle-based economy, duly primed for a rise in livestock value, proved especially prone to, and intolerant of, cattle theft. Lexicographic analysis of the Old English laws has identified stealing as by far the most common of problems and cattle theft as the most common of all. This increase in crime had important consequences for the old connections between customary law and the honor system. For instance, home invasion became the most dreaded of crimes; it was an act of overt terror that diminished the security of peasants and damaged their productivity.

In an epic poem such as *Beowulf*, Anglo-Saxon settlers behave as though they value above all else honor, hospitality, and the right of refuge. And they consider the pursuit of revenge as legitimate social behavior, for violence against the living was a way to keep faith with the dead. This may have been a reality in the more distant Anglo-Saxon past when those in conflict had perhaps learned to channel rage and payback into the clarity of an organized, if bloody, tit-for-tat to settle scores and supposedly reach closure in their conflicts. The codes present another view of violence in the Anglo-Saxon world, and they raise doubts that the honor system ever worked quite as celebrated in the literary sources. Sometime before the seventh century, for instance, customary law developed ambivalent attitudes toward the blood feud or vendetta as an instrument of conflict management. Instead of shedding blood, people became willing to atone, or to make good, for injuries and offenses by means of "composition," a complex grid of monetary reparations graded by the respective rank of contending parties in order to arrive at an amount known in Old English as *bot*, or in the special case of killing, a *wergild*. Yet more telling about the challenges of this era are its laws governing *hamsocn*, or home invasion, wherein the taking of life came to be viewed as an affront so much worse than murder itself as to become "bootless," which meant not "compound-able" at all. Such a death, in other words, was utterly unredeemable. *Hamsocn* became a royal plea that left perpetrators at the uncertain mercy of the king.

The laws may have substituted cash for blood penalties, but they still set a value on body parts based on their function as fighting tools. Payments for an anatomical universe of injuries may have suited an ordinary Anglo-Saxon villager eager to vent rage or pettiness or bad temper legitimately but on the cheap. He or she might be tempted to pay the tiny price of a nasty small act like tearing off the toenail of an adversary. Just a little more money must have seemed fair value for inflicting a bruise hidden by cloth-ing. A nice black shiner in an exposed body part called for no more than a slightly higher penalty, one that just happened to match the composition for ripping off a person's great toenail (Ethelbert 59, 60, 72). Containing the impulse to lash out does not seem to be the point of such minutely detailed rules. What served at one time as an elaborate list of outlets for rage among fighters with a low threshold of tolerance for blood-letting afforded later and perhaps softer generations of individuals a chance to pick and choose some tolerable level of penalty for inflicting humiliation and sometimes quite terrible pain.

When he compiled his laws sometime between 885 and 899, King Alfred confronted the haphazard nature of customary laws found in Christian synod-books that had "gathered the compensations for many human misdeeds...here one law, there another." He tried to impose some kind of order and made additions as he thought fit (Alfred 49.7–10). Detailed rules about the mechanism of the vendetta retaliation supported the old rules while carefully regulating retaliation against anyone shelter-ing someone at home (Alfred 42). For instance, he placed at the center of the system "oath-worthiness," a status or capacity without which a person would become legally defenseless. Wrongful oath-taking, he explained in his preface, was worse than proper oath-taking gone wrong, a distinction quite possibly lost on the majority of his subjects.

Quoting Alcuin of Northumbria (d. 804), who told a Mercian ealdor-man of the late eighth century that "times of tribulation are everywhere in our land," King Edmund (939-46) issued a document "Concerning the Blood Feud" with a preamble in which he deplored the widespread prac-tice of private vengeance. He sought to advance Christianity by controlling a plague of "illegal and manifold conflicts." It was not enough to follow custom at such a time with "loyalty declining, truth silent, malice increasing," and people contriving "something new and unsuited to human nature." He aimed to regulate the blood feud by restricting vengeance to monetary compensation and by placing the whole financial burden of a feud on the killer. If kindred would not help, as older rules demanded, to pay the full *wergild* within 12 months, they would be exempt from compensation, and it would be up to the "the leading men" (*witan*) to see that payment was made (Blood Feud 7).

The tone of the written laws shifts quickly thereafter. King Edgar the Elder (962-63) abandons the archaic style of his predecessors, mentions contemporary events, and makes no attempt to hide his eagerness to propel society into a more Christian atmosphere. The importance of Church tithes, for instance, as a superior kind of legal duty is implied in the injunction that "secular rights be in force ... as good as can best be devised, to the satisfaction of God and for my full royal dignity and for the benefit and security of poor and rich ... to the end that poor man and rich may possess what they rightly acquire, and a thief may not know where to dispose of stolen goods" (Whitbordesstan 2.2). About 35 years later at Wantage, King Ethelred issued laws "for the improvement of public security" and "in order that his peace may remain as firm as it best was in the days of his ancestors." He rails about "deceitful deeds and hateful abuses ... false weights and wrong measures, and lying witnesses and shameful frauds, and horrible perjuries and devilish deeds of murder and manslaughter, of stealing and spoliation, of avarice and greed, of over-eating and over-drinking ... of deceits and various breaches of law, of injuries to clergy and of breaches of the marriage law" (Ethelred 24–25). Indeed, through the prism of the laws, Anglo-Saxon society seemed to be spinning out of control, its rulers unsure what to do about it. Kings were short of funds and lacking organized chanceries; customary law, too, remained helpless. If we take these law codes at face value, they suggest that almost half a millennium of royal efforts to regulate society had tried and failed to bring back the good old, if not better, days. Their means were few; their very goals barred any hope of a general civil peace.

In essence, personal customary law worked best in a local setting where people knew each other and their everyday — no less than their deviant — behaviors quite intimately. Sanctioned only by moral pressure, each self-regulating community could police itself and enforce its decisions only in the immediate neighborhood of the offender and the offense committed. It could therefore be quite flexible and fluid rather than the rigid system it can sometimes appear in the document, for even in partially written form, as in the Old English law lists, custom never amounted to anything like a legal code. It looked after a community of people. It focused on clashes between private individuals and families. And it held kin responsible for an individual's misdeeds. It also reinforced status differences within that community. Rank based on class and gender permeate the penalty structure, for at the most basic level the *wergild,* a fixed sum paid to kin wronged when a member of their kindred was killed, measured a person's value, but such distinctions could be fluid. A thegn could have a degree of rank denoted by *wergild* that differed from the king's perception of his value as measured by *wite,* a penalty paid to him or another authority. And there could be further ambiguities, for up to the time of King Alfred custom also tolerated the concept of a "half-free" person (Ethelbert 26).

The wiggle room within customary law lay not merely in the categories into which people fit. Some of the core concepts within the Anglo-Saxon world, concepts reflected in the laws, were more malleable than rigid. For instance, custom recognized only possession rather than outright ownership and contracts of the sort central to both Roman and modern law. Those in conflict over property could therefore bargain more easily to negotiate compromise rather than risk an all-or-nothing contest. Likewise, the processes and methods of establishing proof—such as ordeals—may appear more rigidly procedural in the formulas by which we glimpse them than in the ways they functioned. We may never know how idiosyncratic they were, for most of what was said and done in villages and even in the king's courts will never be heard.

A small corpus of Old English lawsuit documents (some within charters) provides narrative clues to both actual litigation and the circumstances under which Anglo-Saxon kings wrote down excerpts from customary law. In one rare case, a cattle-thief of questionable oath-worthiness was convicted in part through commonsense, in part by such physical evidence as hoof-tracks and bramble scratches. This was not supposed to happen under a kind of law by which guilt or innocence depended on the subjective "oath-worthiness" of accuser and accused. Most of the Anglo-Saxon lawsuits, however, reflect the policy-making apex of society in developing courts. These courts ran cases more or less as laid down by royal authority, and their proceedings still seem to have been very much an oral process and have thus left little documentary trace. Written laws, it has been suggested, could have been useful as an abstract symbol of justice or Christian belief of the day. Or rulers may simply have wanted to look like proper kings by flourishing an impressive document.

For better or worse, Anglo-Saxon rulers unsure of their goals seemed disinclined to make a clean sweep of custom's edifice of offense and penalty and to substitute another based on Roman notions of crime and punishment. Kings continued to resurrect the good old law that made amends by setting a community back on an even keel. At the same time, as representatives of divine justice, those same kings sought to create a moral climate in which customary law and the Christian faith might coexist in a shared aversion to bloodshed. On one level, searching for more efficient methods of conflict management, reforming Anglo-Saxon kings and their counselors may have wanted to raise the bar of customary law's more positive achievements by seeing to it that nobody lay beyond its reach, that is, by toughening standards of conduct, curtailing deviance, and dealing harshly with recidivists. Yet archaic arrangements for expiation must have seemed inadequate to a Christian whose worth was not measurable in *wergild,* to one who ought not to shed another's blood in vengeance or for any other reason since Christ had already paid the full price for everyone and everything. Appealing for care "earnestly to be taken that those souls be not destroyed which God bought with his own life," in his so-called Code of 1008, King Ethelred urged "life-sparing punishments to be devised for the benefit of the people" because "God's handiwork and his own purchase which he paid for so dearly is not to be destroyed for small offenses" (Ethelred 3, 3.1). Ordinary people struggling with natural forces against unimaginable odds and barely Christianized, if at all, were unlikely to grasp the idea of redemptive justice that might lead to transformation and liberation. Words expressing such ideas were not even in their vocabulary. Kings asked too much of their subjects by calling on them to inhabit, at one time, two discrete dimensions.

It took a drastic change in circumstances to break the impasse. In post-Conquest England, common law replaced customary law. Alongside the rise of canon law (that of the Church) and a revived knowledge of Roman law (the codified system of the former Roman Empire), English Common Law propped up the state as an end in itself and used the state's coercive power and the law's own sanctions to put law itself into effect. It evolved in the post-Conquest period primarily as a state-based system, retaining elements of customary law only by default.

It is hard at the best of times to disentangle the ethics of any legal system from its value as a tool for creating order, and the last five brutal centuries of the first millennium were far from the best of times. In the Anglo-Saxon laws of that period we see evidence of a crisis between incompatible concepts of justice. Today, early in the third millennium, law and justice everywhere are coming under pressure, as Anglo-Saxon custom once did, to become an instrument for redemption instead of punishment. It is chilling to look back and see that it took half as long to compile the Old English law lists as it took to reach the present level of global and technological expansion, more chilling still to watch the legatees of customary law strain to catch up, like dreamers running.

Bibliographic Note

Parenthetical citations within the essay refer to the law texts found in *English Historical Documents*, Vol. 1: *c. 500–1042*, ed. D. Whitelock, 2nd ed. (London: Eyre Methuen Limited, 1979). The short titles I use (usually the name of the king who issued a particular law code, but also "Blood Feud") refer to the chapter titles used in Part Two of Whitelock's collection; the numeration refers to particular items within the code.

The standard works on English law, in English, are those by F. Pollock and F.W. Maitland, *The History of English Law Before the Time of Edward I*, 2nd ed. (Indianapolis: Liberty Fund, 2009 [1895/1898]), and Fritz Kern, *Kingship and Law in the Middle Ages*, trans. S.B. Chrimes (New York: Praeger Publishers, 1956); to them, we must add the more recent work of P. Wormald, *The Making of English Law: King Alfred to the Norman Conquest* (Oxford: Blackwell Publishers, 1999), as well as Lisi Oliver, *The Beginnings of English Law* (Toronto: University of Toronto Press, 2002). Also useful are R.V. Colman, "Domestic Peace and Public Order in Anglo-Saxon Law," in *The Anglo-Saxons: Synthesis and Achievement*, ed. J.D. Woods and D.A.E. Pelteret (Waterloo, ON: Wilfrid Laurier University Press, 1985); and E.G. Stanley, "On the Laws of King Alfred," in *Alfred the Wise: Studies in Honor of Janet Bately*, ed. J.R. Roberts and J.L. Nelson with M. Godden (Woodbridge, CT: D.S. Brewster, 1997). For textual analysis and an extensive bibliography of the field, see J.R. Schwyter, *Old English Legal Language: The Lexical Field of Theft* (Odense: Odense University Press, 1996); and D. Bethurum, "Stylistic Features of the Old English Laws," *Modern Language Review* 27 (1932): 263–79. For the mid-sixth-century volcanic eruption, see D. Keys, *Catastrophe: An Investigation into the Origins of the Modern World* (London: Century, 1999).

EIGHT

Conversion, Miracles, and the Creation of a People in Bede's *Ecclesiastical History*

Jay Rubenstein

Bede's *Ecclesiastical History of the English People* seems an entirely sensible work, compelling in its simplicity and clarity. The Anglo-Saxon monk Bede wrote it around the year 730 in the north of England, where he had passed all his life, a little over a century after Gregory of Tours had written his comparable *Ten Books of Histories* discussed above in Chapter 4. Compared to sixth-century Francia, this northern English landscape was a backwater, not having benefited from the continuous exposure to Roman culture that so heavily shaped Gregory's world. Despite the relative isolation of his setting, however, Bede's history seems, in comparison to Gregory's, an almost modern book. To a degree, this deceptively familiar character is a tribute not only to Bede's talents as narrator but also to his mastery of chronology. In his determination to calculate the correct date for Easter — a passion apparent throughout the *Ecclesiastical History* — he popularized and nearly perfected the *anno domini* calendar system. When Gregory of Tours writes, as he occasionally does, that "the next thing which happened was" (5.26, 7.28, 9.9), it is usually difficult to see where he is coming from or where he intends to go. With Bede, the connections in and between his stories are transparently logical. This historical vision is also a reflection of Bede's own personality. His soft-spoken and academic character fills his narrative just as much as does Gregory's tendency toward sharp and ironic commentary. When at the end of the book Bede describes his life, passed entirely at the monastery of Wearmouth and Jarrow, he observes, "it has always been my delight to learn or to teach or to write," and none of his words give us reason to think otherwise (5.24).

The story that Bede tells seems very much in harmony with his self-portrait. It is a tale of conversions to Christianity, of relapses from it, and of returns to the faith, until by the fifth and final book, which is set at the time of Bede's life, the English had embraced their faith with permanence, if not perfection. Christianity first reached the island during the Roman occupation, and Roman Britain, just like every other part of the empire, witnessed spectacular acts of martyrdom from its initial converts, most notably by Saint Alban, who was beheaded and whose own blood, Bede writes, served as baptismal waters (1.7). Christianity soon became the accepted religion of the island, but when the Roman frontier collapsed in the early fifth century during the time of barbarian invasions — famously, according to Bede, the Angles, the Saxons, and the Jutes — the strength of Christianity similarly waned. Bede vividly describes the Christians' fate: "Public and private buildings fell in ruins, priests were everywhere slain at their altars, prelates and people alike perished by sword and fire regardless of rank, and there was no one left to bury those who had died a cruel death" (1.22). It was not an entirely unjust end, as Bede reminds his readers, for the Britons "never preached the faith to the Saxons or Angles who inhabited Britain with them" (1.22).

A two-pronged process of conversion followed these disasters. In 597, in the south of the country, missionaries dispatched from Rome by Pope Gregory the Great arrived. Gregory had apparently become concerned for the fate of the Angles before he was elected pope. As Bede relates the story, the future pope saw some boys being auctioned as slaves and remarked upon their "fair complexions, handsome faces, and lovely hair." He asked who they were and, hearing that were Angles (*Angli*), felt inspired to make one of the most notoriously bad puns in all of the Middle Ages: the *Angles* "have the face of *angels*, and such men should be fellow-heirs of the *angels* in heaven" (2.1). Immediately after becoming pope in 590, Gregory set into motion a plan to bring this people and their neighbors into the fold. Led by a monk named Augustine (not to be confused with Saint Augustine of Hippo), his missionaries established a tenuous foothold for Christianity and for Roman culture in Kent, establishing an archbishopric at Canterbury. At the same time, Irish missionaries led by Aidan, dispatched from the famous monastery at Iona and eventually made bishop of the church at Lindisfarne, were evangelizing the north of the country. Their brand of Christianity was in its origins Roman, but because Rome had abandoned Britain a century and a half earlier, they were not, in Bede's eyes, well enough informed about current doctrinal practice, particularly about the date of Easter and the form of a monk's tonsure. But Irish Christians' piety and their charity held a greater appeal for their audiences than did the better-educated Romans (3.5), their rude simplicity almost certainly the more appropriate message for an audience of barbarian warriors than was the theological precision of Augustine of Canterbury.

This process of conversion was not always smooth. Romans in particular nearly abandoned the island altogether after the deaths of Augustine in 604 and of Ethelbert, their royal patron, a decade later (2.5–6). And a recourse to idolatry was often only one disaster away, as when the East Saxons abandoned Christianity after an outbreak of plague. But Bede's narrative moves with a kind of logical inevitability, as each missionary group progresses through the various tribes and kingdoms until they finally meet and try to sort out their doctrinal differences.

Bede's presentation of these events seems surprisingly sophisticated. Modern readers readily appreciate his impulse to set the stage for his story through a geographic and cultural overview of England in his opening chapter. Unlike many of his contemporaries and like many of his successors, he begins not with the Creation or with the foundation of the Church or with an event from mythic history like the Trojan War, but rather with the arrival of the Romans in Britain. And Bede feels as haunted by Rome and her ruins as does any modern tourist: the Romans, he writes, had lived on the island for 470 years, "an occupation to which the cities, lighthouses, bridges, and roads which they built there testify to this day" (1.11). Historians also feel a kinship with Bede because of the care with which he identifies his sources and because of his reliance, whenever possible, on primary documents, many of which he copies directly into his work. Bede may have never traveled far from his monastery, as he tells us at the conclusion to the *Ecclesiastical History*, but he did dispatch a research assistant to Rome, a priest from London named Nothelm who brought back to England a wealth of archival material (preface).

The style of Christianity and the methods of preaching likewise sound, in Bede's descriptions, tolerant and humane but no less appropriate for the warlords who embraced the faith. Pope Gregory, for example, urged Mellitus, a potentially overzealous spokesperson for Rome, to destroy pagan idols but to leave the pagan temples in place to serve as churches: in this way the Anglo-Saxons could feel comfortable practicing their new religion in the old places (1.30). To King Ethelbert, on the other hand,

Gregory could offer exactly contradictory advice: "Increase your righteous zeal for their conversion; suppress the worship of idols; overthrow their buildings and shrines; strengthen the morals of your subjects by outstanding purity of life" (1.32). If there were to be extremism in the Christianization of the Anglo-Saxons, it would come from the local leaders and not from meddling outsiders.

Bede further presents his conversions as processes more spiritual, made only after careful consideration and soul-searching, than does Gregory of Tours. Kings do not impose Christianity on their subjects as much as they arrive at it together through mutual consultation. The pattern of conversion begins in Bede in a way familiar enough to anyone who has read the account of Clovis and Clotild in Gregory's *Histories,* in which the Christian queen Clotild introduced her pagan husband to the new faith around the year 490 (2.29–31). Ethelbert of Kent, to take the first example from Bede, had married a Merovingian princess named Bertha, and she brought with her from Gaul a chaplain named Liudhard, whom Bede describes as a bishop (1.25). It was this continental connection that enabled Augustine to land safely at Kent and begin his missionary work in a relatively secure atmosphere. Similarly Paulinus, Archbishop of York, would be able to begin his conversion of Northumbria in 625 because its king, Edwin, had married another Christian princess, in this case Ethelbert's daughter Ethelburh (2.9). Thus, the religion spread about in the upper levels of lay society through a series of familial and cultural alliances, with women acting as bridges to the new faith. As in Gregory's history, Christianity is the religion of a warrior aristocracy.

At this point Bede shifts his focus away from the barbarian leadership to barbarian society in general. Augustine and his followers "preached the word of life to as many as they could." Audiences marveled at "the sweetness of their heavenly doctrine" and were baptized. King Ethelbert, too, eventually accepted their message, as did his followers, though he compelled no one to convert (2.26). Edwin in Northumbria famously agonized over his decision, despite letters from Rome and despite a heavenly vision early in life when he lived as an exile (2.10–12). His conversion finally came after he had consulted with his "loyal chief men" — "*leudes,*" Gregory of Tours would have called them in his *Histories* (2.42, 3.23, 8.9, 9.20) — and found that they favored the new beliefs too (2.13). Thus, in the eyes of the Anglo-Saxon monk Bede, bishop, king, and community worked together in harmony to reach spiritual truths. It is an ideal he presents with schematic clarity in his depiction of the relationship between the Irish missionary Aidan and the Northumbrian king Oswald, who had once lived among the Irish as an exile: "It was indeed a beautiful sight when the bishop was preaching the gospel, to see the king acting as interpreter of the heavenly word for his ealdormen and thegns, for the bishop was not completely at home in the English tongue, while the king had gained a perfect knowledge of Irish during the long period of his exile" (3.3). It is impossible to imagine any of Gregory's kings and bishops doing the same. It is equally difficult to imagine Gregory or his readers attributing sanctity to the Christian kings as frequently as Bede does. In Bede's world the old categories of Roman and barbarian, bishop and king, warrior and saint do not hold. No one group maintains a monopoly on divine favor.

Bede's vision of a Christianity whose message both king and community heard no doubt reflects his own outlook as a monk. Raised in a monastic community from his seventh year, Bede spent his life in a world whose form was not unlike the warrior mead hall in *Beowulf,* with an abbot holding the position of an ecclesiastical warlord surrounded by a loyal band of followers. Instead of thinking that Bede's religious upbringing and monastic isolation blinded him to the harsh political realities of barbarian life, therefore, we might think instead that it gave him a unique understanding of barbarian society, one that had eluded Gregory of Tours. Gregory, steeped as he was in Roman culture, found the customs of the Merovingians self-evidently inferior. Bede, on the other hand, scatters throughout his narrative the gritty physical and psychological realities of Anglo-Saxon life. His stories contain the flavor of heroic myth, as when Coifu, King Edwin's pagan high priest, volunteers to be the first to renounce the pagan religion. To do so, he mounts a warhorse, charges at an altar, and hurls a spear at its idol. The anecdote sounds like the stuff of legend, but it also sounds like the sort of legend on which a barbarian priest would want to model his behavior (3.13). Some of Bede's scenes, unsurprisingly, recall *Beowulf,* as in the speech given just moments before Coifu's ride, when a follower of Edwin compares life on earth to the flight of a sparrow through a mead hall—a fleeting moment of light and warmth, preceded and followed by darkness and the unknown. If the new religion can provide answers to these mysteries, the soldier advises, then the king should listen to the missionaries (3.13). In Bede's world as in Beowulf's, the mead hall is the symbol of safety and community, and every warrior who lives in it, no matter how formidable he may be, knows enough to fear death.

Other sidelights onto tribal life can be surprisingly endearing, as in the story of the poet Caedmon (4.24 [22]). Caedmon lived at the monastery of Whitby, and some evenings during feasts, the monastery's servants would pass a harp to one another and sing songs. Caedmon, however, had no musical training and would bashfully retire from the meal to hide in the stable with the cattle. On one of these nights, after abandoning the feast, he fell asleep among the animals and heard a voice telling him to sing. He at first refused, essentially claiming to be tone deaf, but the voice persisted. When Caedmon finally did obey, he found himself singing a new song about Creation. The gift of music had come to him as if in a dream. The monks and the abbess—for in Bede's world, more often than not, it is a woman who governs religious houses composed of both men and women—recognized his talent and nurtured it. His skill was such that no Englishman in Bede's day ever matched it. Bede offers a paraphrase of one of Caedmon's songs but not a translation, for, as he observes, "it is not possible to translate verse, however well composed, literally from one language to another without some loss of beauty and dignity" (4.24 [22]). It is a rare and wonderful moment, when one of the Middle Ages' greatest scholars observes that the written language of choice, the language inherited from Rome, cannot match the beauties of a Germanic tongue.

Bede was not blind to the difficulties inherent to this conversion process, entailing as it did the integration of barbarian values and barbarian culture with a Christianity that was, one way or another, Roman. Consider his example of the relationship between King Oswine of Deira and Aidan, the Irish missionary dispatched from Iona (3.14). King Oswine, Bede tells us, gave to Aidan one of his finest horses. Although the king knew Aidan preferred to walk, he felt that the horse could serve him well from time to time in case he needed to reach a destination quickly. Aidan, however, gave the animal away to the first beggar to ask for alms. Oswine understandably felt upset. He had, in the best traditions of *Beowulf*, offered a fine gift to a valued friend, and the valued friend had treated the gesture with indifference. Aidan's training, on the other hand, with its emphasis on poverty, had caused him to see no real distinction between ceremonial gifts and worldly pomp, and he made use of the occasion to deliver an edifying lesson on the subject before the king and his warrior followers. The lesson did not take hold immediately. After these words, in a scene whose setting again appears to have been plucked from *Beowulf*, they went in to dine. The missionary sat down in his own place, and the king, who had just come in from hunting, stood warming himself by the fire with his thegns. Suddenly he remembered Aidan's words; at once he took off his sword, gave it to a thegn, and then hastening to where Aidan sat, threw himself at his feet, and asked for his pardon. "Never from henceforth," he said, "will I speak of this again nor will I form any opinion as to what money of mine or how much of it you should give to the sons of God" (3.14). When Aidan heard these words, he raised the king to his feet and urged him to resume his former demeanor. Later that evening, Aidan wept. When one of his followers asked him why, he answered, "I know that the king will not live long; for I never before saw a humble king." Aidan had, in effect, preached too well. He had created a king too Christian to survive a warrior's life. It is this tension that explains why so many kings in the later pages of the *Ecclesiastical History* decide to abandon their office altogether and to die as pilgrims in Rome rather than continue with the contradictions inherent in being a Christian warlord (5.7, 5.19).

So humane is Bede's narrative voice that readers can easily overlook those occasions when his instincts appear remarkably different from their own. Most immediately notable are the miracle stories that mark almost every page of the *Ecclesiastical History*. The fact that Bede tells of supernatural events from Roman times is not surprising, since for him and his readers these incidents occurred in an age already shrouded in legend. But miracles do not grow less frequent after the deaths of the original martyrs. If anything, they grow more numerous, until, by the fifth and final book, the *Ecclesiastical History* has become a dream-like series of supernatural occurrences —resumés of the deaths, lives, and afterlives of saintly men and visions of hell and heaven experienced by people led to redemption or ushered off to damnation. These stories reached Bede largely through rumor or oral reports from a teacher named Trumbert, a doctor named Cynefrith, or simply an anonymous "those who say" (4.3, 4.19 [17]). About such stories, however, Bede merely writes, "For in accordance with the principles of true history, I have simply sought to commit to writing what I have collected from common report, for the instruction of posterity" (preface).

The last element of this statement is probably the most important: everything that Bede included in his history—including the miracles— was intended for the reader's edification. But what lessons did he mean to impart? The answer is not always clear. Modern readers naturally expect miracles to be rewards for virtue on the part of the suppliant or else for faith in God or even for devotion to a particular saint. But this is not always the case. Bede tells, for example, of an unnamed man whose horse suddenly collapsed, foaming at the mouth and to all appearances about to die. Fortunately for the horse, it happened to roll onto a spot where King Oswald — by then Saint Oswald — had died in battle, and the animal suddenly leapt up healthy (3.9). Obviously Bede does not intend us to believe that God had rewarded the horse's devotion or, for that matter, that of the rider. The horse's owner simply noted where the miracle occurred, saw that the grass was somewhat greener there, and reached the apparently logical conclusion that some special sanctity was associated with the place. The line between a miracle story and a bit of magic appears fine indeed.

In another story, Bede tells of a cross set up by Oswald before a battle. The cross, including splinters cut from it and moss scraped off it, became a source of healing power for those who visited it, such that, when a monk named Bothelm had broken an arm, he asked one of his brothers passing by to bring him some part of it, just as a sick person today might ask a friend to stop off at the pharmacy to pick up a prescription. The brother collected the moss, and Bothelm placed it carefully inside his cloak. That night, however, he forgot the relic and fell asleep lying on top of it. "At midnight he awoke feeling something cold close to his side and, putting his hand down to find out what it was, he discovered that his arm and his hand were as sound as if they had never pained him" (3.2). Bothelm did not maintain a vigil and pray long and earnestly over his relic. Rather, he forgot that it was there and slept on it, and the relic worked of its own accord. The power of God was in the moss or in the soil, radiating impersonally, regardless of the faith or the rationality of the recipient. It was worthy of respect for what it was, but it is not for human power to control or channel such force.

Just as striking is the easy accessibility of these relics to the Anglo-Saxons. Gregory's saints, and certainly their bodies, stick close by their churches in his *Histories*. The pride that Gregory takes in his possession of Saint Martin's bones is immediately obvious. He owns them and controls access to them (5.14). In Bede's world, by contrast, relics and saintly power are everywhere. Oswald's body provides the most striking evidence, for it ends up scattered in many locations. The main part came to rest at a monastery called Bardney, its arrival marked by a column of heavenly light (3.11). His head and hands — cut off after his death in battle and displayed on stakes — eventually reached Lindisfarne (3.12). His arm, incorrupt because blessed by Aidan, went to still another church (3.6). This liberal sprinkling of bones, some still in an envelope of flesh, does not take into account the cross left by Oswald in a field, nor does it include the soil where he died. The cross, as we have seen, provided souvenirs to all who venerated it, and the death site was so popular that a hole appeared there "as deep as a man's height" (3.10). In most places Bede seems to celebrate the orderly, hierarchical Christianity of Rome, but here he is barbarian. The saints and their power were treasures to be shared by the whole community, not sparingly doled out by a bishop.

Thus, the miraculous functioned in Anglo-Saxon England, but we have yet to determine what educational purpose Bede intended it to serve in his narrative. He gives at least one clue in his description of the hole created at the site of Oswald's death: "Nor is it to be wondered at that the sick are cured in the place where he died, for while he was alive he never ceased to care for the sick and the poor, to give them alms, and offer them help" (3.9). The efficacy of a relic bears no connection to the recipient of the miracle. The men and women who visit holy places in Bede's England are not pilgrims in the later medieval sense of the term. They do not undertake a difficult journey to a shrine in order to honor a saint and in expectation that the saint will help them. Bede's miracle recipients are simply people who, one way or another, experience the power of God. And the miracle story (like the miracle itself) is a demonstration of this power and of the character of the heroic saint with whom it is associated. Oswald, anticipating Charlemagne, saw his responsibilities as king not just in terms of conquest but in terms of taking care of his subjects. And through his miracles Oswald reminded his family and his followers of that obligation.

However much an extraordinary act of healing might impress a pagan audience or a group of recent converts, in Bede's eyes the grandest signs pointed toward elementary goodness. If the bodies of saints smelt of perfume and gave no indication of decay, it was a reflection of the purity of the saints' hearts (3.8, 4.19 [17]). If Oswald's arm did not decay, it was not because Bishop Aidan had cast a spell-like blessing over it but because the king used that arm to distribute charity (3.6). If Archbishop Mellitus turned back flames from his city, it was only fitting: "So brightly did the man of God burn with the fire of divine love, so often had he repelled the stormy powers of the air from harming him and his people by his prayers and exhortations, that it was right for him to be able to prevail over earthly winds and flames and to ensure that they should not injure him or his people" (2.8).

The greatest miracle in Bede's history, though, is the one with which we began this essay: conversion itself. Like many miracle stories that include a struggle between holy men and demons, this process grew out of a battle against a terrifying foe — not just the abstract system of beliefs that was paganism but rather against very real scourges of God, men like King Penda of Mercia who devastated Christian Northumbria and East Anglia, massacred the Britons, and killed Edwin and Oswald. By the end of the *Ecclesiastical History*, Oswiu, King of Mercia, has finally succeeded in killing Penda, and the same Oswiu has presided at the Synod of Whitby (664), where the correct method for dating Easter was formally decreed for all of the Anglo-Saxon tribes (3.24–25). So significant is Oswiu's accomplishment that one is tempted to overlook his murder of his Christian brother Oswine in order to steal his half of the kingdom (3.14). As Bede tells the story of the Synod of Whitby, Oswiu listened patiently to the cases for both methods of calculating Easter, with Colman, Bishop of Lindisfarne, arguing for the Irish and Wilfrid, Bishop of York, arguing for the Romans. After all of the astronomical and calendrical niceties had been gone over, the king cut to the chase and asked, with a warrior's good sense, whether Saint Peter, leader of the Roman Church, really did hold the keys to heaven. "They both answered, 'Yes.' Thereupon the king concluded, 'Then I tell you, since he is the doorkeeper I will not contradict him'" (3.25). Colman and his followers left the country in protest, but a few dozen pages later, even the Picts and the Irish had begun to see the light (5.21–22). The quality of learning among the English in the 730s had at the same time begun to surpass that of their continental teachers, thanks mainly to the educational work of Archbishop Theodore of Canterbury, originally of Tarsus, who brought Greek learning to England and who involved the country in international debates about the shape of Catholic orthodoxy (4.17 [15], 5.20). So sound is Anglo-Saxon doctrine by the end of the fifth book of the *Ecclesiastical History* that English monks have reversed the original journey of Augustine. In Bede's lifetime it was his own brethren who were traveling east to the Continent to convert the Saxons still practicing pagan rites (5.9, 5.11).

It is a rich and satisfying conclusion to our story. Anglo-Saxon England is a virtuous and prosperous land. It remains essentially a tribal world, but it is a world unified by its religious culture. These political and religious landscapes, however, are not nearly as settled as Bede's version suggests. Many commentators have noted the different picture of the Anglo-Saxon England that Bede paints in his letter to Egbert, written at the very end of his life, where he defines with precision the various shortcomings in contemporary religious practice. One finds there a sense that the English have fallen away from the heroic standards of their ancestors, not that they are making rapid advances upon them. But simply to note that the end of Bede's story is misleading is to miss both the purpose of his history and the sophistication of its conclusion. The five books of the *Ecclesiastical History* parallel deliberately the common Christian model of the Five Ages of the world that came before Christ's birth. At the end of the Fifth Age, Christ had appeared for mankind, just as at the end of the fifth book Christianity has established itself in England. The Sixth Age, the world after Christ and the world of Christianity, was still very much in progress in the 700s, just as a sixth book of ecclesiastical history in England was, in Bede's day, yet to be lived and thus yet to be written. And Bede recognized as much as anyone else that his story was not over, that there were cliffhangers to be resolved. About Ceolwulf, king of the Northumbrians and the man to whom Bede dedicated the *History,* he writes, "The beginning and the course of his reign have been filled with so many and such serious commotions and setbacks that it as yet impossible to know what to say about them or to guess what the outcome will be." In the same passage, about the growing popularity of monasticism among the warrior class, he writes, "What the result will be, a later generation will discover" (5.23).

These passages at the end of the history may be misleading, but they nonetheless point us towards Bede's greatest miracle and his most enduring achievement. In the convoluted tribal world in which he lived, he imagined a single people, a single nation. This idea was born out of a hybrid mix of Old Testament sensibility and Christian piety—of a people chosen by God, whose character He tests, whose shortcomings He punishes, and whose virtue He sometimes rewards. The name Bede chose for these people and used in his title is not the one generally favored in history books: Anglo-Saxon. They were, simply, the Angles. No particular historical reason demanded this label. Most likely it was a tribute to Gregory the Great and the first Roman missionaries, those who had decided to seek out not *Angli,* but *angeli.* And it was this name that would stick to the country: Angle Land or, with the passage of time, England. It is evidence less of the power of Gregory's joke and more of the power of Bede's vision that this conception of the island and its people has remained dominant. We accept the name and we accept the reality of the people because Bede has trained us to do so, to imagine a land not of angels but of Angles.

Bibliographic Note

The *Ecclesiastical History of the English People* is available in many translations. I recommend that of Judith McClure and Roger Collins (Oxford: Oxford University Press, 1999), which is based on the earlier edition by Bertram Colgrave and R.A.B. Mynors for the *Oxford Medieval Texts* series. Anglo-Saxon England is rich in the number and quality of primary sources available in English. Bede's *Life of Saint Cuthbert* and the earlier anonymous life have been published as *Two Lives of Saint Cuthbert*, ed. Bertram Colgrave (Cambridge: Cambridge University Press, 1940). Eddius Stephanus, *Life of Bishop Wilfrid*, also edited by Colgrave (Cambridge: Cambridge University Press, 1927), offers a different perspective on events in the *Ecclesiastical History*. For Bede's own upbringing and time, see *The Lives of the Abbots of Wearmouth and Jarrow* and the anonymous *History of Abbot Ceolfrid*, both translated by J.F. Webb in *The Age of Bede* (London: Penguin Classics, 1983).

The best introduction to Bede's world is Benedicta Ward's marvelous *The Venerable Bede* (London: Geoffrey Chapman, 1990). On the *Ecclesiastical History* itself, one should see J.M. Wallace-Hadrill, *Bede's Ecclesiastical History of the English People: A Historical Commentary* (Oxford: Oxford University Press, 1988). Any study of the Anglo-Saxon world should begin with Frank Stenton's classic *Anglo-Saxon England,* 3rd ed. (Oxford: Oxford University Press, 2001) and be supplemented by James Campbell, Eric John, and Patrick Wormald, *The Anglo-Saxons* (London: Penguin, 1991 [1982]), as well as by Eric John, *Reassessing Anglo-Saxon England* (Manchester: Manchester University Press, 1996). Barbara Yorke examines the political landscape in *Kings and Kingdoms of Early Anglo-Saxon England* (London: Routledge, 1990). David Rollason, *Saints and Relics in Anglo-Saxon England* (Oxford: Blackwell, 1989) is highly recommended. Finally, the archaeological finds at Sutton Hoo and the more recently discovered Staffordshire Hoard are invaluable.

NINE

Between Two Empires
Einhard and His Charles the Great

Jason Glenn

Charles the Great, a.k.a. Charlemagne, is one of the towering figures of the Middle Ages. During his long reign as king of the Franks (768–814), Frankish rule spread throughout northern Europe and, after the pope crowned him "emperor and augustus" in Rome on Christmas day 800, southwards into Italy (28). But his military conquests and the expansion of his rule tell only part of the story of the growth of Frankish power and influence under Charles's leadership. As the most prominent and well-recognized member of the family who, in the words of one modern historian, "forged Europe," Charles has been labelled both the "father of Europe" and the "father of a continent."[1] However grand such labels may be — and however much they speak to historians' inclination to search for origins and to identify individual figures as the leading agents of change — it is undeniable that, together with the members of his court, he initiated an ambitious program of reforms that would transform not merely the political but also the religious and intellectual landscape of the European lands. He also left an impression on the historical identity and consciousness of the Franks that has endured to this day. Indeed, modern

---

[1] Pierre Riché, *The Carolingians: A Family Who Forged Europe,* trans. Michael I. Allen (Philadelphia: University of Pennsylvania Press, 1993); D.A. Bullough, "*Europae Pater:* Charlemagne and His Achievement in the Light of Recent Scholarship," *English Historical Review* 85 (1970): 59–105; Alessandro Barbero, *Charlemagne: Father of a Continent,* trans. Allan Cameron (Berkeley: University of California Press, 2004).

French and German scholars have both traced their nation's ancestry back to the Franks and claimed as their own the great Charles and the achievements of his Carolingian (from the Latin "Karolus" for Charles) family.

Given such a legacy, it is perhaps difficult to believe that his first biographer feared that, had he not put ink to parchment, Charles's memory might fade away. And yet Einhard, who had come to Charles's court in the early 790s, says in his preface that he decided to describe the king's life, character, and accomplishments since he was not sure that anyone else would. "I thought it would be better to write these things [that is, his personal observations] down," he goes on to say, "along with other widely known details, for the sake of posterity, than to allow the splendid life of this most excellent king, the greatest of all the men in his time, and his remarkable deeds, which people now alive can scarcely equal, to be swallowed up by the shadows of forgetfulness" (preface). It may appear to us that Einhard is somewhat overly dramatic here, as aspects of Charles's reign are preserved in other sources and documents. We know, for instance, that many of the events in which Charles participated — including many to which Einhard alludes — are described in the *Royal Frankish Annals,* a running account of events and circumstances that was kept in his court. Likewise, archives throughout the Frankish lands would have had copies of administrative records that emanated from his court; some of these records still exist today and reveal much about his reign. We might also suppose that his legend would have endured and grown by word of mouth, even if Einhard had not written the biography. And there is evidence that it did — one need only think of the *Song of Roland* (discussed in Chapter 12 below).

Nevertheless, let us not be overly hasty to dismiss Einhard's stated concern. We do not know when he composed the text. He may have done so as early as 817, that is, early in the reign of Charles's son and successor Louis. Some scholars have argued that he wrote it in the early to mid 820s, when some of the less savoury aspects of Charles's personal life and his warlike ways came under posthumous critique. Others have made the case that the text was composed in 829/30, or even as late as 836, the year in which we find the first reference to it in the work of another author. This is not the place to explore the relative merits of the dates proposed, but if the text does date from the mid 820s or later, as I suspect, Einhard's concerns about the memory of Charles and his sense of urgency to preserve it are perhaps understandable.

Einhard was a younger contemporary of the king, who was about 25 years his elder. A decade after Charles's death and a quarter-century or so removed from the emperor's crowning moment in Rome, Einhard would therefore have been in his mid fifties. Although it was not uncommon for men his age to live another couple of decades — Charles died at the age of 70 — Einhard had surely seen many of his older contemporaries from Charles's generation and, likewise, a number of his own peers take their appreciation for the king to the grave. In this context, his claim that "no one could write about [Charles's deeds] more truthfully than me, since I myself was present and personally witnessed them, as they say, with my own eyes" resonates (preface). So, too, does his concern for Charles's legacy. After all, we have no evidence that anyone before Einhard sought to write an account of the king's life.

Had he not done so, it is therefore possible not only that the types of details Einhard shares about Charles would have faded into the shadows and been forgotten but also that Charles would not have occupied such a privileged position in the history of Europe. Indeed, Einhard's account influenced the political imagination — and thus the actions — of subsequent generations. It circulated widely within the Frankish lands during the ninth century and was copied into manuscripts over and again for centuries thereafter. It inspired other men to write about other kings and shaped the ways people throughout the Middle Ages remembered the great Charles and thought about royal and imperial rule. In short, Einhard's *Life of Charles the Great* was then, as it is today, a monument to the Frankish past.

It should be, albeit not so much for what it tells us about Charles as for the insight it offers into the Frankish world of the early ninth century. That insight has much less to do with the life and deeds of the king per se than with the intellectual culture he helped to shape. Indeed, when we scratch the surface of Einhard's text, the transcendent figure of the great king and emperor dissolves somewhat from view. As we consider in the following pages how and why Einhard selected what material he would record and how he was inclined to present it, some of his sensibilities come into greater focus. More precisely, we shall see that his *vita* represents an innovative attempt to fashion a new type of ruler suited for a new type of empire.

Einhard maintains an elusive presence throughout the work. Unlike, say, Jean de Joinville, who could be accused of using his own great king as a vehicle for telling his own story in the early fourteenth-century *Life of Saint Louis* (see Chapter 22 below), Einhard offers nary a thread of auto-biographical information. Indeed, he seems to have intended for his own identity to remain unknown. The text originally circulated anonymously and did not bear his name until after his death in 840, when a younger contemporary, Walafrid Strabo, expressed his appreciation for Einhard's great literary talents in a prologue he affixed to the text — Strabo also added to the *vita* the chapter divisions cited throughout this chapter. It is unclear why Einhard preferred not to identify himself. Scholars have speculated that he was perhaps being politically cautious since he wrote and circulated the text within court circles during the reign of Charles's son and successor, Louis the Pious — the text has been read both as sympathetic to and critical of, Louis. Whatever his reasons for anonymity, Einhard nevertheless impresses himself into his text in ways that betray his aspirations for the Franks.

Einhard begins the *vita* with three brief chapters in which he offers the back-story to Charles's reign, that is, his family's rise to royal status and his succession to the throne. In so doing, he underscores the impotence of the last Merovingians, the family of kings that had ruled the Franks "without any vitality for a long time and [had] demonstrated that there was nothing of any worth in it except the empty name of 'king'" (1). As "mayor of the palace" (*major domus*) Charles's father Pepin, like his own father Charles Martel before him, had held great power within the kingdom. He was made king in 751 after the last Merovingian was "ordered deposed" by the pope. When he died in 768, the realm fell to his two sons, Charles and Carloman. The latter, named for Pepin's brother, died not long thereafter, in 771, and Charles ruled his lands from that point forward.

Einhard offers only a few suggestive details about the fate of Charles's brother. Carloman and Charles had agreed to a division of the Frankish lands so that the former received the lands his namesake uncle had controlled when he shared the office of *major domus* with Pepin. They ruled together in peace despite the fact that "many on Carloman's side sought to drive the brothers apart." But, Einhard insists, "the threat of [war] was more suspected than real." We might then ask why, according to Einhard, Carloman's family and the nobles who supported him fled to Italy when he died (3). Why did his widow "spurn" Charles and seek protection from the king of the Lombards (3)? And what does it mean that Charles wore down that king and "accepted complete surrender" from him shortly thereafter (6)? Perhaps there is a hint in Einhard's earlier treatment of their uncle. In the chapter before the younger Carloman died, the uncle Carloman had "walked away from the oppressive chore of governing an earthly kingdom" and retired to a monastery in Rome "to live a contemplative life" (2). We are thus left with the distinct impression that Einhard has put a spin on events between Charles and his brother, events that had taken place more than half a century earlier. This impression is reinforced by what little we know about what happened from other sources and, more generally, about the dimensions of Frankish power dynamics.

The history of Frankish kingship from the sixth century through the reign of Charlemagne and into the tenth century could be told as the struggle of kings to maintain their rule against rival claimants or, perhaps as often, factions of elites who rallied behind someone ·of royal stock. Toward the end of this period, those rivals often came from other families, and the stories of the conflicts were less likely to end in the murder or tonsure of a claimant than at the beginning, when the threats often came from sons or brothers and had more gruesome endings. Indeed, for those familiar with the anecdotes Bishop Gregory of Tours tells of the sixth-century Frankish kings in his *Ten Books of Histories,* the flight of royal relatives and the withdrawal to monastic life is not unfamiliar. But the ways in which it happens in Einhard's presentation most certainly is. Gregory presents us with countless examples of menacing kings forcing the flight of other Franks of royal blood, at least those whom they don't kill or tonsure — without long hair, their rivals were no longer king-worthy and were forced to withdraw to monasteries. He almost revels in telling such tales. Indeed, after detailing Clovis's cunning and ruthless consolidation of his rule, in a passage noted in Chapter 4 of this volume, Gregory's Clovis laments toward the end of his life that he had no more relatives alive to help him in the face of danger. Gregory explains that he did so not because he grieved their loss but, rather, because he hoped to find more living relatives (that is, potential challengers to his rule) to kill (2.42).

In contrast, Einhard's Pepin and Charles seem more passive agents in their own ascent to singular rule; indeed, they appear mere beneficiaries of the decisions and misfortunes of the two Carlomans. Even when Charles's good fortune does not come at the expense of others — as when he reluctantly accepts the imperial title (28) — he is not aggressive in the pursuit of power. In those cases where he does encounter challenges to his rule, he is no Clovis. For instance, in the case of his son Pepin the Hunchback, who conspired against his father "with certain leading Franks" in 792, Einhard reports, "After the plot was uncovered and the conspirators were condemned, [Pepin] was tonsured and allowed to pursue the religious life he had always wanted" (20). Likewise, Einhard uses the passive voice to distance Charles when his punishment against other conspirators was more harsh: "Its perpetrators were sent into exile; some blinded, others unharmed. Only three conspirators lost their lives, since to avoid arrest they had drawn their swords to defend themselves and had even killed some men. They were cut down themselves because there was [simply] no other way to subdue them" (20). Charles, implicitly the victim, is nowhere to be found here.

It is certainly possible that Charles had less violent impulses than had some of Gregory's kings. But it would appear that what distinguishes Charles from them most is the vision and idiosyncrasies of the man who chose to write his biography or, perhaps more accurately, the differences between the visions and idiosyncrasies of the two authors and between the larger political and intellectual cultures in which they wrote. After all, the two men came to their work and the Frankish kings they describe from vastly different perspectives. The Gallo-Roman bishop Gregory had to negotiate a world that was becoming increasingly Frankish in his day as members of the Frankish elite exercised growing authority in both the secular and ecclesiastical domains. As we shall now see, Einhard, through and through a Frank, had a particular fondness for a Rome that had faded into the past. He sought to resuscitate it, to introduce and integrate Roman traditions and legitimacy to Carolingian rule. And he set out to articulate a vision for a Frankish ruler who ruled not merely a kingdom but an empire.

After the opening chapters draw to a close with the death of Carloman and the establishment of Charles as sole king "by the agreement of all of the Franks," Einhard offers a description of the "plan of the work." In a brief note, he explains that he will not bother to recount the king's youth because "there is no one alive now who can give information on it" (4). Instead, he proposes to describe the deeds of Charles — that is, his military achievements — "at home and abroad," then to turn to his character, and, finally, to his administration and death. As his words quoted above from the preface suggest, Einhard had a "constant friendship" with the king, his "foster father," after he came to live at the court. It is therefore not surprising that, as we read through the *vita* — particularly the section about his character — there are moments when he seems to offer privileged insight into Charles's qualities and ways of life. Let us look, for instance, at one such passage in which he describes, among other things, the king's eating and drinking habits:

> [Charles] was moderate when it came to both food and drink, but he was even more moderate in the case of drink, since he deeply detested [seeing] anyone inebriated, especially himself or his men. But he was not able to abstain from food, and often complained that fasting was bad for his health. He seldom put on [large] banquets, but when he did it was for a great number of people on special feast days. His dinner each day was served in four courses only, not including the roast, which his hunters used to carry in on a spit. He preferred [roast meat] over all other food. While eating, he was entertained or listened to someone read out the histories and deeds of the ancients. He was fond of the books of Saint Augustine, particularly the one called the *City of God*.
>
> He was so restrained in his consumption of wine and other drinks, that he seldom drank more than three times during a meal. After his midday meal in the summertime, he would eat some fruit and take a single drink. Then, after he had removed his clothes and shoes, just as he did at night, he would lie down for two or three hours. While sleeping at night, he would not only wake four or five times, but he would even get up. [In the morning] while putting on his shoes and dressing, he not only saw friends, but if the count of the palace informed him that there was some unresolved dispute that could not be sorted out without his judgment, he would order him to bring the disputing parties before him at once. Then, as if he were sitting in court, he heard the nature of the dispute and rendered his opinion. He not only looked after cases such as this at that time, but also matters of any sort that needed to be handled that day or to be assigned to one of his officials. (24)

I quote this passage at some length for several reasons, not least because it provides a sense of Einhard's authorial voice. He presents detail, interesting detail, in a rather matter-of-fact way that can lull the reader into an uncritical reading. Indeed, it is easy to believe that its author has, as he claims in the preface, recorded "truthfully" the king's "deeds" — as well as his "life" and "character" — and thus dutifully completed the task he set for himself. There is perhaps reason to believe that some, indeed many, of the details Einhard furnishes here may well describe the habits of the king at one point or another in his life — let us leave aside a concern that such a composite sketch is inevitably more static than habits, tastes, and inclinations tend to be over the course of a lifetime. But there is also reason for some caution in accepting such details as straightforward descriptions of Charles's behavior.

The habits of the ruler described in this passage bear a striking resemblance to those of Augustus Caesar (63 BC–14 AD), at least as they were described by a Roman imperial official named Suetonius in the early second century. Suetonius's Augustus "ate sparingly" (76). He was "sparing in the use of wine" and "used to drink only three times at supper" (77). He also took naps after lunch and would get up two or three times at night (78). It is intriguing to think that Charles had himself been so enamored with an account of Suetonius's depiction of the emperor that he emulated Augustus. If so, perhaps Einhard merely described what he witnessed. But the many similarities between the descriptions of the two emperors — along with further thematic and narrative similarities throughout the two texts — suggest that however much Charles knew about or emulated Augustus, Einhard drew on the work of Suetonius to develop his own account of Charles's life.

Let us note, however, that he did not merely ascribe to Charles all of the details he found in Suetonius's sketch of Augustus. Rather, he seems to have adopted the basic framing of the Roman author's passage. Thus, he comments on fasting, the frequency of eating in large groups, and favorite foods. Yet he replaced not merely the name of his subject but also many of the details about him. So Charles's taste for roast replaces Augustus's preference for the "food of the common people": coarse bread, small fish, hand-pressed cheese, and figs (76). The infrequent banquets of Charles contrast with the frequent dinner parties of Augustus (74). And whereas Suetonius notes that Augustus took his post-lunch nap "without taking off his shoes and socks" (78), for his siesta Einhard's emperor removed his shoes and clothing, "just as he did at night." It is therefore reasonable to suppose that Einhard took cues from Suetonius about what of an emperor's behavior and habits were worthy of record and then set about to record details of such behavior and habits in Charles.

As we consider such a possibility, let us recognize that precise knowledge of Charles's eating, drinking, and napping or the particularities of his diet only gets us so far in our understanding of the Frankish world of the late eighth and early ninth century. Einhard's authorial choices and their implications, on the other hand, open a number of opportunities to reach a deeper understanding of the world in which both Charles and Einhard ate, drank, and slept.

In that world — and in his *vita* — Einhard at once expresses a pride in his Frankish identity and attempts to transform it, to infuse it with a legitimacy and authority drawn from a Roman world gone by. In Chapter 29, for instance, he enumerates reforms and programs Charles undertook after he became emperor. He had songs of the deeds of early Franks written down for posterity and a grammar of his native tongue put together. Using that language, he gave names to the months and the winds that had previously existed only in "Latin and barbarous names." And he systematized Frankish laws.

Our records of Charles's reign suggest that his legal, administrative, educational, and other social reforms date from well before his imperial coronation. Einhard's presentation suggests, however, that they were undertaken under the guise of an imperial reform program, for it is immediately after becoming emperor (in Chapter 28) that Einhard has Charles undertake these reforms that so flaunt his Frankish heritage. Indeed, Einhard seems intent on making clear to his readers that the imperial title — a title that, incidentally, he claims Charles did not want and only reluctantly accepted — did not threaten Charles's commitment to his Frankish identity. So, although he may have slipped into Roman garb when Pope Leo crowned him emperor, this man, who "normally wore the customary attire of the Franks" and rejected the "gorgeous" clothing of foreigners (23), was unlike previous Roman emperors. This "emperor and augustus" ruled a Frankish empire. And this new empire required a new type of Frankish ruler. It is such a Frankish emperor that Einhard, inspired perhaps by the imperial coronation of 800, sought to create. In the process, by drawing on the Suetonian exemplar of the first emperor of the Romans, he offered his contemporaries and subsequent generations a new way to think about and to present the deeds of a ruler.

It is hardly uncommon to find deeds of kings recorded within earlier medieval histories and chronicles. There is, for instance, much biographical information in the vivid portraits of the Frankish kings that emerge from the pages of Gregory's *Histories*. But the biographical genre per se had been used almost exclusively for the lives of holy men and women for centuries before Einhard. Indeed, Einhard had hagiographical works at his disposal as he sought to organize his thoughts about Charles and did draw on the late-fourth-century *Life of Saint Martin* by Sulpicius Severus, among others, as he developed his *vita*. From Sulpicius, he may have borrowed language to express his prefatory concerns that the memory of Charles might fade away if he did not take up the task of the biography; his impulse to remain anonymous may also have been informed by the preface of Sulpicius, who offers a harsh critique of secular biography. But Einhard's *vita* represents the first biographical sketch of a secular ruler since the fourth century, when the rule of emperors spanned the lands of Europe and the Mediterranean.

Let me repeat this point since it may shock our modern historical sensibilities steeped in traditions of secular biography: no one in the lands of the western Roman Empire or the Frankish kingdoms that emerged in their place beginning in the fifth century—or anywhere else in Europe—thought to write a biography of a ruler. Perhaps it is therefore not surprising that Einhard turned to the work of Suetonius to help organize his thoughts. Or was it that his familiarity with the work of Suetonius and, for that matter, other Roman authors inspired him to undertake the *vita*? Whatever the case, as I suggest above, Einhard did not necessarily use Suetonius to transform Charles into a Roman emperor. He used the work of the Roman author as a guide for the types of information he might offer about an emperor or, more precisely, for the types of information he might use to frame a portrait of a Frankish ruler as an emperor rather than merely a king.

The very decision to write a biography was an innovative move on the part of Einhard. Apparently it was also a self-conscious one. Although he does not refer to Suetonius in his preface—he does cite and quote from the work of Cicero—he feels compelled to justify his decision to write the *vita*:

> I have attempted not to omit any of the facts that have come to my attention, and [yet I also seek] not to irritate those who are excessively critical by supplying a long-winded account of everything new [I have learned]. Perhaps, in this way, it will be possible to avoid angering with a new book [even] those who criticize the old masterpieces composed by the most learned and eloquent of men. And yet, I am quite sure that there are many

people devoted to contemplation and learning who do not believe that the circumstances of the present age should be neglected or that virtually everything that happens these days is not worth remembering and should be condemned to utter silence and oblivion. Some people are so seduced by their love of the distant past, that they would rather insert the famous deeds of other peoples in various compositions, than deny posterity any mention of their own names by writing nothing. (preface)

These words suggest that Einhard thought of his offering as somewhat more than a mere record of the past he feared would otherwise be lost. Indeed, they suggest a self-conscious move toward innovation by one who sought to break with tradition. Or, perhaps more accurately, he sought to distinguish his aims and intentions from those practiced by at least some contemporary thinkers and writers whom he held in low esteem. Einhard intended to create something new. At the same time, we sense here and throughout the preface that, in his mind, to draw on the "old masterpieces composed by the most learned and eloquent of men" was far more than a return to the old. And if this is an allusion to the works of antiquity that shaped his *vita,* Einhard reveals here and in the very structure of his work a reverence for classical Rome and what it had to offer the Franks as they developed their own empire. Such a reverence is otherwise evident in Carolingian architecture, literature, and even the affectionate nicknames members of the Carolingian court had borrowed from Roman figures and used to refer to one another.

Given the appreciation for Rome and its empire that Einhard shared with Charles and their contemporaries, it is perhaps somewhat ironic that, by looking back to them — that is, to Rome and its empire — for inspiration and validation, in many ways it was in their own lifetimes that the story of that empire more or less draws to a close. Whether or not Charles was the father of a continent or his family forged Europe, his coronation, together with the reforms and ideology that emanated from his court, marked the beginning of a new age, a new empire. This is not to suggest that the Franks who lived in the Frankish lands before the reign of Charles imagined themselves as Roman. Quite the contrary, they were likely less self-conscious about Roman ideology and their relationship to that empire than were Charles, Einhard, and their contemporaries. But just as Einhard's

Charles looks quite different from the Augustus of Suetonius, the attempts to make sense of what it meant to become imperial—and how those attempts were shaped by the ways members of the Frankish elite understood the Roman world—essentially led to an empire that no longer resembled its model. In other words, the efforts among the Frankish elite to create an imperial identity modeled on Rome were perhaps the final nail in the coffin of the western Roman Empire itself.

Einhard's work is emblematic of this moment and the larger transformation it marks. Indeed, by drawing on texts about and traditions of Roman rulers to offer a portrait of a new type of emperor, he ended their direct influence on the minds of subsequent authors who sought to record the deeds of secular rulers. Charles's son inspired two biographies. Thegan's *Deeds of Emperor Louis* is based closely in structure on Einhard's *vita.* In his *Life of Emperor Louis,* the so-called Astronomer was clearly quite conscious of Einhard's text, even if he diverges from it structurally and conceptually. At the end of the ninth century, Einhard's work also served as a model for the Welsh author Asser's biography of the West Saxon king Alfred, who established his dominion over the whole of the Anglo-Saxon kingdoms in England. And in the middle of the tenth century, a Saxon author named Widukind drew significantly on the *vita* as he elaborated the deeds of rulers from a new imperial dynasty, the Ottonians, east of the Rhine. Decades earlier, Notker, a monk in the east Frankish lands that would come under that Ottonian rule, wrote another original biography of Charles, a work intended to instruct his own king on how to rule. He did not rely on Einhard as a model for his work. And while these other authors, who did, did not merely mimic the *vita,* they all nevertheless wrote and worked within a new tradition of secular biography of rulers, a tradition begun by a man whose appreciation for the Roman imperial world helped to bring it to a close.

Bibliographic Note

There are numerous English translations of Einhard's *Vita Karoli Magni* and Suetonius's *Life of Augustus.* For the latter, I have used the one in Suetonius, *The Twelve Caesars,* trans. Michael Graves and Robert Grant (London: Penguin Books, 2007), 45–107. For the former, I prefer Paul Dutton's translation, which appears in his *Charlemagne's Courtier: The Complete Einhard* (Toronto: University of Toronto Press, 1998). Together with Dutton's *Carolingian Civilization: A Reader,* 2nd ed. (Toronto: University of

Toronto Press, 2004), *Charlemagne's Courtier* offers an excellent point of departure for studying the Carolingian world. Two other recent translations introduce nicely Einhard's text: Thomas F.X. Noble, *Charlemagne and Louis the Pious: Lives by Einhard, Notker, Ermoldus, Thegan, and the Astronomer* (University Park, PA: Penn State Press, 2009); and David Ganz, *Two Lives of Charlemagne* (London: Penguin Books, 2008).

This essay has drawn significantly on many of the excellent recent studies of Einhard's work that are listed in the helpful bibliographies for these translations. In particular, I'd like to acknowledge here the work of Roger Collins, David Ganz, Matthew Innes, Matthew Kempshall, Rosamond McKitterick, and Matthais Tischler. Otherwise, for Einhard's use of Suetonius, see B. Townend, "Suetonius and His Influence," in *Latin Biography*, ed. Thomas A. Dorey (London: Routledge, 1967), 79–111, and the earlier study by Edward K. Rand, "On the History of the *De Vita Caesarum* of Suetonius in the Early Middle Ages," *Harvard Studies in Classical Philology* 37 (1926): 1–48.

Readers interested in Charles the Great might turn for basic orientation and further bibliography to the recent biographies written by Alessandro Barbero, Matthias Becher, Roger Collins, and Rosamond McKitterick. There are also many fine essays and a good bibliography in Joanna Story, ed., *Charlemagne: Empire and Society* (Manchester: Manchester University Press, 2005).

TEN

Divine Lessons in an Imperfect World
Bernard of Angers and *The Book of Sainte Foy's Miracles*

Kathleen Stewart Fung

Bernard of Angers, in composing a collection of the miracles of Sainte Foy, the young third-century martyr whose relics were housed at the monastery of Conques in southern France, claimed to present only those miracles most worthy of the reader's attention. Thousands of stories clamored for inclusion, yet he could present only a small sample. Bernard was not the only author overwhelmed by the saint's profligate miracle-working. In the half-century after he composed the first two parts of *The Book of Sainte Foy's Miracles,* multiple authors would add to the collection, creating the patchwork text we have today. The complex textual history of the *Book* and the differences between Bernard's presentation of the saint and that of the later anonymous authors are fascinating in and of themselves. In this chapter, however, we will limit ourselves to the first two books by Bernard and focus particularly on his selection and presentation of miracles that show Foy taking "revenge on evil-doers" and performing feats that were "in some way new and unusual" (1.9). In making such a selection, Bernard created a unified set of narratives that warned his clerical audience of the sin of pride, the violence it brought to the world, and the divine justice that the saint imposed in response.

We have little historical evidence for the existence of Sainte Foy or the beginning of her cult. The earliest source to mention Foy, whose name in English simply means "Faith," is the sixth-century *Hieronymian Martyrology.*

This document, meant to ensure that saints were celebrated on the proper day of the liturgical year, states only that she was martyred in the city of Agen (in southern Gaul) and that her feast day fell on the sixth of October. A tenth-century text, the anonymous *Passion of Sainte Foy*, provides more details. Its accuracy, however, is highly questionable since the author of this work seems simply to have cribbed much of his information from another text about a different martyr. Nonetheless, the *Passion* at least shows us something about who the faithful in this period thought Sainte Foy was. In the eleventh century, according to the *Passion*, she was widely believed to have been a young girl killed by the Romans for refusing to renounce her belief in Christ. Sometime in the fourth century, according to the text, the bishop of Agen enshrined her bones in a local church of his city.

While the background of the cult of Sainte Foy is murky, our knowledge of her association with Conques is more secure and begins with the theft of her relics over a century before Bernard wrote. During the mid-ninth century, the monks of Conques were involved in a dispute with the neighboring monastery of Figeac. The possession of a saint's relics would have provided the monks with a powerful patron to whom they could appeal for assistance and who would attract donations and devotion from the local lay community. While we do not know how the dispute with Figeac was resolved, the monks' strategy seems to have been successful in at least one sense. The monastery's records show a rise in donations shortly after the theft of the relics. Only at the end of the tenth century, however, did Foy's full potential as a patron become clear. Then, a man named Guibert claimed that she had restored his missing eyes. Numerous other individuals made similar claims, and Foy's fame as a miracle worker began to spread. By the year 1010, rumors of these events had reached as far north as Chartres, where they attracted the attention of Bernard of Angers, a cleric and scholar.

Miracle collections were an immensely popular genre of religious literature in the eleventh century. Clerics at saints' shrines would routinely record miracles and collect them in texts. *The Book of Sainte Foy's Miracles* is one such work. Bernard came to Conques in 1013; it was then that he composed the first book of miracles. He seems to have initially intended the 34 chapters he wrote to stand alone as a complete text, but sometime in the period between 1013 and 1020 he returned to Conques and added what now represents the first six chapters of the second book. After a final journey to Conques in 1020, he composed the final nine chapters of

Book Two. He likely died shortly thereafter. Sometime between 1020 and 1050, an anonymous monk at the house of Conques took up Bernard's notes and composed Book Three. A number of anonymous authors, all monks at the house of Conques, contributed to Book Four sometime around the middle of the century. Additional monastic authors added individual narratives to the collection until around 1075. Thus, at least five authors, and maybe more, contributed to *The Book of Sainte Foy's Miracles* over a span of 65 years.

There was some genuine interest in the work. Indeed, the monks of Conques seem to have distributed the *Book* to other monastic houses throughout Europe. And Bernard himself tells us that he showed copies of his first book to colleagues and other dignitaries in the north. He assured the monks that while he himself was responsible for the book, Reynold, whom he describes as "the master of the school of Tours" and a man "highly educated in the liberal arts," had seen the work and thought so highly of it that he used it to cure an illness (1.34). Nor was this all. Bernard tells us that his friends Wantelme and Leowulf, two clerics who were "distinguished as much by the reputation of their ancestral stock as by their own refined wisdom," were so struck by the work that they demanded their own copy (1.34). When Bernard showed the work to several bishops, they swore that they would establish new altars in Foy's honor. Thus, it appears that, while the collection as a whole had a largely monastic audience, Bernard originally intended his work for a slightly different group: scholarly clerics like himself.

One of the most striking aspects of Bernard's work, in fact, is its pedagogical tone. Bernard, as he frequently mentions, was not from the area around Conques. He describes the monastery's inhabitants as foreigners who speak a different language and follow strange customs. It is therefore not difficult to sense that he did not write solely as a promoter of Conques and its saint. Indeed, his accounts of the miracles reflect his more general concern with the sin of pride and its concrete consequences in his society. In the dedicatory letter to Fulbert, Bishop of Chartres, Bernard writes that he first heard rumors of Foy's miracles in the year 1010 while he was a student. Because "common people" were reporting "new and unusual" miracles, he initially dismissed them as "so much worthless fiction" (Letter to Fulbert). Yet within three years he decided to go to Conques himself to see the martyr's relics. While there, he investigated the many reports of Foy's miraculous power and decided that they were true. At the end of Book

One, Bernard even includes a letter to the abbot and monks of Conques informing them that he had distributed the work to a highly educated circle of clerics to the north.

Bernard presents his age as one of overwhelming violence. In one episode, the abbot of Sainte Foy's monastery is saved from attack only when his attackers are set upon by another group of marauders; Bernard himself describes seeing abbots dragged from their monasteries and killed (2.9). Throughout the text, warriors emerge from fortified towers to terrorize the populace. While there is some reason to be cautious about taking such descriptions as transparent windows onto a chaotic world, they do suggest that local lords had great power and that, given the paucity of formal governmental institutions, people often turned to the saints for supernatural assistance.

Bernard's decision to compose a miracle collection was particularly appropriate given his concerns with church property. Contemporary charters show that individuals who made donations to churches in this period made them not to any human figure but rather to the saints who were their patrons. Since the saint of any given church was understood as the possessor of its land, it was the saint's duty to protect it. So Bernard explains to his audience, "There is no more serious offense against Sainte Foy, none that will lead more surely to sudden disaster, than to intend evil against the affairs of her domain" (2.5). Bernard describes how the monks took active steps to ensure that lay people were aware of this fact. When Foy's land was threatened, the monks would carry the statue containing her relics in solemn procession around the borders of the contested property, invoke the saint's power, and perhaps leverage community pressure against those who threatened her (2.4). Faced with these elaborate processions of the monks carrying lamps and the holy gospels or sounding horns whenever Foy performed yet another miracle for peasants gathered around, lay people would likely have thought twice about enforcing their claims against the saint or exploiting the peasantry who worked her lands. The monks' prayers could never have overcome armed troops, but they appear to have been at least partially effective; indeed, a village rose up around the monastery during the eleventh century as peasants sought to take advantage of its protection.

Sainte Foy aided and protected her community directly through miracles. According to Bernard, to attack the monastery's property is to wage war against God. Recalling a man who was struck by lightning after seizing monastic property, Bernard, with almost unseemly glee, taunts the saint's victim: "Your corpse can't even serve as food for wild animals and birds" (1.12). Bernard shows this dispute over monastic property as a test of divine power. Although the monks initially meet with their foes in a public hearing, justice is only done with the warrior's gruesome death at the saint's hand. Even though human justice failed, Foy's ability to enforce right did not.

God's enforcement of justice here points out a key aspect of both the text and Bernard's world view. Bernard describes those who attacked Conques in eschatological terms. They are not simply thugs but "Antichrists" whose violent tendencies can be corrected only by the saint. "No trace of divine vengeance can be seen in their lives and therefore they think that what they hear about Christ's return as an avenger is false," he writes (1.11). Bernard's text presents a world in which God's actions are directly visible in history. So he accounts for the sudden death of the warriors who wreak havoc on the land as proof of divine judgment and uses it as a lesson about divine vengeance. After telling a lengthy story of a sinful warrior named Rainon, who had dared to claim land belonging to the monastery and who subsequently died in a fall from his horse, Bernard addresses his reader directly: "Understand these things, you who have proud hearts. Now is the time to come to your senses from your wickedness and learn to do right" (1.5). Again, after relating how Foy miraculously killed another warrior who threatened her property, Bernard addresses the saint's victim: "Oh, bold fighter, oh fearless warrior, oh, most outstanding of men, you who exalted yourself up to the heavens, you who considered the very saints of God as if they were nothing, where is your power now?" (1.12).

Bernard's text, however, was more than just a cautionary tale for those who might consider despoiling church property. Rainon, according to Bernard, was not simply a warrior, he was the very embodiment of Pride. His death was not simply the punishment of a man who dared attack Foy's monks but, instead, the defeat such vice must always receive. Educated readers would have recognized Bernard's Rainon as modeled directly on the description of Pride contained in one of the most popular works on virtue and vice in this period, Prudentius's *Psychomachia*. "You should rejoice, scholar," Bernard writes, "that now Pride, not in imagination as you have read in Prudentius' *Psychomachia*, but actually and in human form, was overpowered by the whirlwind of her own speed and lay there dead" (1.5). In short, for Bernard, current events demonstrate God's divine power and teach his clerical audience the dangers of pride and its consequences.

Bernard as a scholar and cleric was deeply interested in spiritual reform. His work on the cult of Sainte Foy served his interests and permitted him to make particular points. However true to life his depiction of Rainon may have been, it was articulated by Prudentius's work. Thus, Bernard shaped his material to promote his particular spiritual agenda. Indeed, his ideological slant is particularly evident when we examine his work next to the monastery's cartulary, which is full of charters that commemorate warriors' donations of land, or to the later portions of the miracle collection composed by members of the monastery in the generation after him. In Books Three and Four, warriors are much more sympathetic figures. The monks of Conques show them attacking church property but also caring about their wives and children and showing great devotion to Sainte Foy (3.9). In Book Three, a knight who threatens one of the monastery's villages, for example, is not killed by Foy but rather is converted (3.10). After experiencing Foy's power, the monks even depict the man as a defender of the village church against all enemies. The monks had a different agenda than had Bernard, who was an outsider concerned with more general reform. The monks were more concerned with their local constituents who often included warriors who were among their greatest supporters. Their different circumstances and goals resulted in different portrayals of Foy's cult.

But even Bernard does not describe all lay people as bad. In fact, his larger goals are perhaps most apparent when he is faced with such a complex character as Raymond II, Count of Rouergue (2.5). Sainte Foy, Bernard tells us, struck down the count, killing him because he was planning to build a tower above the monastery. Raymond's death at Foy's hands, however, presents a dilemma for Bernard, as Raymond had also donated a great deal of wealth to Conques over the course of his lifetime. Bernard's mixed feelings about Raymond lead him to equivocate about the precise meaning of the count's death while en route to Jerusalem. On the one hand, Foy, solicitous in the protection of her monastery, caused Raymond to die; on the other, thanks to Raymond's past generosity to Foy's monastery, God allowed the count to die in a blessed state. The saint's actions were not always clear, and Bernard's text offers multiple interpretations of the events he records. Raymond, while done in by pride, is also the beneficiary of divine mercy.

The recognition of Bernard's aims allows us to re-examine his text with a new eye. Many of the disputes over land that he records were in reality not one-sided affairs. The families of those who donated property clearly often felt that they had a legitimate claim to the land. Such was the case in the narrative of Rainon. Although Bernard describes him as the raving personification of Pride, Rainon may simply have been asserting his right to his family's land (1.5). The rather stark divide that Bernard draws between the warriors on the one hand and the monastery on the other does not appear to be true to life. Many of the monks that he mentions were once warriors themselves and likely from local families. Giving land to the monastery might thus seem less of a complete transfer than Bernard suggests it was. The Church's expectation about property was changing at this time, so both the warriors and the monks may have felt they were in the right. The monks of Conques could not have been all that different in culture and expectations from their families who lived in the area and who maintained close social and economic ties with the monastery. In short, there were multiple sides to the stories he tells, but Bernard flattens the complexity of the local context in order to teach a more general lesson.

Lay people are not the only object of Bernard's critique; he also sought to criticize clerics like himself. For instance, he tells a story of the monastery under the power of a family of abbots (2.5). Urged on by their wicked uncle, the bishop of Clermont, these abbots plundered the abbey's goods. Because they were acting wickedly, Bernard writes, the miracles of the saint came to a halt. With these passages, Bernard demonstrates that not even Foy's own monks are immune from her corrective authority. More generally, they articulate his message that divided loyalties are not acceptable to the saint: monks must stop acting like members of their clan and instead become loyal members of Foy's family. This plea for the complete separation of monks from their birth families was part of the movement of clerical reform current in this period.

Bernard's focus on spiritual reform is even more clear in those passages in which he writes about Foy's reliquary statue. He explains that it is the custom of the people in the areas south of the Loire River to make reliquaries in the shape of the saint whose bones they contain and that to learned people this may seem like paganism — no more than simple idolatry. Indeed, when he and Bernier, a fellow teacher, first visited the reliquary of Sainte Foy, Bernard reports how "with a sidelong smile," he looked at Bernier, "thinking it absurd, of course, and far beyond the limits of reason that so many rational beings should kneel before a mute and insensate thing" (1.13). Bernard, however, then laments how wrong he was and informs his reader how Foy had beaten "a certain cleric named Odalric, who was considered a prig and held himself somewhat above the others" by ridiculing the saint's image (1.13). Despite initial appearances, those who disparaged the statue were wrong. Like the warriors of the other stories, Bernard himself was exhibiting the sin of pride on his first visit.

Again in the second book, Bernard, apparently not having learned his lesson, reports how he berated the monks at Conques for allowing peasants to spend the night in vigil at the church. While the literate clerics would sing the psalms and masses in the evenings, the peasants, unable to participate in the formal service, would simply sing whatever "peasant songs and other frivolities" they knew (2.12). In response to Bernard's criticism, the monks replied that they too had thought that allowing the peasants to keep vigils was inappropriate and that they had repeatedly barred the church doors at night. Despite their efforts, however, Foy kept unlocking the door to let the people in. Faced with divine approval of the peasants' actions, Bernard states, he was forced to re-evaluate his assumptions: "I was refuted by my own thoughts, just as if I had been slaughtered by my own sword in battle, for I had been out of my senses to believe that God's goodness is subject to human judgment" (2.12). It is not the song itself, Bernard concludes, but "the hardship of keeping vigil and the goodwill of simple people that please Him" (2.12). As Bernard explains, "God turns His gaze to the devotion of our hearts and shows good will toward human ignorance and simpleness, because God Who sustains us has a father's compassion for human frailty" (2.12). Just as the warriors are wrong when through pride they attempt to take Foy's land, so those learned men who scoff at the peasants' true belief are simply arrogant. Bernard's Foy shows his readers that the peasants' belief is more worthy than that of many a learned scholar. Bernard repeatedly displays his learning throughout the *Book* and shows no lack of pride in his own achievements. He happily boasts of the awed reception his writing received and speaks with disdain of those who are less learned (1.34). He clearly expects his audience to be as learned as himself. Yet, even as he flaunts his education, he also argues against ridiculing religious faith.

The many stories Bernard tells of resurrected mules and miraculously healed eyes take on even more meaning when we consider them in light of the larger rhetorical purpose of the text. Bernard puts the argument of those against whom he writes into the mouth of a man who ridiculed his text: "For how could any reasonable person believe things about eyeballs torn out and afterward restored, and animals brought back to life? I have heard of other kinds of miracles that other saints and—rarely—Sainte Foy worked now and then. But mules!...No one who is mentally stable can or ought to expound such things" (1.7). Bernard shows that this is not true. God is in everything, he writes, and his messages are visible everywhere if only the faithful will look. Revived mules show the faithful the truth of the doctrine of bodily resurrection; a man who repeatedly loses his sight and regains it is proof of the need to reform one's ways and not backslide into lust and greed. The educated who doubt these stories are simply so proud that they ignore God's will; their learning leads them astray since they care more about outward appearances than inner belief.

Foy's miracles, in Bernard's hands, are a demonstration of divine power in everyday life. They demonstrate the dangers of pride and the punishment for ignoring God's commands. Writing for the clerics of the schools of the north, Bernard presents a world in chaos, one in which warriors violate the property of the Church, clerics care more about learning than devotion, and even monks hide crimes underneath the cover of their habits. Foy's violent retribution shows the results of such sins, and her healing intervention the reward for the faithful. As Bernard describes his friends and colleagues snatching the book out of his hands and declaring it the work of a genius, it would seem that his message found an eager audience (1.34). Indeed, Bernard was pleased enough with his writings that he returned to Conques twice more and continued his narrative of Foy's power. Having experienced the transformative power of Sainte Foy's miracles himself, Bernard promoted the same spiritual journey to his audience as well.

Bibliographic Note
Pamela Sheingorn offers an excellent translation of *The Book of Sainte Foy's Miracles* as well as the anonymous *The Passion of Sainte Foy* and several other texts of related interest—including the "Letter to Fulbert" from which I quote above—in *The Book of Sainte Foy* (Pennsylvania: University of Pennsylvania Press, 1995). The introduction to this collection, together with Pamela Sheingorn and Kathleen Ashley, *Writing Faith: Text, Sign, and History in the Miracles of Sainte Foy* (Chicago: University of Chicago Press, 1999), provide background on Bernard, his work, and the cult of Sainte

Foy. Both works, on which I have drawn significantly here, have useful bibliographies and are a great resource for further study.

More generally, the scholarship on the cult of saints is vast. A good introduction to the subject can be found in Peter Brown, *The Cult of the Saints: Its Rise and Function in Latin Christianity* (Chicago: University of Chicago Press, 1981); and Thomas Head, *Hagiography and the Cult of Saints: The Diocese of Orleans, 800–1200* (Cambridge: Cambridge University Press, 1990). For the use of relics in enforcing monastic property rights, the collection of articles in *The Peace of God: Social Violence and Religious Response in France around the Year 1000,* eds. Thomas Head and Richard Landes (Ithaca: Cornell University Press, 1992), is helpful, as is H.E.J. Cowdrey's classic article, "The Peace and Truce of God in the Eleventh Century," *Past and Present* 46 (1970): 42–67. Finally, for Bernard's intellectual milieu, see the first volume (*Foundations*) of Richard Southern, *Scholastic Humanism and the Unification of Europe* (Oxford: Blackwell, 1995).

ELEVEN

William of Poitiers Talks about War

Jay Rubenstein

"King William will live long, he will live too in our pages, which we are happy to write in a simple style, so that a great many people may easily understand such shining deeds, particularly since you will find that the greatest orators, who have a special capacity for writing impressively, employ a plain style when they are writing about history" (157–59). No one will ever mistake William of Poitiers for an objective observer. He is a propagandist. His goal is to glorify William, Duke of Normandy, bastard son of his predecessor, and King of England (1066–86). He examines events throughout William's life, but his work is most famous for its description of the Battle of Hastings in 1066. As chaplain to William the Conqueror, William of Poitiers was well placed to obtain accurate information about events that day, even though he was not there and even though he is so clearly biased. But, perhaps more importantly, because of his biases we can learn much about medieval attitudes toward war and its place within the political and imaginative landscapes of eleventh-century Europe.

We know very little about William of Poitiers himself. We can surmise that he was born about 1020 and probably lived until at least 1087. He was born in Normandy, but his surname derives from the fact that he studied in the south, in Poitiers, before he returned to his homeland, where he spent much of his career as archdeacon at Liseux. The character and quality of his education appear readily in the pages of his book. Orderic Vitalis, the twelfth-century Anglo-Norman writer, describes it as a "clever imitation of Sallust." He praises William for his style and his judgment, but one senses in Orderic some impatience with his predecessor's continual accolades and inflated eloquence. "I have not tried to include all that he says," Orderic admits, "or to imitate his artistry."[1] Perhaps because of this artistry, the *Deeds of William* seems not to have appealed to a wide audience. It reaches us only through a single incomplete manuscript, missing both its opening pages and probably many more pages at its end; the manuscript was transcribed in the seventeenth century but has since been lost, probably destroyed in the same fire that damaged the sole manuscript exemplar of *Beowulf*. It is therefore somewhat by chance that William of Poitiers's fulsome praises of William the Conqueror have reached us at all.

The fact that only one copy of his book survives is surprising. It is an example of court propaganda, exactly the sort of thing that King William and his heirs would have wanted distributed throughout their territories. It portrays King William as an unusually brilliant prince of an exceptionally warlike people, a man whose military feats equaled and perhaps surpassed those of Julius Caesar (169–75). Indeed, the conquest of England was, according to the *Deeds of William,* an epoch-making event on a par with the creation of the Roman Empire and the destruction of Troy (143). No doubt the author would be gratified to learn that modern scholarship has generally accepted his assessment. The year 1066 has long stood as the central moment and the central problem in English history, a cultural turning point when continental influences and Romance languages aggressively reshaped the Anglo-Saxon universe. The tendency to view the Conquest as the fulcrum of England's history is made all the more irresistible by the Bayeux Tapestry, the eleventh-century pictorial record that, like William of Poitiers, both explains the Conqueror's claim to the throne and describes his battle with Harold. One of the Tapestry's more famous images, when the Normans and the English first meet on the field of Hastings (plate 65), is especially evocative. The Anglo-Saxons, massed together on foot in their shield-wall formation, appear the embodiment of an early medieval warrior band, the last gasp of the world as dreamed by the *Beowulf* poet. The Normans, by contrast, mounted with spears at the ready, darting out against the English forces, trying to entice them from the safety of their numbers, appear to herald the onset of the age of chivalry, the first glimmer of the world to be imagined by Chrétien de Troyes a century later. Historians who do not accept this interpretation — who downplay the abilities of the Conqueror and the achievement of the

---

[1] Orderic Vitalis, *Ecclesiastical History,* ed. and trans. Marjorie Chibnall (Oxford: Clarendon Press, 1980), vol. 2, 261.

Normans, who deny the backwardness of late Anglo-Saxon society —
argue not just against their contemporaries or against a modern historical
school of thought. Rather, they attack a tradition whose roots lie in the
1070s. The year 1066 belongs not just to William the Conqueror but also
to his chaplain William of Poitiers. When we react to the Conquest, we
react to him. His narrative thus merits an especially close examination.

William of Poitiers's book pretends to be a wide-ranging overview of all
the events of the Conqueror's life. It is in reality a sustained piece of careful argument with one goal in mind: the justification of the duke's somewhat tenuous claim to be king of England. The opening line of the book,
as it reaches us today, makes this point: "[When Cnut lost his life], he lost
also the English kingdom, which he owed not to others but to his own and
his father's conquest" (3). The narration, in the guise of relating a fact, makes
an argument about the legitimacy of kings. The Danish Cnut who ruled
England from 1016 to 1035 had already set a precedent for rule through
conquest alone. William of Poitiers is plainly critical of him, describing
him and his first successor Harald as ruling "by cruelty." The misdeeds of
Harald, Cnut's son, include one especially notable crime: together with the
Anglo-Saxon nobleman Godwine, he conspired against and murdered
Alfred Etheling, the potential Anglo-Saxon claimant to the throne.
Murdered with Alfred were the members of his Norman entourage.
Godwine, the criminal, was the father of Harold, the future king and Duke
William's rival for the throne in 1066. William of Poitiers describes Harold
as his father's "equal in cruelty and perfidy. By your [Godwine's] treachery
you shed the innocent blood of Normans, and in your turn the blood of
your men will be shed by the sword of the Normans" (7).

Right of conquest is, therefore, by itself enough to legitimize rule, but
William of Poitiers does not stop there. He emphasizes, and almost certainly exaggerates, the closeness of the relationship between King Edward
the Confessor (1042–66) and William when, before his reign, the former
was living in exile on the Continent. Duke William, it seems, all but put
Edward on the throne of England single-handedly: "For the English, when
they had discussed the question, agreed that William's arguments were the
best and acquiesced in the just requests of his envoys to avoid experiencing the might of the Normans" (19). Our author William further argues
that Edward named Duke William his heir, a claim that is by no means certain. William was a blood relative to Edward. Queen Emma, Edward's
mother, was the sister of Richard II of Normandy, and therefore William's

great-aunt, but this connection did not make him an obvious claimant to the throne. An argument based on kinship is not crucial to William of Poitiers, since he does not even mention it until after the coronation (151). More crucial, and more dramatic, is that not only had Edward wished Duke William to succeed him, but he had also sent his brother-in-law, Harold Godwineson, as emissary to Normandy to confirm this succession and to swear on relics personal loyalty to the future king. Later, in a gesture heavy with spiritual and political symbolism, William would ride into battle wearing around his neck the very relics upon which Harold had taken his broken oath (71, 115).

The case as presented by William of Poitiers looks compelling, however contrived and emotive it might be. And other texts generally confirm it. The Bayeux Tapestry, for example, shows Harold making his oath on relics and conferring with Edward before departing on that trip to Normandy (plates 27, 1). The tapestry, however, does not specify what words Harold swore, only that he made an oath, and it does not indicate that Edward was sending him on a mission. It is equally possible to read Edward's extended index finger in the tapestry's opening image as a gesture of warning and to see in Harold's slouching posture and upraised hands, upon his return to England and to Edward's court, a gesture of apology or of acknowledged failure (plates 29, 30). Whether Harold journeyed to Normandy as Edward's emissary or on his own behalf to negotiate the release of some of his relatives who were being held hostage at the duke's court — an extremely plausible explanation — must remain a mystery (69). William of Poitiers's carefully constructed arguments do prove that all of these points were very much in contention in the 1070s, as he assembled his chronicle, and that the case was not nearly as secure as either he or the subject of his book would like us to believe.

These insecurities about the legitimacy of William's claim to rule, combined with William of Poitiers's own academic training, make him an author especially conscious of questions of legality. His effusive praises of William play directly into this polemic. As Duke of Normandy, William fulfilled the key duty of a medieval ruler: he kept the peace, enforced justice, and brought rogue lords more firmly under his control than did any comparable contemporary leader. The narrative of William of Poitiers in this respect anticipated the mid-twelfth-century biography of Louis VI by Suger of Saint-Denis. As Louis would later do, William sought to discipline the out-of-control petty castle lords, or castellans, who lived within reach of his authority. As he set about imposing peace on his duchy, some people, according to his biographer, "preferred to enjoy their accustomed liberty, retaining their own possessions and seizing those of others at their pleasure" (9). Historians have generally considered eleventh-century leaders failures when it comes to maintaining peace among their followers. Victims of aristocratic violence looked instead toward ecclesiastics, who created the so-called "Peace of God." Under the Peace, warriors vowed not to harm the persons and property of the unarmed, whose number included churchmen, women, and the poor. Duke William, however, took his duties seriously enough to impose the Peace, or more precisely the Truce of God, thereby restricting the times and circumstances when the warrior aristocracy could engage in acts of violence on his people (81). Or at least he used these principles as reasons to strike out against adversaries, like William of Arques, whose predatory leadership caused Duke William sadness: "The goods of churches, the labours of country people, and the profits of merchants were unjustly made the booty of men-at-arms. He thought he was summoned by the pitiable lamentations of the unwarlike masses, which always arise in time of war or sedition" (37). One might contrast this situation to the climate in Normandy a few years later as William massed his own army to invade England—and William of Poitiers no doubt expected his readers to draw this comparison: "The crops waited unharmed for the scythe of the harvester, and were neither trampled by the proud stampede of horsemen nor cut down by foragers. A man who was weak or unarmed could ride singing on his horse wherever he wished, without trembling at the sight of squadrons of knights" (103–5).

What William of Poitiers wishes to stress in these passages is not just that Duke William was an effective administrator or that he successfully restored peace to his duchy. He also wishes to show that, from the start of his rule, William exercised nearly royal prerogatives. The description of William's program sounds very much like a portrait of an ideal king: "From this time he began with the utmost zeal to protect the churches of God, to uphold the cause of the weak, to impose laws which would not be burdensome, and to make judgments which never deviated from equity and temperance" (9). His protection extended to churchmen, peasants, and merchants, necessary for the spiritual and economic well-being of his people (13–15). William of Poitiers makes the case that the dukes of Normandy were to all intents and purposes kings, when he describes the reason for King Henry of France's jealousy of William: "Normandy, which had been under the kings of the Franks from the earliest times, had now been raised almost to a kingdom" (44). The immediate reason for making this observation is to justify William's war against Henry, but the underlying point, and probably the more important one, is to explain anew the Norman Conquest. To raise oneself from duke to king, with only the slightest justification through royal blood, was an act of hubris, and no one was more aware of the point than the legally trained William of Poitiers. To become king was to take on not just a new office or a new character trait but rather an entirely new persona. So significant is this change for William of Poitiers that he attempts throughout his narrative to avoid describing his subject as "king" until after the coronation in London on Christmas Day, 1066. The Conqueror became on that day "a most worthy king — a title which our pen gladly takes up in place of that of duke" (151–53). So profound is the change wrought in William by the coronation that upon his return to Normandy all of his subjects, most of whom had presumably gazed upon him before, rushed out from the remotest places just for "the chance of seeing the king" (175–77). We should underestimate neither the significance of such a transformation nor the audacity of the bastard duke in claiming to have undergone it.

To secure the arguments for these claims, William of Poitiers fell back on his academic training, particularly on what he knows of so-called "just war theory" from the classical world and probably as well from the writings of Saint Augustine of Hippo. From Cicero, William would have learned that a war may justly be fought to restore rights or lands lost because of a broken contract. He certainly had evidence for this point ready to hand, in the form of Harold's broken oath to help the duke accede to the English throne. He might have learned as well from the same classical sources that wars needed to be fought according to specified rules. A leader must, for example, make a formal declaration of war and not attempt to catch his enemy off guard through a surprise attack. William of Poitiers finds the duke's adherence to this principle during skirmishes on the Continent particularly noteworthy: "still more astonishing, he does not attack this enemy without warning while he is unprepared, but informs him forty days in advance where, when, and for what reason he will come" (51). From Augustine, William of Poitiers would have learned that a soldier must enter into a conflict not violently, or in a rage, but with an appropriately Christian temperament, with God firmly near the forefront of his thoughts. And again, William certainly fulfilled these criteria:

"Even while he was active in arms did not cease with his inward eye to gaze in awe on the eternal majesty" (81). As Augustine advises, the duke fought both to right wrongs and to create peace but never to advance his own personal status. It is probably to illustrate this point that William of Poitiers makes one of his more outlandish claims, that William was reluctant to accept the crown upon the defeat of Harold: "He desired the peace of the kingdom rather than the crown" (149). This portrait of William is unreliable and perhaps even deliberately misleading, but its exaggerations of William's virtues serve a particular end: to demonstrate that the Conqueror met all accepted criteria of what constituted a "just war" in eleventh-century understanding.

A just war, as the name implies, is about justice, the same sort of justice an eleventh-century person would hope to find in a trial. This connection forms another crucial aspect of William of Poitiers's polemic. Readers cannot fail to notice his frequent use of courtroom metaphors. As the battle begins, "The Normans swiftly and boldly took the initiative in the fray. Similarly, when orators are engaged in a lawsuit about theft, he who prosecutes the crime makes the first speech" (129). As the battle wore on and the English began to tire, they "grew weaker, and endured punishment as though confessing their guilt by their defeat" (133). The Battle of Hastings was very much, for both William of Poitiers and William the Conqueror, a legal procedure, a substitute for a regular trial. Harold had, according to our writer, committed a crime. He had stolen away an inheritance that William had been promised and to which Harold had assented. With all the flair of a high-priced lawyer, William of Poitiers turns to the witness stand and levels accusations directly against Harold: "Just a few words, o Harold, will we address to you! With what intent dared you after this take William's inheritance from him and make war on him, when you had with both voice and hand subjected yourself and your people to him by a sacrosanct oath? What you should have suppressed you perniciously stirred up" (77).

Harold does, in this narrative, offer up some defense. Edward the Confessor — or so Harold claimed — named him his heir upon his deathbed, and according to English law dating back to the time of Saint Augustine of Canterbury in the late sixth century, deathbed bequests were treated as inviolable (119). Here in essence are two apparently valid (though unwritten) wills: an earlier one in which Edward named Duke William as heir and a later one in which he named Harold. Complicating things is the fact that Harold seems to have signed on, orally, to the earlier version of the will, apparently invalidating his own later claim to the throne. Whose cause was the more just? The Conqueror, we are told, offered to forego battle and to let the dispute be resolved in court, either by English or Norman law (121). Harold preferred to settle the issue by combat. The result of the battle served as God's own verdict. Or, in William of Poitiers's words, "Your end proves by what right you were raised through the death-bed gift of Edward" (141).

Although the *Deeds of William* makes no secret of its author's interpretation of events, it is noteworthy that Harold does at least have this small claim to legality. The question of the succession to the throne of England is a debatable point, one that might be resolved through a trial in which the competing claims might never be satisfactorily sorted out. When such an occurrence happened in an actual lawsuit in the eleventh century, as opposed to a battle, the litigants did have a procedure to fall back on, namely, the ordeal, useful for reaching a verdict when all other avenues proved inadequate. To take one of the most famous examples of an ordeal in the Middle Ages, Peter Bartholomew, the visionary crusader who led the Christian armies to the Holy Lance of Antioch in 1098, had to prove the truth of his visions by walking through fire. Clearly in Peter's case only God could vouch for the truth or falsity of what he had seen. God, however, remained coy. Peter died from his burns, but not immediately, thereby allowing both his followers and detractors to claim victory.

Another variation of the ordeal, acceptable by eleventh-century legal standards, was trial by combat, where representatives from each side would fight a duel. Whichever side's champion remained standing would be the victor at law as well as in battle. One technical term for trial by combat, in fact, was simply *bellum,* or battle. What the Battle of Hastings was, and what most medieval battles were to some degree, was a judicial procedure. A plaintiff and a defendant pressed their claims and trusted the result to God. In addition to a more formal hearing, Duke William also offered this sort of trial to Harold: "He did not wish the English to die as enemies on account of his dispute; he wished to decide the case by risking his own head in single combat" (123). This understanding of the Battle of Hastings is also evident in the Bayeux Tapestry. Where the Tapestry depicts the beginnings of the battle, as the Normans ride toward Harold's forces, the upper margin contains images of two nude men preparing to wrestle, champions set to determine through physical prowess an unknown and otherwise unknowable truth (plate 56).

This point leads to another important conclusion about William of Poitiers. While he certainly is a writer steeped in the best classical and Augustinian learning that his world had to offer, he was also very much a product of early medieval culture, his mind steeped in the same traditions as the near contemporary *Song of Roland* (discussed in Chapter 12 below). This epic old-French poem ends with a trial by combat, as Pinabel, on behalf of the accused traitor Ganelon, fights Thierry, who represents Charlemagne and the cause of his stepson Roland, whom Ganelon had betrayed. Perhaps more crucially for this comparison, legal-judicial language litters even the earlier combat scenes in *The Song of Roland,* as first Roland and then Charlemagne do battle against Saracen armies. The issues may be religious, but the language is straightforwardly litigious. As the French prepare for the final fight, they exclaim, "Help us now, Almighty God! King Charles is in the right — we mustn't fail him" (241). As the battle begins to turn against the Saracens, Baligant, their emir, "begins to understand somewhat that he is wrong and Charlemagne is right" (257). Still, Baligant moves in to duel Charlemagne, in a scene modeled precisely on the legal principle of trial by combat, about which the poet comments: "The battle cannot ever be concluded till one of them confesses he is wrong" (259). As with the ordeal, the battle resolves itself when God intervenes, sending the archangel Gabriel to give Charlemagne the strength needed to cleave Baligant's skull in two. The verdict is thus rendered: the Saracen cause is wrong; the Christian cause is right.

William of Poitiers fits easily into this intellectual world. His account of the Battle of Hastings is the story of an ordeal — a trial by combat with the trappings of classical and Augustinian just war theory. Some historians have attempted to distinguish in the Middle Ages two types of war, holy and just. The *Song of Roland* would appear to exemplify a holy war, laying the groundwork for the crusades in the Holy Land. William of Poitiers, on the other hand, describes, if you accept his explanations, a just war. But as the overlap between *The Song of Roland* and the *Deeds of William* indicates, we cannot draw any such clear division. Justice is the prerogative of God. Justice, truth, and righteousness are all the same thing, as Saint Anselm, one of William the Conqueror's most renowned churchmen, would argue. If one seeks the truth in a legal setting or in a military setting, one seeks simultaneously the will of God. It is only natural, therefore, that Duke William would ask the approval of Pope Alexander II before he invaded England and that he would carry the papal banner into battle

(105). It is also for this reason that it would not appear incongruous that a churchman, William's half-brother Odo, Bishop of Bayeux, would ride alongside the duke into battle—no more than it appeared incongruous to the audience for Roland that Archbishop Turpin fought so ruthlessly against Saracen enemies. "No tonsured priest who ever sang a mass performed such feats of prowess with his body," the poet writes without any apparent irony (121). Finally, it is because of this essential blending of religion, law, and warfare that William, like Roland and Charlemagne, carried relics into battle (125). William's relics had the added propaganda value of being connected to Harold's oath, but this connection only further highlights the perfect overlap of piety, justice, and the field of battle.

The sacred and judicial character of battle also explains one of the more unusual—and I would say implausible—features of William of Poitiers's battle narrative. If we accept the version of events in the *Deeds of William*, then we must necessarily believe that the Normans went into battle with no discernible plan, apart from how they would order the troops, and no apparent tactical advantage. To seek the upper hand was characteristic of Harold, who cunningly sent forth spies and who attempted to catch the Normans off guard through a night attack (107, 125). Even the most obvious of the Normans' advantages—the fact that the English had just fought a major battle at Stamford Bridge against a Scandinavian army allied with Harold's own brother Tostig—was in William of Poitiers's analysis further indication of the miraculous character of the Norman victory. The probable interpretation of events is that Harold's army was exhausted after a long and bloody battle fought in the north of England and that the army that William faced in the south was far less formidable than it normally would have been. But for William of Poitiers the carnage at Stamford Bridge only proved that the Anglo-Saxons were the fiercest of men, perhaps invincible (117, 137). One might speculate further still: William, using his own intelligence network, had delayed his invasion until he learned that the Norwegian king, Harold Hardrada, had already invaded England. William thus knew that whichever King Harold won at Stamford Bridge, his own Norman army would face an exhausted and ill-prepared force when it landed near Hastings.

As for the battle itself, the Anglo-Saxons are said to have fought in a "shield wall" formation, with soldiers packed so closely together that if someone died, he had no room to fall (133). In order for the badly outnumbered Normans to win, they needed to draw the English out of this formation. They did so, but fortuitously, for, William of Poitiers writes, rumor spread among the army that Duke William had died. The soldiers panicked and began to retreat. The story again resonates well with the world of Roland, where all action ultimately centered upon the hero in battle, either Roland or Charlemagne or, here, William the Conqueror. When Duke William realized what had happened, he threw back his helmet, rallied his troops, and ordered them back into the fray. And as the Normans regrouped, something nearly miraculous happened. The English had rushed forth to cut down their retreating foes. As a result, the Normans could use their advantages of speed and height, brought about because they had ridden horses into battle, to encircle their enemies and to cut them apart (129–31). Twice more the Normans feigned flight, and twice more they suddenly reversed themselves and butchered the Anglo-Saxons. "So a combat of an unusual kind began, with one side attacking in different ways and the other standing firmly as if fixed to the ground" (133). By the end of the day, the English could only admit their defeat and their guilt. Harold Godwineson's cause was wrong; William's was right.

Thus, if we are to believe William of Poitiers, the Normans stumbled onto the one tactic that could overcome the fearsome Anglo-Saxon shield wall. Surely it is more likely that the duke, who "succeeded more by good planning than by chance" (173), had entered the battle with the intention of using feigned flights to draw his adversaries out of their formation. But if that were the case, why would William of Poitiers not give due credit to his hero? Or why would he not praise the duke for the way in which he had delayed his invasion of England until he could take advantage of Harold's losses at Stamford Bridge? Sound strategy and clever tactics intended to minimize one's own casualties are highly lauded in modern military history, but in the eleventh century there was something almost indecent about planning ahead. The tyrant Harold tried to gain the upper hand over William through cunning, in spite of his overwhelming advantages. The reason why William of Poitiers avoids these topics — although Duke William's strategies are readily apparent — is that to engage in trickery before battle is the equivalent of engaging in trickery before God. If battle is a form of the ordeal, trial by combat, then anyone who enters into it less honorably, less openly, or less recklessly than did Roland is someone who is trying to beat the ordeal. Battle is about justice, and a combatant must rely not on strategy, as did Harold Godwineson, and not upon numbers, as did Harold of Norway, but upon the will of God, as did William the

Conqueror—the will of God which is the same as righteousness and justice, which in turn are what battle is all about.

William of Poitiers's text is high propaganda. It is frequently implausible and often misleading. He does, however, give us more than enough evidence to reconstruct adequately the events of Hastings. More importantly, his deceptions and his unapologetic propaganda are by themselves informative, for they allow us to reconstruct beliefs about battle, justice, and how the imaginative world of Roland gave shape to the course of political events in eleventh-century Europe.

Bibliographic Note

The most important of sources related to the Norman Conquest and the centerpiece of this essay is William of Poitiers, *Deeds of William,* ed. and trans. R.H.C. Davis and Marjorie Chibnall (Oxford: Oxford University Press, 1998), supplemented by the Bayeux Tapestry, which is available in a variety of facsimile reproductions—in my parenthetical references above, I refer to the plates as numbered in *English Historical Documents,* ed. David C. Douglas, vol. 2, 2nd ed. (New York: Oxford University Press, 1981 [1953]). I have also cited, by laisse, passages from *The Song of Roland;* see Chapter 12 in this volume. Other crucial primary sources include Orderic Vitalis, *Ecclesiastical History,* 6 vols., ed. and trans. Marjorie Chibnall (Oxford: Clarendon Press, 1968–80); William of Malmesbury, *History of the Kings of England,* 2 vols., ed. R.A.B. Mynors, R.M. Thomson, and M. Winterbottom (Oxford: Clarendon Press, 1998, 1999); Eadmer, *History of Recent Events in England,* trans. Geoffrey Bosanquet, with a foreword by R.W. Southern (London: Cresset Press, 1964); and William of Jumièges, *Deeds of the Norman Dukes,* 2 vols., ed. Elisabeth M.C. van Houts (Oxford: Clarendon Press, 1992–95). Another possibly contemporary source is the poetic description of Hastings published as Guy of Amiens, *Carmen de Hastingae proelio,* ed. Frank Barlow (Oxford: Clarendon Press, 1999), though its authenticity has at times been questioned.

For contrasting views of how "Viking" the Normans were, compare David Bates, *Normandy Before 1066* (London: Longman, 1982) and Eleanor Searle, *Predatory Kinship and the Creation of Norman Power, 840–1066* (Berkeley: University of California Press, 1988). A recent examination of this question is Emily Albu, *The Normans and their Histories: Propaganda, Myth and Subversion* (Rochester: Boydell Press, 2001). Also see R.H.C. Davis, *The Normans and Their Myth* (London: Thames & Hudson, 1976).

TWELVE

Epic Values
The Song of Roland

Susan P. Millinger

*T*he *Song of Roland* is the greatest of the *chansons de geste*, that is, "songs of deeds" written down in France in the twelfth and thirteenth centuries. It is an epic tale, a symbolic story of the conflict between Good and Evil that celebrates the great deeds of Roland, his companion Oliver, and the Franks against the Saracens (Muslims) in the battle of Roncesvaux. At the core of this story is the memory of a real battle in 778 mentioned by Charlemagne's biographer Einhard, who wrote of an ambush by Christian Basques of Charlemagne's rearguard as the Franks returned from an unsuccessful campaign in Spain.[1] In the hands of the poet some four centuries later, however, the story has been transformed.

It begins *in medias res,* when, after seven long years of war in Spain between Charlemagne and the Saracen king Marsile, the latter hatches a plan to promise the former his faithful service and conversion to Christianity if he'll abandon Spain and return to France. Charlemagne receives Marsile's messengers and takes counsel with his own men to determine who among them will head off to Spain with his response. At Roland's suggestion, the emperor selects Ganelon, Roland's stepfather, for this perilous task. Ganelon fears that the Saracen king will not permit him

---

[1] Compare the ninth chapter of Einhard, *The Life of Charles the Great*—for references to translations, see the bibliographic note to Chapter 9 in this volume—to the only other early medieval account of the event: *Royal Frankish Annals,* an. 778, in *Carolingian Chronicles: Royal Frankish Annals and Nithard's Histories,* trans. Bernhard Walter Scholz with Barbara Rogers (Ann Arbor: University of Michigan Press, 1972), 56.

to return to the Franks and will have him killed. To save his skin, he sets in motion Marsile's plot to ambush the rearguard and, when he returns to Charlemagne, suggests that Roland be its leader. Once Charlemagne and the majority of the Franks withdraw from Spain, Oliver sees the Saracens' advance and urges Roland to blow his horn so that Charlemagne can come back to help them fight. Roland dismisses Oliver's suggestion for fear that it will shame him, his family, and the Franks. After a rousing speech by Archbishop Turpin, in which he says that those who die fighting will be absolved of their sins, the Franks enter battle and fight valiantly until it becomes clear that they cannot withstand the Saracen onslaught. Roland then decides, this time against Oliver's objections—their roles have been reversed!—to blow the horn. They continue their valiant battle but cannot fight off the inevitable. By the time Charlemagne returns, Roland, Oliver, Turpin, and the Franks are all dead. Charlemagne fights the remaining Saracens and prevails in battle before returning to France, where he puts Ganelon on trial for treason. Ganelon admits that he orchestrated the death of his stepson but insists that he is innocent of treason since he was pursuing a private dispute with Roland. Nevertheless, he is ultimately found guilty, drawn, and quartered as the poem draws to a close.

Developed around the time of the First Crusade (1096–99)—hence the transformation of the Christian Basques into Saracens—this vivid and glorified adaptation of the events that led to the death of Roland and his companions, like the *chansons de geste* in general, was quite popular among medieval audiences. Indeed, already in the late eleventh century, people were naming their sons Roland and Oliver, and Roland is depicted in stained glass and sculpture in twelfth- and thirteenth-century cathedrals. The number and variety of the languages of the surviving versions— there are German, Norwegian, Welsh, and Latin versions and fragments from versions in Castilian, Middle Dutch, and English—presumably only a small portion of the versions that were once in existence, seem only to confirm a widespread appeal. However, it was not until the modern period that it came to be viewed as a piece of great literature. To its medieval audiences—perhaps warriors, perhaps clerics as interested in moral tales as deeds of glory, or perhaps a mixture of both—*Roland*, like the *chansons* in general, was little more than entertainment.

The *chansons* are conventional in style, and *Roland* is no exception. Perhaps due to their origins in oral performance, they typically have certain components: descriptions of arming before battle, insults, hand-to-hand combat, the prayers of the heroes, etc. It is impossible not to notice recurring phrases and to think about why they recur. All of the *chansons de geste* have the same basic organization. Each stanza, called a *laisse*, has a chosen vowel sound found in the last accented syllable of every line, a technique called assonance. In addition, each ten-syllable line is subdivided by a break after the fourth syllable (or sometimes sixth, as in the case of *Roland*). Each half of the line tends to have two stressed syllables. The need to fit this pattern and provide assonance helps to explain the poets' or reciters' use of stock phrases. And the use of stock components and language, like the repetition that is a frequent feature of the poems, probably appealed to audiences, just as we enjoy (and expect) certain conventions characteristic of different genres of modern entertainment, such as the car chase in the detective film or the shoot-out in the western. As the most popular and widely recognized of its genre, the *Song of Roland,* like popular modern literature or films, can present the historian with insight into the society in which and for which it was produced.

Roland is indeed a rich source for the study of the eleventh and twelfth centuries. Our earliest and best version of the poem, found in manuscript Digby 23 of the British Library, dates from the late 1090s. It reveals a very secular kind of Christian clergy. The warlike Archbishop Turpin is not atypical of the bishops of the eleventh century. For instance, he is akin to Bishop Odo of Bayeux, half-brother of William the Conqueror, who may have been fighting at the Battle of Hastings in 1066 and is represented as leading troops into combat in the Bayeux Tapestry. In the epic *The Cid* (see Chapter 15 below), which dates from the twelfth or early thirteenth century, Bishop Don Jerome, who is described as "learned in letters and with much wisdom/ and a ready warrior on foot or on horse" (78), asks the Cid for the right to strike the first blow in a battle against Muslims and is granted that right (94). Such clergy, who share the values of the knights, are respected within the *chansons.* Not all are. Turpin comments to Roland as, after a pause, he returns to killing Muslims, "A man in battle should be fierce and strong—/For one who isn't, I wouldn't give two cents./ Instead of fighting let him become a monk/And spend his days praying for all our sins" (141). Here, fighting for God is superior to praying for sin. Critical remarks about clergy who are not warriors in the flesh can be found elsewhere in the *chansons de geste.* Thus, the poem has interesting things to tell us about knightly views of the clergy.

Roland also offers insight into contemporary attitudes toward women, even if it gives less space to them than do some other *chansons.* Bramimonde, the Spanish queen, is the most important woman to the poet, perhaps because she provides a vehicle by which the Muslims' decisions about fighting the French can be criticized by an insider. No Muslim knight or counselor tells King Marsile (188) or later the envoys of his overlord Baligant (195) that they are doomed to defeat, but the queen does. Later, she is the token Muslim converted by persuasion, while the other survivors are converted by force (290). However, Alde, Oliver's sister and Roland's betrothed, is mentioned only twice in the poem. The first reference to her comes in the second argument between Roland and Oliver about whether or not to blow the horn. Oliver tells Roland he can't marry his sister if he disgraces himself by asking Charles for help (130). Later she receives two laisses of attention when she dies of grief at hearing of Roland's death (268–69). She is clearly low on the heroes' list of priorities. *The Cid* provides an interesting contrast, for in it the hero's desire to provide his wife and daughters a home with him is a major motivating force for his actions.

The male/female relations of the *chansons* are traditionally compared with those of the romances of Chrétien de Troyes or the *lais* of Marie of France (see Chapter 17 below), in which pleasing women is a major motive for men's actions. It has traditionally been supposed that the changes in the role of women between epic and romance reflect real change in women's status in society. For contemporary students of women's history, however, whether the change from epic to romance mirrors any improvement in the status of women is controversial.

While *Roland* is informative for what it shows us of women and clergy, historians have tended to be most interested in mining the text as a source of information about "feudal values" and "feudal institutions." "Feudalism" is one of those "ism" words that, as modern creations, grossly oversimplify and perhaps distort the complex realities of the past (or present). Nevertheless, *The Song of Roland* provides an opportunity to explore the presence and importance of feudal values and institutions. How important is the fief in the lives and minds of the characters? What is the relationship between man and lord we call "vassalage"? Does the king share governmental powers with his great vassals who hold fiefs from him? Is the king's power limited by his nobles? We need to explore also the importance of other social and governmental elements that might be considered "non-feudal." Not all important personal relationships or aspects of royal power are feudal ones. Indeed, it may ultimately be more useful to talk of the "knightly" rather than the "feudal" society revealed by the poem.

In this knightly society—and in the poem—the bond between lord and his man is essential. Roland talks of suffering and dying for his lord:

"Ben devuns ci ester our nostre rei:/ Pur sun seigneur deit hom susfrir destreiz/ E endurer e grand chalz e grans freiz,/ in deit hom perdre e gel quir e del peil"; "Here we will stand, defending our great king/ This is the service a vassal owes his lord:/ To suffer hardships, endure great heat and cold,/And in a battle to lose both hair and hide" (Terry 79). The word Roland uses is "hom," the root of the word homage, that is, the ceremony that makes one a man of a lord. Note that the "hom" of the poem has become "vassal" in Terry's translation. This is rather typical of the sloppiness with which the poem's "feudal" language is usually translated. "Hom" may serve as a synonym for vassal, but it need not. Like "lord" it is a broad term that can have a number of connotations, in the way that "man" does in modern English.

Roland later repeats these words almost exactly (88). After talking about the need of a "hom" to suffer much, to endure heat and cold, to lose hair and skin, Roland encourages Oliver to strike hard, as he himself will with the sword Charlemagne gave him. He says: "Se jo I moerc, dire poet ki l'avrat/ ... que ele fut a noble vassal." Compare two translations: "And if I die, whoever takes my sword/ Can say its master has nobly served his lord" (Terry 88), which emphasizes the feudal bond between lord and man, and the more general, "If I die, who has it next can say/ ... that it belonged to a noble knight" (Brault 88), which suggests that "vassus" means a noble knight. Assumptions about what terms mean may cause us to see "feudal" relationships as more important in the poem than they were when it was recited. The poet and his audience may have understood these terms more as qualifications of a certain type of man than as articulations of a formal relationship.

That is not to say that a close relationship between lord and man is not important in the poem. However, does it mark a society as feudal? The leader/follower bond can be traced in its general outlines back through early medieval society to the "comitatus" Tacitus describes in the *Germania*, discussed above in Chapter 3, although scholars today dispute the accuracy of this description. In the barbarian warband, a proven warrior collected about himself younger men who served him in battle, men whose need for rewards may indeed have at times driven the lord into battle. Tacitus describes the followers as men who willingly die in battle for their lord, as can also be seen, for example, in late Anglo-Saxon society in an eleventh-century poem, "The Battle of Maldon," a poem that makes for an interesting comparison with *Roland*. Yet the term "feudal" is not applied to these other instances of close relationships between lord and follower.

The loyalty of Roland to Charlemagne, which is reciprocated by Charlemagne's love for him, is reinforced by familial relationship. Roland is the nephew of Charlemagne (15), one of many famous nephews who appear in the *chansons de geste*. There are, for example, numerous nephews to be found in the cycle of William of Orange, a series of *chansons* set in the ninth century about William and his family. We can wonder whether the importance of one's sister's son can also be traced back to the barbarian peoples, where it may reflect traces of an earlier matrilineal society. According to Tacitus, Germanic men valued their sisters' sons as highly as their own.[2] In the patrilineal societies of western Europe in the High Middle Ages, sisters' sons might be trusted by their uncles because, unlike the sons of brothers, they have little if any claim to inherit power or land; sisters' sons had no reason to hasten their uncles' deaths. There is also the issue of blood kinship. We always know that our sister's sons are indeed our kin, but we can never be quite sure who fathered the children attributed to our brothers.

The blood tie between Roland and his lord — a bond visible also in *The Cid*, in which several of the Cid's most loyal men are his kinsmen — is a reminder of the importance of family in the medieval world. Hatred within a family, such as that between Ganelon and his stepson Roland, which brought about Roland's death, balances the love that leads Charlemagne to avenge it. Family love is evident again in Ganelon's trial; after one of his kinsmen dies fighting for him, a group of his relatives and supporters share Ganelon's fate. If we focus too closely on the bonds between lord and follower, we risk missing the importance of family bonds.

The relationship between and among knights is no less significant in the poem. Roland and Oliver could disagree with one another without permanent damage to their closeness. Roland's concern for the dying and dead Oliver (148–51) shows that he matters to Roland as his sister, Roland's betrothed, does not — Roland himself does not even mention her. Roland and Oliver may be the closest of friends, but they are not the only good friends. The attention of the 12 peers to one another's exploits and one another's deaths show that this group is, indeed, a band of brothers. Perhaps camaraderie among men who fight side by side is a natural human psychological response, but note how much more visible it is in *The Song of Roland* than, say, in *Beowulf* or "The Battle of Maldon." Male

---

[2] Tacitus, *Germania*, trans. J.B. Rives (Oxford: Clarendon Press, 1999), 20.3.

friendship—to be cemented by marriage, in the case of Roland and Oliver—
is an important social relationship in this world.

The relationship between lord and man is important, yet so too are
family relations and friendship. But what of that other important aspect of
feudalism, the land held on conditional terms from a lord? How important
is the fief in this world? We encounter it in what Ganelon claims is the
planned disposal of the Spanish lands. Marsile, the Muslim king of Spain,
will hold in fief (*en fiu*) only half of Spain from Charlemagne (33). Later,
we seem to get the actual plan of Charlemagne's court, when Ganelon
reports to him that Marsile, as arranged, will come to France, become a
Christian, and "Jointes ses mains iert vostre comandet,/ De vos tendrat
Espaigne le regent"; "His hands placed between yours, he will become your
vassal/ He will hold the kingdom of Spain as a fief from you" (Brault 54);
"Both of his hands he'll place between your own,/ And do homage for all
his lands in Spain" (Terry 54). In other words, Marsile does homage and
gets his lands back in return. The French lords remember their "fiefs and
honors" ("fius e des honurs") as they ride homeward (e.g., 66). As Baligant
musters his men for the last great battle between Muslims and Franks, he
offers his son land (231). Although this is sometimes translated as a fief, as
Brault does, the Old French speaks only of a "gift," and Terry, for example,
does not use the term "fief" in her translation. Thus, the poem does mention fiefs, although not as often as the translators may.

Translators sometimes assume the presence of feudal institutions, and
therefore they refer to them when the text may not. It is therefore extremely
useful to have an Old French version to consult. Even if one's understanding of the language is minimal or non-existent, with a little practice one
can identify whether or not words like "hom" and "vassal" or "fiu" are being
used. Of course, that doesn't help us understand what such terms meant at
the time. The verb we usually assume to indicate a feudal holding, "tenere,"
usually translated "to hold," can mean simply "to have." And, in any case,
most lands were regarded as belonging to families, whether or not they
were called "fiefs" and theoretically held from a lord. It is important to
remember that the poet was driven by considerations of rhyme and rhythm,
so reading too much into the precise words chosen can be a mistake.

Roland does not focus on property as much as some of the other *chansons de geste* do. It is not about winning wealth in land and objects, as is, for
example, *The Cid*. Perhaps as an indication of their wickedness, the
Muslims talk more about wealth than the Christians do. See, for example,

the list of treasures Marsile will offer Charlemagne (3), the gifts Ganelon receives for betraying the French (48–52), or the gifts offered by Baligant to his son and his men (245). Note, though, that Charlemagne also refers to gifts (246). It is easy to miss the reference to the booty the French have taken: "His knights rejoice, for great is their reward—/ silver and gold, and costly gear for war," translates Terry (8). While material rewards do not loom large in the poem for the Christians, the battle gear of both sides is described in very conventional language as made of precious metals and jewels. These are certainly objects well worth looting! That there is so little talk of material gain among the Christians, whether loot or rewards of land and objects, may reinforce the suggestion that Digby 23's original may have been written by a cleric for clerics. The moral and religious lessons of the tale do seem very important.

But this is a tale about warfare, and the descriptions of arming for battle and of combat in battle, conventional though they are, can be read for information about medieval fighting tactics. The splendor of weapons and armor is grossly exaggerated, as are the force of blows and the numbers killed. Nevertheless, we can see the basic outlines of the fighting of the age. Note the indication of what men value in a horse in the description of Turpin's steed (126). That swords, like horses, have names is one indication of their importance to the peers. The poem shows us the progression from fighting with spears to fighting with swords, as well as how these weapons are used. The picture of Roland ready for battle and laughing for joy is unforgettable (91).

Government is inevitably a part of the *chanson*, as the king makes decisions at the outset that set the story in motion and holds a trial for Ganelon the traitor in the end. In decision-making, it is notable that the king holds council with his great men and relies on their suggestions. Indeed, in the choice of an envoy to the Muslims, he seems bound by his council's decisions (17–24). He can veto nominations, but he does not initiate any. Similarly, when Charlemagne at the head of the vanguard hears Roland's horn in the distance, he relies on his intimate advisor Naimes to tell him what to do (133–36). In the trial of Ganelon, too, the king must rely on the workings of the judicial system (271–89). His power lies in his reputation, in the love and loyal service of his barons—in part at least a response to his loyalty to them as seen in the section sometimes called The Vengeance of Charlemagne (177–267)—and his special religious status. It is possible to argue that the Charlemagne of *The Song of Roland* is the knight or baron's ideal ruler, that is, a great warrior who has God on his side and takes his barons' advice. But note that in Ganelon's trial, Thierry espouses a concept of *lèse majesté*. He argues that in betraying Roland, Ganelon was not just carrying out a personal vendetta, he was harming the king whom Roland serves as a commander (277).

The Charlemagne of the *chanson* is not much like the Charles of Einhard's biography or William the Conqueror as seen by contemporaries. On the other hand, he is not a "first among equals" leader such as the twelfth-century Anglo-Norman King Stephen (c. 1096–1154). He is set apart from and above his barons in status. If we might be tempted in the first part of the poem to see him as a weak, limited, stereotypically "feudal" king, we need to pay attention to the power he displays in the second part (177–291), in which he is shown as a great warrior who is also so close to God that a miracle is worked for him. Yet there has been scholarly disagreement about whether the "Baligant episode," which occupies much of the second half of the poem (177–263), is a later addition, not integral to the poem. This long episode in which Charlemagne, Roland's lord, fights and defeats Baligant, Marsile's overlord, might have been added to present an image of the king as a powerful soldier and man of God.

Let us set the picture of Charlemagne in *The Song of Roland* against the background of other *chansons de geste*. Most of the *chansons* are categorized as belonging to one of three great cycles: the cycle of the deeds of the king (usually Charlemagne), to which *Roland* belongs; the tales of rebellious vassals (including, for example, *Raoul de Cambrai*); and the cycle of William of Orange and his kinsmen. All show the bravery in battle of the heroes, but not all show the king as admirable in the ways that Charlemagne appears in *Roland*. William of Orange and his family, for example, are unfairly treated by the weak king they serve, Louis the Pious, son of Charlemagne. In considering what we can learn from *The Song of Roland* about the society in which it was produced, we must therefore be aware that we are drawing conclusions from one exemplar of a genre, one that in some ways may be atypical. Did *Roland* appeal to nineteenth- and twentieth-century Frenchmen because it was a battle between the forces of Good and Evil, not between French political rivals, or because its heroes, both Roland and Charlemagne, are men of great worth? *Beowulf*, too, avoids in its main plot line the usual conflicts of epics between human enemies; its hero tackles a monster and a dragon. Roland fights the human version of Grendel in his battle with the Muslims — indeed, his enemies are in part described as non-human monsters.

For modern readers, the poem's portrayal of Muslims (the "Saracens") is disconcerting, to say the least. There are only two kinds of Muslims mentioned: either they are men who are described as great warriors, who would be great knights "if only they were Christians" (72, 228), or they are semi-human monsters, "big-headed men from Misnes—/They have stiff hairs growing along their spines/ Just like the bristles along the backs of pigs" (Terry 232). The lineage of many medieval "monsters" can be traced to Pliny's *Natural History*. Pliny expressed the belief, for example, that the heat of the south burned its inhabitants black. A French chronicler contemporary with Digby 23, Benoît of Sainte-Maure, believed that those who lived in the south were deformed both physically and morally; that they were hairy and black, chinless and horned; and that they had large feet and long noses.[3] The poem's Saracen Chernuble of Muneigre at least partially fits that description (39). However, the portrait of Abisme, "The fiercest man in all that company./ Evil in heart, and guilty of great crimes,/ He has no faith in Mary's holy Son/ This pagan's skin is black as melted pitch/ . . ." (Terry 125), may also reflect the common late antique and medieval image of the devil as black.

The poem is typical of most of the *chansons de geste* in that it shows ignorance about Muslim beliefs as well as Muslim society. It is interesting to compare the Muslims of *Roland* with those of *The Cid*. Although the Christian Cid does spend much of his time fighting Muslims in Spain, he also has Muslim allies who help him in his conflicts with other Christian lords. His main Muslim ally is shown as extremely kind and generous in his treatment of the Cid's womenfolk. In short, the Cid is fighting for his reputation, wealth, and power; his main enemies are Christian. Roland is fighting "evil"; his main enemies are the enemies of Christianity.

The values of *Roland* are the values of a society of warriors, specifically of Christian warriors in a Christian society. Prowess in battle, loyalty to lord and fellow fighters, and concern for the fate of their souls after death are all important. The speeches in which Roland explains his refusal to blow his horn and summon help suggest additional values or at least raise questions about them. Does or does not the poet intend us to criticize Roland for refusing to summon help? Is he "proud" in a bad sense? A similar question concerns the behavior of Ealdorman Brythnoth in "The

---

[3] Benoît de Sainte-Maure, *Chronique des ducs de Normandie*, ed. Carin Fahlin C. Fahlin, (Uppsala: Almqvist and Wiksells, 1951–67), vol. 3, ll. 141–43.

Battle of Maldon": is the poet criticizing him for allowing the Vikings to cross the causeway and fight the assembled English army? As we develop our own answers to such questions, it is essential to avoid seeing the poem through twenty-first-century perspectives. Avoiding death in battle has not always been as important as it seems to be for us today, especially in societies that believe wholeheartedly in rewards in the next life for those who have lived (or died) well.

Many different societies have produced epics, whether primary (the products of early pre-literate societies, which circulated orally for centuries before taking written form) or secondary (creations in fully established civilizations by writers influenced by the epic tradition, such as Virgil or Milton). To explore what is distinctively western European in epics such as *Beowulf* or *Roland*, it may be fruitful to compare them with the Japanese *The Tale of the Heike*, or the Indian *Mahabharata* and *Ramayana*, or the Iranian *Shahnameh*, or the West African *Sundiyata*, or even modern western equivalents. Is Tolkien's *Lord of the Rings* a modern example of a secondary epic? And what of the *Star Wars* cycle: is it an epic in a non-literary medium? To answer these questions, we need to probe beyond explorations of the values and institutions above to ask what human needs epics appear to meet. But here we may be leaving the sphere of the historian.

Bibliographic Note

I have used two translations for this essay: Patricia Terry, *The Song of Roland*, 2nd ed. (New York: Macmillan, 1992) and Gerard J. Brault, *The Song of Roland: An Analytical Translation* (University Park: Pennsylvania State University Press, 1978). My parenthetical citations refer to the appropriate laisse of the text, which is the same for both translations; where I have quoted a translation, I include the name of the translator in the parenthetical reference.

For the comparative study of the epics cited above, see *Poem of the Cid*, trans. W.S. Merwin (New York: New American Library, 1975), discussed in Chapter 15 of this volume; *Guillaume d'Orange: Four Twelfth Century Epics*, trans. Joan Ferrante (New York: Columbia University Press, 1974); *Genji and Heike: Selections from The Tale of Genji and The Tale of the Heike*, trans. Helen Craig McCullough (Stanford, CA: Stanford University Press, 1994); and "The Battle of Maldon," widely available in collections of Old English verse, such as in Kevin Crossley-Holland, *The Anglo-Saxon World: An Anthology* (Oxford: Oxford University Press, 1999).

Studies of *The Song of Roland* as a work of literature are abundant. Here I note only Andrew Taylor's two articles, "Was There a Song of Roland?" *Speculum* 76 (2001): 28–65 and "The Myth of the Minstrel Manuscript," *Speculum* 66 (1991): 43–73, which discuss Digby 23 and the issues of authorship and readership. Likewise, my discussion of feudalism draws on a long-standing scholarly reflection on the use of the term. As a point of departure, see Elizabeth A.R. Brown, "The Tyranny of a Construct: Feudalism and Historians of Medieval Europe," *American Historical Review* 79 (1974): 1063–88; Susan Reynolds, *Fiefs and Vassals* (Oxford: Clarendon Press, 1994); and a debate in *Past and Present* that began with Thomas N. Bisson's article in vol. 142 (1994) and was continued in vols. 152 (1996) and 155 (1997).

THIRTEEN

Galbert of Bruges
The Notary as Poet

Lawrence R. Jannuzzi

"The traveller who has gone to Italy to study the tactile values of Giotto, or the corruption of the Papacy," wrote E.M. Forster, "may return remembering nothing but the blue sky and the men and women who live under it." So, when Forster's English heroine found herself in Florence without her tourist guidebook — "In Santa Croce with No Baedeker" — it turned out to be a windfall because "the pernicious charm of Italy worked on her, and instead of acquiring information, she began to be happy."[1]

Reading history from original sources is like that, the balance between acquiring the Baedeker information and something more personal. One of the tricks of learning history directly from the sources is not to ignore the facts, certainly, but to get past the initial, panicked urge for the Baedeker information, to forget for a while the nagging feeling that someone else can look at something — a fresco in Forster's case, or a text, or a human being for that matter — and see things that we cannot see. It is important not to succumb to the suspicion that others can see in color while we are limited to black and white. That kind of fear causes us to scramble for the guidebook, but it only gets in the way. It actually blocks out the color. On the other hand, let the world of a writer become real and personal, and the color floods back into it. Information can follow, but the point is the act of noticing and the spirit with which things are noticed.

An example: if the thirteenth-century historian Matthew Paris wrote that he was writing while sitting in his Benedictine monastic cloister, a lecture or a footnote can tell us about monks and cloisters. However, when

---

[1] E.M. Forster, *A Room with a View* (New York: Barnes and Noble, 1993), 16–30.

a reader cares to notice, say, that Matthew was writing under a pear tree behind a cloister wall in the drizzling English rain, and that the Franciscan historian Salimbene (see Chapter 21) was, at almost the same moment, walking through the shade of an olive tree on a sunny Italian roadside, then immediately the two worlds, and the two books, of those two dead men will begin to bounce off each other and split open.[2] When readers care about Matthew and Salimbene, they can begin to wonder what the English rain or the Italian sunshine can do to the mind and the pen of a writer, how olives and pears can make different lunches and different attitudes toward an afternoon of writing, how thinking on the road and thinking behind a wall might result in different thoughts and different books.

The phrase "cares to notice" is not rhetorical, for caring for the writer — and caring in some personal way — is a good way to get past the urge to turn immediately to the guidebook. Studying a medieval writer is difficult. Respecting him (in this case I am speaking of a "him") is much more difficult. Liking him (or disliking him, which is another way to care) can be almost impossible. But that is where the fun is, where much of the history is.

And that is what makes so enriching the study of a book like *The Murder of Charles the Good*, written by a twelfth-century notary named Galbert. This is a book that lets us care about the writer in a particularly personal way, although the reasons for caring about Galbert may seem odd. This book is appealing not because it is a history (although it is a superb one), but because it is a history written by a notary. The very word "notary" fills the mind with images of accounting records and wills and deeds, lists of things that need to be (literally) itemized, acts that must be witnessed and recorded, dry facts — always someone else's facts — that must be scheduled, collated, calendared. But with Galbert, the reader who cares can begin to see, dimly, into and through the words of this otherwise mundane functionary. Here the student who listens can hear, a little, the cracking sound that the notarial voice makes when it must speak of things that stretch and break the lists and categories by which it had lived. When we can see the poetry in the book, we can care for its writer; we can look at this notary and see — if we care to — not black-and-white notarial entries, not *jurats, items, incipits,* and *explicits,* but "the color of men's souls."[3]

---

[2] This example is taken loosely from Robert Brentano, *Two Churches: England and Italy in the Thirteenth Century* (Berkeley: University of California Press, 1988 [1967]), 326–45.

[3] Robert Brentano, *A New World in a Small Place: Church and Religion in the Diocese of Rieti, 1188–1378* (Berkeley: University of California Press, 1994), 4.

In what sense is Galbert a poet? A modern poet, writing about Galbert's contemporary Hildegard of Bingen, describes Hildegard's "discipline" of writing poetry much as Galbert saw his own "discipline" of writing: "In composing a poem, one often seems to move directly from ignorance to revelation, instantly from a muddled sense of things to a clear picture, with only the vaguest sense of how it happened.... But if visionaries and poets are at the mercy of what they see, they are also called to articulate it. And this requires them to employ another form of knowledge, the linear thought that enables them to communicate their experience to others."[4] In the words that lie at the intersection of different forms of knowledge, and in their disciplined use, lies poetry. "The discipline of poetry teaches poets, at least, that they often have to say things they can't pretend to understand.... We [poets] experience words as steeped in mystery, forces beyond our intellectual grasp."[5] In Galbert, we can discern application of words in just this way, as a salve to deep, even inexpressible wounds, but applied according to the linear discipline of the notary. It is that very underlying notarial discipline that makes his book a work of poetry. And when we see the poet nestled inside the notary, interesting things begin to happen.

The linear, Baedeker account of the cataclysmic events Galbert witnessed is quick in the retelling. Galbert was a notary of Bruges, a city in the county of Flanders, in what is now Belgium. In 1127 his lord, Charles, who was Count of Flanders but of Danish descent, was hacked to pieces by assassins while attending Mass in his church. The murder was not only grucsomc (although Galbert's description of it is restrained compared with some others), it touched off a series of violent aftershocks.

The killers, headed by Charles's provost, were members of a disgruntled local family who, Galbert says, felt its social position and legal status as free citizens threatened by Charles. Overconfident after the murder, they immediately set about finishing off Charles's supporters. The count's family and faction, routed at first, rallied and counterattacked. Lynch mobs set off in search of the conspirators and besieged most of them in the count's own church and castle, his parceled body still inside. The canons of the defiled church armed themselves to fight in the choir against removal of the new "martyr's" body, as miracles were already being associated with the remains.

A martyr's relics are powerful things, and the bishop of Noyon, Charles's brother-in-law, showed up to claim the body. A band of men

---

[4] Kathleen Norris, *The Cloister Walk* (New York: Riverhead Books, 1996), 10–11.

[5] Norris, *The Cloister Walk*, 1.

from Ghent arrived to punish the perpetrators and, incidentally, also to claim the body. The burghers of Bruges, also wanting control of the body, found themselves fighting the men of Ghent, the bishop, the count's cronies, and the forces of the king of France, whose vassal Charles was. The French king had important dynastic and political interest in Flanders, and therefore, of course, the English king, with unabashed glee, started to put forward rival claimants to Charles's position. Amid all this, Galbert hints throughout that it was the count's vast treasure, as much as his miraculous remains, that was the target of these combating groups.

When the murderers or those associated with them were caught, they were disposed of in ostentatiously humiliating ways, usually ending with the unfortunate body, dead several times over, dumped in a sewer. The few survivors among the besieged were thrown alive from the top of a high tower and smashed on the pavement below (29, 81, 57).

Lurid violence always makes a good story, the more so when it is combined with greed, ambition, and religious passion. But Galbert at first glance seems simply to note the violence with the bloodless precision one would expect of the notary, the recordation of a dispassionate, professional witness documenting observations solely for the use of others. Galbert certainly promises a dispassionate "notarial" account of the killing and its aftermath: "I do not seek to embellish" the story, he tells us at the outset; rather, he wants to tell "only the truth of things, and even if my style is dry" (1).

So it is not surprising that Galbert calls our attention to the exact physical posture of the count as he was attacked, the exact point of the liturgy at which it happened, and his exact glance and gesture when he died (15). It was the sixth Nones of March, the day between the second and fourth days of the second week of Lent (Tuesday, 2 March 1127). In the lunar liturgical calendar, it was the fifth Concurrent and the sixth Epact, at dawn. Count Charles was kneeling in the gallery of his own church, his eyes fixed on the psalm he was reciting, the liturgical office of Terce having reached precisely (and ironically, as Galbert will tell us) the words "our father." Charles's chaplain had placed beside him pennies to be given to the poor, and the count's right arm was extended to dispense those alms when it was severed by the murderers. At the moment of death, Charles lifted his eyes and hands to heaven "as well as he could amid so many blows and thrusts of the swordsmen" (15).

This is the notarial stuff we might expect, the minutely precise recordation of bare, if sensational, facts. So Galbert says, in various ways. As he begins his description of the count's death, he advises that his intent, more than anything, is to find order in, or impose order on, the chaotic events dividing the subject "by days and the events of those days" (14). He later underscores that it was he, "Galbert, a notary," who wrote this book, as if to remind his readers that the profession of the author is to provide unembellished facts, facts that were, as he says, "transcribed" more than composed (35). In this way, the reader, who is given a "true and reliable" account of the life and death of the count and the subsequent furor — the facts of the case — can pray appropriately for the dead count (14).

But order in things like this is hard to come by. The harder Galbert tries to reflect on these events, the less possible it becomes for him to make sense of the disintegration he saw around him at the time. When he later added a passage describing the events leading up to the beginning of the blow-by-blow account, he still spoke of his "dry style" and his purpose of writing simply "for the memory" of his readers; he still described the events as simply "strange" (Intro.). Yet here, at the beginning of the book but at a later stage of the writing process — the book as it exists now was not written front to back — he knows, and he knows that we readers know, that stenographic exactitude has proven inadequate for the task at hand.

Galbert describes how he came to that conclusion, and the process is revealing of his core and the core of his book. Immediately after the events, in the midst of so many burning roofs, roofs torched by flaming arrows fired from the besieged castle, he had "no suitable place for writing." He was surrounded by such rampant looting and burning, so disturbed at heart by the calamity — indeed, the whole town was so badly rent with fear — that writing was nearly impossible. He had to force himself "almost unwillingly" to put pen to paper (35). He realized that the problem in writing was not the turmoil but his own fear. He had to worry more about finding some order within himself than finding some nonexistent order in a disordered world. He says that he had to find some mental peace, to "subdue" and "compose" his mind, which was "as unquiet as if it were tossed about in Euripus." Only then, he says, could he engage in what he, like our modern poet, calls the "discipline" of writing (Intro.).

It is with this confession that we begin to see this book as more than a "transcript" and watch it become a work that tells us not only about Flanders but about Galbert and also about ourselves. It is at that point — when Galbert is forced to look within himself, when the overwhelming disorder of the world forces him to examine his own internal order —

that his words quickly exceed his linear mind's grasp, when he becomes a poet.

Galbert recognizes and speaks of exactly this process. He tells us that, rather than eloquence, he began striving for "the truth," which he committed to paper for the memory of the faithful. As he did so, composition was no longer satisfied with simple remembrance of the events. The truth demands more. "In this distress of mind," he writes, "a little spark of love, warmed and animated by its own fire, set aflame...my bodily self, which had been seized by fear, with the freedom to write" (Intro.). Love, then, casts out fear and creates freedom to write. What he is aiming for now is no longer only memory, and it transcends recordation and the craft of writing itself. Now he asks his readers to experience "fresh wonder" at the workings of the world (Intro.).

This later-added introduction reveals a transforming syllogism that Galbert discovered within himself. In searching for the truth, "distress of mind" prompts memory; memory—the notarial act—gives the spark of love; love leads to freedom; freedom allows discipline; discipline leads to art; and art creates wonder. Once a reader has seen this Galbert—this process working within him—a new, personal connection between him and the reader has been made; it is impossible now not to care for Galbert, impossible to read his book in the same way, and impossible not to see Galbert's world in some of the colors he saw.

As we watch Galbert set aflame with freedom, then, he ignites us a little in return, but some cautions are in order. It is not possible to trace a trajectory through the pages of his book, to watch while Galbert literally turns from notary to historian to poet. In the first place, he did not simply write his book from the first page to the last, changing as he went. We can see the hand of much revision, rethinking, and redrafting in the pages. The book must be considered as a whole. But, more important, to look for such a change is to miss Galbert as a writer and as a human, and to misunderstand his process. Galbert did not turn from a notary into an historian or a poet; he never ceased to be the notary. The notary remains intact, as he must if he is to exercise the linear discipline that gives expression to the inexpressible, if he is to have a frame for his words. Yet, as we read, we can become and remain conscious of the growth that Galbert is experiencing, and we can see that growth in the subtle layering of things that he sees and of ways that he sees.

In other words, the fact that Galbert was a notary should not be substituted for some other fact as "the" fact to be noticed, the kind of "mediating" Baedeker observation that I have mentioned, the kind that, if it is taken as "the" color of the text, allows that color to drain away. It is a typical entry in a guidebook. What I am trying to suggest is one way for the new reader to explore without the guidebook, to engage the writer personally and see what questions and imagination are generated from that engagement. Galbert's "purpose" — in the sense of some objective thing he wanted to accomplish with his book — is indeed not clear, and to wonder about it is valid and necessary. But let us explore first what that effort in the search for form and order in his world — and thus in his writing, too — might tell us about Galbert himself. In doing so, some of his unstated purpose might very well become apparent, but what will certainly come into greater clarity is Galbert's real existence in a real world, his real world.

As we get to know Galbert, the drama he saw around himself, the confusion, the deeply ambivalent feelings he had for those involved in the murder become increasingly apparent. One poem the reader might find in this book is the dawning awareness that Galbert's city and country (his *patria*, or fatherland) had somehow transformed itself from "home" into a threatening, dangerous, even evil place. "Home" is considered in many ways by Galbert, and it is revealing to observe how he employs the pronoun "we," because for him, Bruges — home — is not just another place but the place where "we" live. Nevertheless, the word "we" is a surprisingly elastic term. It occasionally refers to the Flemish as opposed to the French or English, but it also refers to the people of Bruges as opposed to the men of other towns of Flanders, such as Ghent or Ypres. On occasion, "we" even means some groups within the citizenry of Bruges, such as the merchants as opposed to the unfree serfs. Yet it does not appear that Galbert is at all uncertain about who "we" are. Rather, it seems that he locates himself within a set of concentric circles, the larger outer ones embracing and yet dependent on the smaller inner ones. In that way, when the count, standing somewhere very near the center circle, is killed, the dire international implications demonstrate to Galbert that the very order of nature has been disturbed and no part of it can avoid the effects. Galbert uses his observational, notarial skills to write something of what we might call a prose poem describing the indescribable — nothing less than a blow aimed at the center circle of natural reality and therefore at the natural order itself.

If this is correct, we can begin to explain what may otherwise seem to be puzzling choices. One of these is Galbert's habit of describing things that his readers must already know. At one point, for example, he carefully describes the church occupied by the traitors after the murder and besieged by the count's loyalists (37). It was a church everyone in Bruges must have seen every day, the color, shape, and history of which was part of their lives. But Galbert tells them about it anyway: "There stood the church of Saint Donation, built round and high, roofed over with earthenware material, its peak vaulted with hollow jars and bricks, for the original roofing of the church had been made of wood but when the structure of the bell-tower was erected, the basilica itself had been covered with this man-made material" (37). This long discussion of the architecture and building material of the church is related only slightly to the siege of the church itself, thrust somewhat oddly into a more practical description of the site of the battle and the defensive possibilities of the place. This description is notarial, and, being notarial, on the surface it seems random. But Galbert's decision to include these details is not random. He has also inserted a revealing statement about that building: "From this place it dominated the scene in the splendor of its beauty like the throne of the realm; in the midst of the fatherland it called for safety and justice everywhere in the land through security and peace, right and laws" (37).

In this insertion, Galbert offers his reflection on his own material observations. He must add what that physical building means to him, what is important to him when he looks at the church in his mind and writes about it. The church building reminds the people of the "throne of the realm," the throne now vacant. It reminds the people that the man whose church it was — the father of the fatherland — has been treacherously killed within it. The physical building — the monument — reminds the people of safety and justice, security and peace, right and law, all of which lie in ruins thanks to those who retreated inside it. In short, the church stands as a reproach, a standing contradiction, harboring within itself the very denial of everything it promises.

Inside this building, which had stood for the safety offered by good government but had given the count no safety, the traitors "labored day and night to make themselves safer" (37). Thus, turning from the physical building to its occupants, Galbert contrasts the safety that the church once stood for with the false promise of safety it now offered the very destroyers of safety. For that safety was not only an ironic perversion of the safety the building was meant to guarantee, it was in fact nonexistent, and those inside knew it.

Thus, from irony comes drama, and drama requires invention. As these wretched outlaws labored to build defensive barricades, Galbert tells us of their fear, quoting conversations he could not have heard and motives he could only have guessed. They worked so hard "because they had now learned that they would have to fight against the whole world." The conspirators remember that they had once said that if they killed Charles, there would be no one to avenge him. Galbert turns that statement into a revelation of the fear and desperation the conspirators felt trapped inside the church: "Then finally they could remember their own saying, 'If we kill Charles, who will come to avenge him?' But, in fact, those coming to avenge him were infinite" (37).

The foundation of this chapter, then, is a dispassionate and thorough discussion of the physical building in which the battle was shaping up. But that description, coming from Galbert the notary, is inadequate for Galbert the poet; important to him is the metaphorical significance of the building itself, and this leads him to build a dramatic and imaginative scene of the fear and despair felt by those trapped within. Galbert in this way paints exquisite portraits in dramatic terms in order to tell a good story. But like a painter, he does so by composing carefully observed real objects in combinations that never existed in nature. In that way, he tells not only a good story but a true one.

See the way Galbert tells us of the day the count was killed (12). First, he sets the mood. The day dawned "so dark and foggy that you could not distinguish anything a spear's length away." Galbert then (adding sleepless nights to sleepless knights) brings us into the count's bedroom and even into his mind. Portentously foreshadowing his fate, Galbert reports that the count had not slept well the night before, tossing in bed, "now lying on one side, now sitting up again on the bed." He was "so disquieted" that he seemed "quite exhausted, even to himself" (12). As with the conspirators' conversation inside the church, Galbert could have had no way of knowing that the count did not sleep well, much less what he had been thinking. This is pure dramatic invention. The literary conceit continues as the count rises to go to the fatal church service and the conspiracy swings into action. Spies placed in the castle pass word of his movements. Reaching the church, Charles kneels in prayer, and the killers approach from behind with drawn swords hidden beneath their cloaks. The count chants, and the killers fan out behind him to cut off his escape. They raise their treacherous swords…but at that exact moment of final, fatal betrayal, Galbert stops dead in his tracks. "Now it should be known," he says, "what a noble man and distinguished ruler those impious and inhuman serfs betrayed" (12)!

Galbert leaves us panting, with the count tied to the figurative railroad track, to tell us about the moral aspects of the moment. He wants to hold us in supreme dramatic (almost melodramatic) suspense while he speaks of Charles's piety and humility, and the perversity of the ringleader's character (13).

At that moment, on one level, he wants to tell us what a noble count has been killed and about the "impious and inhuman serfs" who have committed such heinous crimes. Good and evil stand dramatically poised on the verge of their fateful clash. But one of the things that most vexes Galbert is what could possibly have been going on in the hearts of those who inhabited his home, both of the good and of those who so violently breached the peace and safety of Flanders. Simple moralizing is too simple.

Galbert goes on to tell us that Bertulf, the chief of the band of murderers, is the son of Erembald who in his own time had gained the high office of castellan by treachery and murder (71). Galbert certainly means, as he says often enough, that the mark of Cain was on the family and that Bertulf was working out the destiny of the sins committed by his father. But the story of how Bertulf and his contemporaries fell out with the count is not a cosmic condemnation. Instead, it is a source of compassion. The count had declared that the Erembald family was originally—and therefore by nature—serfs and not free, and that privileges of free citizens were to be taken away from them (7). In this way, we are not allowed to rest sanguine in their malice. We can begin to see that there is another side to their story.

And there is a hint that the count's reasons may not have been altogether noble either. We are told that the count, "wishing to reestablish proper order in his realm," set out to "find out who...were servile and who were free men in the realm." But he had chosen to "find out" who was free at precisely the moment that he was engaged in restoring the prosperity of the realm, namely, his own wealth (7). The veiled connection between Bertulf's legal status and the count's profit cannot help but suggest that Charles was seeking to fill those treasury coffers in which everyone was so interested as soon as he was dead. Galbert hints broadly that the count was embarking on a political offensive against the Erembald clan, using the skeleton in its family closet—its prior status as serfs—as a pretext for reducing their power and seizing their property.

In this way, Galbert reminds us that as evil as the murder of the count was, the Erembald clan was part of Bruges society, a part of "we." If its free status and history were attacked, its identity and place in the larger family were also attacked. The Erembalds could either resist or be excluded. Galbert offers a hint of sympathy for Bertulf's dismissive reference to Charles as "that Charles of Denmark" (8), that is to say, an outsider to Bruges society. The clan may have unjustly "usurped" their own liberty, and they certainly acted unjustly in killing the count, but if we cast this other light on them, we have new sympathy for Bertulf's preference "to perish together with the whole line of his nephews rather than be handed over in servitude to the count" (8). There is sincerity in Bertulf's cry: "Let him try as much as he wants, we shall be free and we are free, and there is no man on earth who can make us into serfs!" (8). If this is a prose poem about the *patria,* about "we," it was the count himself, perhaps, who was attacking the established "we."

Having carefully given us the detailed "facts," Galbert could have been content with simple condemnation of the evildoers. Instead, he shows us the depths of these human hearts in complexity and perspective, with more than a little portion of grandeur even in the midst of perfidy. More important, whether he believes the actions were justified or not (and he certainly does not), Galbert has found here a way to explore his underlying questions: "who are 'we' and how did 'we' come to this?" He declines the easy answers and embraces instead the ambiguous. In his answers — or rather, his hints of answers — Galbert has hit upon something that he sees in the human heart. He seems to be telling us that treachery and treason, and the universal chaos they engender, can have their roots in noble, and even universal, human impulses. In that sense, "we" is all of us.

We see in Galbert something of his idea of home, family, clan, safety, order, and the ripping at the seams those things have suffered in his presence. When Galbert speaks of "we," he is speaking of his people and the sense of loss and betrayal he feels when members of his "family" turn on one another. Perhaps, in the final analysis, that is the "we" that Galbert is driving at. It is certainly the "we" about which poets write.

Bibliographic Note
For this essay, I use James Bruce Ross's translation of Galbert's text: Galbert of Bruges, *The Murder of Charles the Good* (Toronto: University of Toronto Press, 1993), which is a reprint of the translation originally published by Columbia University Press in 1959; for the references, I cite her chapter divisions. Galbert's writing process is more deeply and formally

explicated in Jeff Rider, *God's Scribe: The Historiographical Art of Galbert of Bruges* (Washington, DC: Catholic University of America Press, 2001). For the times and places with which Galbert was concerned, a good starting place is David Nicholas, *Medieval Flanders* (New York: Longman, 1992). M.T. Clanchy writes deeply on notaries, literacy, and their effects on a medieval society, although not Flanders, in *From Memory to Written Record: England, 1066–1307* (Oxford: Blackwell, 1993). Notarial culture and training and their influence on personality and events was also a recurrent theme in the thought, writing, and teaching of Robert Brentano. See, for instance, his "Notarial Cartularies and Religious Personality: Rome, Rieti, and Bishop Thomas of Secinario (1339–1341)" in *Sources of Social History: Private Acts of the Late Middle Ages*, ed. Paolo Brezzi and Egmont Lee (Toronto: Pontifical Institute, 1984), 169–83.

FOURTEEN

Odo of Deuil's *The Journey of Louis VII to the East*
Between *The Song of Roland* and Joinville's *Life of Saint Louis*

Rudi Paul Lindner

In the twelfth century, the expansion of Europe was well underway. Universities arose in Italy and then across the Alps to the north. Administrative kingship grew steadily in France and England as a papal establishment emerged in Italy, headed at first by monks and, by the end of the era, by lawyers. Romanesque style flowered even as the Gothic materialized. And a recovery of interest in the ancient world's legacy accompanied these developments. The century began with crusaders ensconced in the Holy Land, having triumphed over distance, disease, discord, and Muslim ways of warfare. It ended with the crushing defeat of the crusader kingdom's knights in 1186, Jerusalem again in Muslim hands in 1187, and the failure of the Third Crusade, the crusade of three kings, to redeem the dream of Outremer. But it is on the middle of the century and the Second Crusade (1146–48) — or rather, on a text produced in the middle of the century about the Second Crusade — on which we shall focus in this chapter.

In 1144 the furthest outrider of the crusader states, the County of Edessa, centered on what is today's Urfa in southeast Turkey, fell to a Muslim army. When news reached western Europe a year later, calls for a new crusade arose, and the expressive, pressing preaching of Saint Bernard of Clairvaux (1090–1153), the leading light of his generation of Cistercian monks who sought a greater austerity in monastic life, brought forth volunteers. The First Crusade (1095–99) had been an expedition of barons; the

Second Crusade to the East involved two kings, Conrad of Germany and Louis VII of France. The Second Crusade failed, and it failed badly. The First Crusade had called forth a large number of knights; the Second was undermanned. There had developed a good deal of cohesion and order during the First Crusade; the Second advanced with split forces, a larger German and a smaller French contingent, and the Turks in Asia Minor had the pleasure of defeating separate expeditions. The Muslims in 1096 were divided; in the 1140s, both in Asia Minor and in the Holy Land, they were united. Only a fraction of the knighthood that began the Second Crusade managed to struggle across Asia Minor, not enough to have a serious effect on the military balance in northern Syria. Neither crusading army was successful in the end, but the story of Louis's crusade is worth examination.

There are at least two reasons for this: one is the subject, Louis VII (b. 1120), and the second is the author, Odo of Deuil (1110–62). Louis ruled as king of France from 1137 to 1180 and was an object of considerable interest to the great abbot, royal biographer, and royal propagandist, Suger of Saint-Denis (c. 1081–1151), Odo's patron. During his reign there was much friction between him and the king of England, Henry II (1133–89), who rarely allowed an opportunity to pass that would increase his power and influence at the expense of Louis. It did not help that Louis's first marriage, to the great heiress Eleanor of Aquitaine (1122–1204), was not a success and that she then married Henry. Louis is generally considered to have been a devout man, better suited to a career in the clergy or, perhaps better, to a life of monastic virtue. However, in the work of Odo, as we shall see below, we encounter him just before and during his crusade in a slightly different light, as a transitional figure in the history of religious expression and emotional response.

Odo of Deuil was a protégé of Suger, ultimately his successor as abbot of the great monastic house at Saint-Denis (outside Paris) and royal chaplain. We are exceptionally fortunate that he wrote an account of the crusade for Suger. It is a work of medium length — about 75 pages in a modern edition — dedicated to chronicling the Second Crusade. He attempts to explain what happened and why, and he makes Louis a central figure: heroic, self-sacrificing, a model of both policy and action. It was probably written in 1148 and does not contain the final episodes of the crusade. Odo writes at sufficient length that we can form not only the image that he had of his monarch, but we can also see Odo himself, and even more, we can measure the distance between the two as we march along with them from Paris to the Damascus road. And that is why it is such a wonderful work from which to learn.

Odo's text, *The Journey of Louis VII to the East* (hereafter, *De profectione*), sits neatly between the late eleventh-century *The Song of Roland* (discussed above in Chapter 12) and Jean de Joinville's early fourteenth-century *Life of Saint Louis* (discussed below in Chapter 22). There is, from a generation back into the past, a hero too proud to blow his own horn. A few generations into the future, there is a hero who wishes to imitate Jesus while counseling the killing of Jews. From another perspective, 20 years earlier, in his *Murder of Charles the Good*, Galbert of Bruges (see Chapter 13 above) finds it necessary to explain just why, according to God's plan, the bewildering kaleidoscope of deeds he witnesses really did make sense; Odo will try to perform the same task, but he will fail. Odo, a very conventional man, feels far more comfortable with the swirl of ceremonial as Louis takes his leave of Saint-Denis than he does waiting for his monarch outside a leprosarium (5).

But in whatever niche the *De profectione* sits, we have a choice of direction from which to study it. We could look back at it from the fourteenth century, in which case Odo's talk of failed markets, supply and demand, and his concern to avoid unhealthy water places him just before things get really interesting and quantifiable economic history becomes possible. Moving forward from the early Middle Ages, however, Odo's account appears one of the jewels of the twelfth-century renaissance, a text in which personality, the distance between Odo and Louis as individuals, and a changing religiosity come to the fore and suggest that a new world has taken shape. Whereas in *Roland* the last pages contain a debate about how to try the traitor Ganelon and, more generally, how to obtain justice, in Odo's account there is little doubt about how justice ought to proceed (37–39). For those whose hearts lie in the thirteenth century, this work is a wonderful bud not yet ready to flower, a truly transitional work, a work in movement, first, from Paris to Palestine, and second, from the king as Caesar to the monarch as Jesus. Odo puts it rather differently; taking the conventional view, he sees the Second Crusade as a failure: "the flowers of France withered before they could bear fruit in Damascus" (119).

One of the most interesting aspects of Odo's text is the plain difference between author and subject. When readers open Einhard's ninth-century *Life of Charles the Great* (see Chapter 9 above) and look at his Charles, they see almost immediately the narrow distance between ruler and author.

Einhard goes to great lengths to show this distance to the reader, not least with the use of material from Suetonius. But at the same time Einhard does not express wonder or bewilderment at his patron. While he is clear about the greatness of the emperor, he is also clear about his understanding of those qualities: he does not find it odd that Charlemagne should be irritated at Leo III after the imperial coronation on Christmas in 800 (28). It seems in character for Charlemagne to act thus. In *Roland,* there is a famous discussion between the hero and his comrade Oliver about the advisability of blowing the horn to recall Charlemagne and the rest of the army: Oliver thinks it wise; Roland thinks it unmanly. The poets who established the text (c. 1095) feel comfortable with both sides of the argument between Roland and Oliver, a tension that makes the text even more interesting as witness to a sense of a set of practices in flux. We might make a similar argument that the fascinating discussion at the end about how to judge and punish Ganelon, to which I have already alluded, represents a tension between competing views of loyalty and obligation. In other words, although these texts are quite different from one another, their creators seem to be in sympathy with or, at least, to understand and appreciate the motivations of the figures they craft in their writing.

Despite their apparent closeness, Odo has no such understanding of his principal figure. Let us return to Louis in the late spring of 1147, at the beginning of the crusade: "Upon setting out, he did a praiseworthy thing, which few, perhaps no one of his lofty rank, could imitate; for, first having visited some monks in Paris, he went outside the gates to the leper colony. There I myself saw him enter, with only two companions, and shut out the rest of his great retinue for a long time. Meanwhile his mother and his wife and countless others went ahead to Saint-Denis" (17). Odo does not understand just what is going on, nor does he understand why, even though he considers it noteworthy. A king visiting a leper colony is, to him, out of place and beyond his understanding. He notes it as anomalous but shows no curiosity as to its meaning. He describes what happened but does not attempt to describe it fully, perhaps because he may not know what the significant parts of such a description would contain. Looking back from the early fourteenth century, Joinville is able to describe what Louis IX does in the middle of the thirteenth century. And he can fit it into a better understanding of what those acts mean and just why they comprise greatness. Joinville has no hesitation in pointing out Louis IX's imitations of Jesus and he lets us know what they mean, even when he finds them acts of which he is incapable. When Louis IX asks Joinville whether he washed the feet of the poor on Maundy Thursday (the Thursday before Easter), Joinville responds, "I will never wash the feet of such lowly fellows." Louis reminds him not to scorn an act that Jesus had performed (169). Joinville does not miss opportunities to drive home the point, even pointing out that Louis's death occurred at the same hour as that of Jesus (349).

Odo, however, who was the king's chaplain, recounts but does not understand. He simply cannot comprehend the spirituality of Louis VII, a spirituality that, set against that found in the later works of Joinville or William of Rubruck (see Chapter 20 below), is moving in the direction of that imitation of Jesus to which, in various degrees, many thirteenth-century figures after Saint Francis (1181–1226) aspire. This distance between author and subject is a wonderful thing for readers who seek to understand just what it means to see through a glass darkly. What I mean here is that, as one reads a textbook—and many history textbooks are written to be memorized rather than to be puzzled through—one receives a clear image of the characters, great and humble. In this particular chronicle we can watch Odo watching Louis, sometimes knowing his man, sometimes puzzled. At the end, for example, Odo is sad, overcome in fact, both conscious of failure and willing to apportion blame. He does not show us a Louis VII for whom, or so it seems from Odo, the act of crusading was itself sufficient reward (119, 143).

But Odo is not incapable of understanding. Indeed, there are within his text other figures, also conventional, whom he understands very well indeed. Chief among these is Godfrey de la Roche, the bishop of Langres (1138–62/63), who was an original monk of the Cistercian house of Clairvaux. Odo very much appreciates Godfrey. The bishop is "pious and spirited" and, later, the possessor of "wise intellect and saintly piety" (27, 69). But he seems more like Archbishop Turpin of *Roland,* who bade the warriors to kill as penance, who was himself a successful warrior, and who counseled those who did not have the stomach for killing to become a monk (89, 126, 141). For those who prefer their bishops to be monks rather than the lawyers they would be in the thirteenth century, Godfrey is a nice piece of work. He is in favor of punishing the Byzantines by seizing their lands and their great city of Constantinople (59, 69). This is not a momentary inspiration. The bishop of Langres has a plan. He has noticed that the land walls of the city are weak, and some of them in poor repair. Moreover, he suggests that the supply of fresh water could be cut with ease.

Furthermore, the conquest of Constantinople would lead to the capitulation of the other communities of the Byzantine Empire.

It is in the midst of his reverie that Odo praises his "saintly piety," which he illustrates by attempting to quote Godfrey's justification, which is that the Byzantine emperor Manuel was installing Greek Orthodox prelates in those parts of southeast Anatolia and northwest Syria over which he had gained control. Odo is in agreement about the perfidy of the Byzantines. Godfrey's suggestion, in his view, is only doing God's work. We wonder whether Aelred of Rievaulx (1110–67) or Bernard or any of the representatives of the newer, more self-searching monks of the generation after the founding of the Cistercians would have agreed. I suggest that Odo's piety was more formal than self-examined and that this concern for outward form helps us to understand the one moment of generosity he shows toward the Byzantines, when he describes the ceremonial of the feast of Saint Denis as celebrated in Constantinople (69).

When we weigh the representation of the bishop of Langres against Louis VII, we see the developing forms of religiosity in the middle of the twelfth century just as, in the judgment of Ganelon, we can see the different definitions of justice with which the audience was experimenting at the end of the eleventh century. Perhaps it can be put another way. From the eleventh through the twelfth century, Jesus appears more and more human, less and less distant in crucifixion imagery. Or, if we look at the means by which thoughtful men and women sought to learn about God, there seems to be a movement across the twelfth century toward a time when the journey to know Him is an inner one, a Platonic voyage of abstraction that can be taken while seated in a darkened room. Louis VII seems unaffected by the failure of the crusade, and perhaps he is moving in the direction of a faith that is less externalized. We do not see him among the lepers; a generation earlier, Galbert's Charles the Good (d. 1127) presents pennies to the poor without eye contact, in a ceremony to be seen but perhaps not felt (3). It is this sense of flux that the *De profectione* illustrates so well.

And it is flux not only in the ebb and flow of sentiment. The Second Crusade shows us a society, an army, a government on the march. Some of the crusaders lead; some of them lag. They find it difficult to preserve their customs, so they form and reform them in response to changing circumstances. As Odo remarks, "[Louis] enacted laws necessary for securing peace and other requirements on the journey, which the leaders confirmed by solemn oath. But because they did not observe them well, I have not preserved them either" (21). Some of the knights, many of the knights, end up on foot, bereft of the horse that is their mark of status and wealth. Each day on the march forces consideration of a different solution to the problem of food. Is there a market? What are the prices? Is it possible to forage? Is it legitimate to take what they find? If the pickings are slim or the prices high, what does that mean (97)? Who is responsible? Odo takes delight in blaming the Byzantine emperor for failures far beyond his central control, even though he sees how difficult it is for the crusaders to keep themselves in good order over a much shorter distance (87, 109, 113). Sometimes without guides, sometimes with guides they do not trust, sometimes without a clear sense of direction, the army moves across Anatolia in ways that defy modern attempts to plot their path on a map (87, 91). Further, they travel in winter, which forces them closer together and renders them easier prey. Odo makes plain the difficulty of organizing a moving society, and he highlights the breakdown of traditional, settled forms when he brings in officials of the Templars, a military religious order dedicated to ensuring the safety of the persons and goods of pilgrims to the Holy Land, to put things right again towards the end of the debacle (125).

All this affects Louis, but we do not see him as we see the German emperor, full of anger, confusion, and self-pity at his first attempt to force his way across the Asia Minor peninsula (99–101). In fact, Louis is remarkably less predictable than most of the other players whom Odo has established for us — and here is another contrast with the parties whom Galbert describes 20 years earlier. He is Odo's hero, but he is not at his best in Odo's mind until the end, having come through the terrible ordeal still decent and caring. This is a man with whom Odo may sympathize. But he struggles to understand that a court on the march is not a court such as the one, say, Joinville conceives a century later, with his king sitting beneath a leafy oak to dispense justice in a garden (177). The broken, surprising landscape of Pisidia (115, 117) becomes much like the unexpected behavior of Louis, for whom the unfinished journey seems a personal success, a testament to a religiosity far in advance of his biographer.

Success matters to Odo. Success fortifies his attachment to ways of thinking and to conventions not unlike those we glimpse in *Roland*: trial by combat ends with the just man winning; God displays the right through military victory; and the right side wins. Odo knows how to ring the changes and is familiar and comfortable with all of *Roland*'s clichés. The distance between him and his king is therefore most stark when Odo must deal with defeat and failure. Louis VII saw the crusade as a pilgrimage, with the suffering, defeat, and humiliation as a part, perhaps a necessary part, of taking on the burden. From early on, the image he has before him is that of a pilgrim, and even when the responsibilities of a pilgrim differ from those of a shrewd ruler, we can see him privilege the impulse to act as a pilgrim above all else. This is the real point of the story of Boris, the pretender to the throne of Hungary: "Our king said that the king of Hungary was his friend, but, nevertheless, that he must not do on behalf of the king anything which ill became a pilgrim" (37–39). Odo needs to find another way to explain what happened to the crusaders, and the perfidy of the Byzantines gives him (and others) a superb way out of his dilemma.

Odo will not have much of this. He thinks in terms of an older concept, still well maintained, the concept of vengeance: "Let no one think that I am taking vengeance on a race of men hateful to me and that because of my hatred I am inventing a Greek whom I have not seen" (57). He understands retribution well, and when he tells stories of crusaders who misbehave or of people who misbehave while in their cups, he understands perfectly well the ways in which they receive their just deserts (75). Joinville's Louis IX will wrestle with this problem on his own crusade. However, in this work, as in that of Galbert, vengeance is an integral part of justice. But whereas Galbert sees it all as part, if necessarily a convoluted part, of God's plan and therefore must make sense — thus, Galbert explains inconsistencies away — Odo looks as well to the future for justification and judgment from above. This may explain in part why his work appears to break off *in medias res* in the Holy Land before the end and return to France.

We might ask whether what we have is an incomplete work that would have received further editing (although Odo lived for more than a decade after the return to France). For someone who has read the lengthy descriptions in Joinville, who describes grain sprouting from mounds of wheat and the golden amphorae at the court of the Sultan of Turkey (197, 199), or William of Rubruck, who takes the trouble to measure the length of the axle of a Mongol cart in the account of his journey east (2), Odo's descriptions of place and person seem spare and unsatisfactory. However, he does not seem to see the world as worth detailing in and for itself. He has little to tell us about Queen Eleanor, and in fact this is a work in which the world is populated by males. After mentioning that the Byzantine empress wrote to Eleanor, Odo immediately comments that "then the Greeks degenerated entirely into women" (57). Eleanor of Aquitaine serves here not as a person but as a point of departure.

As I have noted, we do not learn very much about the men's appearance. We know that the Turks are archers, but we do not know what any of them looks like. Nor do we learn much about the appearance of the Byzantines, except insofar as the Byzantine emperor becomes something of an "icon" himself in the telling of the story. We learn none of the detail about personal appearance that William of Rubruck recounts in the thirteenth century. So we learn what the Turks do and what the Byzantines do, but we learn no more about the persons themselves. Odo does not comprehend a Louis VII, but instead he relies on detailing what he does; he may call someone great, while he may also be at a loss at explaining wherein that greatness lies. This is a very far cry from the account of Rubruck. Rubruck does not understand the Great Khan, but he plays with his descriptions of the khan and of the others with whom he has continuing contact, looking for an explanation, seeking understanding, much as he lets his reader know his understanding of the workings of the Mongol cart or the way in which *cosmos* (mare's milk) derives its kick. In short, Odo paints the outlines of a picture without throwing a bright light everywhere as a modern reader might like. His landscapes and personalities are drawn without relief or cross-hatching, perhaps to remind him of their full impact, perhaps to spare the reader everything but what Odo feels is crucial to his understanding. In any case, we are left to wonder whether Louis VII's crusade is more akin to Beowulf's (much earlier) expedition to fight Grendel rather than William of Rubruck's travels to Mongolia.[1]

If we take the *Song of Roland* and Joinville's *Life of Saint Louis* — or, for that matter, other works separated by Odo's generation — as boundary markers, this is a transitional work. The bishop of Langres is the person whom Odo understands best. On the other hand, he struggles to describe Bishop Arnulf of Lisieux (1141–81). Arnulf was not only an early champion of Gothic architecture in northern France, but he was also papal legate to the crusade and later proved his prowess as conciliator when he arranged for Thomas Becket's safe return to England during the archbishop of

---

[1] I owe this comparison to Professor Richard Helmholz, who suggested it as an examination question when we taught under Professor Brentano, and I confess that I have used it mercilessly ever since.

Canterbury's deadly quarrel with Henry II. When Arnulf went to negotiate with the Byzantine Emperor Manuel, Odo saw his success as that of
one who charms the poisonous adder (75, 77). And Louis VII is something of a mystery. For Odo, military victory is necessary and should be
pre-ordained. For Louis, the act of pilgrimage, the suffering and depriva-
tion, is sufficient unto itself. It is no wonder that this work was not widely
copied, and only one manuscript is known; the manuscript contains
a number of other works as well, all of which exist in multiple copies
(xxxv–vii). The person who should be the hero becomes a person for
whom heroism is a thing apart, or at least he does not act as the hero did
during the preceding century — he is not the William the Conqueror
(d. 1086) that William of Poitiers (fl. 1070s) so exalted (see chapter 11); he
is no Roland. We are at the beginning of a transition to a world in which
there is more color, more flashy clothing, and items described in loving
detail, items for which a reader may have no use — for instance, William of
Rubruck's ideas about Mongolian cuisine (2). We cannot know for sure
whether Louis VII really saw himself as an imitation of Jesus, but as we
approach texts of a century later, we should not be surprised at such an
imitation. Louis's strength lies in what he does not show us, what is left to be
wondered at, what is left unsaid, rather than those crusaders for whom the
display of might and power are crucial. For Louis, as we see once he comes to
Antalya on the south coast of Anatolia, the goal is not victory, or even survival, but penitence and trial (131). This is a different kind of power.

The *De profectione* is not an easy book from which to derive lessons.
The descriptions are so bland, the expressions so conventional, that it is
easy to glide over what is happening, what is being expressed, what is being
misunderstood. It is not as obviously rich a text as *Roland* or Joinville's *Life
of Saint Louis*. But the figures lurking in the background are significant,
and some of them deserve close attention, such as the bishop of Langres
and Arnulf of Lisieux. They help us to think about what a reforming
church would look like and, with them in mind, offer us a precious view of
Bernard, whose words are quintessentially agricultural in Odo: sermoniz-
ing in the field outside Vezelay, his words fertilizing the expected rush of
crusaders and watering the seed with his own exhortations (9). So this is a
good book from which to take quick brush-stroke pictures of a number of
supporting players.

It is practically impossible to form a picture of Louis VII without thinking in terms of the thirteenth century and the desire to walk in Jesus's foot-

steps so common in it. Louis VII is not quite there yet: he does not appear to have the curiosity of a Rubruck. At the same time, he is far different from the nobles who went on the First Crusade, and that is very important. There is danger in thinking that Louis VII leans solely in the direction of Rubruck or Louis IX. It is Odo—and, in his own way, Joinville—who gives us pause, who allows us to see the paths crossing in different directions, one conventional, the other not. In fact, we might cease to beg the question and ask what is "conventional" about Odo, and to compare him more directly with such figures as Galbert and Charles the Good. After all, it does appear that there were more men like Odo than like Louis on the march up country in 1146.

Finally, the reader may ask how Suger, to whom *De profectione* is dedicated—and thus the intended reader of the account?—might respond to the various pieces of it. What would surprise him? What would he expect? How would he feel about the defeats? How would he respond to the account of Byzantine perfidy? And how would he feel about the ironic qualities that Louis displays throughout the account? We do not and cannot know. But there is perhaps something to be said for the notion that the work survives not in a Saint-Denis manuscript but in a manuscript put together at Clairvaux. Louis VII was perhaps not the hero that Suger had in mind when he himself wrote the life of his father, Louis VI. Perhaps it was for this reason that Odo never went back to revise or complete the account.

Odo's book is not a complete work about a complete historical figure, nor is the author someone who stands out elsewhere in the twelfth-century tapestry. At the same time, the book seems to be about movement and effort, not only on crusade, but movement from one sort of leadership to another, from one sort of vantage point to another, from men standing puzzled outside a leprosarium to flowers yet to bear fruit. I have found it an acquired taste.

Bibliographic Note

The sole English translation of Odo's work is *De profectione Ludovici VII in orientem,* ed. and trans. Virginia Gingerick Berry (New York: Columbia University Press, 1948). For other readings that go along with this book, Richard Southern, *The Making of the Middle Ages* (New Haven: Yale University Press, 1953) is central, although it demands a very good humanistic education of its readers. To see how historians worked with material during the past century, it is useful to look at sculptural programs at

Romanesque churches and compare them as narratives with Odo. In particular, the program at Autun is a good place to start, on which see Linda Seidel, *Legends in Limestone* (Chicago: University of Chicago Press, 1999). On Odo himself the best work is Jonathan Phillips, "Odo of Deuil's *De profectione Ludovici VII in orientem* as a Source for the Second Crusade," in *The Experience of Crusading*, eds. Marcus Bull and Norman Housley (Cambridge: Cambridge University Press, 2003), 1: 80–95. On the Second Crusade, there is only one thorough study: Jonathan Phillips, *The Second Crusade* (New Haven: Yale University Press, 2007). For a general history of the crusades, the latest big book is Christopher Tyerman, *God's War* (Cambridge, MA: Harvard University Press, 2006). On the wider world of the twelfth-century renaissance, there is still much to savor in the very accessible (and avuncular) volume of Charles Homer Haskins, *The Renaissance of the Twelfth Century* (Cambridge, MA: Harvard University Press, 1927); and Colin Morris, *The Discovery of the Individual 1050–1200* (London: SPCK, 1972). See also the more recent R.N. Swanson, *The Twelfth-Century Renaissance* (Manchester: Manchester University Press, 1999); and R.I. Moore, *The First European Revolution, c. 970–1215* (Oxford: Blackwell, 2000).

FIFTEEN

Encountering the Cid

Helen Nader

The *Poema de Mío Cid* is a masterpiece of European literature. It is the oldest poem in the Spanish language, and for many Spaniards — especially Castilians — it is the finest, not only as poetry but also as national history. The poem lauds the deeds of a real person, Rodrigo (Ruy, for short) Díaz de Vivar, whose vassals called him *Mío Cid* (my lord). Because of his youthful success in battle, his contemporaries also called him *el Campeador* (the warrior or battler). To the degree that *The Cid* records the deeds of a great hero who is a faithful vassal of his king, like the *Song of Roland* (discussed in Chapter 12 above), it belongs to the category of *chansons de geste*. Since it can in many ways be compared with *Roland*, let us touch here lightly on *The Cid* as epic.

The Cid joins together two different stories. In the first half of the poem, called "The Exile," *The Cid*, like the *Aeneid*, is a comeback epic. Before the poem begins, King Alfonso VI (1040–1109) exiles the Cid and his family from the Kingdom of Castile, leaving them without a home, income, or security. The Cid must make a living by looting Muslim towns (20–54). Never defeated in battle, he accumulates booty and, the greatest prize of all, the Muslim city of Valencia (64–76). Finally rich again, the Cid reconciles with his king (82). So, in a sense, *The Cid* is that most appealing of all plots, a rags to riches story.

The second story, called "The Outrage at Corpes," links *The Cid* to such themes in *Roland* as the family quarrel, the vengeance brought about by the quarrel, and the assembly. After the Cid is pardoned and welcomed back by Alfonso, the king marries the Cid's daughters, Elvira and Sol, to the Infantes (heirs) of Carrión, allies of the Cid's old enemy (102–11). These two young men show themselves to be cowards when confronted by a lion (102), and to avenge their public humiliation they beat their wives and abandon them in the oak forest of Corpes (128–30). Though the women are rescued by one of the Cid's men (131), the Cid seeks vengeance. King Alfonso calls his vassals to sit as a court of justice in the city of Toledo (133). The assembly and the king decide that the Infantes should go through trial by combat. The Cid's champions win the combats, and Elvira and Sol marry the kings of Navarre and Aragon (149).

The Spanish poet also employs literary conventions used in *Roland*. The most frequent is the epic epithet: "he who girt on his sword in a lucky hour," "the excellent Battler," or "he who in a lucky hour was born." *The Cid's* poetic unit is the single line of verse that has a sharp break, or two half-lines. Modern editors have grouped *The Cid's* 3,730 lines into 152 stanzas or laisses of varying size. In contrast to the quite strict beat of French epic poems with four syllables to the half-line—in *Roland*, occasionally six— the Spanish poem has an irregular beat in which each half-line may have as few as four syllables or as many as 14. When the poem was sung, only an expert musician could overcome the difficulty of such a wide variety of beats.

The lines within each laisse usually have the same assonating, accented next-to-the-last syllable, but the assonances are less strictly observed than in the French poems. Sometimes their irregularity appears to serve a poetic function by heightening a moment of particular emotion or excite- ment. There are frequent and striking changes of tense in a single line. All of these irregularities help to avoid monotony and to make *The Cid* much less somber than *Roland*. To hear the beats and assonances, try saying the first lines out loud:

> De los sos ojos tan fuertemiento llorando,
> tornava la cabeça e estávalos catando;
> vio puertas abiertas e uços sin cañados,
> alcándaras vazías, sin pielles e sin mantos
> e sin falcones e sin adtores mudados.[1] (Michael 1.1–5)

---

[1] Translated by Rita Hamilton and Janet Perry as "Tears streamed from his eyes as he turned his head and stood looking at them. He saw doors left open and gates unlocked, empty pegs without fur tunics or cloaks, perches without falcons or moulted hawks." *The Poem of the Cid: A Bilingual Edition with Parallel Text* (Harmonds- worth: Penguin Books, 1984), 23.

These opening lines give a taste of one of the most important features of The Cid — its striking images. These are almost always of a physical nature. A literal translation of the first two lines, "Eyes crying copiously he turned his head," sounds awkward in English but provides a powerful image in Spanish. At other places, the poet speaks of "mouth speaking" and "eyes gazing." The Cid's physicality poses difficult problems for translators, who must choose between literal or poetic equivalents. Look, for example, at the Cid's physicality in laisse 4 and how two translators choose different ways to express body action: "Aguijó Mio Cid, a la puerta se llegava, / sacó el pie del estribera, una ferídal' dava" (Michael 4.35–36): "The Cid spurred his horse, rode up to the door and, drawing his foot from the stirrup, gave it a kick" (Hamilton); or the more muscular "Mio Cid dug in his spurs, raced up to the door, pulled one foot out of the stirrup and gave it a helluva kick" (Blackburn). This physicality adds verve to action scenes and intensifies emotions. When the Cid says goodbye to his wife and daughters, for example, their emotional pain is as vivid as a wound. "Llorando de los ojos que non viestes atal, /assís' parten unos d'otros como la uña de la carne" (Michael 8.374–75): "Weeping bitterly, they parted with such pain / as when the finger-nail is torn from the flesh" (Hamilton).

A feature that still delights Spanish readers are the jokes. When the Cid releases Count Ramón, he says "Ya vos ides, conde, a guisa de muy franco" (Michael 62.1068). In Spanish, this is a pun on the word *franco* (free); the Cid frees the count, who is a franco (Frank). The pun does not exist in English, so translators have to use two different words, and the joke is lost: "Now, be off with you, Count, frank and free" (Blackburn 56); "You are off now … like the free Frank you are" (Hamilton 79); "You are leaving us, count … free as a Frank" (Simpson 44)!

Whether The Cid was composed only for oral performance before an audience or ever sung in its entirety are matters of debate. Some of its formal features seem to lend themselves to song or oral performance. In the Middle Ages the copyist divided the poem into three sections, which suggests that the whole poem was too long for a single performance. Each section was labeled a *cantar* (song). The *cantares* do not start or end at natural breaks in the story. For example, "The Outrage at Corpes" begins about halfway through Cantar Two. This technique of introducing a new story before the end of the first one may serve the poetic purpose of enticing the listener to come back for the performance of the next cantar.

We do not know the exact identity of the composer of *The Cid*. Like the author of *Roland*, the Spanish poet employs both learned and popular language. The poet carried out some research in chronicles and official documents and uses their legal and formal language, as well as some historical information. There are phrases of legal or ecclesiastical origin and phrases with Latin grammatical construction. This raises many questions — and debates — about the author and his setting. Some scholars argue that only the clergy were literate and knew Latin and, therefore, that the author of *The Cid* must have been a priest.

Certain events in the life of the historic Cid suggest the possibility that the poet could have been a layman. Many people, though not the majority, had experience with legal documents in medieval Castile. The historic Cid himself was literate and, during the periods when he served as a member of the king's retinue, he signed as a witness to royal decrees and other legal documents, all of them in Latin. In fact, by some miracle, one of the Cid's own documents has survived; shortly before he and Jimena married, Rodrigo signed a contract in which he gave her an *arras,* a bride gift, of 27 properties. Another argument in favor of a lay poet comes from the nature of clerical writing in medieval Spain. The chronicles composed by priests have two distinctive characteristics: they are written in Latin and they present the Reconquest — that is, Christian efforts to retake Iberia from the Muslims from the early eighth century forward — as a religious crusade. Laymen who actually fought the battles also wrote chronicles in the vernacular and interpreted the Reconquest as a war for profit.

Whether he be priest or layman, many places claim to be the home of this poet. The Benedictine monastery near Burgos, San Pedro de Cardeña, where the historic Cid was buried, claimed that one of their monks composed the poem. During the twelfth and thirteenth centuries, this monastery carried on a profitable business from tourists, many of them pilgrims who made a detour to visit the Cid's tomb. The monks "discovered" several relics of the Cid and sponsored re-enactments of the Cid's battles and performances of the many Cidian ballads that flourished after his death.

In contrast to our lack of evidence about the poet's occupation and identity, the poet's geographical origin is well known from evidence within the poem. Scholars point to the poet's knowledge of geography to identify his hometown. On this evidence, he was from the town of Medinaceli. One thing is certain: he was a Castilian. His dialect, his geographical knowledge, and his preference for Castilian subjects all identify his nationality. The classic explanation of how *The Cid* was composed derives from the monumental studies of a Spanish philologist, Ramón Menéndez Pidal. A short Latin poem composed during the Cid's lifetime, the *Carmen Campi Doctoris,* celebrated the Cid's victory over Ramón, Count of Barcelona.[2] According to Menéndez Pidal, from that point on many authors composed short vernacular songs or ballads while the events were still fresh in the public consciousness during the 50 years after the real Cid's death in 1099. As they sang the poems, *juglares* (male performers) and *juglaresas* (female performers) introduced revisions, improvements, repetitions, and additions. By 1140, according to Menéndez Pidal, these ballads coalesced into one long song, *The Poem of the Cid,* sometimes called *Cantar de Mío Cid* (*The Song of the Cid*). Menéndez Pidal also believed that, at the end of the· twelfth century, a single *juglar* knew the entire poem by heart and sang it to a clerk, who wrote it down for the first time. In May 1307, a man who signed himself as Per Abbat finished copying that now-lost manuscript. Per Abbat's parchment copy, the sole surviving manuscript, was preserved in the town hall of the Cid's home town of Vivar.

Recently, scholars have proposed an alternative method of composition and chronology, one that dates the poem's composition later and Per Abbat's manuscript earlier. Instead of many authors, they believe that there was one and that he wrote it down himself. They reject Menéndez Pidal's dating based on language because, they believe, the poet deliberately used language already antiquated in his own lifetime, a fairly common poetic technique (a similar technique was followed by W.S. Merwin in his English verse translation of *The Cid*). They have concluded that the poem could not have been composed before 1201. This date is based on a literal reading of lines 3724–25 of laisse 152 where the poet tells us that "today the kings of Spain are related to him." The Cid's descendants did not become kings until 1201. In contrast to Menéndez Pidal, most scholars now believe that Per Abbat made his copy in May 1207, not 1307. This narrows the time frame of the oral composition to the years between 1201 and 1207.

Menéndez Pidal, working directly from the Per Abbat parchment, which is now in the Biblioteca Nacional of Madrid, established a much more complete and accurate transcription of the manuscript than any published before. His text remains the starting point for all subsequent editions and translations of the poem. Ian Michael began with Menéndez Pidal's text and then took advantage of scientific technology to read the

---

[2] Roger Wright, "The First Poem on the Cid — the *Carmen Campi Doctoris,*" *Papers of the Liverpool Latin Seminar* 2 (1979): 213–48.

parchment manuscript under ultra-violet light to give us the finest edition yet of *The Poem of the Cid.*

These textual misadventures did not keep the Cid's deeds from being known. Although Per Abbat's manuscript lay almost forgotten in the Vivar town archives, the Cid's story remained popular and well known from other medieval ballads and chronicles. According to Menéndez Pidal, medieval Spaniards considered the Cid a model hero and composed numerous popular ballads, legends, and other tales elaborating his story until the historical Cid became completely obscured by this fanciful literature. For example, many towns and cities in central Iberia proudly claimed that they had been conquered by the Cid. In most cases, they based their claims on the ballads about the Cid's youthful battles; they accepted the Cidian ballads as history.

Menéndez Pidal determined to rescue the real Cid from these fables. Over the course of a 30-year quest to find the historic Cid, he found documents in church and town archives, read manuscript chronicles written in the Middle Ages, and bit by bit tore away much of the accumulated fantasy that for centuries had obscured the real Rodrigo Díaz de Vivar. His research culminated in the publication of his masterpiece, *La España del Cid,* which offered a new interpretation of medieval Spain. It has superseded all the Cidian ballads as a source for the Cid's story.

Menéndez Pidal succeeded in establishing which parts of the poem were or were not historical. In "The Exile," the first half of the poem, the incident with the Jewish moneylenders has no basis in reality, and as a financial transaction it makes no sense (8–11). The poet probably uses the two moneylenders to show the fate of those who doubt the Cid's innocence; the Jews believe that the Cid, though unjustly accused, is guilty. The Cid, therefore, is free to trick them. The rest of "The Exile" does have an historical basis in the life of the historical Cid, though the poet took liberties to achieve his own purposes.

None of the second story, "The Outrage at Corpes," has any basis in a past reality. The historic Cid's daughters, in reality named Cristina and María, married a prince and a count, not kings. There were no Infantes of Carrión, no first marriage, and no outrage at Corpes. As literature, however, the story contains some of the highlights of the Spanish language, such as the spectacular insults exchanged during the assembly and the gory details of the trials by combat.

Menéndez Pidal lived during a period of history that devastated the self-image of Spaniards. He began his quest for the historical Cid after the humiliating loss of the last bits of the Spanish Empire when the United States had needed only three months (June–August 1898) to conquer Cuba and the Philippines in the Spanish-American War. Spain was left weak and discredited, and Menéndez Pidal's generation of intellectuals— called "the generation of '98"—longed for a national hero and a heroic past to restore Spanish pride. In Menéndez Pidal's hands, the Cid became that hero, and the medieval Reconquest became Spain's heroic past. We must therefore be alert to this national bias if we use *The Cid* as a source.

For Menéndez Pidal, the Cid symbolized Castile, a new, dynamically expanding kingdom that led the Iberian Peninsula into the mainstream of European Christian society. As a frontier kingdom, Castile needed and rewarded men of merit who could contribute military and economic leadership in the Reconquest of Muslim Spain. As a result Castilians were more democratic, more innovative, more open to diversity than the older, more conservative Kingdom of León from which Castile had sprung. The frontier society encouraged social mobility, with men of ability and proven success moving up the social and economic ladders until they achieved the status of royal vassals. Even Alfonso VI shed his Leonese conservatism after he became king of Castile in 1072 and introduced change; a great admirer of all things French, the king brought Cluniac monks from France to reform the Spanish Church along the lines proposed by Pope Gregory VII in the eleventh century and suppressed the traditional hispanic liturgy and priests. The king also married a daughter of the Duke of Burgundy and gave high positions to Burgundian knights who married two of his daughters. With these French priests and knights came a cultural integration of Castile into the wider European currents of religion, art, and song. In short, Pidal's Spain of the Cid displayed the virtues and strengths that "the generation of '98" needed.

For British scholars, *The Cid* has been a favorite subject of study ever since 1808, when an English army under the command of Arthur Wellesley (the future Duke of Wellington) occupied Portugal to "liberate" Spain from the French forces of Napoleon Bonaparte. While we are fortunate to have the extraordinary research and analysis of British authors writing today about *The Cid*, we must also take their biases into account. Richard Fletcher has a gift for turning scholarship into lively expeditions into the unknown. Fletcher and most other twentieth-century British scholars have seen medieval Castile as a society dominated by class conflict. Rodrigo's Castilian enemies hate him because he is an upstart acting as an aristocrat, when he is actually an overly ambitious lower-class knight of undistinguished origins (maybe even a bastard!). British authors have developed some unflattering descriptions of the Cid: "that unpleasant mercenary thug," and "this unsavory character"; his vassals have been called "a gang of thugs."[3] In his own work, Fletcher deftly targets the Christian and Muslim documentary evidence to give us a medieval Castile that is reactive—responding to outside stimuli from the Arabs rather than innovating through its own national genius.

In the Cid's lifetime, the military situation in Iberia changed suddenly. For almost a century, al-Andalus (Muslim Spain) had no central government; each Muslim city was an independent kingdom, called a *taifa*. The *taifa* kings fought each other as often as they fought Christians, and this enabled the Christian kings of León and Castile to intimidate them into paying tribute in exchange for peace. This situation seemed intolerable to Muslim religious reformers in northwest Africa, particularly after Alfonso VI of Castile conquered the Muslim city of Toledo in 1085. In June 1086, the Almoravid ruler, Yusuf ibn Tashufin, came to al-Andalus from Africa at the request of the *taifa* king of Seville, who could no longer tolerate Alfonso's demands for tribute. In October, the Almoravids inflicted a disastrous defeat on Alfonso (Battle of Sagrajas), and a few months later Alfonso restored the Cid to his favor. In 1089, he exiled the Cid again, this time for not joining the royal forces on time in a battle against the Almoravids. The relationship between Alfonso and the Cid, in other words, developed in relation to the actions of the Muslims.

For Fletcher, this suddenly disastrous series of Castilian defeats also explains who wrote *The Cid* and why. He argues that the poem had a single author who composed it as a call for unity after the Almoravids soundly defeated the Christians at the battle of Alarcos in 1195. In view of this historical setting, Fletcher poses this question: "A Cid presented as a Castilian, a Christian and a loyalist, as embodying virtues at once martial and civic, a law-abiding citizen as well as a good family man and a brave soldier, in a poem composed towards the end of the twelfth century, was a Cid who could appeal to—whom?" His answer: the establishment.[4]

Who made up the establishment? For British writers that establishment clearly would have been warriors, the military aristocracy who would be

---

[3] A sharp-witted review by another British historian of medieval Spain, Roger Collins, gathers these insults in *History Today* 52 (2002): 118–19.

[4] Richard Fletcher, *The Quest for El Cid* (London: Hutchinson, 1989), 187–205; quotation from p. 194.

inspired by the battle scenes and by the loot. Traditionally, scholars assume that *juglares* sang *The Cid* in royal and aristocratic courts to knights who were vassals of the king or other lords. That may fit the situation in medieval France, which is sometimes described as comprising three separate but interdependent societies: those who fight (warriors), those who pray (clergy), and those who work (peasants). So it's traditional to think of the *Song of Roland* as sung to knights and their courts. But Castile is different, at least as American historians describe medieval Spain. Americans see the Spain of the Cid as a frontier in which geographical restlessness and social mobility combined to create a classless society. There, all adult males were warriors. Everyone lived in small farm cities and towns, and these municipalities were organized for war. The wars against the Muslims were carried out almost entirely by ordinary farmers and merchants. Every able-bodied male citizen of a city or town belonged to the municipal militia. Each man had to appear at an annual muster in the town square with his battle equipment in good fighting condition. Municipal militias answered the call to battle when the king and his vassals led an expedition to attack a major Muslim city.

Royal campaigns, however, were rare. Most of the fighting between Christians and Muslims took place at the initiative of municipal militias, without reference to or participation by the king. A Christian city council would decide that their citizens needed an infusion of capital, so they would call up the militia and head off to attack a Muslim town — sometimes hundreds of miles away — to acquire booty. They divided up the loot according to strict rules in their municipal ordinances, such as the *Code of Cuenca,* always sending one-fifth to the king. If the poet composed the *Cid* to appeal to warriors, that audience would include every farmer in Castile.

This raises other questions: were the Cid and his men acting like military aristocracy in the poem? Or were they acting like the municipal militias? Royal vassals accompanied the king in battle and in military expeditions against both Christian and Muslim rulers. They safeguarded the king, advised him, and carried out his orders. Is the behavior of the Cid and his vassals that of knights? Or is it the behavior of farmers? Might their looting be a measure of how far they have fallen in social status as a result of having been expelled from their king's service?

Movement permeates the action in the *Cid,* and it reflects the mobility of medieval Spaniards. The hero experiences social mobility, first downward, then upward. He moves spatially almost constantly, covering hundreds of miles through a Spanish landscape dotted with real cities and towns and accurately described in sharp detail by the poet. He rides south through small river valleys to raid Muslim towns, north to the mountains and city of Zaragoza, and southeast to Valencia on the Mediterranean coast. He moves from the cold north of Burgos to the sunny beaches of Valencia.

The Cid, his men, and his wife all pray frequently and thank God for their good fortune. They are pious Christians who frequently call upon God to assist them in their crises and endeavors. Although the Cid has been blessed by God, in the appearance of the angel Gabriel (19), the Castilians do not speak of their military actions as a crusade. They are in this war for the loot; if they killed their prisoners, they would receive no ransom. They plan ahead for this primary objective of their battles. Before attacking Castejón, the Cid instructs his commander of the advance guard to range all through the Manzanares Valley to gather up the spoils (23). The loot that they prize most is war equipment — weapons, armor, saddles, horses, and tents — but they profit most from hard cash in gold coins and from prisoners of war who can be ransomed for cash. The Cid thanks God for making him rich but at no point in the poem does he express religion as his motive for fighting Muslims.

In contrast, the only Frenchman in the poem — the priest Jerome — does perceive the Reconquest as a holy war and says he is fighting a religious crusade. The poet of *The Cid* himself makes this distinction (78). This character is based on an historic French Benedictine monk, Jerome of Perigord, one of many Frenchmen who came to Spain to fight against the Muslims after popes announced a crusade. The historic Cid appointed him as the first bishop of Valencia. After the Cid's death, his wife Jimena ruled the city until King Alfonso VI abandoned Valencia to the Muslims in 1102, and Jerome became bishop of Salamanca.

Other foreigners in *The Cid* do not receive such generous treatment. The Cid tricks the Jews in the first cantar, probably in the tradition of his youthful pranks and insults. Jews in Spain were not citizens of the cities or towns where they lived; only Christians could be citizens. Instead the Jews formed their own community within the city, governed by their rabbi and rabbinic law. They were subjects of the king and under his protection but exempt from royal and city laws. Because they were not subject to the royal cap on interest rates, they could charge much higher interest than Christians. For this reason, they might have more cash on hand than Christian lenders would. Muslims also lived in Christian cities as subjects of the king but with the same laws and judges they had when the city was ruled by a Muslim.

Women frame *The Cid*; they play crucial roles in the opening and closing incidents. A nine-year-old girl speaks for the people of Burgos, explaining to the Cid the citizens' conflicting desires to help him and to save themselves from the king's wrath (4). The welfare and prosperity of the Cid's wife and daughters provide his motive for raiding Muslim towns, especially Alcocer (26–8) and Castejón (23). The Cid's conquest of the city of Valencia is not complete until he brings his wife and daughters to see and enjoy what he has accomplished for them (87). The great trial scene, in which the Cid amazes the onlookers with his physical fierceness and his grasp of complex legal procedure, grows out of his desire to see justice for his daughters (139–45).

Does this emphasis on women and the family reflect some historical reality in the society of Castile in the twelfth and thirteenth centuries? How could an historian investigate this question? An American historian of medieval Spain examined law codes and discovered that women took responsibility for managing the farms, household, and economy during the militiamen's absence on war campaigns.[5] After her husband's death, a Castilian widow continued to possess and manage her own property. An occasional widow on the frontier administered her late husband's government post, just as Jimena governed Valencia after the Cid's death. What does that tell us about the position of women in medieval Castilian society? How do the women in *The Cid* differ from those in *Roland*?

To his contemporaries, the Cid's respect and love for his wife and daughters further enhanced his reputation as a knight. Whether or not he was a faithful vassal of his king is a matter for debate. In fact, King Alfonso VI exiled the historic Cid twice, first from 1081 to 1087 (not mentioned by the poet), then again in 1089, when he charged him with disloyalty. Essentially, by exiling him, Alfonso relieved him of his obligations as a vassal. Being exiled, according to custom, gave Rodrigo the right to earn a living for himself and his followers, to claim authority over whatever territory he conquered, and even to wage war against his former lord.

The Cid never did fight against Alfonso; in fact, he repeatedly sent the king the traditional one-fifth of his spoils even while in exile (100). Furthermore, the Cid is himself a lord of vassals, who voluntarily join him in exile and benefit from his superb military leadership and generosity. For these reasons, the poet tells us "What a good vassal, if only he had a good king" (3).

---

[5] Heath Dillard, *Daughters of the Reconquest: Women in Castilian Town Society, 1100–1300* (Cambridge: Cambridge University Press, 1984).

Bibliographic Note

I draw on several versions of *The Cid* in this essay. For general references to the text I cite merely the appropriate laisses. When I refer to a particular edition or translation, I include the editor or translator along with the particular laisse (and sometimes lines within the laisse) of the poem.

Of the many translations, I prefer *The Poem of the Cid: A Bilingual Edition with Parallel Text* (Harmondsworth: Penguin Books, 1984), with Spanish text by Ian Michael and English prose translation by Rita Hamilton and Janet Perry, or the Lesley Byrd Simpson prose translation *The Poem of The Cid* (Berkeley: University of California Press, 2007). I also appreciate *Poem of the Cid*, ed. Ramón Menéndez Pidal and trans. W.S. Merwin (New York: Meridian, 1959), for its verse translation that captures the rhythm of the original, and the lively translation by Paul Blackburn, *Poem of the Cid: A Modern Translation with Notes* (Norman: University of Oklahoma Press, 1998). A facsimile of the Per Abbat manuscript is available on CD-ROM: *Manuscrito de Per Abbat: Cantar de Mío Cid* (Madrid: Biblioteca Nacional, 1998), as well as in a paper facsimile with the same title.

Studies of the *Cid* are too numerous to list. For an introduction, see Ian Michael, "Spanish Literature and Learning to 1474," in *Spain: A Companion to Spanish Studies*, ed. P.E. Russell (New York: Pitman Publishing, 1973), 200–204. Richard Fletcher, *The Quest for El Cid* (London: Hutchinson, 1989) is entertaining as well as carefully researched. And although most of the work of the great philologist Ramón Menéndez Pidal is in Spanish, English readers are fortunate to have access to Harold Sunderland's translation of his *The Cid and His Spain* (London: Frank Cass, 1934).

SIXTEEN

Wondrous Crusade Encounters
Usamah ibn Munqidh's
Book of Learning by Example
Adnan Husain

Among the most widely appreciated anecdotes about Arab or Muslim experiences of the crusades are Usamah ibn Munqidh's entertaining impressions of the "Franks," as all the Latin Christians were collectively named in Arabic sources. These stories offer an invaluable external perspective from the vantage of an Arab-Muslim combatant against, diplomatic envoy to, and even occasional ally of, the Latin crusaders. Usamah's vivid and humorous sketches of the Franks and their strange habits provide some balance against the caricatured portrayal of the "Saracens" (Muslims) in European historical sources and literary representations of crusade encounters, early examples of what could be called "Orientalism." Moreover, for many students of the crusades unfamiliar with Middle Eastern history, Usamah's recorded encounters with and views of the Franks have often come to serve as a typical voice representing "the other side," namely, the Arab-Islamic cultural and religious attitudes and responses toward the invading Latin Christians. Since these stories are often approached in isolation and excerpted from Usamah's understudied auto-biographical text, *The Book of Learning by Example*, interpretations of his views can easily resolve into the somewhat simplistic or anachronistic but, nevertheless, contradictory ideas about the historical character of crusade-era encounters between Arab Muslims and Latin Christians.

Did Usamah exemplify through his many amicable dealings and contacts with the Franks the unexpected possibility of cross-cultural understanding and friendship, even inter-religious tolerance, during this era of conflict? Or do his apparently wry criticisms of the seemingly uncivilized and superstitious mores of the Franks reveal, on the contrary, a hostility and sense of superiority comparable to the Latins' own violent hostility toward the Saracens—that is, does he betray an "Occidentalism"? Alternatively, do Usamah's representations simply reflect uncomprehending and superficial impressions that demonstrate the rather narrow limits of cross-cultural interchange between medieval peoples and religious communities, the impasse of a "clash of civilizations"? These are all real, debatable possibilities that can find support in the array of anecdotes Usamah assembles about the Franks. A more fundamental question, however, concerns the extent to which his experiences and impressions are typical: what do his perspectives actually reflect individually and historically?

To approach this question, we must place Usamah's accounts of the Franks into a wider context of *The Book of Learning* (*Kitab al-I'tibar*) and the history that surrounds it. A serious attempt at understanding the historical meaning of his encounters with the Franks requires an appreciation of Usamah's life and his times, his social and political world, and the literary culture he shared with his work's contemporary audience. In the light of such a background, Usamah's relations with and representations of the Latin Christians appear quite complex, multi-faceted, often contradictory, and, in some cases, unique to him. While religious identity may seem to us to mark most clearly differences between the Muslim Arab and the Christian Frank during crusading conflict, Usamah's text suggests that other social differences within a horizon of elite warrior culture shared by both Christians and Muslims were perhaps more crucial and meaningful to him and thus greater factors in the ways that he defined the Franks.

Usamah ibn Munqidh was born in 1095, just months before Pope Urban II (1088–99) first preached crusade at Clermont in France. He died at the age of 93 in 1188, the year after the sultan Salah al-Din (c. 1138–93) took Jerusalem back from the Latins. He spent his childhood and youth until 1131 in the precincts of Shayzar, a small city located about 30 miles inland from the Mediterranean coast near Hama in the northwest of modern Syria. Here, on the borders of the Byzantine Empire, in a region populated principally by Eastern Orthodox Christians, Usamah's clan ruled a small principality. The Banu Munqidh was an influential family in the region but had only recently seized the city from Byzantine control in 1080. As lords of the territory, they inhabited the citadel resting high above Shayzar on a rocky promontory nearly surrounded by a curling bend of the Orontes River. Usamah grew up as a member of an elite patrician family of well-known warriors who enjoyed a wide reputation for martial valor, honor, piety, and courtly refinement.

Usamah's father Murshid, himself a copyist of the Qur'an and author of a commentary on the Muslim sacred scripture, insured that his sons were educated both in the arts of war and of literary culture. Usamah remembers that his pious father would order his children to recite from memory their daily assigned portions of scripture while they rode to the hunting grounds (230). Capitalizing on the displacement of scholars fleeing the Frankish conquest of the larger and wealthier coastal cities, Murshid managed to attract famous men of letters to Shayzar to tutor Usamah and his brothers.

Usamah's early education imparted a lasting appreciation for scholarship and an abiding interest in books. Bitterly remarking on the violation of a safe-conduct order from King Baldwin III and the Frankish pillaging of the ship carrying his extended family and household of nearly 50 persons and all their possessions, Usamah wrote, "In the vessel were jewelry, which had been entrusted to the women, clothes, gems, swords, weapons, and gold and silver amounting to about thirty thousand dinars.... The safety of my children, my brother's children, and our *harem* [household] made the loss of money that we suffered a comparatively easy matter to endure — with the exception of the books, which were four thousand volumes, all of the most valuable kind. Their loss has left a heart sore that will stay with me to the last day of my life" (61). It is hard to imagine a lay nobleman in Europe at this time acquiring a comparable literary and religious education or so impressive a collection of books that, even with exaggeration, numbered far more titles than the best monastic libraries of the time.

Beyond exercising and drilling in horsemanship and the use of arms, Usamah's martial skills were honed, like his noble Frankish peers, in the aristocratic pursuit of hunting wild game on horseback in the lush countryside where he would be accompanied by specially trained hounds and falcons. In fact, a large proportion of his autobiographical reminiscences revolve around clearly related experiences of combat and hunting. Usamah writes in similar terms about his exploits as a fighter or hunter and, whether the quarry was a lion or a marauding foe — either of whom might ambush the neglectful — he emphasizes the unpredictability of fate, the expression of qualities of courage and resourcefulness, and the display of skilled technique.

Such martial skills and qualities were crucial to the survival of the Banu Munqidh, whose small, independent principality was perched dangerously with enemies on all sides. Usamah remembers the threats posed by bandits, rival warlords in neighboring towns eager to expand their territories, and the Frankish marauders. In addition to defending their territory militarily, the Banu Munqidh clan negotiated alliances through constant diplomacy with stronger powers; the political demands of survival could easily trump religious differences and unite Frankish and Muslim lords.

The First Crusade (1096–99) established several independent principalities that were technically subordinate to the Kingdom of Jerusalem but operated independently in their diplomatic relations with local Muslim powers. Usamah's early memories of encounters with the Franks occurred in the context of his family's accommodation to the sudden rise of Frankish power in the region, particularly to the bordering principality of crusader Antioch. Usamah's uncle and the head of the clan, Sultan, recognized the conquests made by crusaders en route to Jerusalem and sought a truce with the crusader army. By accepting tributary status, Shayzar was spared the depredations of the crusader army — "pilgrims" in some contemporary parlance — on its path of pillage and conquest. The context for the diplomatic negotiations were mentioned by a Frankish chronicler, Peter Tudebode, who relates that in 1099 while in Ma'arrat al-Nu'man, the Frankish leader received envoys from "the king of Shayzar" seeking an accord and offering tribute. He was said to want to help the Christians and promised to make the "pilgrims secure and free of fear so far as his jurisdiction permitted." He also offered to provide a market for provisions. Tudebode suggests that the army pitched their tents along the river near the town but that the king of Shayzar was alarmed by their nearness to the city and threatened to deny them the market unless they moved further south. He sent two Turkish guides to speed them along. The guides helped them ford the river and come to a well-provisioned valley that the crusaders could plunder. Tudebode notes that the army stayed in this valley for five days and was revived just two weeks after near starvation had driven some of the crusaders to cannibalism — they fed on the corpses of the Saracen inhabitants they had massacred in the nearby city of Ma'arrat al-Nu'man. So Usamah's uncle, who also agreed to provide horses and other supplies after swearing "on his law" (by his religion) that he would not harm the pilgrims, cannily avoided a disastrous confrontation by providing crucial relief and provisions to the crusaders on the last leg of their long march to Jerusalem.[1]

---

[1] Petrus Tudebodus, *Historia de Hierosolymitano itinere*, trans. John H. Hill and Laurita L. Hill (Philadelphia: American Philosophical Society, 1974), 104–5.

As a result, an uneasy period of truce, interspersed with raids and skir-mishes, protected Shayzar and led to occasional contact between the Banu Munqidh and the rulers of Antioch during Usamah's youth. These rela-tions with the crusaders provide the backdrop for many of the early encounters Usamah had with the Franks and reflect not only conflict with the alien invaders but also political alliance and cooperation across reli-gious boundaries.

The Banu Munqidh ended up being fairly loyal tributaries of the prin-cipality of Antioch for a period. The clan provided guides through their territory on the path to Jerusalem and subsequently had to furnish services to their overlords and to pay a substantial annual tribute. One such serv-ice rendered to a later prince of Antioch, Roger of Salerno (1112–19), involved escorting one of his messengers headed for Jerusalem. Although Usamah describes Roger as "a devil of the Franks" (148), the practical ben-efits of the alliance were evident, as the Frankish messenger himself was remembered to have observed in a conversation with Usamah's uncle Sultan: "'My lord has dispatched me on business and a secret mission, but seeing that you are an intelligent man I will disclose it to you.' My uncle said, 'How do you know that I am an intelligent man when you have never seen me before this moment?' The knight replied, 'Because I noticed that the whole region I passed through was in ruins, except for your domains which are flourishing'" (117). The Banu Munqidh clan also developed a relatively close and amicable relationship with King Baldwin II of Jerusalem (1118–31). He was captured in 1123 and, during the negotia-tions for his release, was a guest of the Banu Munqidh. After receiving gen-erous treatment by his hosts, Baldwin later released them from the obligations to pay the tribute to the principality of Antioch and all burdens his predecessor had imposed on them in 1108. Likewise, the warm rela-tions between Baldwin and the Banu Munqidh clan came to play an important role in Usamah's subsequent career when he was a vassal of the emir of Damascus in the 1130s. During this period, a number of negotia-tions took place between the king of Jerusalem and the emir of Damascus. Because Usamah played a role in them, he had access to Jerusalem and the freedom to cross the frontier into Frankish-held territories.

While Sultan's judicious policies and prudent diplomacy helped to pre-serve the principality of Shayzar from external foes and threats, internal family politics and social tensions would prove more fateful in their impli-cations for Usamah's subsequent career and future. After the death of Nasr in 1098, Usamah's father, Murshid, was the eldest paternal member of the clan and presumed heir to lordship of Shayzar. But, nevertheless, for somewhat obscure reasons, he ceded leadership of the family to his younger brother, Sultan. Murshid nonetheless continued to serve actively as the right-hand man of his brother, who remained childless for several decades. As a result, Usamah and his brothers, as the eldest of the children in the paternal lines of the family, rose to great prominence during their youth and, as they grew older and distinguished themselves in martial prowess and political acumen, eventually posed a potential threat to Sultan's position. As it happened, tensions increased after the birth of a son to Sultan soon after Murshid's death in 1138 when Usamah was approximately 30 years old. Usamah and his brothers were exiled from Shayzar. Consequently, he was absent in 1157 from a family banquet held in the citadel of Shayzar by his cousin when a devastating earthquake struck northern Syria. The castle collapsed and there were not many survivors. The territory was thus lost to its overlord, the ruler of Aleppo and Damascus.

Usamah spent the next 60 years of his life away from his birthplace as an itinerant warrior who plied his skills as a soldier and diplomat for successive lords and patrons. With a life that spanned almost the entire twelfth century from the aftermath of the First Crusade to the eve of the Third Crusade (1189–92) and with a career that led him across Egypt and the Levant, he witnessed countless conflicts among peoples throughout the region. On one side, he saw the Isma'ili Shi'i Fatimid Caliphate established in Egypt and allied fortress communities of assassins scattered from the coastal ranges of the Mediterranean to the mountainous fastnesses of Persia further east. On the other, there were arrayed Sunni powers, the Turkish Seljuk dynasty in Iran and Anatolia, and local emirs in Syria and Iraq. Out of these conflicts, in the second half of the twelfth century, a new political, cultural, and religious atmosphere developed and crystallized in the revival of the discourse of jihad. Warlords like Salah al-Din began to promote this "neo-jihad" by lavishly supporting religious scholars and institutions in order to legitimize their rule as pious defenders of orthodox Sunni Muslims against both the "cross-worshipping" Frankish invaders and the usurping Isma'ili "heretics." While this neo-jihad derived from an older tradition of religious struggle that included martial endeavor in the path of God as well as inner spiritual disciplining of personality and behavior, it emerged in direct response to apparent crusader religious zeal and mirrored, in part, the Christian sanctification of violent holy war. It was, however, conceived as a defensive struggle to protect Muslim society and never considered conversion of the Franks as a conscious objective.

It is easy to exaggerate the importance of religious motives in understanding the complex relationships of conflict and collaboration among
the warlords of the medieval Levant. Yet Usamah's reflections display scant
evidence of the ideological dimensions of the neo-jihad. While pious in
practice and upbringing, he recalls his formative experiences of accommodation and contact with the Franks from the early decades of the century
before a more concerted effort to resist them. Perhaps the nature of his
career, which saw him serve both the Isma'ili Shi'i Caliphate in Egypt and
Salah al-Din, the Sunni champion who toppled it, prevented him from
adopting too inflexible a sensibility.

Despite decades of distinguished military service and noteworthy political involvement, contemporaries celebrated Usamah as much — if not
more — as a man of letters and distinguished poet. He composed dozens of
works, most of which unfortunately do not survive. They range across different genres of Arabic scholarship. He wrote works on poetics and composed his own poetry. He penned a piece on dream interpretation and a
compendium of useful stories called the "Kernels of Refinement" that
expressed the proper manners and behavior of refined gentlemen of his
age. Broadly speaking, although a few works of religious instruction are
attributed to him, Usamah's written work encompasses broadly the category of *adab*, that is, the secular kinds of knowledge of the cultured elite —
everything from history, geography, and poetry to knowledge about
genealogies and the natural world, and the like. *Adab* was supposed to be
simultaneously entertaining and instructive, and Usamah's most celebrated work, *The Book of Learning by Example*, certainly qualifies.

Much like Jean de Joinville's early fourteenth-century *Life of Saint Louis*
(see Chapter 22 below) written by a lay nobleman who participated in a
crusade and reflected back on it at the end of his long life, Usamah's memories cluster around formative moments of his life and his adventures as a
young man. His anecdotes tend to be drawn from before his exile from
Shayzar and to deal with a relatively small number of themes. They are
intended as noteworthy examples and entertaining wonders to be contem-
plated. Usually he offers pairs of thematically related stories. When he
includes a story about a wild lion that was so destructive on one hunt that
it completely ravaged the large hunting party that he led, he offers a contrasting account about a tame lion that a trainer brought to the castle for
the amusement of the court. They released this lion into a courtyard with
sheep, expecting to enjoy the spectacle of the lion pouncing upon them.
Instead, to the astonished mirth of the men, the sheep aggressively butted

the lion and sent it scurrying away to seek safety (136–37). These pairings of thematically related episodes, which balance stories about good virtues with bad qualities—and likewise between positive morals and negative consequences, between expectations and surprises—form a very large part of the book.

One of the major themes of the work concerns the unpredictable fortunes of warfare and hunting. For instance, Usamah includes a number of stories of unexpected outcomes when someone who was given what appeared to be a devastatingly mortal blow by a lance thrust or sword cut nevertheless somehow manages to survive and return to battle, whereas others who receive very light wounds or a tiny scratch inexplicably perish (70, 127–28, 134–35). With such examples, Usamah draws out and explores lessons about the variability and inscrutability of fate as determined by God's will and decree. As a work of *adab*, the exemplary stories are meant to be entertaining and thus memorable in conveying a particular moral lesson or ethical principle to an audience consisting of peers or younger generations of his social world.

Innovatively for this genre, Usamah uses his own experience or those of people close to him—i.e., family or those bound to him—to provide the anecdotes that exemplify and illustrate the moral lessons he explores. Although the book is often described as his memoirs, like many pre-modern works, it cannot properly be understood as autobiography. It does not follow a continuous narrative of his life, starting with his birth and ending with his final reflections in old age. Instead, the text is organized around these loosely connected anecdotes that convey an ethical idea or cultural principle. What distinguishes his work from other examples of *adab* literature is the autobiographical character of the anecdotes and the personal reflection that guides their selection and organization.

It is in this broad context of *adab* literature that we can understand Usamah's approach to his encounters with the Latin Christian crusaders. The Franks are only one group among many that he situates in his complex world. For instance, he has as many stories about animals and their habits and activities as he does about the Franks. In fact, there is generally an important interplay between his descriptions and observations of animals and his ethnography on the morals and manners of the Franks. As a warrior and patrician, Usamah enjoyed complicated relations with the animal world. We might expect him, as a hunter and warrior, to have expert knowledge of falconry and horses. So, for example, he is capable of talking very specifically about the habits of horses, which often play important roles in his anecdotes and thus in his imagination and that of his fellow warrior elites (126–28). Like falcons, they are described in martial terms, display courage, and are honored for their performance in battle or hunt. Both were highly valued, had names and distinct personalities, and were sometimes given as important gifts in diplomatic arrangements between the princes of the region (253). It is striking to read his perceptive accounts of wild animals in the environment of Syria, at the time a lush and verdant habitat for a dizzying variety of wildlife, including leopards, gazelles, and a number of unknown species that have not survived (135–41, 236–53). Like the falcons and horses, these animals in Usamah's accounts have traits that mirror human qualities and hold social roles mirroring those of humans.

While the complexities of political relationships during the era of the crusades distinguished the Franks from the animal world, Usamah tends to see them, like the animals, as part of the natural landscape, as one group among many that he encounters. In general, he describes them as having few cultural refinements and as essentially unmarked by civilization, that is, they lack the types of habits and customs that for him and other members of his society defined proper social relations. Instead, the Franks are fierce warriors who have a kind of wild, almost animal sort of strength. And, as he does with his accounts of animals, he counterposes scenes about the Franks to help distinguish socially acceptable and aberrant behavior.

For example, he distinguishes Franks who were new arrivals from those who had spent a long period of time in the Levant and had adapted to local customs. During one of his visits to Jerusalem as an honored guest, Usamah was permitted to visit the Dome of the Rock, the major Muslim shrine that was then under Templar control. Performing a prayer there in Muslim fashion, he faced the direction of Mecca, to the south of Jerusalem, but was immediately accosted by a rude Frank who insisted that he pray eastward, as was Christian custom. The Frank grabbed Usamah and turned him roughly before the Templars managed to intervene to allow him to continue unmolested. The Templars later explained to Usamah that the Frank had only recently arrived and had not previously seen anyone praying in any direction other than east; they thus sought to exonerate the newcomer's hostile behavior as ignorance of the diversity of religious practice in the region. "Thereupon I said to myself I have had enough of prayer," Usamah relates, "so I went out and have ever since been surprised at the conduct of this devil of a man, at the change in the color of his face, his trembling and his sentiment at the sight of one praying that is south towards Mecca" (163–64).

Usamah contrasts this harsh and unbending ignorant attitude of newly arrived Franks with long-time Latin residents. About these latter, whom he sometimes calls "settled," "coastal," or "Syrian" Franks, he had a number of observations that indicate that they were capable of adapting rather completely to the lifestyles of an eastern household. In one case, Usamah accepted an invitation to dinner from one of the early crusaders who had stayed—a Frank with whom Usamah had a great deal of business—but upon being seated at the table, he refrained from partaking of the meal due to concern about whether the food was licit according to Islamic dietary law. His host quickly perceived the reason for Usamah's hesitation and set him at ease by revealing that he never ate anything except what had been prepared by an Egyptian woman whom he had had installed as his household's cook and that he never allowed pork to come into his home. Although he admits that he was still a bit cautious about eating, Usamah was relieved and also perhaps somewhat surprised and impressed by this Frank who had become eastern in his habits (169–70). Together, these anecdotes show the various possibilities for kinds of Frankish identity in the Latin crusader kingdom and demonstrate an awareness on Usamah's part of distinctions that could be drawn among them. Despite such appreciation for Franks who had managed to adapt to local circumstances, in some cases Usamah betrays a belief that deeper differences endured. These differences were based more on a socio-cultural or ethnic basis than on religious identity alone, and they prevented Frankish assimilation to the multi-religious society of the eastern Mediterranean.

Many of Usamah's stories are self-consciously humorous and may have been shared in an inter-religious and cross-cultural environment, so we may lose in translation layers of social meaning. They nevertheless give us a sense for how Usamah and his peers may have perceived Latin Christians and provide insight into gendered notions of honor for both Muslims and Christians. Usamah is, for instance, struck by the lack of marital jealousy among the Frankish men and, more generally, by their lack of concern for protecting and preserving feminine honor:

> Here is an illustration which I myself witnessed. When I used to visit Nablus [a city under Frankish control], I always took lodging with a man

named Mu'izz whose home was a lodging house for the Muslims. The house had windows which opened to the road, and there stood opposite to it on the other side of the road a house belonging to a Frank who sold wine for the merchants. One day this Frank went home and found a man with his wife in the same bed. He asked him, "What could have made you enter into my wife's room?" The man replied "I was tired so I went in to rest." "But how," he asked "did you get into my bed?" The other replied "I found a bed that was spread so I slept in it." "But," he said "my wife was sleeping together with you." The other replied "Well, the bed is hers. How could I therefore have prevented her from using her own bed?" "By the truth of my religion," said the husband, "if you should do it again you and I would have a quarrel." Such was for the Frank the entire expression of his disapproval and the limit of his jealousy. (164–65)

Usamah clearly means for this story to be humorous. While he presents it as a story that he himself witnessed or heard from Mu'izz, it has the character of a stock sort of joke. If so, perhaps it was a story that circulated in Nablus as an example of the dumb husband, ignorant of the fact that he has been cuckolded — this was a common theme of bawdy tales in Europe known as "Fabliaux." Usamah might have missed the way in which this Frankish tale was an invented story. Whatever the case, he interprets it in a critical manner to show some of the failings of the Franks, which he takes as typical, to illustrate that they had a very different conception of jealousy and feminine honor. Now, such an interpretation is really quite unreasonable since at this time the behavior of the husband described in this humorous anecdote doesn't reflect anything like the common practice or attitude by men in an equally patriarchal Latin Christian society. However, as an extreme example of a comparative difference that Usamah perceives, the story serves to dramatize and exaggerate a point about Frankish sexual laxity and lack of sexual jealousy over women that is fundamental to the distinctions Usamah draws between his society and that of the Franks.

In contrast to this Frankish laxity, Usamah recalls his uncle's attitude toward the modesty of a woman he had long since divorced by the time she was captured in a Frankish raid on her father's fortified castle. The uncle apparently declared that he would spend an exorbitant sum on ransoming her from the Franks because he could not tolerate having a woman who had unveiled herself to him being their captive. In other words, it contradicted his own sense of masculine honor to have a woman so distantly associated with him subjected to such an apparent humiliation (100). Such urgency to protect the honor of women, particularly when they were captured by the Franks, is a theme that runs through the text. It was a grave concern for the society of men engaged in conflict with Frankish knights, a concern that went far beyond that for warriors captured in raids and battles for which a regular system of ransom and prisoner exchange was in place. As a fundamental set of cultural associations in the patriarchal world of Usamah, this gendered notion explains his characterization of the Franks as a paradoxical pairing of martial skill and prowess, even valor in feats of arms, with no similar sense of jealousy over women's honor. In short, for Usamah, the Franks are fierce warriors but lack the socio-cultural basis of masculine virtue and honor.

Usamah sees this as a contradiction, for he understood masculine virtue as the jealous and rigorous protection of feminine honor. Men were motivated to adopt the heroic posture of valiant combat and to demonstrate their bravery and courage by protecting the dignity of women and guarding zealously their modesty. These sets of associations define perhaps most fundamentally the distinction—a socio-cultural rather more than a simply religious difference—Usamah perceived between his society and that of the culture and habits of the Franks.

The Franks were a curious and instructive mystery for Usamah, despite the somewhat simple and humorous characterizations he applied to them. They violated the specific cultural and social logics he understood. And while over time they might adopt local practices of living or even convert to Islam, they maintained their identity fundamentally as Catholic Franks, quite unlike Arab Christians. Usamah tells the story of a Frankish youth who was captured and fostered in his father's house where he accepted Islam. Usamah judged it a sincere conversion based on his practice—the young man fasted and prayed. He learned stone-cutting and was thus relatively successful economically and socially. He was married off to a woman from a pious family—Usamah's own father paid the costs for the wedding and for establishing the new family in a home. They had two sons, but when the boys were about five or six years of age, their father took them with their Arab-Muslim mother and everything in his house and joined the Franks in Afamiyah, where he was re-baptized as a Christian (160). Here and elsewhere, Usamah suggests that Frankish conversions to Islam somehow could not be considered final since, rather surprisingly to him, despite social and cultural integration into life in the East and even Muslim religious culture, they often revert not only to Catholic Christianity but to Frankish society. Perhaps even more mystifying to him is the case of a captured Frankish woman who was married off to a Muslim lord, had a son and heir with this man, lived a life of great luxury, and managed to become very important and influential in the affairs of the territory. And yet she gave it all up and left her son, the lord of the Castle of Ja'bar, to escape and return to her own people; thereafter, she lived with a Frankish shoemaker at a humble, if not abject level of both social and economic status (159–60).

Alas, Usamah seems to have assumed that the Franks would have wanted the same things that he and his fellow Muslim elites desired, that they would conceive of honor as he did. But his conclusion about this Frankish woman most likely applies more generally to the Frankish population in the crusader kingdom as a whole and expresses his lingering disappointment that things could not be otherwise: "The Franks are an accursed people, members of which do not assimilate except with their own kin" (160).

Bibliographic Note

The English translation used in this essay is Phillip K. Hitti, *An Arab-Syrian Gentleman and Warrior in the Period of the Crusades: Memoirs of Usamah Ibn-Munqidh* (Princeton: Princeton University Press, 1987). Some passages from Usamah's other writings relating further anecdotes on the Franks are translated in Francesco Gabrieli, *Arab Historians of the Crusades: Selected and Translated from the Arabic Sources,* trans. E.J. Costello (Berkeley: University of California Press, 1978). A new translation that includes these excerpts has recently become available, *The Book of Contemplation: Islam and the Crusades,* trans. Paul M. Cobb (London: Penguin Books, 2008).

The biography by Paul M. Cobb, *Usama ibn Munqidh: Warrior-Poet of the Age of Crusades* (Oxford: Oneworld, 2005), provides a comprehensive bibliography and detailed account. For a full treatment of Muslim responses to the crusades, consult Carole Hillenbrand, *The Crusades: Islamic Perspectives* (New York: Routledge, 2000), which also has a helpful bibliography; see also John V. Tolan, *Saracens: Islam in the Medieval European Imagination* (New York: Columbia University Press, 2002), for medieval images of Islam in crusade-era sources. For a general introduction to the history of Islamic societies, see Marshall Hodgson, *The Venture of Islam: Conscience and History in a World Civilization,* vols. 1 and 2 (Chicago: University of Chicago Press, 1974). And for the concept of "Orientalism," consult Edward Said's *Orientalism* (New York: Vintage, 1979).

SEVENTEEN

Between History and Literature
Chrétien de Troyes's *Lancelot* and Marie de France's *Lais*

Amy G. Remensnyder[1]

Whatever is the historian to do with the magical worlds Marie de France and Chrétien de Troyes depicted with such artistry in the second half of the twelfth century? Worlds in which ebony boats with silk sails glide unguided across the sea, courtly kings soar through the air in the shape of hawks, and the mythical King Arthur, Queen Guinevere, and the knights of the Round Table pursue their endless adventures in an enchanted landscape. Delight at this shimmering world of possibility would not be an unreasonable reaction. After all, it's what the contemporary audiences of these texts felt. So read these poems with all the pleasure that great literature has to offer the reader fortunate enough to encounter it. Then stop to reflect on the history of the magical worlds Marie and Chrétien present.

Both authors drew from the rich stock of Celtic folklore that until the early twelfth century circulated mostly as oral stories and songs. By then, King Arthur and his knights loomed large in such material. Arthur's historicity is certainly questionable, for he appears only fleetingly in written sources predating the twelfth century and even then in suspiciously legendary contexts. But many medieval people didn't doubt that he had existed, even if they didn't always believe the fanciful adventures attributed to members of his court. By the first half of the twelfth century, Arthurian

---

[1] While writing this article, I held an ACLS/SSRC/NEH International and Area Studies fellowship. I thank all three foundations for their support.

legend had gained such stature that carved figures of the king and his knights sometimes gallop along church façades, enjoying places usually reserved for saints and biblical heroes.

Arthur's full emergence into the limelight of written history occurred in approximately 1138, when the learned cleric Geoffrey of Monmouth composed his *History of the Kings of Britain*. In this sprawling text recounting the illustrious if almost entirely legendary history of Britain's founders, King Arthur's exploits form the centerpiece. Geoffrey's widely circulated book boosted the mythic ruler's renown. Soon a flood of narrative poems — first in French and then, by the end of the twelfth century, in German and later in Italian, Spanish, and other European vernaculars — brought Arthur and his entourage to medieval audiences.

In writing about the Arthurian world of courts, quests, knights, ladies, and love, Marie and Chrétien were thus producing a vision of history, much like the *jongleurs* (minstrels) who sang of Charlemagne and his peers in *chansons de geste* such as the *Song of Roland* (see Chapter 12 above). Like the historical landscape of the *chansons*, this was a landscape celebrated in the vernacular. For while Geoffrey of Monmouth wrote his *History* in Latin — the language of authority and of the Church — both Marie and Chrétien wrote in what we call Old French but what they and their contemporaries usually termed *romanz*. Hence, modern scholars call texts such as the *Lais* and *Lancelot* "romances" not because they are about love but because of the language in which they were composed.

Like most writers of romance, Marie and Chrétien put their names on their works. Unfortunately, they reveal little else about themselves. Chrétien identifies himself as author in five extant romances: *Erec and Enide, Cligés, The Knight with the Lion, The Story of the Grail,* and *The Knight of the Cart,* otherwise known as *Lancelot*. In the prologue to *Cligés,* he tells his audience that he wrote other tales, none of which survive. Marie claims as her own the *Lais,* a retelling of Aesop's *Fables,* and a translation into *romanz* of a Latin text, Henry of Saltrey's *Tractatus de purgatorio de sancti Patricii*. Both authors also say where they were from. Chrétien, who several times writes that he is "from Troyes," is more forthcoming than Marie, who offers only the meager information that she is "from France."

Although scholars have scoured the archives in Chrétien's hometown, they have turned up few details about him. We don't even know where or when he was born and died. Because Chrétien says so, we do know that he wrote *Lancelot* for one of the most powerful women in late-twelfth-century France, Marie, Countess of Champagne, and *The Story of the Grail* for another of the great princely powers of the era, Philip, Count of Flanders. So Chrétien may have embarked on his literary endeavors as early as 1159, the year of the first extant reference to Marie as countess. In any case he certainly had taken quill in hand sometime before 1191, the date of Philip's death.

Whenever Chrétien wrote, the impressive range of his literary allusions indicates that he must have been able to read not only *romanz* but also Latin. He probably acquired these skills at one of the cathedral schools, the nuclei from which universities later developed. In the twelfth century, ambitious young men attended these increasingly popular urban schools where they received instruction in Latin and were exposed to the great pagan classical authors and the canonical Christian writers. Men who received this education — as most male writers of romance seem to have — enjoyed the title of cleric (*clerc*) and the authority that went along with it, even if they were only in minor orders (the lowest ranks of the ecclesiastical hierarchy).

As a woman, Marie certainly wasn't called "*clerc*," nor could she have attended a cathedral school. But she did acquire a good education, perhaps from private tutors or at a monastery. In her prologue to the *Lais*, she even presents herself as a learned author who can legitimately claim the same kind of authority as her male counterparts. She carefully underlines her access to written Latin culture. First she refers to Priscian (*Prologue* 10–16), whose book on Latin grammar belonged to the standard curriculum of the schools. Then she describes how she wished to undertake a "weighty work" and "began to think about composing some good stories and translating from Latin to Romance" (*Prologue* 25–30). Only after establishing her credentials in the realm of literate knowledge (or *clergie* as her contemporaries called it) does she explain how she decided in the end to work from oral instead of written sources.

As a literate woman, Marie was unusual — but not unique. Nuns and abbesses read and wrote Latin. Some were even prolific and renowned authors. Laywomen too might command Latin well enough to write it, although more rarely. But unlike most women, Marie chose to write in the vernacular. As far as we know, she is the first female author of romance, perhaps even the earliest woman to write poetry in *romanz*. And like Chrétien, she was one of the pioneers of the genre: she wrote the *Lais* sometime between 1160 and 1199, most probably before 1170.

Who exactly was this accomplished woman? Marie's identity remains as murky as Chrétien's—no dates of birth or death, no biographical information in contemporaneous texts. Again, we have to piece together the person from the poetry. Although Marie identifies herself as "from France," most scholars believe that she lived and wrote in England, where in the wake of the Norman invasion of 1066, French had become the language of royal and princely courts. The "noble king" to whom she dedicates the *Lais* might therefore be Henry II (*Prologue* 43). The "Count William" whom she mentions in her *Fables* poses more of a challenge, given the bevy of counts by this name in late-twelfth-century England. More important than the identity of the count or even the king is the fact of Marie's relation to these powerful men. If she could write for them in the role of a court poet—an unconventional role for a woman—then she moved in the milieu of the great courts of England and most probably was herself a noble. Scholars have therefore scrutinized all the aristocratic Maries linked to the royal family whom they can find in twelfth-century England. Yet they cannot say which—if any—of these women composed the *Lais*.

Dominating the foreground of these sketchy portraits of Marie and Chrétien are people as crucial as these authors themselves to the development of romance literature: the princely patrons who funded the work. In the twelfth century, aristocrats such as Marie de Champagne and monarchs such as Henry II surrounded themselves with writers and artists in order to showcase their power and set themselves apart from their subjects. Some patrons involved themselves personally in their poets' labors—Chrétien insists, for instance, that Marie de Champagne gave him the subject matter for *Lancelot*. So strong was the association between patron and literary production that in several manuscripts of the romances (including one of *Lancelot*), the text opens with a portrait of the poet's benefactor.

All of these portraits happen to be of female patrons. Romance may have been a genre dominated by male authors, but these writers sing the praises of queens and countesses as patrons almost as often as they laud the generosity of kings and counts. Often, too, the poets address themselves to an audience that they describe as including women or as composed of women. Manuscripts of romances are even sometimes listed as prized possessions in inventories of aristocratic women's property.

Both the female and the male audiences for the romances came from the same elite social stratum as these texts' patrons: knights and ladies, counts and countesses, kings and queens. Yet while literacy was increasing among aristocrats, not all of them—probably not even most of them—could read, even in the vernacular. So they would gather around a person who had mastered the art of letters and listen as he or she read out loud the adventures of Eliduc or Guigemar or Lancelot. This combination of literacy and orality also characterized how many people in the twelfth century encountered other kinds of written texts. It wasn't a method of reading particularly easy on the books, for they must have been passed around for people's delectation, particularly if they were illustrated, as many of the manuscripts of Chrétien's works were. In fact, most of the extant Chrétien manuscripts are battered, some of the pages even food-stained, the illuminations worn down as if caressed by too many eager fingers.

As they listened to the romances, courtly audiences would have seen themselves as if in the most flattering of mirrors. The characters of the romances consist almost exclusively of nobility and royalty. Only occasionally is the homogenous landscape of knights and ladies interrupted by a burgher (town dweller), and even then he or she is assimilated to the aristocratic class in attitude and behavior. As for priests and monks and nuns, few do more than help to move the plot along, such as the bishop of Dol who makes and dissolves marriages in Marie's *Le Fresne* or the "elderly monk" who shows Lancelot the tomb inscribed with his destiny (*Lancelot* 230–31). And peasants hardly ever rear their heads to intrude into the realm of romance.

The world of romance then is unreal not only because it plays with magical motifs from Celtic folklore. It also refuses the actual social landscape of the twelfth century, where towns hummed with people, commerce, and trade as they had not since Late Antiquity; members of the ecclesiastical hierarchy wielded considerable and visible power; and peasants, as almost always in any medieval culture, constituted the bulk of the population. In romance, these social actors fade away, leaving only the aristocracy. Romance is a literature of class—the aristocratic class.

The ideals romance proposes through its exemplary knights and ladies are intended for this class. In fact, the twinned codes of chivalry and courtliness—both clearly delineated by Marie and Chrétien as by most authors of romance—constitute a boundary elevating the aristocracy above all other social groups. To ignore these codes is to slip in status—authors such as Chrétien stigmatize knights who commit this error with the derogatory term *vilain* ("boorish"), the same word used for peasants.

Scholars disagree about the origins of chivalry and courtliness. But almost all agree that in this period, these codes were no more than ideals. Outside the pages of the romances, it is rare to encounter a late-twelfth-century knight whose conduct could be called chivalric or courtly by any stretch of the imagination. It would therefore be a mistake to read the romances as a direct reflection of actual aristocratic behavior. Yet the magical world of the romances was not entirely divorced from reality. Instead, the mirror of romance into which aristocratic audiences gazed offers the modern reader a looking-glass view of the historical circumstances, preoccupations, and anxieties of this class in twelfth-century northern France and England.

Romance, for example, existed in dialogue with one of this period's major political developments: the emergence of increasingly centralized administrative monarchies in England and France. Innovative rulers such as Henry II of England and Philip Augustus of France built on structures they inherited from their immediate predecessors in efforts to establish themselves as sovereigns, as supreme monarchs. In the process, these kings whittled away at the powers of the great lords of their realms. Both Henry and Philip enlarged the system of royal courts with the aim of restricting the right of magnates to adjudicate cases. To help in the administration of royal justice—and of the equally expanded apparatus of royal finance—these rulers needed not men of war like knights, but instead men who could read and write, men who had been educated in the schools—in a word, clerics. Indeed, while great nobles might attend royal courts especially on ceremonial occasions such as Christmas or Easter, it was clerics who increasingly assisted rulers in the daily management of the realm.

The contrast between real high medieval courts and the courts of romance is a stark one. At Arthur's court in *Lancelot,* as at the royal courts in the *Lais,* knights serve and counsel their king who, in turn, rewards them for their fidelity. No account-keeping cleric disturbs this harmonious relationship between knight and monarch. Nor does the ruler in any way curb the power of his magnates as Henry and Philip were doing. Rather, he functions as a traditional monarch, content like the kings of *Beowulf* to distribute largesse to his faithful knights.

We might then read the courtly romances as bittersweet, nostalgic evocations of the political configuration that the aristocracy wanted but saw vanishing. Many of the manuscripts of Chrétien's romances in fact come from just those regions of France where nobles felt the most pinched by the expansion of Capetian royal power. Given the realities of the twelfth century, courts dominated by the aristocracy could exist nowhere else than in literature. The gulf between political actualities and the ideal order cherished by aristocratic fantasy gaped so wide that it could be bridged only by the magical language of the unreal favored by the romances.

It is also possible, however, to read the romances positively rather than negatively in relation to the royal ambitions of this period. Rulers themselves could be the patrons of romance, as was "a noble king"—perhaps Henry II himself—of Marie's *Lais*. And in the *Lais*, Marie endows kings with exactly the right that Henry II claimed as his prerogative: the dispensation of justice. Royal justice may be rough, as it is in *Bisclavret* where the king, along with restoring the werewolf's lands and human form, tortures and exiles the unfaithful wife, or as in *Lanval* where Arthur unfairly places the hero on trial. But Marie openly locates justice with the king and not with the knights who people her poems. Indeed, she implicitly disparages a king who ignores royal duty and allows his seneschal to administer justice in his place (*Equitan* 21–28, 195–97). She even punishes this king with a gruesome death for his failure to understand that, as a monarch, he cannot play the same adulterous love games as his knights. In other words, he is to act like a sovereign   like Henry II, like Philip Augustus—rather than like a mere knight.

Marie also insinuates that good monarchs have the power to order the world. So in *Bisclavret*, it is the king who re-establishes the order perturbed by the wife's betrayal of her werewolf-husband. Chrétien even more strongly delineates the royal court as the space from which order emanates. In his romances, right order—that is, peace—prevails at Arthur's court. Beyond the court lies the forest, often in medieval thought the refuge for people whose identities confound traditional social categories. In the Arthurian forest live hermits such as the elderly monk Lancelot encounters (*Lancelot* 230–31), the holy man beloved by Eliduc (*Eliduc* 889–915), and madmen such as Yvain, hero of another of Chrétien's romances. In *Lancelot*, the forest is also the site of danger, of violent encounters between knights, and of enchantments such as the Underwater Bridge that defy natural order (*Lancelot* 269–70). In short, disorder reigns outside the court. Only where the king holds power can order and peace be found. Surely this imaginative geography would have pleased rulers such as Philip Augustus and Henry II.

Glorification of the sovereign on the one hand or, on the other, the urgent expression of the knights' desire for a place at court—which then is romance? It is perhaps not necessary to choose between these interpretations of romance's relationship to the centralization of royal power. Romances after all are not polemical texts written to argue one point of view. They are literary texts, layered with the ambiguities of the human psyche. In its own tensions, romance reveals the fault lines of a social class adapting to changing political circumstances.

Relations between kings and knights belong to the world of men. But what of the women who crowd the romances? Most appear not as independent figures but as the lovers and wives of knights. Indeed, the romances are most often about what we in the twenty-first century would call romance: heterosexual love and marriage. These relations between men and women provide the profound structure for the romances. Not coincidentally, love and especially marriage also conditioned how aristocrats experienced their world, how they presented themselves, and what they thought about.

In the twelfth century, heterosexual love appears to have been a favorite topic of discussion among the aristocracy. Knights and ladies were familiar with the amorous exploits of romance characters. And in the short lyrical poems of the troubadours, noblemen and women heard of the painful longings aroused by more contemporaneous love affairs. This genre of love poetry emerged in southern France in the twelfth century but spread quickly to other areas, just as the romances did. Its aristocratic authors, mostly male but sometimes female, sang in sensual language of impossible love between a young knight and a married woman of higher social stature. This passionate poetry appears to exalt women, describing male lovers serving their ladies as vassals served lords.

This literary and aristocratic preoccupation with love had its spiritual counterpart in the form of a newly affective Christian piety. Depicted increasingly in text and image as approachable human figures, Mary and Christ inspired love in their devotees rather than only the awe aroused by their more forbidding representations in the early Middle Ages. Love became as central to spirituality as it was to literary discourse.

If romance and lyric poetry reflected the affectivity of the twelfth century, they surely did not mirror the realities of aristocratic marriage. Neither love nor the elevation of women is much evident in non-literary descriptions of marital unions among the nobility, for marriage served this class above all as a strategy to augment power and establish alliances useful to one or both parties. Accordingly, marriage was often one of the building blocks utilized by great twelfth-century magnates to consolidate territory and power.

Love of the sort depicted in the romances was obviously not the motivating factor for such marriages. So far removed from passion were aristocratic marital politics that alliances were often cemented through the betrothal of children, even infants. Sons as well as daughters could be pawns in this game of marriage. Yet marital strategies most often involved the exchange of women between men, often men a good deal older than the woman — the elderly husbands of Marie de France's *Guigemar* (209–17) and *Yonec* (17) were not mere figments of romance imagination.

Of course, there were aristocratic women who actively shaped their marital fates. They could even wield considerable power. Nonetheless, the balance of power within marriage did not often resemble the troubadour conceit of the woman as sovereign served by the man — Lancelot's courtly obedience to Guinevere in *Lancelot* was as fictional as the hazards of the Sword Bridge. And while aristocratic men could esteem beauty and wit in a potential mate, in her person they often saw above all the property she would bring to the marriage — heiresses were highly desirable wives. In the romances, the knight's quest — which often ends in marriage — poetically expresses the need of young landless knights to acquire wealthy women as their brides.

Due to shifts in French aristocratic inheritance practices, in the twelfth century there were perhaps more such knights and fewer such heiresses than before. Earlier, both sons and daughters received shares of their parents' property, but in twelfth-century France fathers increasingly wished to bequeath everything to their sons. Usually one son was favored above all — the eldest, who might receive everything, leaving not only his sisters but his brothers with little or nothing. These changes occurred as the French aristocracy began to conceive of family as patriliny, an unbroken succession of men stretching back into the past and forward into the future. Narrative genealogies composed in northern France thus blithely present family as a chain of men begetting other men, often seemingly without the intervention of a woman. Such texts rarely mention wives or daughters, and even more rarely dignify them with names. The dearth of female names in these genealogies is a disturbing echo of Marie de France's reticence to name her female characters in the *Lais*.

If family was patrilineal, then one of the functions of aristocratic marriage was to produce legitimate sons to succeed their father. In *Le Fresne,*

Gurun's vassals press him to marry because he needs "an heir who could succeed to his land and inheritance" (319–21), while in *Yonec*, a wealthy elderly man "took a wife in order to have children who would come after him and be his heirs" (17–20). Marie de France does not need to specify that the desired heirs must be male and legitimate. This would be obvious to any aristocratic audience in an era when husbands regularly repudiated wives who failed to bear boys.

Given this emphasis on legitimate sons, why ever did the romances celebrate adulterous love so frequently? Chrétien was the first author to detail the adulterous affair of Guinevere and Lancelot, but he had many imitators. This pair rapidly became synonymous with guilty if glorious love. Hardly less famous as paragons of adulterous passion were Queen Iseut and Tristan. In *Chevrefoil*, Marie de France captures a fleeting moment of their love, but other authors dedicated entire romances to Tristan and Iseut. Of Marie de France's 12 *lais*, only three — *Chaitivel, Les Deux Amanz*, and *Le Fresne* — don't involve adultery. In seven *lais*, Marie depicts adultery positively; that is, she as author does not punish the characters for their transgressive love. Only in three *lais* does she draw obviously negative portraits of adultery or attempted adultery: *Bisclavret, Equitan*, and *Lanval*. The troubadour poetry, too, sang frequently of adulterous love.

Here, yet again, the romances appear to part company with reality. There is little evidence suggesting that adultery (particularly on the wife's part) was tolerated in aristocratic circles — the twelfth century was no era of free love. Heavy legal penalties punished adultery, and it was socially acceptable for cuckolded husbands to repudiate errant wives and enact bloody vengeance on their paramours. The valorization of adultery in the romances and lyric love poetry cannot then be read as a simple stamp of approval on such amorous relations. Something else must be behind this literary preoccupation.

One clue lies in the typical structure of the adulterous affair in romance and troubadour poetry. Literary adultery in the romances usually takes shape as a triangle consisting of one married woman and two men, her husband and her lover. Another structural constant is that the woman is generally of higher social status than her lover, an inversion of the hierarchy established through their gender. The lover professes to serve and obey the woman, as Lancelot does even when Guinevere commands him to fight his worst (*Lancelot* 276–80). This is of course a further inversion of the normal hierarchy between men and women.

But in concluding that romance adultery elevates the woman, we would be wrongly omitting the third member of the adulterous triangle, the woman's husband. Like his spouse, the husband enjoys higher social station than the male lover. And often the male lover owes service to the husband, though not of the amorous variety offered to the wife: the wife's lover is the husband's vassal. Lancelot, for example, is one of King Arthur's knights and Tristan is the nephew and favored vassal of Iseut's husband, King Mark. In other words, the adulterous triangle often assigns the husband and the wife structurally analogous positions in relationship to the wife's lover.

The motif of adultery therefore is perhaps as much about relations between two men mediated by a female figure as it is about relations between men and women. The knight (male lover) needs his lord's affection and the material and social rewards it brings. In the romances, this desire for the lord's favor is sublimated in the lover's passion for his lord's wife. Of course, the most important lord for a knight to be close to—especially in twelfth-century England and France—was the king. Therefore, the most desirable woman in romance and the one often the object of knightly affections is the queen. The adulterous queen is in fact a stock character of romance. Her adultery becomes almost a normative feature of her husband's court, for it keeps the knight who loves her in her husband's service.

The adulterous triangle in romance thus can express the intensely homosocial nature of knightly culture, founded as it was on relations between lords and vassals. This homosociality appears in other types of romance triangles involving two men and one woman. The customs of Logres described by Chrétien in *Lancelot,* for example, figure women as objects that men violently exchange in order to prove their prowess to each other (*Lancelot* 223).

Yet important as bonds between men were in the world of romance and in the world of knights, they were not the only factor in the romance predilection for adultery. Behind adulterous queens lies a discourse on royal power no less important than the one mediated by the figure of the king: in literature, as in reality, those people who wished to question the monarch's legitimacy might accuse his wife of adultery. Like Guinevere in *Lancelot,* most adulterous queens of romance face a moment when they must prove that they are faithful to their husbands. Of course, these queens are guilty as charged. Yet they always manage to pull off some ruse, as Guinevere does, to prove their innocence and thus to validate their husband's power (*Lancelot* 264–69).

The romance motif of the adulterous queen also functions as a veiled meditation on how much power it was proper for a queen herself to wield. Through her body, a queen had access to royal power, a power rooted in her ability to bear children, particularly sons. Such power could be easily shaken by accusations of adultery. Accordingly, romance queens who betray the marital bond serve as metaphors for the danger posed by women's proximity to royal power. Especially strong warnings came in the shape of a figure borrowed from the Bible (*Genesis* 39): the queen who actively attempts to seduce one of her husband's knights, as Arthur's nameless wife does in *Lanval.* Spurned by the knight who has no wish to break his fidelity to his lord (*Lanval* 270–74), this queen is also foiled in her attempt to make the king punish the knight. The seductress queens of romance are thus both sexually and politically transgressive: they try to meddle in royal government by interfering in the king's relations with his vassals. Unlike adulterous but politically passive queens such as Guinevere, the seductress queens are punished or restrained so that right order may prevail in the political hierarchy.

It is no accident that the romance motif of the adulterous queen peaked in popularity exactly during the period in France and England when royal power was increasingly defined as a male prerogative, leaving queens relegated to the secondary role of consort rather than monarch. And when in the early fourteenth century the exclusion of women from inheriting the throne was articulated as legal principle in France, the adulterous queen vanishes from French romance.

Bonds between men, affirmation of male sovereignty, restriction of queens' power — such interpretations of romance adultery render this motif an expression of male concerns. This makes sense. After all, romance was a male-dominated genre, and love and marriage were social conventions structured by patriarchal norms. Yet as is often the case in patriarchal cultures, aristocratic men and women did not always have congruent experiences or expectations of marriage. These differences must have influenced how men and women listened to and understood the depiction of love, marriage, and adultery in the romances. Perhaps these differences extended to the authors as well as the audiences of romance. In her presentation of adultery, did Marie de France, the lone female author of this genre, speak in a voice different from that of her male counterparts, or did she simply express the conventions of the genre and the age?

Marie doesn't seem terribly interested in the theme of the adulterous queen. *Lanval* and *Chevrefoil* are the only two romances in which she plays with this motif. The other adulterous situations she describes don't lend themselves to interpretation as homosocial triangles through which a knight becomes closer to his lord. The knight-lovers in *Yonec, Milun, Guigemar,* and *Laüstic* certainly do not need the patronage of the woman's husband—*Yonec* and *Milun* even end with the husband's death. Instead of projecting a message about relationships between men, Marie's exploration of adultery is often about women themselves. In particular, Marie is concerned with the very real constraints women faced in the realm of marriage. Many of the adulterous women in the *Lais* are as unhappily wed as countless aristocratic women of the period actually were. These fictional women escape their marital plight through affairs with men they love. Adultery thus serves as a metaphor for a power that women often did not have in any world but the fictional one created by Marie: the ability to choose one's mate.

In the real world, aristocratic men could exercise marital choice by repudiating one wife to gain another. Yet even in the fantasy world of the *Lais,* women's ability to select their partners is hemmed in with all sorts of difficulties. At best, Marie's adulterous women must endure long years of separation from their lovers before being reunited with these men (*Guigemar, Milun*). Other female characters are less lucky. The passion both Guilliadun and Guildeluec feel for the unworthy Eliduc leads them to a nunnery, while the woman in *Laüstic* loses her lover all together. In *Yonec,* the woman must even watch as her lover meets a bloody death on the sharp spikes prepared by her jealous husband. Non-adulterous women don't always fare much better. The female character in *Chaitivel* is robbed of the possibility of choosing among the knights who love her, and in *Les Deux Amanz,* the girl's beloved dies before she can wed him.

Only Marie's most fantastic female creation can escape the conventions of the aristocratic world and truly choose her mate: the fairy woman of *Lanval.* She rides off with her beloved Lanval to Avalon, a magical island as different from the rest of the world as this woman herself is from other women. Even a fairy woman must seek an enchanted realm that lies beyond the realm of the court, Marie seems to be saying, if she wishes to live happily ever after with her lover. To be free from the court and its patriarchal structures, women must take refuge in a magical world. That world exists only in the imagination: Avalon is as unreal, if as seductive, as the lovers who materialize magically in *Yonec* and *Guigemar* to liberate women from the prisons of bad marriages. Yet here, as almost always in the romances, the language of magic isn't mere escapist fantasy. Marie de

France uses it to make room for a female voice amid the constraints imposed by twelfth-century aristocratic culture and by the genre of romance itself.

Romance authors such as Marie and Chrétien flirted with reality, suffusing it with the glow of magic. The enchanted landscapes they created entertain and delight audiences in the twenty-first century as they did in the twelfth century. Yet it must never be forgotten that behind the playful language of romance lay the very real hopes, fears, and longings of twelfth-century women and men.

Bibliographic Note

All citations of *Lancelot* refer to Chrétien de Troyes, "Knight of the Cart (Lancelot)," in his collected works: *Arthurian Romances,* trans. Carleton Caroll (London: Penguin Books, 1991), 207–94. Citations of Marie de France refer to lines in her *Lais,* trans. Joan Ferrante and Robert Hanning (Grand Rapids, MI: Baker Books, 1995).

A good general introduction to Chrétien and his works is provided by Joseph J. Duggan, *The Romances of Chrétien de Troyes* (New Haven: Yale University Press, 2001), while R. Howard Bloch gives a comprehensive analysis of Marie de France's works in his *The Anonymous Marie de France* (Chicago: University of Chicago Press, 2003). Close textual analysis of the literary and rhetorical strategies employed by Chrétien, Marie, and other authors of twelfth-century romances appears in Matilda Tomaryn Bruckner, *Shaping Romance: Interpretation, Truth, and Closure in Twelfth-Century French Fictions* (Philadelphia: University of Pennsylvania Press, 1993).

For orientation in the study of the ideals of courtliness and chivalry that permeate Chrétien's and Marie's work, see C. Stephen Jaeger, *The Origins of Courtliness: Civilizing Trends and the Formation of Courtly Ideals* (Philadelphia: University of Pennsylvania Press, 1985); Maurice Keen, *Chivalry* (New Haven: Yale University Press, 1984); and Joachim Bumke, *Courtly Culture: Literature and Society in the High Middle Ages,* trans. Thomas Dunlap (Berkeley: University of California Press, 1991). In addition to the work of the scholars cited here, I am indebted to the following scholars who have worked on various aspects of the romances and the cultures that produced them: John F. Benton, Georges Duby, Jean Dunbabin, Michelle Freeman, Kathryn Gravdal, Sandra Hindman, Sharon Kinoshita, Roberta Erich Köhler, Roberta L. Krueger, Jacques LeGoff, Peggy McCracken, and Karl D. Uitti.

EIGHTEEN

Walter Daniel's *Life of Aelred of Rievaulx*
The Heroism of Intelligence and the Miracle of Love

Katherine Christensen

In the twelfth century, European society was engaged in renewal and ref- ormation. New intensity of thinking, feeling, and expression show up in such diverse forms as the development of schools that would become universities; new religious communities; the honing of law and procedure in Church and kingdom; an effervescence of literature both Latin and vernacular; and a fresh emphasis on the individual—on motivation, emotion, and responsibility. Out of this environment, or rather from a very specific nexus within it—the juncture of Cistercian monasticism and Anglo-Norman Yorkshire—comes Walter Daniel's *Life of Aelred of Rievaulx*.

Like the more famous Jocelin of Brakelond, who wrote his chronicle about the monastery of Bury Saint Edmunds a few decades later in the early thirteenth century, Walter takes the reader into the cloister of Rievaulx to watch a bit of the life within, particularly, and with particular intensity, the life of its abbot. Unlike Jocelin, who had some ambivalence about his abbot, Walter introduces the reader to a much-loved friend whom he believed to be a saint as well, a man whose life was shaped by the heroism of intelligence and marked by miracles, above all the miracle of love. In the process, he reveals one possible interplay of individual development and community life, as well as an example of authority and leadership that was part personal charm, part institutional tradition, part spiritual power. In his work, one can see how some of the characteristic tendencies of the twelfth century blended uneasily and also why such blendings were as popular as they were. One such instance is the popularity of early Cistercians, monks who felt that contemporary Benedictine monks had strayed from the sixth-century *Rule of Saint Benedict* and who felt thus compelled to live under a more literal interpretation of its precepts.

Aelred was the third abbot of Rievaulx, one of the monasteries founded in a spectacular burst of enthusiasm for Cistercian life in the north of England in the first half of the twelfth century and mother to five other houses by the time of his death in 1167. Early Cistercian history abounds in stories of recruits who left interesting and successful lives in the world to embrace the severe asceticism, back-to-the-*Rule* simplicity, and God-smitten silence of this new monastic order. Aelred's story is one of them. Born about 1110 into an Anglo-Saxon priestly family, he spent part of his youth at the court of the king of Scotland and was a valued official there when he entered the novitiate in 1134. He served as novice master at Rievaulx, its representative at the order's principal house in Cîteaux and in Rome, and as abbot of a new foundation, Revesby, before being elected abbot of Rievaulx in 1147. Aelred was a figure of importance in his order, as abbot and writer, and in the ecclesiastical and political life of his region and nation. The early Cistercians tried to minimize their entanglements with the world, yet his responsibilities, like those of any abbot of his day, were both temporal and spiritual.

Benedict's *Rule* lays a heavy charge upon an abbot: he is to be father, teacher, spiritual mentor and example, and ruler and administrator, although the last is clearly a lower priority for Benedict. Faithful fulfillment of those responsibilities could leave little trace in the kind of sources that survive from the twelfth century. Too often it is mostly the public, external life of an abbot that is visible, the name on charters or in chronicles or on lists in a *gesta abbatum* (deeds of the abbots) of lands acquired, buildings put up. Harder to see is the inner life of the man and his community, including the tensions inherent in the abbot's role in a world where monasteries had significant social, economic, even political functions. Unlike many abbots of his day, however, Aelred can be seen in both the spiritual and temporal spheres, thanks to the survival of his own writings and Walter Daniel's *Life*. The resulting picture offers a dramatic contrast to that of Jocelin's Abbot Samson of Bury, not so much as Cistercian versus Benedictine (although that matters in portraying the nature of the community, its concerns, and the abbot's relation to it and to the outside world) as a contrast in the personalities and priorities of the abbots and their observers.

Born around 1125 of a knightly family, Walter Daniel had significant academic training that might otherwise have led to opportunities in the secular world had he not joined his father at Rievaulx around 1150, that is, a few years after Aelred had become abbot. In the last decade of Aelred's life, Walter was secretary and caregiver to the abbot, whose energy and movement were increasingly limited by disability and pain. Indeed, in his *Lament for Aelred* (141–42), Walter referred to himself as having served Aelred *in officio medicus,* which may or may not indicate medical training or a formal position as the abbey's infirmarian. Apart from Aelred himself, Walter may have been Rievaulx's most productive author, contributing a variety of works to the abbey's library. Of his own career, little is known beyond what he provides in the *Life,* in which he shows enough of himself that one can take the measure of the man.

Walter was very much part of the story he was telling. Genuinely learned without being a first-rate intellect, he was devout without having the spiritual depth of his abbot. He was self-conscious (even self-centered), prone to be impatient, and not one to suffer fools gladly—this picture is confirmed by Aelred himself in his affectionately critical depiction of Walter in the second and third books of his *Spiritual Friendship.* Walter could be caustic to the point of rudeness when on the defensive; he sometimes indulged in prolixity and purple prose. But he was also forthright and disarmingly frank in his love and his crankiness. In all, he was a familiarly flawed human being, understandable even when one wonders how far to trust him. What comes through without question is his regard for his abbot and his joy in, and gratitude for, the life at Rievaulx that Aelred nurtured for Walter and others like him.

Walter wrote the *Life* not too long after the abbot's death in order to preserve Aelred's memory, to present him as a model of holiness, and to defend his sanctity in the face of harsher assessments being made of him within and beyond the order. He likewise defended the extent of Aelred's activities outside the cloister in his *Letter to Maurice,* written perhaps to the prior of the Austin canons at Kirkham in reaction to early criticism of the *Life.* Because his portrait of Aelred was shaped with a conscious eye on the critics, he focuses on the abbot at home, in his spiritual role, rather than on the external activities that were drawing the criticism. He enables the reader to slip quietly into the inner circle around Aelred and to watch the abbot through the eyes of a willing and good-hearted, if imperfect, disciple. Despite his evident friendship with the abbot, however, Walter does not present much insight into Aelred's own mind and heart—for that one must read Aelred himself. With its uneven chronological coverage and its studied lack of attention to Aelred's public life, the *Life of Aelred* is not biography in the modern, critical sense.

It is also not hagiography, in either the pejorative sense ("pious fiction" or "exercise in panegyric") that leads some modern scholars to prefer the term "sacred biography," or in the sense of a life-and-miracles dossier that would become part of the formal process of canonization just a generation or two later. There is nothing to suggest that Walter or others sought to have Aelred honored as a saint in the Church at large, although the Cistercians do so among themselves to this day. Walter's text is hagiography in the broader, older sense: an edifying account to preserve the memory of a friend of God and follower of Christ, especially for those of the holy one's own home place. It draws on a tradition that unwinds from Athanasius's and Sulpicius Severus's writing about Antony and Martin to Gregory the Great's stories of Benedict, Bede's account of the abbots of Wearmouth and Jarrow, and indeed Aelred's own lives of Ninian and Edward the Confessor, which Walter may have taken down from Aelred's dictation. Walter in fact drew self-consciously on earlier saints' lives for language and imagery—he discussed his use of Sulpicius (*Letter* 155)— and the echo of scripture is never far away. But Walter's most important source is memory, his own and that of others. As scribe and caregiver he was often at Aelred's side in the abbot's later years, and it is for precisely those years that Walter's account is fullest. He collected memories of others at Rievaulx and elsewhere about Aelred—he later identified his informants (*Letter* 147–51) in response to criticism for not doing so in the *Life*—and he took in Aelred's own recollections of his earlier life as well. But Walter's attention was selective. He was principally concerned with relationships as well as the conditions of body, mind, and soul within the community of Rievaulx.

Walter intended his portrait of Aelred to present an abbot of the sort prescribed by Benedict's *Rule:* father, teacher, model of monastic observance and holiness, and, like Benedict, a holy man of prophetic insight as well as miracle-worker. Walter depicted Aelred as solidly within monastic tradition, yet profoundly individual, shaped by his personal history, gifts, and needs. Central to Walter's work is his conviction that the greatest and most significant miracle of Aelred's life was the love he was able to give, receive, and foster among others, especially his spiritual sons. Behind that miracle of love, at the root of the relationships it sustained and that were sustained by it, lay a heroism of intelligence, as Aelred sought to school and shape thought, emotion, and action — first his own, then those of his pupils — to serve the quest for love of God and others.

Walter portrayed Aelred's spiritual powers as increasing and deepening over time, his intelligence growing toward wisdom, his fatherly solicitude yielding moments of prophetic insight and miraculous action. This is in part a matter of Walter's experience; he knew Aelred only as abbot and most intimately in the last decade of the abbot's life. Yet some key patterns emerge early: one is the way Aelred bent his intelligence to the tasks of dealing with himself, with others (their attractiveness, their needs, and their shortcomings), and with the various responsibilities handed him. Another is his emphasis on love for God and for others, his own need and desire to love and to be loved, and a practical concern for the conditions to make that possible. These two patterns intersect over and over. They almost define Aelred's particular form of sanctity. Aelred's miracles, for all that Walter called them great, were not spectacular but rather were quiet healings of bodily pain or mental turmoil, supernatural insight, and ability to care for the spiritual needs of those who depended on him. His word healed a fever-wracked subprior, his staff straightened a craftsman's crippled arm (*Life* 21, 23); at times he could read the souls of monks, knowing their sins before they confessed them (*Life* 44). What really dazzled Walter was Aelred's persistent *caritas*, which seemed to him more marvelous than raising the dead (*Letter* 156). Perhaps it took another intelligent man, to whom such patient love certainly did not come easily, to see the magnitude of it.

The link between monasticism and heroism was as old as the image of monks as athletes of Christ, and creative intelligence often marked the monastic impulse. Four centuries earlier, the Anglo-Saxon Guthlac transferred his warrior's quest to monastic commitment and, likewise, the desert tradition to the fens.[1] The application of disciplined, heroic intelligence is especially evident among the early Cistercians. They stripped Benedict's *Rule* of comfortable mitigations that had clustered like barnacles. They innovated with the role of lay brothers and the rejection of child

---

[1] *Felix's Life of Saint Guthlac*, ed. B. Colgrave (Cambridge: Cambridge University Press, 1956), xviii–xix (pp. 81–83), xxiv–xxvii (pp. 87–93).

oblates. They struck out into the wilderness, and then they organized a complex monastic network to provide mutual supervision. On the personal level, to choose to be a Cistercian meant looking at one's prospects, whether at court or in the Church, in the schools, or even the familial landholdings, and deciding to do something radically different with one's life.

As a young man Aelred found responsibility and friendship at the royal court of Scotland. Walter presented Aelred's competent, amiable service as steward almost as a matter of course, in language that echoes that of the *Rule* about a good cellarer (*Life* 2; cf. *Rule* 31). But even under the pious king David, it was probably no simple task. Intelligence, as well as Aelred's charity and gift for peacemaking, are revealed in the story of how he patiently endured crude insults from a knight who eventually expressed contrition and respect (*Life* 3). Life at court was comfortable, honorable, and productive, yet Aelred came to be uneasy and was too bright not to recognize what was happening. Walter's account of Aelred's conversion to the monastic life does not dwell on what Aelred himself realized, that is, that part of his motivation was to find a morally safer environment than court life provided, an environment in which to find the love he knew he needed; in his *Mirror of Charity* (1.28), Aelred remembers certain of his relationships from that time in court as morally perilous. Aelred was familiar with religious life at Durham, where he had family connections, but when he heard about the new monastery at Rievaulx, his imagination was fired by the intensity and purity of the monks' observance, including their hardships (*Life* 5). After consulting with Rievaulx's patron, the nobleman Walter Espec, and the archbishop of York, he went to see the abbey for himself. The lyrical description of Rievaulx in the fifth chapter of the *Life* is Walter's, not Aelred's, yet given the latter's penchant for the outdoors, he was probably equally enchanted. But the real enchantment was spiritual. Aelred had found his true home, and he never looked back. He did not share Samson of Bury's regret at not having had the option of the schools instead of the cloister (Jocelin 33).

Walter depicted Aelred's formation in monastic life as a development of virtue already present within him and of self-mastery through loving submission to the will of others. It also entailed a new disciplining of mind and body that called the intelligence into play: steeping the mind in Scripture, especially the psalms, sustained meditation, and adjustment to a physically demanding life without either slacking or overdoing (*Life* 12). Monastic maturity brought new responsibilities as Aelred's gifts for persuasion and for assessing situations were recognized and put to use: there were calls to advise the abbot, a journey to Rome to present Rievaulx's concerns about a disputed archiepiscopal election at York, and service as novice master (*Life* 14). Aelred rose to each challenge in turn and at the same time was finding new dimensions to his concepts of love in his own prayer and study (particularly of Augustine's *Confessions*) and in friendships he developed within the cloister (*Spiritual Friendship* 3.119–27). At the urging of Abbot Bernard of Clairvaux (c. 1090–1153), the Cistercians' most influential leader, Aelred started to reduce some of his thoughts to writing in the *Mirror of Charity* (cf. *Life* 17).

When he was elected the first abbot of Revesby, Rievaulx's daughter-house, Aelred confronted an avalanche of external duties, as well as all the cares of a new institution. He dealt with local magnates, preached to clergy, and dealt with gifts and donors, all the while training his obedientiaries and building up the numbers and spiritual life of the community (*Life* 20). If this busy routine had perturbed Aelred, Walter does not know it. He did, however, sense that Aelred's critics thought him all too comfortable with such worldliness. Aelred's experience at court would have taught him to view such duties as service and to rate the necessary socializing with the great and the good no more highly than it deserved. Rather like Gregory the Great in the sixth century, he had some aptitude for administration. He might regret the spiritual distraction involved, but he did not agonize over the task. As abbot of Rievaulx, Aelred was a good enough manager to double the house in numbers and resources (*Life* 30), but it must have entailed plenty of the dealings with outsiders of which Walter complained in the second book of *Spiritual Friendship*. With the General Chapters (meetings of the abbots) at Citeaux, supervisory visits to Rievaulx's related houses, and occasional involvement in secular and ecclesiastical issues, he was also away from the monastery a good deal.

The story of Martha and Mary (*Luke* 10:38–42) provided a common medieval metaphor about the respective roles of action and contemplation, a metaphor that Aelred himself once used in a sermon.[2] Although Walter preferred not to stress these dimensions of Aelred's life, the importance of that practical "Martha" side of an abbot's vocation was widely

---

[2] G. Constable, "The Interpretation of Mary and Martha," in his *Three Studies in Medieval Religious Thought* (Cambridge: Cambridge University Press, 1995), 1–141. For Aelred's sermon, see p. 88 of Dutton's introduction to the *Life*.

acknowledged. An abbot who was too much "Mary," immersed in contemplation but without good judgment and management skills, could let a community drift into disorder and confusion. Yet one cannot imagine Aelred preferring to be away from Rievaulx as Samson of Bury was said to prefer his manors or favoring practical-minded obedientiaries over more contemplative types (Jocelin 32, 37). Samson's mirror was his account book (Jocelin 27), while Aelred's was a discussion of love, love for God and one's neighbor. How Aelred made an environment of love a reality at Rievaulx is what Walter is most intent to show.

As novice master, then as abbot, Aelred had the authority and opportunity to apply his concern for love to the shaping of monastic community. The office of novice master was particularly important in an order that accepted no child oblates and was forming intense young men, often brought up to a life of action and privilege, to lead lives of contemplation and austere equality. Not all of them took to it as readily as had Aelred. He could go to great lengths to support a wavering vocation. One unstable monk was twice miraculously restrained from leaving by Aelred's prayers. The first time the monk returned, having wandered in a circle, the novice master Aelred bent the rules and did not tell their abbot of the incident (*Life* 15). When the monk later attempted to leave again, he was miraculously unable to pass through the abbey gate while Aelred, then abbot, prayed (*Life* 22). In the end, this monk who had caused Aelred such anxiety died safely in the habit, his head in Aelred's hands (*Life* 28). Aelred dealt seriously with the struggles younger monks had with the difficulties of the life they had chosen, and he seems to have encouraged the kind of friendships he himself needed and enjoyed.

Aelred wanted his monks to treat one another gently and took care to provide them an example. He considered it the glory of the house that it taught "tolerance of the infirm and compassion with others in their necessities" (*Life* 29). Under his rule, Rievaulx was a place of second chances for those who needed mercy, those who had failed to persevere in the monastic life elsewhere. Walter insisted that he never knew Aelred to expel anyone (*Life* 31), yet the abbot's legendary patience did have limits. The visiting abbot of a daughter-house once drew Aelred's anger in words so harsh Walter initially interpreted them as a lethal curse, although he later backed away from this judgment (cf. *Life* 37 and *Letter* 149). It was the visitor's abusive speech that provoked Aelred. He was, admittedly, its target, but he seemed to respond to more than a personal attack. It is likely that the visitor was defending himself against Aelred's correction and that Aelred heard in his intemperate rant an attack on truth and justice, as well as on the Cistercian discipline. It was an appalling example to give to the monks of Rievaulx. Taking to heart the admonition of the *Rule* that an abbot should strive to be loved rather than feared (*Rule* 64.15), Aelred understood that the abbot set the tone of the house, and he realized how much harm an abbot could do through his own sin or stupidity. In the *Pastoral Prayer*, written late in his life, he prayed that his own monks would love and fear him in such measure as God knew to be beneficial to them (3, 9).

As he aged, Aelred had to determine how to deal with his own physical infirmities since they affected his official and personal life and the kind of leadership and example he could provide. He could have retired. Walter's portrait of the frail, pain-ridden abbot of Aelred's last years is of a man wracked by kidney stones and arthritis but still very much in charge. Eventually Aelred's poor health required drastic concessions. The General Chapter gave him wide discretion to mitigate an abbot's normal daily routine and travel, and Aelred submitted to being cared for, though he was uncomfortable about being exempt from the common observance (*Life* 31). He used this dispensation as grounds to have a small chamber built near the infirmary, where he could carry on as best he could with minimal disruption to the community. He may have intended to keep the community's everyday problems at arms' length; instead, his monks crowded into this place "and talked to him as a little child prattles with its mother" (*Life* 31). The scene is charming, yet it is not difficult to imagine that providing such a motherly presence was tiring for Aelred and that Walter may often have wanted to shoo his brethren away. Only a fraction of the by-then sizeable community at Rievaulx could have actually spent much time in their abbot's company this way, and this may have produced tension and division. It may also have been a means by which the abbot's words radiated out from his room into little clusters of conversation all around the abbey. In the *Pastoral Prayer*, Aelred prayed that, since he could not edify his monks by vigils and fasts, he might do so by humility and charity, patience and pity (7). Being available to them was one way to do so.

Through the curtailment of his travel and outside activities, ill health gave Aelred back to his monks, and Aelred himself may have welcomed that. Although sometimes in pain at the slightest touch, he was not entirely an invalid or cut off from normal community life (*Life* 31). Walter recalled an occasion when the abbot, sitting in the orchard with the cellarers, got painfully to his feet and hurried in the fading light, without his staff, to the side of a monk who was thought to be dying (*Life* 36). It was no more than any abbot was supposed to do, but Aelred's monks surely knew how much even such ordinary tasks cost him. He was not idle either. Walter asserted that many of his writings and a voluminous, now-lost correspondence date from this period. In time and despite his frailty, to Walter's obvious anxiety, Aelred intensified his austerities and was increasingly absorbed in contemplation. Yet from that period of Aelred's life Walter recalled several instances of miraculous knowledge of the state of the souls of various monks within the community. Their ailing abbot was, in some ways, more present than ever (*Life* 44–46).

He was also vulnerable, and not only to ordinary trials like the cold of a Yorkshire winter. Walter's memoir has little to say about challenges to Aelred's authority, yet there was quiet heroism in choosing to govern as Aelred did. He was available to his monks and committed to dealing with them with alert intelligence that discerned and made allowance for weaknesses even in the face of serious faults. This comes through with painful intensity in an event Walter did not include in the *Life* but made the concluding tale in his *Letter to Maurice*. A monk (whether deranged or just belligerently out of control is unclear) once stormed into the abbot's room, berated him, and literally pitched Aelred into the fire. Walter himself in fury tackled the assailant before other monks helped restrain him, but, before Walter's eyes, Aelred, who moments before had huddled in pain by the fire "like a leaf of parchment," was instantly Father Abbot, asserting the full authority of his office with every expectation of being obeyed. Blessing and soothing the culprit, he insisted to his outraged rescuers that the monk was ill and was to be treated gently. This show of kindness Walter could only call, in amazed wonder, "the most perfect pledge of love" (*Letter* 158). The abbot who was prepared to defer to the opinion of his monks about admitting new recruits would not relinquish his right to discipline them with charity (*Life* 30).

When he realized his life was nearing its end, Aelred calmly set about his final abbatial duties, to leave the community in good order and comforted by his love for them. His final chapter talks left them in tears and him exhausted, and he grieved when he had to send away monks who had come to deal with some business because he was simply too tired to speak (*Life* 49). Finally he summoned them all to ask their permission and their prayers to leave them, this time not on some errand overseas or at court, but for eternity. He blessed them, asserting that he loved them "as a mother," and admonished them about the election of his successor. Specifically he cautioned the younger monks to take guidance from the elders, aware, given the growth of the community, that for many this would be their first experience of electing an abbot (*Life* 50). He also bequeathed them the treasure-hoard that had delighted him over the years: three books (a glossed psalter, John's Gospel, and Augustine's *Confessions*), a collection of relics (perhaps from his family home at Hexham), and a cross that had belonged to Henry Murdac, the severe fellow Cistercian who became archbishop of York when Aelred and others had successfully lobbied for the deposition of his predecessor over 20 years earlier (*Life* 51). The collection says much about Aelred. The books had shaped his life as a monk and his most important insights into the spiritual life, while the relics spoke of his conscious connection to the holy landscape of the past, both remote and recent.

The love Aelred had fostered in his community enfolded him as he died. To keep vigil with a dying brother was standard monastic practice, but Walter recounted that 12, 20, 40, 100 monks crowded into the abbot's room, "so vehemently was this lover of us all loved by his own" (*Life* 53). They took turns at his side through a long, weary process of dying and watched him slip away from them, his attention more and more fixed on eternity. "Festinate, for crist luve," he murmured in a mingling of Latin and English meaning "Hasten, for the love of Christ" (*Life* 54). Near the end, cradling Aelred's head in his hands, Walter directed his abbot's gaze to the crucifix and whispered, "Let your eye be where your heart is" (*Life* 57). It was one last chance to lead by example, and Aelred roused himself to speak, as Bede had, not in the English of his childhood, but in the liturgical Latin that had shaped his prayer by day and night for over 30 years. His final affirmation of faith and hope used the language he shared with all his monks, whatever their background (*Life* 57).

"Blessed is that abbot who deserves so to be loved by his own," Walter observed, remembering how the monks of Rievaulx had sat at Aelred's deathbed and how Aelred himself had cherished that love as the greatest blessing of his life (*Life* 53). Not every twelfth-century abbot could have been so sure of such love, not all would have been so eager for it, and not all would have deserved it. Obviously, not everyone at Rievaulx loved Aelred and responded well to his approach to monastic community. It has long been suggested that Walter's depiction of Rievaulx under Aelred was tinted by a rosy glow of idealization or memorialized a golden sunset that soon faded, that Aelred's governance by love had led to a lack of discipline that later abbots, competent and devout as they were, had to meet with a stricter regime.

It may be true, yet, if so, that reality may have less to do with Aelred's policy, strictness, or lack thereof, than with other issues. The first generation of Cistercians were all but gone, and many movements find it hard to sustain their initial intensity as later generations find themselves needing to settle down into routines with structure and regularity. At Rievaulx and elsewhere, success itself took a toll, as sheer numbers made it hard to maintain the close relationships of earlier days. Moreover, the context of religious life was changing, not just at Rievaulx and among the Cistercians, but in western Christendom generally. The monastic orders would continue to flourish and to serve, but the growing cities and the intellectual climate of the schools were raising new issues, providing new paths. One cannot know how Aelred might have adjusted, had he lived to govern Rievaulx for another decade or two, how he might have applied his intelligence to the task of inviting yet another generation into Cistercian life, or what new forms he might have found for miracles of love. Walter Daniel wanted to make sure that the memory of his example would remain.

Bibliographic Note

For this essay, I have relied on Walter Daniel, *The Life of Aelred of Rievaulx,* ed. and trans. Maurice Powicke (Oxford: Oxford University Press, 1979 [1950]), which includes the *Letter to Maurice.* It has been reprinted, albeit without the Latin text, as Walter Daniel, *The Life of Aelred of Rievaulx* (Kalamazoo, MI: Cistercian Publications, 1994), adding the previously untranslated *Lament for Aelred* and an insightful introduction by Marsha Dutton.

For further study of the themes addressed here, there is no substitute for reading Aelred himself. See *The Mirror of Charity,* trans. E. Connor (Kalamazoo, MI: Cistercian Publications, 1990); *Spiritual Friendship,* trans. M.E. Laker (Kalamazoo, MI: Cistercian Publications, 1974); and *The Pastoral Prayer,* trans. R.P. Lawson in *Treatises* I (Kalamazoo, MI: Cistercian Publications, 1971). Walter's *Life of Aelred* invites comparison with the other great monastic memoirs of the period; in this chapter, I have used Jocelin of Brakelond, *Chronicle of the Abbey of Bury St. Edmunds,* trans. D. Greenway and J. Sayers (Oxford: Oxford University Press, 1989).

Secondary literature on Aelred and his world is extensive. Dutton's references in *The Life of Aelred* to her own and the work of others are helpful, as is T.J. Heffernan, *Sacred Biography: Saints and Their Biographers in the Middle Ages* (Oxford: Oxford University Press, 1988). For broader context, see Janet Burton, *The Monastic Order in Yorkshire* (Cambridge: Cambridge University Press, 1999); Peter Fergusson and Stuart Harrison, *Rievaulx Abbey: Community, Architecture, Memory* (New Haven: Yale University Press, 2000); Brian McGuire, *Friendship and Community: The Monastic Experience, 350–1250* (Kalamazoo, MI: Cistercian Publications, 1988), and its 2nd ed. (Ithaca: Cornell, 2010); and Brian McGuire, *Brother and Lover: Aelred of Rievaulx* (New York: Crossroad, 1994). Aelred Squire, *Aelred of Rivaulx: A Study* (Kalamazoo, MI: Cistercian Publications, 1981) remains the standard study of Aelred.

NINETEEN

Richard of Devizes
The Monk Who Forgot to be Medieval

Nancy Partner

The author of the little history covering the first three years of the reign of King Richard I of England (1189–92) inserted his given name, identifying place of origin (the twelfth century's substitute for a surname), professional affiliation, and home address into the first lines of his book: "Richard, called 'of Devizes,'" "our church at Winchester," and "the cloister at Winchester." Richard was a common name and this particular Richard did not want to be confused with any other. The dedication and remarks that make up a kind of preface to the historical narrative beginning with the royal coronation of 1189 freely use first-person singular verbs, so many that "I" occurs in translation 21 times in fewer than two-and-a-half pages of text, and personal possessives stand out as well: "my request," "my leaving," "my exercise," "my work," "my writing" (1–3). This Richard, who came from the town of Devizes and announces himself a monk and writer residing in the monastery of Saint Swithin and serving the cathedral church of Winchester, is a man of frankly expressed personal wishes: "I often had a strong desire to follow...and certainly to see for myself"; "I wonder at another thing"; "I wonder at a third thing"; "Oh how happy I would be if..." (1–2).

A more assertive personality—or the crafted persona of one—occupies the foreground of our entry into this text than is usually the case with medieval authors, especially authors of histories whose narrative personas were conventionally earnest, studious, pious, and modest. The long-established conventions of authorship in the genre of history were self-effacing: the book was produced as a service to others, often an act of obedience with the author purportedly writing only to fulfill the direct request of a superior. John of Salisbury (c. 1115–76), one of the most distinguished intellectuals of his era, gracefully gave credit to a friend for deciding that he should write a work of history: "And so, my dearest friend and master, I gladly obey your command."[1] If the historian was a monk, religious earnestness and personal modesty—authorship as an act of obedience and not pride—was the expected posture. The historian Orderic Vitalis (1075–c. 1142), born in England and living in a Norman monastery, even suggests that his abbot may change anything he finds inadequate: "I began this work at the clear command of the venerable old abbot, Roger, and am now offering it to you, Father Warin...so that you may delete what is superfluous [and] correct its infelicities."[2]

In medieval Europe after the eighth century, history was synonymous with Bede, whose Ecclesiastical History of the English People, discussed in Chapter 8 above, set the standard for intellectual and literary accomplishment. History served serious moral purposes by illustrating the virtues and vices of men: "Should history tell of good men and their good estate, the thoughtful listener is spurred on to imitate the good; should it record the evil ends of wicked men, no less effectually the devout and earnest listener or reader is kindled to eschew what is harmful and perverse."[3] Bede was not the first Christian historian to regard history as a mode of moral instruction, but his influence made nearly all succeeding historians accept a responsibility to moralize history. In this tradition, William of Malmesbury (c. 1095–1143), a monk-historian writing some 50 years before Richard, notes: "For what is more to the advantage of virtue or more conducive to justice than learning the divine gentleness to the good and vengeance upon traitors?"[4]

A rather more ambitious goal was to apply biblical exegesis to the ongoing events of the world, which was regarded as God's Book in which the

---

[1] John of Salisbury, Memoirs of the Papal Court, trans. Marjorie Chibnall (London: Nelson and Sons, 1956), 3.

[2] The Ecclesiastical History of Orderic Vitalis, ed. and trans. Marjorie Chibnall (Oxford: Clarendon Press, 1980), vol. 1, 133.

[3] Bede, Ecclesiastical History of the English People, trans. Leo Sherley-Price (London: Penguin Books, 1990), 41.

[4] William of Malmesbury, The Historia Novella, trans. K.R. Potter (London: Nelson and Sons, 1955), 1.

divinity "writes" by influencing events. The techniques used to decipher the hidden spiritual meanings of Scripture could be adapted by highly educated and serious historians to uncover God's purposes and judgments in the life of the created world. Indeed, all the historians Richard of Devizes might have known invoked moral reasons for writing history as the self-introduction to their putative readers and masked their personal literary ambitions in higher purposes.

Richard, a monk by profession and obviously well educated, immedi-·ately invokes several of those conventions, but his words betray to even the uninformed reader of medieval histories an oddly flippant disrespect for them. He dedicates the book in the first line: "To his venerable father and always his master, Robert, formerly prior of Winchester...if what he has begun is good, may he persevere in it" (1). Something rings a little odd in the "formerly prior" and that "if" attached to the conditional "good." We learn immediately what the questionable enterprise is—Robert had left Winchester to join the Carthusians, a new monastic order whose way of life was so strict and demanding that it accepted only mature men who were already successful monks of other orders. Richard spends the rest of his prologue describing a visit he made to Robert's new home "to see for myself...by how much a Carthusian cell is loftier and nearer Heaven than is the cloister at Winchester." He adopts the attitude of a naïve enthusiast whose illusions are crushed by the absurd reality he discovered. Carthusians live in individual cells with "one door, which you are allowed to open as you like, but through which you may not go out, except in such a way that one foot always stays short of the threshold and inside the cell." The other foot may go wherever it likes. "There must be some great and profound mystery," Richard comically exclaims about this open door and one-foot policy (1–2). Carthusians recoil from worldly contact so much that they refuse to offer the traditional monastic hospitality of meals and beds to travelers. Richard wonders loudly how it is that such isolated men always know the latest gossip, everything that happens, "and sometimes you know about it in advance" (2). And even though Robert has joined this spiritual elite and no longer needs mere human information, he has asked Richard to write a very worldly book for him so that he can be reminded how vile the world is "and so that these letters might bring back the memory of your friend to you again"—a friend he will rarely or never see (2). In this prologue the moral purpose of history is perversely to display the world at its most wicked and corrupt, to remind an elite monk of what he is supposed to forget and also of the pleasures of sophisticated conversation with the worldly friend he has left behind. The preface speaks the hurt feelings of a rejected friend who hardly conceals his scorn for extremist and pretentious religious zealotry.

Modern medievalists may not admit this, but even quite sophisticated readers encounter certain ingrained resistances in themselves when reading a serious medieval text whose author doesn't seem to conform to the paradigmatic notions of "the medieval": sober intentions, a religious motive informing every subject and assertion, subjection of individuality to a collective religious or social standard, and so forth along these too familiar lines. Currently, historians tend to disdain these stereotypes, but describing medieval personalities in markedly individualist terms sounds "too modern" to many ears. In Richard of Devizes, we find a monk who sounds sometimes petty and angry, allows personal hurt feelings to show, makes jokes in bad taste, adopts irony as his favorite stylistic tone, hardly mentions religion or morality at all and then in confusing ways, and ridicules another stricter religious order. No salvational morality is discernable in Richard's book, and he seems cynical in a sophisticated way but without the moral vision of true satire. The common medieval attitude called *contemptus mundi* — disdain for worldliness in view of eternal values — does not fit this text. The usual strategy for approaching medieval texts, by placing them in their institutional and cultural context (here monastery life, monastic religiosity, and contemporary concerns with Church governance) does not work exceptionally well for reading this author.

———————

There are any number of reasons for reading a twelfth-century history, and most of those reasons apply to Richard of Devizes's book: factual information, inaccurate information that reveals contemporary attitudes, and comparison with other writers and sources of information. Richard's history is fairly brief; its subject matter is chiefly the political machinations in England during the long absences of King Richard I, with interpolated scenes of the king on crusade and a few interesting digressions on other topics. But reading for this sort of information assumes that the historian-author fits the conventions of historical authorship we have learned to expect, conventions that in turn allow us to adopt the expectations of history-readers, albeit critical modern ones. Reading in this way, we tend to let the narrator's personality sink into the background. But something persists in telling us that to read Richard of Devizes in this same conventional way is to do something wrong, something the narrator is signaling to us not to do. We are plainly being asked to acknowledge this man, this personality, and not a generalized historian like any other, as a central experience of reading his book. That much is clear. But what personality, what person is this? The only person we can know is in this voice, this style, its tone, and its boldly displayed tastes, all of which constitute a distinct and major subject matter of the book. In this twelfth-century history we encounter a narrative voice that seems to be self-consciously and deliberately different from contemporary literary norms. Perhaps just reading that and accepting what we hear opens a new and additional kind of information: we have the promise of an individual personality, and that is what Richard's book can be about, at least for one kind of reading.

No one reads a twelfth-century author without some sense or anticipation of his medievalness, and when we know that an author was a professional of the Church our sense of his primary identity is virtually complete: "medieval" plus "ecclesiastical" construct what counts as a person. This is a shallow notion of a person, but it is often accepted as enough for medieval authors. The context for reading a specific medieval history is whatever array of contemporary culture we can reasonably attach to an author—whatever the evidence about political, social, religious, and intellectual life suggests about conditions in his lifetime and locale, we try to tailor to fit our author. The specific traits that make William of Malmesbury different, say, from John of Salisbury do not tend to be personality traits in this conventional approach. It feels sufficient to note that one was a Benedictine monk and the other had a varied career in the secular Church and to trace the extent of their education, knowledge, and intellectual opinions.

The "medieval" component is the more diffuse and unquestioned presumption that all literate Christians held certain religious beliefs, a particular world view involving supernatural forces, concern with salvation, sin, and non-worldly values. Adding "monk" to the mix raises the intensity and scope of the medievalness by a significant degree. Parish priests were often ill-educated and apparently never wrote books. Bishops were primarily chief executive officers of the Church. But monks stand for self-abnegation, spirituality, and lives completely immersed in a religious collective. This outdated, idealized sense of medievalness, so hard to specify, so hard to get rid of, lights up with self-conscious awkwardness as we read Richard's quirky book, and that too is valuable, something learned from reading. In a provisional sense, what does this narrative voice sound like? To what sort of person do we imaginatively attach the Richard-voice, composed as it is from a multitude of highbrow literary allusions, often inappropriately elevated for the events they describe, the constant denigrating commentary on nearly all the persons mentioned, and the vicious, selfish behaviors disconcertingly described for their entertainment value?

Personality types, at least the aspects that can be deliberately cultivated and that certain institutions can select and encourage, are subject to fashions, more demanding in their cultivation than clothing styles but equally amenable to conscious choices. Richard's style is not a current style, but something of it sounds familiarly like a novel. The personality fashions of the moment do not emphasize ironic detachment and humor that depends on classical allusions. Ironic detachment as an aspect of high cultivation is not the same as the "cool" aligned with being hip or with-it, although irony as a tone and personal stance are aspects of both. Richard's deliberately over-stylized voice is an older style. It involves a constant jokey play of clever satirical humor (often involving erudite allusions or wordplay) and an assertive idiosyncrasy, layered over a deeply conservative attachment to institutions, upper-class values, and high culture. Such an Oxbridge donnish mode of the earlier twentieth century resonates in some of Richard's self-conscious classicizing wit and his disdain for men who grub after power too openly and unsuccessfully. But Richard was neither a scholar nor a serious-minded intellectual.

Richard's Winchester was an insider's place. As the wealthiest episcopal diocese in England, its bishop was close to the centers of ecclesiastical and secular political power, a player whether he liked that role or not. The men privileged to belong to the monastery attached to the cathedral (a tradition unique to a few of England's dioceses) lived in a center of information about the most important men and events of the day, and they often witnessed them directly. One of the first events Richard describes is the arrest of a high royal official forced to pay (or repay) huge sums of money for his freedom. Deliberately—and sarcastically—dwelling on the weight of the contrast he presents, Richard says, "That great and powerful man...was seized and put in chains and brought to Winchester, where he was made a spectacle … weakened by hunger and loaded down with chains" (4–5). Richard also reports the exact sums he was forced to pay and in what currency. A major confrontation was planned between John, the king's brother and impatient successor, and William Longchamp, the king's designated representative — "the place, outside Winchester" (33). The new bishop of Winchester in 1189 was Godfrey, son of a high royal official and thus powerfully connected in his own right. Richard admires his bishop without reservation for his intelligence, political skills, and his strong sense of what was owed to Winchester's prestige, and he praises him in wholly secular terms as everything a bishop should be. Bishop Godfrey, "having secretly given the king 3,000 pounds of silver," recovered some land his church had lost, "nor did this circumspect man forget to make a fine [a good-will payment] with the king to guarantee the safety of the treasure of his church" and a variety of other rights and possessions (8).

King Richard combined chivalric glamor with royal ruthlessness and a complete lack of interest in governance or the welfare of England. His coronation set off a massive fund-raising effort to finance his expeditionary force for the Third Crusade: "[The king] made this jest: 'If I could have found a buyer I would have sold London itself'" (9). What Richard intends to convey about the king through this cynical quip is not that he was prepared to give away the chief city of his kingdom, but that he was prepared to take money from anyone stupid enough to think he could get bargains from the king. With his insider's knowingness, Richard chronicles royal amorality with a certain amusement and total acceptance.

Credulous, greedy fools squandered fortunes buying their fantasies of power from the cynical, obliging king who "unburdened all those whose money was a burden to them, and he gave to whomever he pleased whatever powers and possessions they chose" (9). But Godfrey of Winchester knew how things worked, understood his king, and expended money only for rights he could enforce. Other men were publicly confounded to discover that King Richard had sold them conflicting royal orders, but never Bishop Godfrey. This is the sort of power player the historian admires.

Confined to the first three years of Richard I's reign, Richard of Devizes's history is made up of political insider stories when the scene is in England and romantically exaggerated partisan accounts of King Richard on crusade, the point of which is invariably to show up by comparison the contemptible French king, the contemptible French in general, and the more contemptible Byzantine Christians of all ranks. Scenes back home seen from the perspective of Winchester, close to the action and insider gossip, are interlaced with scenes abroad set in Sicily, Cyprus, and Acre, connected only with the unstated, implied sense of "meanwhile." Richard's account is entirely secular whether it concerns the crusade or the institutions and clergy of the Church. The frenzied maneuvering for power, personal advantage, and opportunistic advancement during the king's indeterminate stay abroad (and the unsettling but exciting possibility of his never returning) was ideal for Richard's insider stories—his knowing reports of who said what to whom—and bolstered his confidence to invent fictional speeches for important men at moments of high stress. Unconcealed raw ambition among the power brokers in England during the king's absence—their little dramas of public self-assertion and humiliation, such as letters, conversation, and crass maneuvers for control of castles and high position immediately after the king's departure—is Richard's literary world.

With a combination of slightly absurd classical quotations, he renders these events in which men, who are frequently both bishops and public officials with control of castles, blatantly try to bully and outwit one another. Here, he drops in Horace and Virgil: "The sacred letter of the king, greatly to be revered, was brought forth to be proclaimed. 'The mountains are in labor; a ridiculous mouse will be born' [*Ars Poetica*]. It was ordered that complete silence be kept before the king's mandate. 'All were still and kept attentive silence' [*Aeneid*]." There, he turns to sarcastic, knowing gossip: "The letter, which would have been more impressive if its contents had not already been known, was read in public" (12). The real world that Richard decorates with classical quotation is rendered in bluntly straightforward lines such as, "John, the king's brother, who had kept his ears open, so that he knew for certain that his brother had turned his back on England, now went about the country with a larger following. He did not prohibit or restrain his followers from calling him the king's heir" (29–30).

This twelfth-century author is no moralizer about the vanity of the world. There is no pious recoil of distaste from the power politics of life in a nearly ungoverned kingdom where conflict between the absent king's impatiently ambitious brother and the resented but legitimate royal deputy, the chancellor William Longchamp, turned tiny provocations into high stakes gambles. It is clear that Richard of Devizes, speaking from a conservative center of wealth and power, was loyal only to his king and

William Longchamp, the king's chosen man in England. He felt contempt for opportunist semi-traitors: "The face of the realm was altered at the king's departure" — it was done with secret letters and secret promises. Richard draws on his elegant secular learning, not biblical verses, when he ornaments scenes of double-dealing and public humiliation. At the showdown that drove William Longchamp out of England, Richard lends him a pithy line from Juvenal to begin his defiant speech: "Am I always to be only a listener, and shall I never answer?" And with powerful men incriminating themselves without restraint, only Bishop Godfrey had political acumen and sense: "Although he [Godfrey] was more eloquent than most, [he] kept silent all the time" (49–51).

Richard's chronicle is not the sort of medieval narrative in which invisibly embodied moral forces, the devil or satanic impulses, are invoked to supply motives to men making greedy and destructive bad choices. Richard knows exactly why men want what they want, and he implicitly writes for readers who understand the world in those same terms. Interjections of pious shock, despair at the evil ways of the world, biblical allusions, and moralizing clichés would feel tiresome, intrusively naïve, beside the point, or priggish in this context. Elevated notions and idealism of a limited sort are directed to the king on his chivalric adventures far away. Richard writes for adults in the career-track institutions of secular and ecclesiastical life for whom power and wealth, gained and lost, make unashamedly interesting reading.

In his narrative voice, Richard is conservative, a man who understands the value of established institutions, both secular and ecclesiastic, and feels that life within these organized and long-standing arrangements offers as much satisfaction and personal expression as any civilized and well-judging man should want. The sort of impulse that took his friend, Prior Robert, to a more ascetic, inward mode of religious life would merely seem excessive to Richard. The word "cynical" seems a crude fit for his style of mind; he is not disabused and disillusioned. His is a worldly conservatism that offers ample space for the free play of personality, wit, humor, personal friendship, and more impersonal loyalties to city, nation, and king. Irony, different from cynicism in many important degrees, is the natural tone of this sophistication, which allows for occasional sentimentality and romanticized loyalty.

The mental map of Richard's world could be drawn in a kind of frankly anachronistic analogue to the mental map of an inside-the-beltway

Washington professional, someone near but not in the inner circles of high power, a career professional in an agency or department, privy to good-quality gossip, yet not himself a player. He sounds like the kind of man for whom the institutions that channel the vast reservoirs of real power (royal or public) into narrower streams are what describe reality at its most meaningful level. Insider gossip about winners and losers in the endless maneuvers to attain and extend the reach of personal influence, and privileged information about the struggles among the great, are the shop talk, endlessly enthralling, of his social world. The facts that Saint-Swithin was a cathedral chapter with a major bishop as its titular abbot and that Bishop Godfrey of Winchester had access to the near reaches of royal power, with a lot to gain or lose, is crucial for Richard and his insiders' book.

For such a brief book, featuring important men in the Church and secular nobility, Richard wrote at disproportionate length about Jews and did so in a tone that has left his intentions unclear to modern readers. Since his narrative begins with the coronation of Richard I, it is not surprising that he reported the ferocious attacks against the Jews in London, touched off by a confused series of events surrounding the coronation. Murderous attacks on Jews occurred in numerous towns, culminating in a virtual pogrom in York, where 500 English Jews were killed. Richard tells these events in a condensed report written in his characteristic style of amused disdain: "On that same coronation day, at about the hour of the solemnity in which the Son was immolated to the Father, they began in the city of London to immolate the Jews to their father, the Devil. It took them so long to celebrate this mystery that the holocaust was barely completed on the second day. The other towns and cities of the country emulated the faith of the Londoners, and with equal devotion they dispatched their bloodsuckers bloodily to hell. To some degree, but not everywhere the same, this storm against the incorrigible people raged throughout the kingdom" (3–4). The heavy-handed religious language — immolate, the Son and the Father, the Devil, "this mystery," "the faith of the Londoners" — deployed with a cool, removed tone makes the author's personal response hard to gage, except that the stress on "this mystery" and the length of time it took to complete seems very sarcastic. He continues: "Winchester alone spared its worms. They were a prudent and far-sighted people and a city that always behaved in a civilized manner. They never did anything overhastily, for fear they might repent of it later, and they looked to the end of things rather than to the beginnings. They did not want partially to vomit forth the undigested mass violently and at their peril, even though they were urged to do so, when they were not ready" (4). Although the style here of distanced mild disdain and his choice of vomit imagery as a metaphor for persecution are repellant to modern readers, Richard does seem to be praising the citizens of Winchester and associating tolerant behavior with civilized manners. His praise is equivocal: on the one hand, Winchester's peaceful restraint is civilized; and yet, on the other, it is also merely prudent, a cost/benefit analysis that suggests the possibility of short-term loss. There is nothing about tolerance in these sentences; the citizens of Winchester were far-sighted, self-interested, and "not ready." Yet York and the other scenes of looting and carnage were not punished, and Richard expresses nothing but his signature knowing scorn for them and their protracted bloody "mystery."

An entirely original and much longer episode involving Jews is Richard's story of an alleged ritual child murder in Winchester. This is one of the longest single episodes in the book and shows every mark of careful composition. The creation of narrative voice, the sophisticated wit, deliberate echoes of classical learning—together with what sound like spoofs of contemporary sources—and narrative completion demand our attention. The story is deliberately connected with the earlier mention of Winchester's Jews. "Because Winchester should not be deprived of its just praise for having kept peace with the Jews, as is told at the beginning of this book, the Jews of Winchester, zealous, after the Jewish fashion, for the honor of their city... brought upon themselves, according to the testimony of many people, the widely known reputation of having made a martyr of a boy in Winchester" (64). The tissue of sly insults here is so closely interlaced that it is nearly impossible to diagram. Everyone mentioned is tarnished, both the peaceful Christians and the Jews. The cool snideness somehow even touches the "testimony of many people" and the "widely known reputation." Common belief does not count for much from a writer who commented dismissively that "those who do not understand the causes of things marveled greatly" at an eclipse of the sun in June of 1191, while "those who study the working of the world, however, say that certain defects of the sun and moon do not signify anything" (35).

Richard then tells a story with a long build-up. "A certain Jew," unnamed, of Winchester hired a Christian boy from France as apprentice to the cobbler's trade. A French Jew had recommended him for this position, encouraging the boy with a detailed travelogue of what to expect on his travels through England. Richard assumes the fictional voice of the French Jew in a comic tour de force performance in which he satirizes the chief cities of England. London is a sink of exotic depravity and temptations: "Do not associate with the crowds of pimps.... You will meet with more braggarts there than in all France; the number of parasites is infinite. Actors, jesters, smooth-skinned lads, Moors, flatterers, pretty boys, effeminates, pederasts, singing and dancing girls." All the threatening delights of imperial Rome, lifted directly from Horace's first books of the *Satires,* are bestowed on London (65–66). Other cities get their own special insults. Canterbury is impoverished. Rochester is a mere hamlet. Exeter provides the same feed to men and animals. Bath has a smelly climate. York is full of filthy Scotsmen. Ely smells bad, too. Bristol is populated with soap makers. And these cities, with cathedrals, are the best places—all the rest of the towns and villages are filled with crude boors (66–67). Only Winchester, where alone the Jews "enjoy perpetual peace," is civilized, wealthy, refined, gracious, and courteous. Winchester has only one vice: "the people of Winchester lie like sentries"; "nowhere else under heaven are so many false rumors made up so easily as there" (67).

After the long comic prologue, the story proper begins. The Christian boy and his friend work for the Jews, living together "in the same old hut of a poor old woman." Then the boy disappeared around the time of the Passover holiday. His friend looked for him and finally accused the Jewish cobbler of murder: "'You son of a dirty whore,' he said, 'you thief, you traitor, you devil, you have crucified my friend!'" As his shouts attracted a crowd, his eloquence expanded to fit the opportunity: "'O you men who gather together,' he said, 'see if there is a grief like unto my grief.... This man has torn the heart out of my breast.'" More circumstantial details intervene; more hearsay accusations lead to a legal process before judges. But the supposed accusers were disqualified; the Jew offered testimony under oath. "Gold won the judges favour ... and the matter was dropped" (67–69). End of story.

What kind of child-martyr story is this, in which every variety of comic satire is displayed, all the character-narrators are figures of fun or scorn, and an elaborate, circuitous lead-in with all kinds of incidental detail that seems to be building up to some narrative crisis finally goes nowhere? "The matter was dropped." Richard did not treat this episode with any seriousness at all. The only literary sub-category that fits his meandering anecdote is called a shaggy dog story, which is a long, involved anecdote whose humor lies in its digressions and embroideries, the way it is told, and its long-delayed punch line. It is almost nihilistic in its pointlessness, and it deliberately flouts the conventions of folk narrative. There is no point searching for the moral center of this piece of narrative or the author's real opinion. The core of the story, compounded presumably of rumors and gossip, appealed to him as the hook around which to build a serpentine comic performance with a clever self-deflating ending, in other words, a prototypical shaggy dog story.

———————

How exactly are we to register this voice, that of an historian who follows intently the course of political opportunism and near-treason in all their permutations with evident fascination and who uses the information about persecutions and blood libel of the Jews as the ingredients of a stretched-out joke? Richard shows an early form of near-jingoism in his open contempt for the French and his exaggerated idealizing of King Richard I; he admires Queen Eleanor and accepts her as an active political player in her own right. Being a monk in an elite, refined, and wealthy religious center is his career and his status in the world, a high status. It has little to do with piety or excessive moralizing of the sort he clearly finds tedious and silly in the Carthusians. As far as one can judge from this book, his only book, Richard of Devizes was a man who found only one thing worth a continuous and serious attention, and that was politics in all its forms. Power was serious; everything else was passing entertainment, stuff for a shaggy dog story. As an author, this Richard asks us to accept him on his own terms, the only terms he offers, and forces us to rethink everything we thought was medieval.

Bibliographic Note

The best edition and translation of Richard's *Chronicle* is John T. Appleby, *The Chronicle of Richard of Devizes of the Time of King Richard the First* (London: Nelson and Sons, 1963). It is especially interesting to compare Richard with contemporary historians of similar background, to several of whom I refer in the notes for this chapter and who are discussed in Antonia Gransden, *Historical Writing in England, c. 550 to c. 1307* (Ithaca: Cornell University Press, 1974). For a general survey of the common conventions of modesty and self-effacement accepted by nearly all authors of historical works, see her "Prologues in the Historiography of Twelfth-Century England," in *England in the Twelfth Century,* ed. Daniel Williams (Woodbridge: Boydell Press, 1990), 55–81. A different literary-historical approach is found in Nancy Partner, *Serious Entertainments: The Writing of History in Twelfth-Century England* (Chicago: University of Chicago Press, 1977), where I discuss Richard of Devizes at greater length.

Valuable background to Richard's cultural and political world is Richard W. Southern, "England's First Entry into Europe," in his *Medieval Humanism* (Oxford: Blackwell, 1970), 135–57. For further discussion of Richard's representation of Jews within his chronicle, see Anthony Bale, "Richard of Devizes and Fictions of Judaism," *Jewish Culture and History* 3.2 (2000): 55–72; Robert Levine, "Why Praise Jews: History and Satire in the Middle Ages," *Journal of Medieval History* 12 (1986): 291–96; and John McCulloh, "Jewish Ritual Murder: William of Norwich, Thomas of Monmouth, and the Early Dissemination of the Myth," *Speculum* 72 (1997): 698–740.

TWENTY

Mission to Crusade
Friar William of Rubruck's Journey to the Mongols

Adnan Husain

"Now on the third day after we left Soldaia, we encountered the Tartars; and when I came among them I really felt as if I were entering some other world" (1.14). On his return to Acre in the Latin kingdom in Palestine in August 1255, Franciscan friar William of Rubruck wrote these words in a lengthy letter to King Louis IX of France (1226–70). William details both his journey to the Mongol imperial capital of Qaraqorum in inner Asia and his startling experiences in this "other world." But William's letter to the future saint, who had returned to France after his failed crusade (the seventh, from 1248 to 1254), was more than a private account of one intrepid friar's experiences among the alien Mongols. It testifies to and draws significance from a period when many different peoples across Eurasia, not just Latin Christians and Mongols, would come into contact — sometimes violent conflict — in ways that would connect their histories. William's narrative captures a truly global moment in the pre-modern past, one forged both by the spectacular Mongol conquests across Asia and also by the commercial and military expansion of the Latins further east, between which the Muslim-dominated societies of west Asia were caught.

By William's time, Latin Christians ("the Franks" as they were often known among non-Latins), had become involved in Mediterranean-wide ventures of trade, conquest, and settlement. Beginning in the mid-eleventh century, the Normans captured and settled Muslim-ruled Sicily. Castilian and Aragonese sovereigns defeated the Arab and Berber Muslim dynasties of Spain to encompass most of the Iberian Peninsula, leaving only the Castilian tributary of the Nasrid kingdom of Granada by 1238. Crusaders had managed to maintain small and embattled Latin enclaves on the Levantine coast. The Fourth Crusade and the conquest of Constantinople in 1204 had led to the establishment of Latin imperial rule in the Byzantine East until 1261. Consequently, by the mid-thirteenth century, several generations of Latin warriors had established themselves in small principalities in former Byzantine and Muslim provinces across the eastern Mediterranean, along the Greek and Balkan coastline (Morea), and on major islands such as Crete and Cyprus. This increasing presence of the Latins was all made possible by the maritime dominance of Italian cities, especially Genoa and Venice, whose merchants trafficked across the Mediterranean and whose ships ferried people of all sorts: pilgrims, mercenaries, colonists, couriers, diplomats, slaves, and missionaries. In these expanded territories, Latins now ruled over ethnically diverse and religiously heterogeneous peoples: Arab and Berber Muslims, Sephardic Jews, and Greek Orthodox and other eastern Christians. Elsewhere they interacted with people of other ethnicities, such as Turks and Armenians. Indeed, the horizons of medieval European peoples had already expanded well beyond what would become western Europe.

But news of a new people, the Mongols, would provoke truly universalist aspirations and an even wider global imagination. Known typically, though erroneously, to the Latin West as the "Tartars" — the Tatars were a different central Asian tribal group whose name passed into the Latin West in a form recalling the classical name for Hell, *Tartarus* — this nomadic tribal people, the Mongols, had united under the leadership of Chingis (Gengis) Khan (d. 1227) and, through astonishing and often terrifying conquest, had swept across the steppes of Asia to form a vast empire, the largest contiguous land empire in world history. Ruled by Chingis's dynastic successors until the empire slowly fragmented over the course of the fourteenth century — but approaching its zenith soon after William of Rubruck wrote his letter — Mongol dominions stretched from the northern shores of the Black Sea near Hungary and eastern Anatolia in the west to China in the east. Waging a failing effort to defend the Latin kingdom against the Ayyubid successors of the great Muslim warrior Salah al-Din (Saladin), who had recaptured Jerusalem in 1187, crusade enthusiasts recognized a remarkable opportunity in the stunning Mongol defeats of Muslim princes such as the Seljuk Turks of Anatolia and the Khwarazm Shahs in greater Persia.

Although initial impressions of the fearsome Mongol hordes in Latin Christendom were fed by the terrifying accounts of the invasion of Catholic Hungary in the early 1240s, reports circulating among eastern Christian circles, including those of crusade allies such as the Cilician Armenian kingdom in Anatolia, suggested that the religiously indeterminate Mongols were sympathetic to Christians and open to conversion. Such rumors converged powerfully with older legends from the middle of the twelfth century of a Christian king and priest named John who ruled vast territory in the East. In 1248, the Mongol commander in Persia, Eljigidai, sent his own embassy to the Latin West. His eastern Christian envoys reached Louis IX in Cyprus as the king was about to launch an invasion of Egypt; they claimed the Grand Khan Guyuk had converted to Christianity and encouraged Louis to attack Egypt as Eljigidai would begin a campaign westwards in Iraq against the Caliph in Baghdad. Expectations, already high for "the most Christian" king's crusade, soared at this news, and Louis quickly sent off two Dominican friars to Guyuk in Qaraqorum with rich gifts to follow up on these overtures. Over two years later when they rejoined Louis in Caeserea, these high hopes were dashed, and the disappointment was as great as that which had accompanied Louis's disastrous defeat in Egypt the year before, in 1250. Apparently, Guyuk had died in the interim and his desperate widow, acting as temporary regent, had displayed the gifts as tribute and evidence of Frankish submission before an assembly of diplomatic embassies to the Mongol court. Soon thereafter Guyuk's brother Mongke (Mangu Chan) deposed and executed her. Joinville, in *The Life of Saint Louis* (see Chapter 22 below), provides an account of this embarrassing episode and notes that Louis deeply regretted his credulity (178–79, 267). Later rumors of the conversion to Christianity of Sartaq, a Mongol prince and son of Batu, lord of the Golden Horde, would provoke Louis IX to dispatch Friar William of Rubruck with a more cautious letter. William's remarkable journey, his personal narrative of his experiences, and his detailed observations on the "other world" of the Mongols in central Asia thus took shape within this larger context of religious, political, and military ambitions and policies in a period that connected the histories of Eurasia and its peoples.

William's journey would take him first from the crusader states to the western limit of Mongol suzerainty in the spring of 1253. By ship to Constantinople, then into the Black Sea, he journeyed to the port of Soldaia on its northeastern shore, a city under sway of Batu (d. 1255), who

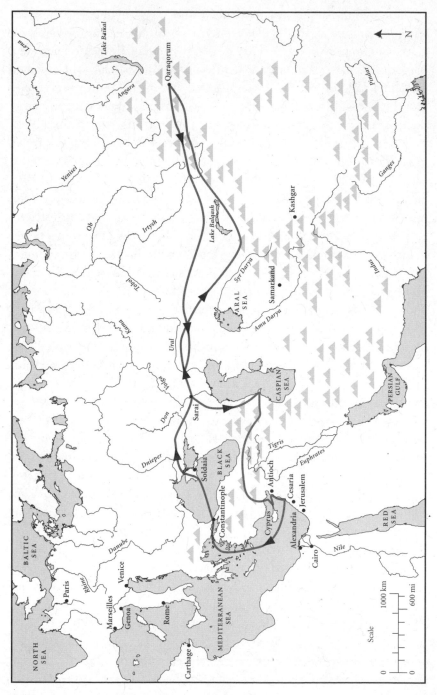

William of Rubruck's Journey to Qaraqorum.

was himself a grandson of Chingis Khan. Soon after departing, the friar would encounter a party of Mongols who brought him to the camp of Batu's son, Sartaq (d. 1256). It would be simply the first stage in an arduous trip across Asia to Qaraqorum, the seat of the Mongol Empire on the far northeastern end of the vast continent. This journey took him a great distance both geographically and culturally from the Mediterranean world, otherwise fairly well known to a Latin audience and, in particular, to the crusading King Louis. It exposed William to unfamiliar customs, foreign languages, and alien religious beliefs and practices.

About William of Rubruck we know very little other than what he tells us either directly or indirectly in his letter. His name suggests that he came from Rubruck in Flanders (modern Belgium), but he seems to have spent enough time in Paris to use it as a frame of reference in his report to King Louis. For instance, he compares the rivers Don and Volga with the Seine (10.14, 18.4) and describes distances in the Mongol capital of Qaraqorum in terms of the location of the monastery and suburb of Saint-Denis (32.1). Perhaps he had acquired his education as a theologian in Paris, allowing him to assume duties upon his return as a *lector* (lecturer in theology), even though he wished to rejoin Louis "and the spiritual comrades" he had in his kingdom (Epilogue.1). And although his text is not showy in displays of erudition—it is written in a pretty straightforward and simple Latin, perhaps for a lay, if royal, audience—he must have been well educated and was on some intimate terms with the king, who was well known to favor the friars as spiritual companions. He admits he was heavy enough that his girth proved to be something of a burden during his arduous journey (21.6).

While we have very few biographical details, the nature of his text and the personal voice that gives it shape reveal much about William, about what he thought and how he reacted to the challenging experiences he faced. In fulfilling his charge from Louis to put into writing "everything I saw among the Tartars" without fear of writing at length (Preface.2), William provides much more than a report on the Mongols; he offers both an autobiographical account of his journey and a very observant, almost ethnographic, report of Mongol material and cultural life.

William's ethnographic observations revolve around the central feature of Mongol society that distinguished it from the settled world he had known—nomadism. Referring to and interpolating a line of scripture— "For we have not here a lasting city, but we seek one that is to come"

(*Hebrews* 13:14) — he labels the Mongols as pagan nomads in his first, dismal judgment about them: "Nowhere have they any 'lasting city'; and of the 'one to come' they have no knowledge" (2.1). Instead, their dwellings of interlaced branches covered over in white felt were lashed to massive wagons that gave the Mongol camp the eerie appearance of a city on the move (2.2–4). He describes as well the kinds of food they ate (3); the brewing of their distinctive drink, *cosmos*, made from mare's milk (4); the way they hunted (5.3–4); their customs of dress (5.5–6), how men and women wore their hair, and how women adorned themselves (6); the division of labor between the sexes (7.1–3); their marriage customs (7.4–5); such matters of political and social importance as the administration of justice and the kinds of laws they established in their society (8.1–2); and, finally, their pagan funerary rituals and the powers of their soothsayers, "who are, as it were, their priests" (8.3–5). Typically detailed, William's portrait is also very visual. At one point, when he despairs at finding the words to convey the image of the carts that married Mongol women used, he admits to Louis that he would have drawn pictures of everything if he had known how (2.4).

Due to his remarkably detailed descriptions of Mongol life and habits, his report has been prized by historians of the Mongols for its accuracy, and he has been treated almost like an early anthropologist who went among tribal natives and provided an organized and complete description of their material, social, and cultural life. Aware of previous missions to the Mongols, including that of Louis's earlier diplomacy and the account of papal envoy and fellow Franciscan, John of Plano Carpini, five years earlier (19.5), even before his journey William had some impressions about the Mongols and the East, including wondrous geographical lore inherited from earlier scholars about dog-headed and one-eyed peoples. However, he was soon to find this knowledge rather wanting: "I enquired about the monsters or human freaks who are described by Isidore and Solinus, but was told that such things had never been sighted, which makes us very much doubt whether the story is true" (19.46). The actual experience of travel thus challenged William's expectations. However accurate or insightful his report on the world he encountered, his text is informed deeply by his interests and concerns. So the work is just as valuable a source of his cultural judgments that mark Mongol difference as it is about these alien others. Indeed, it shows us how a Latin Christian friar coped with the experience of living outside his own culture.

Practicing the Franciscan religious life in this alien cultural environment, for instance, proved to be a social challenge for William. He tells us about his embarrassment when he attempted to go about the Mongol camp barefoot in accordance with the Franciscan rule but was derided by those who gathered round and laughed (28.4). And at other times we see him losing his temper and snapping at his hosts in un-Franciscan fashion when they interrogated him about France, "as if they were due to move in and take it all over forthwith" (28.19).

Given that the journey was so difficult and his experience was at times so traumatic, some basic questions intrude, questions that help to understand the connection between his personal narrative and the wider history of which he was a part. Why did William of Rubruck travel to the Mongol East, what was his purpose, his motivations? Did he travel as a missionary to convert the Mongols, as a diplomatic envoy carrying an official letter from his patron, King Louis, as a Catholic priest to minister to captive Latin Christians in the East, or as a spy to reconnoiter political and military intelligence about a mysterious and dangerous enemy? At every interview at a Mongol court, such questions were posed. Although straightforward and simple, they do not have straightforward and simple answers. Indeed, William made many apparently contradictory or ambiguous remarks about his purpose and role, not only to his Mongol questioners, according to his own account of these conversations, but also in his own reflections throughout the text. In some ways his reasons for his presence in the East depended upon whom he was addressing and the context of their exchange. It is also very possible that he had different but overlapping, at times complementary and at times contradictory, motives or purposes for his journey. As his hope to discover receptive converts among the Mongol elite receded, for example, his purpose and interests may have shifted to more realistic goals. It is perhaps less important to settle on one single explanation than to understand that the various possibilities reveal much about the political dynamics of the cross-cultural encounters in which he participated.

Firstly, there were a variety of reasons for and ways of traveling in the Middle Ages. Besides mercantile and commercial travelers, such as the later celebrated Marco Polo (c. 1254–1324), some people may have wandered to satisfy a sense of exploration and curiosity about the world. However, this was anathema to the disciplinary values of Latin religious culture, especially for members of the religious orders—and principally monks—who were meant to be stable and to remain in their cloisters, unlike the wayward *gyrovagues* who wandered about. Stability was a key component of the monastic vow as articulated in the then-influential sixth-century *Rule of Saint Benedict.*[1] Furthermore, Bernard of Clairvaux (1090–1153), a monastic leader and scholar of the twelfth century, had discussed the first step toward pride and the danger of this sin for monks as the indulging in *curiositas,* which he characterized as a vagrant wandering beyond obedience and authority both in the physical and mental sense.[2] Pilgrimage to the shrines of the saints housing their relics was a more accepted form of religious travel, and the most celebrated pilgrimage site was Jerusalem. Likewise, crusade brought the Latins across the sea or along time-consuming overland routes to the Levant and was thus itself often described as a pilgrimage. Finally, the two forms of travel most relevant to William's case were the exchange of diplomatic embassies or communications through envoys — although he repeatedly denies such a role for himself — and the missionary travel of Franciscan friars who sought the conversion of souls or martyrdom.

As he tells us, William preached a sermon in Constantinople at Saint-Sophia at the outset of his journey and announced that he was not Louis's envoy but rather "was going among these unbelievers in accordance with our Rule" (1.6). He is referring here to the provision in the *Regula Bullata* of 1223 that concerns the mission to preach the Gospels and Christianity throughout the world to infidels.[3] Already by the 1250s when William traveled, a tradition of Franciscan missionary preaching to Saracens had developed following the example of Francis himself (1181/82–1226), whose famous encounter with the Sultan of Babylon (Egypt) in 1219 could be found in the earliest official life of the saint and served as a pious model for Franciscan mission.[4]

An important consequence of William's adoption of the conversion mission as the purpose or mode of his travel east was that it put him very much in contact with the religious communities he encountered. Unlike many earlier descriptions and portraits of the East, he regarded the people

---

[1] *The Rule of Saint Benedict,* ed. Justin McCann (Westminster, MD: Newman Press, 1963), 15–17, 131.

[2] Bernard of Clairvaux, *The Twelve Steps of Humility and Pride,* ed. Halcyon C. Backhouse (London: Hodder and Stoughton, 1985), 47–55.

[3] Chapter 12 of the Rule of 1223 in *The Writings of Saint Francis of Assisi,* trans. Benen Fahy (London: Burns and Oates, 1964), 64.

[4] Chapter 20 of Thomas of Celano's first life of Francis from 1229 in *Saint Francis of Assisi,* trans. Placid Hermann (Chicago: Franciscan Herald Press, 1988), 50–53.

he encountered as souls to save. He seems to have seized any and every opportunity he could to preach to Christian sectarians, Buddhist monks, "Saracen" Muslims, or Mongol polytheists. His success, however, was remarkably limited. In one case he claims almost to have managed to convert a Saracen he encountered on the journey to Qaraqorum, but his efforts were purportedly stymied by the prevailing notion among the eastern churches that one could not be a Christian and drink *cosmos* (12.1–2). He concludes rather pithily about these efforts that he had baptized only six souls. Most of these seem to have been the children of Latin Christian captives, so he was confirming them in their faith by administering the sacrament rather than effectively converting new adherents (36.6).

In fact, ministering to the enslaved Latin Christian captives from Germany and Hungary or to the recently Christianized Alans, a tribal people of eastern Europe, all of whom had been captured during the Mongol incursions in the early 1240s, became William's avowedly chief reason for journeying to central Asia and seeking Mongol permission to remain (33.1, 34.6). Franciscan and Dominican priests similarly provided pastoral care to communities of Latin Christians dispersed around the Mediterranean. For instance, friars in the 1230s and 1240s administered the sacraments and provided religious counsel and guidance to a community of merchants, mercenaries, and captive slaves in Tunis. Like the questions that these friars had posed to canon lawyers to help adjudicate the special circumstances of their position as a small minority in a non-Christian society, William encountered many similar sorts of challenges in trying to provide instruction in Roman doctrine and the performance of the sacraments in the Roman liturgical manner for the small community he found in the extreme east. On one occasion, he remembers the evident joy of finally being able to acquire some of the liturgical instruments and vestments necessary to cobble together a fair performance of the Latin Mass. He was thrilled to celebrate Easter in the Nestorian church in Qaraqorum, not only because he managed to avoid participating in their rite, in his view, but also for the rare opportunity to act independently and celebrate the sacrament using the instruments that a captured French silversmith had fashioned (30.10–14).

His report of these pastoral activities and local involvements — even conflicts — with the diverse religious communities in Qaraqorum suggests a shift from evangelical goals toward pastoral care for the Latin Christians of the Mongol Empire. In one such symbolic triumph, William parades a flag emblazoned with a cross carried high and sings a Latin hymn that causes "the Saracens considerable amazement" (19.43). These activities come to the fore as he grows disillusioned about the prospects for actually converting the Mongol lords and perturbed at his limited opportunities for and success in preaching at the Mongol court, for which he blames his language limitations and a poor translator (13.6 *et al.*). But his failure to influence his hosts after what he took to be a resounding triumph at a debate commissioned by Mongke between representatives of the various religions of his empire seems to have been the final and most decisive point, for this episode and his subsequent interview with the unhumbled khan represent the climax of William's narrative and the collapse of any expectant hopes for missionary success. As he admits, he would have needed to "possess the power to work miracles, as Moses did," were he to have swayed the resistant Mongol emperor. Preaching the Gospels by word and deed simply had not translated across languages and religious cultures successfully, nor had his appeals to seemingly universal theological reason (33.7, 34.7).

Over the course of the narrative, William's perspectives on and expectations about the nature of religious identity become increasingly clear and specific, especially in relation to the various Christian groupings in the East. His principal frustrations are directed at Nestorian Christian priests, who seem embarrassed to display the figure of Jesus on their crosses (15.7, 29.34) and were often drunk (26.12, 29). More importantly they neglected to instruct Mongols in the elements of the faith and thereby to capitalize on their enviable access to and influence with the women of the Mongol households in particular. Instead they accommodated themselves to participating syncretically in Mongol superstition and sorcery when they should have condemned the practices outright (29.42). Although Nestorian Christians and Roman Catholics differed in some points of doctrine about the nature of Christ, William emphasizes these doctrinal differences less than the more observable behavior and practices of the Nestorian priests. He finds their different religious culture, their commitments, and their identity more objectionable and worrisome. Religious identity for William, laboring beyond the cultural world of the Latin West, comes to be crystallized in these concrete ways and not only or simply to be a matter of orthodox belief.

He finds the priests' political accommodation of Mongol practices deeply disturbing. These objections lead him to deny that Sartaq was really a Christian and to explain away reports of his conversion, accepted in

Muslim and Eastern Christian chronicles of the period[5] simply as a matter of the exaggerated claims of the Nestorians (17.2). Equally revealing, William relates that "whether Sartach believes in Christ or not, I do not know." He does not even seem to care. This might seem astonishing since the proximate cause for his journey was to make contact with a Mongol lord in Asia Minor who had been rumored to have converted to Christianity and convey to him Louis IX's letter. The important point for William, however, seems to be that Sartach "does not wish to be called a Christian" (18.1). He reveals that Sartaq's court secretary, a Nestorian Christian named Coiac, had admonished him, "Do not say that our master is a Christian. He is not a Christian; he is a Mo'al [Mongol]." William explains, "For they regard the term of Christianity as the name of a people, and so they have become so arrogant that although they may perhaps believe somewhat in Christ, they have no wish to be called Christians, since they want their own name, Mo'al, to be exalted above all others" (xvi.5; my translation). The Mongols insist on their separate ethnic identity as Mongols, which is also a political status as rulers of an empire founded by their ancestor Chingis, a status that they value above all else. Moreover, the political dispensation of the Mongols, what they refer to as the "Order of Heaven" in Mongke's response to Louis, is as universal as William's Franciscan mission: "In Heaven there is only one eternal God; on earth there is only one lord, Chingis Chan" (36.6).

William carried a letter from Louis to Sartaq, which may suggest some diplomatic or political purpose for the journey. In any case, the Mongols seem to have regarded William and his party initially as official envoys from Louis and required, as was their custom, that he address Mongol lords at his first audiences with them in a gesture of submission on his knees. Yet William was at pains to avoid accepting this status and, when necessary, chose to deny it outright. He repeated constantly that he was a religious monk and priest without gifts, that Louis had written to Sartaq only because he had thought he was a Christian (9.1, 15.2, 28.2, 28.16, 36.13). Eventually, at the Great Khan's court, William was recognized as a holy man rather than an envoy, which meant that he was expected to offer spiritual support and prayers for the khan and his household at all his encounters with them (29, 30.8)

---

[5] Juzjani, *Tabaqat-i Nasiri*, ed. M. Habibi (Kabul: Anjuman-i Tarikhi Afghanistan, 1963–64), vol. 2, 217.

The status and contents of the letter, which William never reveals completely in the text — his audience was, after all, its author — are quite mysterious. Sartaq's secretary told William that the letter "raises certain problems on which [Sartaq] would not venture to act without consulting his father: so to his father you must go" (16.1). William had presented the letter, translated into Arabic and Syriac in Acre, and Sartaq's court prepared its own translation employing Armenian priests (15.7–8). At Batu's court, we learn that Louis's letter contained a request that William and his companion be allowed to stay in Mongol territory (29.9). However, the contents were problematic enough to require referring it, along with William, to the Grand Khan, Mongke. Batu, William learns en route to Qaraqorum, was communicating to Mongke that the French king was asking Sartaq for "troops and assistance against the Saracens." They understood the letter as having significant political and military implications. William, "struck with great astonishment and anxiety too," suspected that the Armenian translators had given the letter "a more forceful rendering" out of their hatred of the Saracens. In contrast, William describes the "gist of the letter" as "urging him [Sartaq] to be a friend to all Christians, to exalt the Cross, and to be the enemy of all who are enemies to the Cross" (27.11). Earlier, in Soldaia, he had explained to local officials serving Sartaq and Batu that all the Christians had been overjoyed at the news of Sartaq's conversion and that Louis, who was waging war against the Muslims in order to wrest the Holy Land from them, wrote to inform Sartaq "of what is in the interests of the whole of Christendom" (1.7).

This last phrase indicates that the conditions on which conversion were understood as real or acceptable by William and Louis were not simply a matter of embracing Christian doctrine. William approaches Mongol converts with expectations that they might be receptive to a political affiliation or identification with the Latins crusading against the Muslims to reconquer Jerusalem, which had been in Muslim hands again since 1187. What William seems to mean by "Christian," it becomes clear, is someone who is culturally and politically as well as religiously a Latin Christian, a "Frank" as Muslims such as Usamah ibn Munqidh might say. These identities overlap closely for William. While he decries Sartaq's inability to recognize Christianity as a faith rather than the name of a people, ultimately how much did the Mongols really misunderstand what it meant to be a Latin Christian and how closely were religious and political affiliations combined for them? Can we imagine William accepting Mongol khans converted to Christianity as his liege lords? He clearly answers no: "I shall gladly urge him (Mongke) to become a Christian, since my purpose in coming was to preach this to all men. I shall further promise him that the Franks and the Pope will be overjoyed and will regard him as a brother and a friend. But that they would be bound to become his subjects and pay him tribute like these other peoples, this I shall never promise, since I should be gainsaying my own conscience" (27.8). Plainly he also refused to accept Sartaq as a true Christian, despite his evidently sincere belief in Christ. Mongols could and did accept various religious adherents among their ruling elite, whether Christian, Muslim, or Buddhist, though they maintained ancestral practices and honored their shamans, whom William calls "soothsayers" (35). But they remained Mongols and accepted the political dominion of only the heirs of Chingis. Realizing that the Mongols were resistant to embracing the political implications of being Christians in his terms and would ever remain committed to their ethno-political mandate of universal conquest, William ends his account by encouraging war on the Mongols (Epilogue.4).

Consequently the instruction that Louis gave and that William seems admirably to have fulfilled, that is, to write down everything that he saw even if it was of great length, appears less and less like the disinterested curiosity of a French king in the Orient interested in a new and strange people. William's thorough and detailed account likewise acquires clear military consequences and political overtones. On his return journey, he remarks that he is glad he had a chance to observe and detail Mongol armaments. He further implies that perhaps the Mongols are not the invincible force their sudden conquests suggest by noting that Sartaq's men were having difficulty subduing the newly Christianized Alans in their mountainous homeland as well as a people called the "Lesgi" (Saracens) living near his return route. Consequently, his account partly takes on the character of an intelligence report, providing updated and useful knowledge to his royal patron on the contemporary political conditions in the Mongol Empire and its military strength.

In encountering this "other world" of the extreme East, William comes to articulate the terms of Latin Christian identity, conversion to which was not simply a matter of adopting a universal set of theological beliefs but also integration into and subordination within a specific political and religious culture. While he began his journey in missionary engagement with "the other" and with hopeful expectations of Mongol conversion, he ended it by preaching crusade against them.

Bibliographic Note

Parenthetical citations within the text refer to William of Rubruck's work by chapter and, where appropriate, paragraph divisions used in both English translations; the more widely available one appears in *Mission to Asia*, ed. Christopher Dawson (Toronto: University of Toronto Press, 1980 [1955]), but the better and more recent translation, which I have used in quotations above, is that of Peter Jackson, *The Mission of William of Rubruck* (London: The Hakluyt Society, 1990), which also offers excellent notes and an informative introduction. Many documents and travel journals of late medieval travelers to Asia have been translated in Dawson's *Mission to Asia* and *Cathay and the Way Thither*, trans Henry Yule and Henri Cordier, 4 vols. (London: The Hakluyt Society, 1913–16). On the general theology of mission, see E. Randolph Daniel, *The Franciscan Concept of Mission in the High Middle Ages* (Olean, NY: The Franciscan Institute, 1975).

A good introduction to the Mongols is D.O. Morgan, *The Mongols* (Oxford: Oxford University Press, 1986), and, for the period of William's journey, Thomas Allsen, *Mongol Imperialism: The Policies of the Grand Qan Mongke in China, Russia, and the Islamic Lands, 1251–1259* (Berkeley: University of California Press, 1987). The most thorough and up-to-date study of Mongol relations with the Latin West is Peter Jackson, *The Mongols and the West* (New York: Pearson Longman, 2005), which contains a very helpful bibliography.

TWENTY-ONE

Saint Francis and Salimbene de Adam
The Franciscan Experience of Family

Victoria M. Morse

When Salimbene de Adam (1221–c. 1289) joined the Franciscans in 1238, he joined an established religious order, with a system of governance and a culture that had been developing since at least 1209/10 when Francis of Assisi (1181/82–1226) presented his first rule to Pope Innocent III (1198–1216). The Order looked back to Saint Francis as its founder and inspiration but had already begun to develop a set of traditions and habits that influenced life in the Order in ways independent of the saint's model. Historians of the Franciscan movement, including contemporaries of Francis himself, have debated vigorously how the religious Order resembled, and failed to resemble, the small brotherhood that had formed around Francis soon after his conversion to the ascetic life in 1208. It has been easy to see the story as one of institutionalization and the decline of the early inspiration and rigor that characterized the first brothers. As the Order grew rapidly from two to a dozen to hundreds of brothers throughout Europe, its structural needs began to outweigh Francis's early emphasis on simplicity and powerlessness. By the later part of the thirteenth century, the Order had begun to split. On the one hand, the rigorists wished to return to what they understood as Francis's original way of life, based closely on the gospel descriptions of how Jesus himself had lived and taught. On the other hand, those who focused on the mission to preach offered to (or imposed upon) them by a series of popes wished to facilitate preaching through study at the universities and through more highly developed institutional·support for the needs of the individual preaching friar.

Scholars have struggled to clarify the tensions within Francis's life and thought, the conflicting interpretations of his life and mission by contemporaries, and the quite various purposes that popes, cardinals, and early ministers general felt the Order could and should fulfill in the energetic, colorful, and highly contested religious climate of the early thirteenth century. These studies have helped us see how the members of the Order might think so differently about their purpose and mode of living. There is, however, another piece to the picture. If we look at the ways in which an individual Franciscan experienced the Order after Francis's death and as Francis's original companions were growing old and dying, we find that the very durability of the Franciscan way of life was a force for change. In spite of the earlier emphasis that Francis had placed on rootlessness and social exclusion, the Franciscans were developing a history, something that even they could not refuse to possess. Taking the historian Salimbene de Adam's extended narrative of his own entry into the Order as a case study, we shall see that to join the Franciscans, far from being the radical renunciation of family that Francis had called for, was to embrace a family tradition of Franciscanism. Family memory and family ties had become central to the experience of being Franciscan in a way that troubled and partly reversed Francis's original emphasis on freedom from family ties and his readiness to approach all people equally as brothers and sisters.

At the outset, let us acknowledge that we must struggle to know what Francis may have "originally emphasized" or what his first intentions may have been. The earliest life of the saint was written by Thomas of Celano as an official text for Francis's canonization after his death in 1226. There also exist writings by Francis himself and a few testimonies by outside observers from Francis's lifetime. But some of the most intriguing evidence concerning Francis's life and attitudes are the writings attributed to his close companions, *The Legend of the Three Companions* and *The Assisi Compilation*. These are complex documents. Neither exists in manuscripts from any earlier than 1311, although the texts were apparently written in the 1240s at the request of the minister general, or administrative head, of the Franciscan Order to help correct perceived deficiencies in the official narrative of Francis's life. The companions exhibit a testy spirit of dissatisfaction with the present state of the Order and a certain degree of nostalgia for the old days. The late date of the manuscripts and the questions surrounding their production urge us to use the sources with caution, yet the authors' apparent closeness to the saint make them hard to set aside. Although these sources cannot offer the definitive word on the early experiences of Francis and his original companions, they provide a useful point of departure for understanding that early period of excitement and experimentation.

The companions wrote of Francis's own conversion to the religious life primarily as the renunciation of money, yet this renunciation is interwoven with his relations with his family and his social standing as the son of a successful merchant. Possessions and status appear inseparably linked. A scene from the beginning of Francis's conversion dramatizes the relationship between profession, money, and power. One day when he was in the shop selling cloth, totally absorbed in business, a poor man came in begging alms for the love of God. Preoccupied with thoughts of wealth and the care of business, Francis gave him nothing. Then, touched by divine grace, he accused himself of great rudeness, saying to himself: "If that poor man had asked something from you for a great count or baron, you would certainly have granted him his request. How much more should you have done this for the King of kings and the Lord of all!" (*Legend* 1). The accusation against business in this text is that it absorbs the mind and leaves little room for consideration and attentiveness to others and to God. Because divine grace intervened, Francis was able to recollect himself and return to a thoughtful awareness of the correct hierarchy of status and power by recognizing that asking in the name of the Lord was superior to asking in the name of a count or baron. The companions record a similar message concerning status when they tell how Francis toyed with the idea of abandoning the merchant status of his father and becoming a knight. He was already known for lavish spending so that "he seemed to be the son of some great prince" rather than a merchant's son (*Legend* 1). Hoping to be knighted, he equipped himself and set off to join a military campaign in southern Italy. A dream soon sent him back to Assisi; it reminded him yet again that God could offer more than any worldly lord to the man who served Him (*Legend* 2).

Although the sources marvel at how Francis's parents put up with his lavish generosity before his conversion, there are several indications of tension, especially with his father. We learn that Francis provided very large amounts of food to the poor, especially when his father was away (*Legend* 3).

When he used the proceeds of the sale of some of his father's cloth to pay for the rebuilding of the dilapidated church of San Damiano, his father pursued him, although the sources show differences of memory or opinion about whether he considered his son mad because of his sudden turn to asceticism or whether he was furiously seeking the return of his money (*Legend* 6). There is agreement, however, about the moment when Francis appeared before the bishop of Assisi, returned the money, stripped off his clothing, and renounced his father, saying, "Until now I have called Pietro di Bernardone my father. But, because I have proposed to serve God, I return to him the money on account of which he was so upset, and also all the clothing which is his, wanting to say from now on: 'Our Father who are in heaven,' and not, 'My father, Pietro di Bernardone'" (*Legend* 6). The simultaneous rejection of the money, his father, and the goods he traded in demonstrates how closely money and goods were associated with the economic role of the father.

When the companions recalled the arrival of Francis's first brothers, they were similarly emphatic about the disposal of worldly goods. One such story shows Francis and his first two companions thinking very much in line with the hierarchy of power that we have seen influencing Francis's own conversion. The men ask Francis how they should return the goods granted to them by God. Using the imagery of the relationship between lord and vassal, Francis says that the goods should be returned to the lord who granted them in the first place (*Legend* 8). This advice is verified and further directed by the three biblical verses that provided the "rule and manner of living" for the first group of brothers: "If you wish to be perfect, go, sell everything you possess and give to the poor, and you will have a treasure in heaven" (*Mark* 10:21); "Take nothing for your journey, etc." (*Luke* 9:3); "If any man wishes to come after me, he must deny himself, etc." (*Matt.* 16:24) (*Legend* 8). As one of his companions, Bernard, immediately sells his possessions and begins to distribute the proceeds to the poor, we are reminded that, for Francis, the way to return goods to God was to give them to God's poor people.

The assumption that returning goods to God meant giving them to the poor helps to explain the profound concern to distinguish the postulant's own natural family from "the poor" in several stories of successful and unsuccessful bids to join Francis and his brothers. When John wished to join, he made it clear that he wanted to follow Francis's advice about disposing of his ox, the share that he claimed as his part of his peasant family's property. The family grieved over the loss of both John's labor and the ox. In recognition of their need and to make them better appreciate the virtue of John's decision, Francis gave John permission to give the ox to his own family, even though he really ought to have given his "goods to other poor people according to the advice of the Holy Gospel" (*AC* 61). In this way, John was able to enter the Order without doing harm to his family. The story emphasizes that he did not ask for this dispensation from the practice that Francis understood as authorized by the Gospels: it was Francis's choice to exempt the family, with discretion, from following the rigor of the letter of the gospel precept. Since the text goes on to portray John as simple and eager to imitate Francis down to his smallest cough or gesture, there is no sense that it was his will to deviate from biblical purity. Francis demonstrated a similar reserve about mitigating the rule for brothers who were ill. Other brothers might provide them whatever comforts they could, but Francis strongly cautioned the suffering brother against demanding these little luxuries (*AC* 45). Patient suffering was the appropriate response to illness just as acceptance of the complete alienation of propriety was the appropriate attitude for an aspiring brother. If suffering or alienation were mitigated by another person, well and good, but that must not be expected or generalized into a rule.

Examples of failed bids to join the brothers underscore the importance of abandoning one's natural family. The companions recalled a man who "led by love of the flesh... distributed all his goods to his relatives" (*AC* 62). This man argued that the goods were necessary to them. The authors' point seems to be that this man tried to make for himself the decision to mitigate the rigor of the Gospel precept, rather than leave the matter to Francis as Brother John had done. Again, Francis's gift of discernment plays a crucial role, as the companions note that Francis perceived quickly through the Holy Spirit that this man was carnal and sent him away with a harsh rebuke. The truth of Francis's perception is warranted; the man simply leaves, rather than change his mind and give his goods to "other poor people." Giving one's goods back to God via his poor is clearly different from giving one's goods to one's kin group.

Another example of a failed attempt to join the brothers helps to clarify both Francis's ability to discern motivations and the nature of relationships with the world and the family. The son of a nobleman from Lucca came weeping to Francis, who rejected him with little sympathy. Once again, the companions recount the rebuke first before going on to show

how fully Francis's discernment was borne out by circumstances. When the man's relatives arrived intent on taking him home by force, the mere sound of the horses and the sight of his relatives caused him to give in without a struggle and return to the world (*AC* 70). The reader is presumably meant to contrast his actions with those of Francis, who demonstrated a spirited resistance to much greater pressure from his own father to abandon his religious life.

To gain further insight into the ways the companions envisioned the relationship between the religious life and secular world of family concerns, let us consider the case of women who wished to pursue a religious life. Women were less able to leave their homes than men were, and the companions recognized that they faced extra obstacles in such a pursuit. Nevertheless, they praised women who avoided marriage, remained at home committed to fasting and prayer, and thus imitated the brothers' way of life, even if they remained physically among their kin. Unsupported by the more experienced "holy and religious people" who would surround and support the male convert, they must find a way to lead a more religious life by separating themselves mentally from the adverse conditions of the household (*AC* 74).

In the companions' writings, separation from kin is closely linked to the other positive steps toward a Franciscan vocation: the renunciation of money and status and, more generally, the abandonment of secular society. They portray the kin group primarily as an economic unit that controls its members in the interest of the collectivity. Francis's own resistance to the economic interests of the family focused on the figure of his father as head of the kin group and primary economic player. Francis's mother, like other mothers of male saints, appears to be more understanding of her son's calling, but she remains subordinate to her husband (*Legend* 68, 73, and 79). Likewise, the poor mother of two of the friars was treated as a part of the community when Francis gave her their only New Testament to sell for her support. The companions recall in passing that Francis "used to call the mother of any of the friars his mother and the mother of all the other friars in the Order" (*AC* 93). Mothers, because of their relative lack of power within the natural family, seem to have been easy to assimilate into the refashioned Franciscan family. But the natural family and larger kin group, associated with paternal authority and worldly wealth, were treated with intense suspicion. In evaluating the sincerity and success of the men who joined Francis and the women who took up the religious life at home, the companions looked for indications of how complete a separation the aspiring friars or religious women had made from the worldly concerns of their natural families.

Within the Order, however, language drawn from the natural family abounded to describe roles and relationships among the friars. Much of this language was traditional, as when the companions refer to Francis as "father" or to the friars as "brothers" or had Francis address a friar as "brother" (*AC* 105–6). In his own writings, however, Francis himself frequently prefers to describe himself as a mother, especially when he provides lovingly for the brothers' needs. The other friars also took on the role of mothers when they were paired up during Lent, one (the son) to engage in contemplation, the other (the mother) to attend to his physical needs and protect him from interruption. After a time, the friars would switch roles, so that each had a chance to pray and a chance to serve.[1] Elsewhere the companions describe the brothers as caring for one another amid the dangers of the road as a "mother for an only and beloved child" (*Legend* 11). The roles of mother, son, and brother were creatively divorced from biological relationships and made available to express the emotional and functional relationships that the friars needed for maintaining a close-knit, mutually supportive community.

Although Francis carefully avoided taking up a paternal role and preferred to be subject to a companion friar, he was prepared to put his gift of discernment at the brothers' service to mitigate, when necessary, the full rigor of the Gospel life that he and the brothers had chosen. The companions recall how he coaxed a sick brother to eat grapes by eating some himself and how he had all the brothers eat with one who had tried to limit his food with too little respect for his body's needs (*AC* 50, 53). Francis's ability to discern motives and to adjust the rigor of his high expectations to the realities of individual capacity were traits of spiritual authority that, nonetheless, seemed to the companions to sit comfortably with Francis's renunciation of temporal authority within the Order.

When Francis did give up control over the Order that he had created and handed its governance over to others so that he could remain a simple friar until the end of his life, he did so as a father returning his family to

---

[1] Francis of Assisi, "A Rule for Hermitages," in *Francis of Assisi: Early Documents*, vol. 1: *The Saint*, trans. Regis J. Armstrong, J.A. Wayne Hellmann, and William J. Short (New York: New City Press, 1999), 61–62.

God. The companions describe the brothers in tears "as they saw themselves orphaned of such a father" and recalled the words of Francis: "Lord, I give back to You the family which until now You have entrusted to me. Now, sweetest Lord, because of my infirmities…I can no longer take care of them and I entrust them to the ministers" (AC 39). His role as "father" to his family of friars is underscored precisely by his renunciation of them: he can no longer protect them and places the burden of ensuring their salvation squarely on the shoulders of the ministers.

In the writings of the companions, then, entry into the Franciscan Order entailed a sharp break with the roles and expectations of the secular family. Francis rejected the natural family and invented a new pattern of roles and functions that he modeled through his example. Even this new family was a burden, however, and a distraction from "minority," the quality of being lesser, more humble, and more subject than other men.

When Salimbene de Adam set out to describe his own entry into the Franciscan Order in 1238, he clearly had Francis's struggles with his father in mind. He wrote his account in the 1280s, almost 50 years later, as part of a long autobiographical and genealogical digression in his chronicle of contemporary events, itself a continuation of an earlier chronicle that ended in 1211. From his account, we learn that Salimbene's father bitterly opposed his son's decision to join the Franciscans. The circumstances of this decision are not fully clear. We do know that Salimbene's older brother, Guido, entered the Order after marrying, having a daughter, and embarking on a career as a judge. Guido's wife and daughter, Agnes, entered the Order of the Clares, the female branch of the Franciscans, presumably at the same time as he became a Franciscan friar. Salimbene never spells out how this family connection affected his own decision; Brother Guido appears in the story of Salimbene's entry into the Order and then largely drops out of the picture. Perhaps having a brother in the Order was more important for his decision to join than for his later experiences of life as a Franciscan (Chronicle 12–13).

From their father's perspective, having two sons join the Order was a disaster. After his brother's conversion to the religious life, Salimbene was the remaining heir, the one person who could continue the lineage and inherit and protect the family property. The family was of high status, and Guido de Adam had been a crusader who remembered proudly that his war horse was accounted best in his company (*Chronicle* 12). Guido fought to retain his son as his heir, complaining to the pope and to the German emperor in the hope of forcing the Franciscans to return him. In a series of dramatic scenes, Salimbene recalls (or invents) his arguments with his father as he countered offers of property and appeals to family affection with biblical passages about the renunciation of family (*Chronicle* 13–15). At first there are striking similarities with the stories of Francis's conversion. The fathers' anger and pursuit of their sons are similar in the two texts, as are the fathers' ultimate reactions to their sons' obstinacy. Francis's father cursed him when they passed each other in the streets of Assisi (*Legend* 8), and Salimbene records a vivid scene of his father prostrate before the brothers and his own lay entourage, cursing him in these words: "Accursed son, I give you to a thousand devils, along with your brother, who is here a friar with you, assisting in your deception. I lay my everlasting curse upon your head and bequeath you to the infernal demons" (*Chronicle* 15). Guido put the finishing touch on his ardent attempts to regain control of his erring son when he sent pirates to try to kidnap him from the convent in Tuscany where Salimbene had chosen to live (*Chronicle* 16–17).

In spite of what he recalled as his steadfast resistance to his father's threats and blandishments, Salimbene portrays his first experiences in the Order as troubling and full of doubts. He was initially rewarded for defying his father with a comforting vision of the Virgin Mary, who invited him to "come forward and kiss my son, whom you confessed yesterday before men" (*Chronicle* 15). This divine vision is clearly meant to offer him a new locus for affection and belonging. His narrative, however, quickly turns to a contrasting encounter with an unknown man from his native Parma who angrily accused him of taking alms away from the real poor and of causing his parents grief. These accusations lead Salimbene to pause and consider what his life would be like in the Order: "I began to turn about in my mind and to think over all those things that I had heard and seen, because if I were going to live in the Order for fifty years as a mendicant, not only would it be a long road for me ... but even, beyond my power, an embarrassing and unbearable kind of labor" (*Chronicle* 19). This passage shows him questioning the discipline of begging, one of the fundamental activities of the Order and one of the key elements of Francis's own commitment to poverty and the renunciation of status (*AC* 150–51). In a striking contrast to the certainty with which he had faced his father and his father's curses, the man from Parma seems to have shaken him and made him reconsider his commitment, probably in part because of the exposed moment in which the encounter took place.

Once again, reassurance comes, but not, in this text, directly from the Franciscan community of which he is now a part. Instead, a dream shows him the Holy Family out begging just like Franciscans, collecting the scraps in covered baskets left at the foot of the steps. This time it is Christ himself who speaks to Salimbene and patiently answers his questions. The dream begins precisely with Salimbene's fears and grief concerning his relationship with his father. He dreamt that he avoided the section of the town where the merchants of Parma lodged because he feared being rebuked as he had been earlier the same day: "I was afraid that the Parmese might speak to me on behalf of my father and cut me to the heart" (*Chronicle* 20). Then he recalls briefly his father's ongoing hostility and the fact that they were never reconciled. To counter these fears, Christ turns to him in the dream and begins to explain patiently, with abundant scriptural citation, his own attitudes toward poverty and how Francis, Christ's "friend and beloved," captured the essence of poverty in his rule (*Chronicle* 20). After a lengthy discussion of these matters (to which Salimbene admits he has added "more words"), he seems to have found the reassurance he lacked (*Chronicle* 29). A final dialogue shows how invulnerable he had become to the wiles of those men sent by his father to lure him back to the world. A man brought greetings from his father and a message that his mother would like to see him and then die, "so little she cares about her own death." These words were meant to move him, but he was able to react with anger and to re-emphasize his distance from his parents (*Chronicle* 29). At last, Salimbene presents himself as fully integrated into the Franciscan Order emotionally as well as intellectually.

The Order that Salimbene joined appears in his *Chronicle* as a very different community than that of the first Franciscans. Although he wrote affectionately of Brother Bernard of Quintavalle, Francis's first companion, and even noted that Bernard told him many things about Francis's way of life, it is striking that he did not choose to record the content of those stories, nor did he reflect on how stories of the founder shaped his own experience in the Order (*Chronicle* 13). Instead, the Order appears in Salimbene's account as a highly professional cadre of men dedicated to a mission of preaching and intervention in the political life of the city-states of Italy. Contemporary authors seem increasingly to describe conversions to the Franciscans in terms of utility to the Order's mission rather than as personal narratives of reorientation. Salimbene shows himself an ardent supporter of the increasing clericalization of the Order in his constant denigration of the lay brothers as useless "extras": they lacked education, were not priests, and could not qualify as preachers.

Nevertheless, this is not quite the whole story. Unlike the radical break with family envisioned by Francis, where kin were left behind and even a biological mother was reconceptualized as the mother of all the brothers, Salimbene, for all his traumatic separation from his parents, joined his kin in the Franciscan Order. His brother Guido and Guido's wife and daughter were already Franciscans when he joined, and although we cannot know the details of this family affair, those conversions must have been in some way crucial to his own. Beyond them, however, is a much larger network of cousins and other family connections: Lady Romagna, a sister in the convent of Saint Clare; Lady Karacossa (sister to Salimbene and Guido), who entered the Clares as a widow; Brother James de Cassio, the son of Salimbene's cousin and a speaker of Arabic (*Chronicle* 12, 30–31). The examples could be multiplied. Even more interesting are the laymen who were associated more loosely with the Franciscans. Salimbene's half-brother, Master John, son of his father's concubine, died in Toulouse "after having confessed to the friars" (*Chronicle* 30). A cousin of Salimbene's mother was a judge in the entourage of Lord Manfred de Cornazano of Parma, who "along with his wife" was "an outstanding benefactor of the Friars Minor" (*Chronicle* 156). Although some of these have loose connections with the friars, the fact that Salimbene meticulously records them offers a sense of how his larger kin network had become interwoven with the Franciscans. Far from the novelty of Francis's experimental mode of life, which entailed a dramatic rupture with family culture as well as family wealth and authority, Salimbene's choice of the religious life seems already, in these early years of the Order, to be marked by a veritable forest of family traditions and connections.

Salimbene wrote movingly of the way in which he and his brother had destroyed their lineage by their choice to abandon the world: "I, Brother Salimbene, and my brother, Guido de Adam, destroyed our house in both the male and female line by entering the Religious Order, so that we might build it up again in heaven. May He deign to grant this to us, Who lives and reigns with the Father and the Holy Spirit forever and ever! Amen" (*Chronicle* 32). This stark statement of responsibility for what was obviously a troubling action is striking, as Salimbene concludes his lengthy reflection on his genealogy with a discussion of the unintentional ways in which he has seen "many families destroyed in many parts of the world" (*Chronicle* 36). Looking on this destruction as divine providence and fleshing out the scriptural passages that should remind the reader of how little control mere men have over their own destinies, Salimbene states that "we ought to be concerned about our salvation while we have the time, that it might not be said of us what is written in *Jeremiah* 8[:20]: 'The harvest is past, the summer is ended, and we are not saved'" (*Chronicle* 36).

In spite of Salimbene's stark acceptance of the destruction of his family line, kinship re-emerges quickly as a motivating force in the chronicle. As Salimbene enumerates the reasons for having written at such great length about his genealogy, his rationale is that Sister Agnes, Guido's daughter, wished to learn more about her father's family so that she might know for whom to pray. He comments that she has been a recluse "since she was small" and wanted to know "as much about her father's lineage as she already knew about her mother's." The idea that a Clare and a recluse from childhood would wish to know about and to pray for her natural family excites no surprise in Salimbene, who presents his motives for writing as self-evidently useful and desirable. The penetration of family knowledge and family relationships across the boundary of the Franciscan Order in this context appears as unproblematic. The fact that Salimbene's mother also ended her life in the Clares puts a final seal upon the Franciscan-ization of his family (*Chronicle* 31). Only his father held out, buried alone in the new family tomb by the new baptistery in Parma, which he had helped to build and which he must have intended as a monument for the future generations of the de Adam lineage that never came into being (*Chronicle* 30).

Conversion to the religious life, for Salimbene, was not only a rejection of his natural family in favor of the brotherhood or of the role of father in favor of the role of priest; it was also crucially a transition to a new view of his lineage, reimagined as a wide network of Franciscan men and women, capable of building up the family anew in heaven. In contrast to Francis's sharp break with familial and religious tradition, Salimbene could and did take his family concerns into the Order with him. His family tradition of Franciscan piety and commitment ensured that, however difficult was his rejection of the father's role and his part in the worldly continuation of the lineage, there could not be for Salimbene quite the same sense of radical otherness about becoming a friar. Family tradition and family history normalized unintentionally even the experience of rupture and conversion.

Bibliographic Note

Quotations from the *Legend of the Three Companions* and the *Assisi Compilation* (abbreviated as *AC*, above) are from *Francis of Assisi: Early Documents*, vol. 2: *The Founder,* trans. Regis J. Armstrong, J.A. Wayne Hellmann, and William J. Short (New York: New City Press, 2000). This collection is the best starting place for studying Francis and the medieval Franciscans. See also Jacques Dalarun, *The Misadventure of Francis of Assisi: Toward a Historical Use of the Franciscan Legends,* trans. Edward Hagman (Saint Bonaventure, NY: Franciscan Institute Publications, 2002). I have drawn on Catherine M. Mooney, "Francis of Assisi as Mother, Father, and Androgynous Figure," in *The Boswell Thesis: Essays on Christianity, Social Tolerance, and Homosexuality,* ed. Mathew Kuefler (Chicago: University of Chicago Press, 2006), 301–33; and P.H. Cullum, "Gendering Charity in Medieval Hagiography," in *Gender and Holiness: Men, Women, and Saints in Late Medieval Europe,* eds. Samantha J.E. Riches and Sarah Salih (London: Routledge, 2002), 135–51.

Salimbene de Adam's chronicle is available in English as *The Chronicle of Salimbene de Adam,* trans. Joseph L. Baird, Giuseppe Baglivi, and John Robert Kane (Binghamton, NY: Medieval & Renaissance Texts & Studies, 1986). An important essay is Adnan Husain, "Writing Identity as Remembered History: Person, Place, and Time in Friar Salimbene's Autobiographical Prose Map," *Viator* 36 (2005): 265–92. My own study owes a great deal to Maria Teresa Dolso, *"Et sint minores": Modelli di vocazione e reclutamento dei frati Minori nel primo secolo francescano* (Milan: Edizioni Biblioteca Francescana, 2001), and Alessandro Barbero, *Un santo in famiglia: Vocazione religiosa e resistenze sociali nell'agiografia latina medievale* (Turin: Rosenberg & Selier, 1991).

TWENTY-TWO

Cities and Kingship in the Medieval West
Joinville's Louis IX and Paris

John Tuthill

Jean de Joinville (1224–c. 1319), lord of Joinville and seneschal of Champagne, wrote his *Life of Saint Louis* as an old man early in the fourteenth century, a generation or so after the death of his contemporary, the great King Louis IX (1226–70). The work was composed in French, written at the request of the queen of France, Joan of Navarre (1273–1305), wife of King Philip IV (1285–1314) who was himself the grandson of Louis IX. As Joinville tells us in his dedication, he intended the book to edify and to instruct the rising generation of French princes, the sons of King Philip (165). He was no doubt convinced that the younger generation had much to learn from the example of their elders, especially that of their saintly great-grandfather who, in Joinville's eyes at least, was a much better model for the boys to emulate than was their own father. The tone of the work is adulatory, as Joinville uses Louis's personal characteristics and comportment to demonstrate the proper ways to behave and rule. His emphasis is on values rather than achievements. In the centerpiece of Joinville's story, the account of Louis's crusade to Egypt during the mid-1240s, the king is a conspicuous failure by any practical measure, having been captured and held for ransom at the hands of his Muslim enemies. Not only does Louis's failure not tarnish his image, but in Joinville's eyes it even enhances it by identifying his hero ever more with the sufferings of Christ.

Joinville's *Life of Saint Louis* calls to mind the *Life* of another Louis known for his personal qualities and Christ-like sufferings, the anonymous Astronomer's *Life* of Louis the Pious (768–840), son of Charlemagne and emperor in the ninth century. Like Joinville's Louis, Louis the Pious was remembered for his generosity, his love of peace, and his faith; and like Louis IX, Louis the Pious kept his reputation for personal holiness, notwithstanding the occasions in which he failed in his reign. Yet in the end, for the anonymous author, the piety of the Carolingian Louis worked against him; his personal characteristics made him appear weak in the eyes of the contemporaries who served him. For Joinville, on the other hand, Louis IX's saintly qualities make him not just a better ruler but a more powerful one as well. While the Astronomer tells us in his prologue that Louis the Pious's mildness led his empire into civil war, Saint Louis's disastrous crusades only enhanced his reputation as a saint and a king, at least according to his chronicler.

These two rulers were judged differently for a variety of reasons, not the least of which is that kingship had changed during the intervening centuries. The economic realities of thirteenth-century France were quite different from those of ninth-century Francia, and the later kings had far more, and more varied, resources at their disposal than did their Carolingian predecessors. Saint Louis's rule especially benefited from the growth of significant commercial cities — most importantly Paris — and the wise exploitation of these cities afforded him resources and opportunities that his pious namesake had lacked. The presence of prosperous cities within his kingdom made Louis IX's saintliness affordable; the king's saintliness also worked to render his cities more loyal, as well as more giving.

Louis the Pious had no such advantage. The Carolingian emperor ruled from royal palaces located for convenient access to hot springs, hunting grounds, food supplies, or strategic sites. The heart of his empire had no significant urban centers. Aside from Rome, always an exception in the early medieval West, the largest "city" in his empire was Metz, and it boasted a population of just a few thousand souls. Louis ruled a predominately land-based empire in which obedience was secured through grants of land and vows of vassalage, and in which money was largely a status symbol. To keep the loyalty of his vassals, Louis's father, Charlemagne, had spent his life fighting to enlarge his realm in order to win new land for distribution to those who served him faithfully. But land was not a renewable resource, and no empire can expand forever. When expansion stopped, late in Charlemagne's career, fissures quickly began to appear in the foundation of the empire, widening into crevices and then canyons during the reigns of his successors. Preserving such an empire was virtually impossible, as his able but luckless son discovered. Late- and post-Carolingian Europe devolved into smaller and smaller political entities, better suited to the economic realities of the time than had been Louis's dream of empire.

Even the smaller realms that emerged in "feudal" Europe were hard to hold together because their rulers lacked the wherewithal to buy consistent support without weakening themselves. Rulership was a constant struggle. In the twelfth century, for example, Suger (c. 1081–51), abbot of the wealthy monastery of Saint Denis, describes the reign of an active and successful king of France, Louis VI (1108–37), who traveled tirelessly from castle to castle to enforce his claims to lordship in the midst of new rebellions that seemed to arise any time he turned his back.

By the time of Louis VI, however, the social and economic structures of western Europe were beginning to change in discernable ways. As commercial cities grew almost everywhere, those rulers who learned to adjust to the new realities enlarged their resources and augmented their power. The career of Louis's contemporary to the north, Count Charles the Good of Flanders (c. 1084–1127), ruling one of the most heavily urbanized parts of Europe, was a harbinger of things to come. Charles, whose life was cut short by treachery, was fondly remembered by Galbert, a notary in Bruges, who recounts his justice, his peacemaking, and his generosity—often in cash—to the urban poor (see Chapter 13 above). Justice, peacemaking, and cash would all have a long history in later European governments, and all three were directly connected to the needs of the urban centers growing up within their realms, so they became important to government in more urbanized Flanders earlier than in less-developed France.

The new cities in the Middle Ages were not terribly big: in fact, medieval people didn't always think of population size as one of the essential features of a city. In a sermon preached on the feast of the Annunciation sometime before 1250, a Portuguese Dominican friar, Pelagius Parvus, never mentions population when he discusses the characteristics of a city. The very first quality of a city he notes is that it is a place of refuge: one could flee to it in times of danger, as medieval cities were fortified enclosures. Secondly, he says, all necessities of life could be found there: cities were market centers. They also ruled their surrounding territory, and it was within cities that the king lived. The medieval city was, in this view, a commercial and political center, enclosed and defended by walls, but also extending out into the countryside, offering protection and opportunity in exchange for domination.[1]

---

[1] John Tuthill, "Fr. Paio and His 406 Sermons," *Actas do Segundo Encontro sobre Historia Dominicana* (Porto: Dominicanos, 1984), vol. 1, 376.

Commerce was indeed the engine that drove most successful medieval cities. Although some manufacturing occurred within them, they were principally places where people bought and sold goods produced there and elsewhere. This commerce could generate great wealth, but it needed certain conditions in order to flourish. Businesses then, as now, needed a degree of security and stability. Predictability made business planning feasible; uncertainty drove potential investors away. Simply put, medieval cities needed law, order, and peace if they were to thrive as business centers. Law, order, and peace, however, had never been the hallmarks of medieval life or government. To nurture their commercial cities, later medieval rulers needed to acquire a new and very different set of skills from those that had made their predecessors successful.

Cities were a phenomenon new to the medieval West of the twelfth century, and, as with most new phenomena, opinions differed as to what to make of them. Some observers found them stimulating and alluring. William Fitz Stephen (d. c. 1190) described London as a city almost breathtaking in its attractions: its wealth, its 13 conventual churches and 126 lesser parochial churches, its disputatious scholars, its horse market, its games and sports, and its restaurant. However, his anonymous countryman and contemporary, who wrote of the crusade against the Moors in Portugal in 1147, found Lisbon thoroughly intimidating. Its countryside, like London's, was rich and healthy; it had fertile fields and orchards of olives and figs and offered good air and waters brimming with fish. Inside its walls, however, in its narrow streets lined with closely packed buildings, "the most depraved people from all parts of the world had flowed as if into a cesspool." It was a "breeding ground of lust and filth" (*Conquest of Lisbon* 94). Attractive or intimidating, a site of opportunity or of danger: the difference could lie in the eye of the beholder, but it also depended on the level of law and order the city was able to maintain.

Preserving law and order was a challenge for city governments. In countryside villages, close family relationships and peer pressure kept people more or less in line. In a community where everyone knew everyone else, where they had all been living together for generations, it was harder to get away with wrongdoing. Growing cities, on the other hand, were filled with transients and newcomers. City people did not always have the same deep personal roots within their community, and that made them both more free and, potentially, more dangerous. To keep the peace, cities had to rely more on impersonal law than on social pressure, yet the enforcement of law posed special difficulties. One very important social group, the clergy, claimed immunity from prosecution under secular law, and clerical immunity extended broadly, including some relatively troublesome types such as university students. Another important group, the knights, while technically bound by secular law, often went unpunished because of their social and political connections. The same could be said for yet another group of growing importance at this time, royal officials. Notwithstanding the immunities or privileges of some of those who lived in them, successful commercial cities needed to enforce the law and maintain the peace, and kings could help. Kings often had both the political clout to stand up to the Church over claims of clerical immunity and the social clout to keep the knights in line. A king who promoted peace and security within his cities could find them highly profitable; a king who did not could suffer the consequences.

In his *Life of Saint Louis,* Joinville shows us a king who models himself, sometimes consciously, to fit a mold required by the new values and needs of his commercial cities, a king who derives power and stature from his relations with them. While Joinville intended to write the life of a role-model king, his account also provides passing glimpses of Paris and of the relations between the city and its king. As Joinville makes clear, for example, Paris was the center of royal government, just as Pelagius Parvus, the contemporary Portuguese Dominican preacher, said a city should be. In Joinville's account, when the king summoned his barons to announce his intention to go on crusade and to ask them to swear to be faithful to his children if anything should happen to him while he was away, he called them to Paris (192). Summoned on another occasion to a meeting of the royal council in Paris, Joinville sought to excuse himself, citing quartan fever as the reason, but Louis would have none of it. The king, Joinville tells us, "sent me word that he insisted on my coming, because there were good physicians in Paris who well knew how to cure such ailments" (345).

Louis saw to it that Paris was full of spiritual physicians as well. Like William Fitz Stephen's London, Paris was a city of churches. Louis IX helped to solidify the city as the ecclesiastical center of the kingdom. According to Joinville, he constructed the Abbey of Antoine near Paris (337), a monastery for the Carthusians outside the city at Vauvert (343), an Augustinian church outside the Porte Montmartre, "a house on the Seine toward Saint-Germain-des-Prés" for the "Sacks" (the Order of Penitence), and another for the "White Mantles," who had "begged him to give them help so that they might remain in Paris...a house and certain old buildings lying round about it...near the old gate of the Temple in Paris, fairly close to the rue de la Tisseranderie." The Brothers of the Holy Cross got "a house in the street once known as the Carrefour du Temple, but now called the rue Sainte-Croix." "Thus," concludes Joinville, "the good King Louis surrounded the city of Paris with people vowed to the service of religion" (344). In the process, the king also increased the prestige of his leading city and extended its influence beyond its walls into the surrounding countryside, as Pelagius Parvus suggested was the norm.

Paris was also the market center of the kingdom, a place where all necessities could be found, again as the Portuguese Dominican would have recommended. When contemplating the damage done when withdrawing Turks set fire to the Damietta bazaar in the face of the advancing crusaders, Joinville reports that "the consequences of this action were as serious for us as if — God forbid! — someone were, tomorrow, to set fire to the Petit-Pont in Paris" (205). Paris produced, as well as sold. When Louis's queen needed to fulfill a vow of thanksgiving for her deliverance from shipwreck, she commissioned Parisian artisans to make for her a silver ship, containing silver figures of the king, the queen, their three children, and sailors along with the mast, rudder, and rigging also in silver, at a cost of 100 *livres* (322).

Parisians got around, too. Their presence and influence were by no means restricted to their own city. Deep within Egypt, surrounded by enemies and deathly ill with dysentery, King Louis was taken to a house occupied by a woman who was "a native of Paris" (241). Later, when the king was taken captive by the Turks, they brought in an individual who promptly castigated the crusaders for daring to eat meat on a Friday; Joinville describes him as "a citizen of Paris" (245). On the return trip home, after the king's release, "certain sons of Paris burghers" held up a foraging party on the island of Pantaleria. They were supposed to be looking for fresh fruit for the queen's children, but they were eating the fruit themselves, while others in the shore party waited for them impatiently (324).

These young men were not the only Parisians who were difficult to control. While Louis's Paris may not have been "a breeding ground for lust and filth," it certainly was a rough and ready place. Joinville reports that on his way to town to join the crusade, he saw the corpses of three royal sergeants killed by an angry Parisian clerk whom they had mugged. After the incident, in a scene worthy of a Hollywood action film, the clerk went home, got his crossbow and sword, and tracked the sergeants down in the street. With his crossbow, he shot one dead through the heart, and the other two took flight with the clerk in hot pursuit. One of the sergeants got stuck trying to escape through a hedge; the clerk severed his leg with the sword, killing him. The other sergeant tried frantically to escape into the house of a stranger, but the clerk caught him and split his skull down to his teeth (193). Royal justice could be rough and ready, too. Joinville heard that the king had once ordered "the lips and nose of a citizen of Paris seared" in punishment for using the name of the Lord and His mother in a wicked oath (336).

Strict and public justice of this sort was very much in the interests of a city needing law, order, and stability, and Louis IX endeavored to give Paris exactly that, and in a very public way. Joinville recounts that the king often had his officials hear judicial pleadings at the city gate known as "the Gate of Requests" in the mornings after Mass (176). The king himself heard the most difficult cases later in the day. Joinville fondly remembers him hearing cases while sitting against an oak tree in the forest of Vincennes or on a carpet in the public gardens in Paris (177).

To satisfy the interests of the cities, justice had to be impartial, as well as strict and public. City governments were often impatient with the claims of immunity or preferential treatment of privileged groups who lived within their jurisdiction. The king, chastened by the realization that he had once given the abbot of Cluny a more favorable hearing because the good cleric had first given him two palfreys, forbade his judges from accepting any gift "from those who have any matter to bring before" the court, lest they be swayed to partiality as he himself had been (327). He further ordered all royal office holders to take an oath "that they will do justice to all, without respect to persons, to the poor as to the rich, and to men from other countries as to those who are native-born" (337). When he went on his second crusade, Joinville reported, Louis ordered his son and heir, Philip, "Deal justly and equitably with your subjects," and he asked him to give the benefit of the doubt to the poor in any legal dispute until the facts of the case were fully clear (348). Pious though he was, Louis pointedly refused to enforce judgments of ecclesiastical excommunication unless he himself reviewed the evidence and agreed with the Church's decision (177–78, 332). As a judge, Louis was capable of ruling even against his own immediate self-interests. When Renaud de Trit produced a defective royal charter giving a county to the heirs of the Countess of Boulogne, the royal council concluded that the charter itself was null and void because its seal was broken. Louis overruled his advisors and honored the grant, since it was clear to him that the charter itself was genuine (178–79).

When Abbot Geoffroy of Saint Urbain argued that the king, not Joinville, had jurisdiction over his monastery, Louis's own investigation upheld the claims of his seneschal, much to the latter's satisfaction (333–34). Louis's practice was in keeping with his advice to Prince Philip: "If through your own act, or the act of your predecessors, you hold anything which should belong to another, and his right to it is proved beyond question, restore it to him without delay. If on the other hand there is some doubt about the matter, have it investigated, promptly and thoroughly, by wise and knowledgeable men" (348).

In the king's eyes, as well as Joinville's, a reputation for fairness and impartiality was somehow more valuable than property, a far cry from the situation Louis the Pious had faced centuries before in his land-based empire. Whereas the Carolingian ruler was weakened by his alienations of royal properties and his empire gradually disintegrated under his heirs, Saint Louis's justice, even when it appeared to sacrifice his own interests, was ultimately aimed explicitly at safeguarding his, and his heirs', position as ruler of the kingdom. Joinville twice recounts the king's encounter with a Franciscan preacher, Brother Hugh, who told the returning crusader that he had never read of a kingdom being lost or changing its ruler unless "justice had been ignored." He went on to say, "Therefore let the king who is now returning to France take good care to see that he administers justice well and promptly to his people, so that our Lord may allow him to rule his kingdom in peace to the end of his days" (176, 328–29).

Like Brother Hugh, Louis IX saw a close connection between justice and peace. As the king himself told his heir: "You must give your attention to ensuring that your subjects live peaceably and uprightly under your rule" (348). And while the *Life* centers on Louis's military crusade to Egypt, Joinville describes the crusading king as a great champion of peace. Twice Joinville reports that the king made peace with King Henry III of England, against the advice of his own royal council, returning territory that the French had justly seized from the English (178, 334). Joinville also tells of three instances in which the king sent some trusted advisor to settle violent disputes among his nobility (335). Royal and noble violence could adversely affect townspeople and their livelihoods. Joinville reports, for example, that in the civil war at the beginning of Louis's reign the count of Champagne set fire to three of his towns to prevent his enemies from seizing the supplies they contained (184).

In promoting peace, Louis both empowered his own government and stimulated his own cities. Instead of facing destructive warfare, those cities with royal courts found themselves full of litigants turning to the king's justice to seek peaceful solutions to their problems. Joinville reports, for instance, "As a result of the king's constant efforts to make peace the people of Burgundy and of Lorraine, whom he had reconciled, loved and obeyed him so well that, on occasions when they had disputes to settle, I have seen them come to plead their suits at his courts of Rheims, Paris, and Orleans" (335–36). Louis himself explicitly recognized the close connection between wealthy cities and powerful royal government in his final advice to his son: "Above all maintain the good cities and communities of your realm in the same condition and with the same privileges as they enjoyed under your predecessors. If there is anything in them that needs reform, do what is necessary to set it right; and keep them ever in your favour and your love. For because of the wealth and power of your great cities not only your own subjects, and especially your great lords and barons, but also the people of other countries will fear to undertake anything against you" (348).

Louis's advice to his son was not just idle; the king knew what he was talking about, having seen first-hand what a loyal and prosperous city and its people could do for him. Joinville relates how the king's barons rebelled when Louis was still a young boy under the regency of his mother. The two were holed up in the castle of Montlhéri and did not dare to attempt to return to Paris until the people of that city came to escort them to safety (182). The city supported the king because it wanted something from him in return.

Louis's greatness and success as a king came at least in part because he recognized the importance of this support and the way in which he could ensure its continuance. The secret, in the end, was money. Paris, like any thriving medieval city, was potentially a source of vast revenue, in cash, for its king. If the king protected his city's business life by means of justice and peace, he could anticipate regular revenue in return and could use that revenue to build a more stable government system, staffed by more professional civil servants, than either France or Francia had ever seen before. Joinville describes the process clearly. Early in Louis's reign, he tells us, it was customary for the office of Provost of Paris to be sold either to a burgess of the city or "anyone else who would buy it." "Those who bought this office," he continues, "condoned all offenses committed by their children or their nephews, so that these young delinquents became accustomed to relying on those who occupied the provostship. In consequence people of the lower classes were greatly downtrodden; nor could they obtain justice against the rich, because of the great gifts and presents the latter made to the provosts" (341). A venal government, with judicial offices for sale, spawned inequitable justice and "downtrodden" lower classes.

As Joinville indicates, however, city people could leave one difficult environment and move to another with a more congenial business climate. "On account of the great injustice done by the provosts, and because of the robberies perpetrated during their term of office, the poorer people dared not remain in the king's own domains, but went to parts administered by other provosts and ruled by other laws" (341). "The poorer people" were the ones who did the work that made a city flourish, and their flight was problematic for the king. Recognizing the problem, Louis stopped selling the office of provost of Paris and instead "arranged a good and generous salary to be given to those who should hold it in future." He recruited men who "would administer justice well and strictly, and not spare the rich any more than the poor." The results, according to Joinville, were both positive and tangible:

> A certain Etienne Boileau ... subsequently maintained and upheld the office of provost so well that no wrong-doer, thief, or murderer dared to remain in Paris, for all who did were soon hanged or put out of the way; neither parentage, nor noble descent, nor gold and silver availed to save them. So conditions in the king's domains soon began to improve, and people came to live there because of the good justice that prevailed. The population so increased, and things were so much better, that goods and property and everything else sold for double their value as compared with what the king had formerly received. (341–42)

Higher city property values and increased city trade meant greater tax revenue for the lord of the city, in this case Louis himself, and while Joinville is not interested in discussing taxation, he is extraordinarily interested in money, how much is spent, how much things cost.

One of the most apparent differences between the crusade of Louis IX and Louis VII's "journey to the East" 70 years earlier (see Chapter 14 above) is the greatly increased role played by money in the later crusade. Joinville certainly shows us more of it. Louis IX began his crusade with "a good store of money in his treasury" as well as a good supply of what money can buy (197). In Cyprus, Joinville saw a huge stack of barrels of wine bought up two years in advance, and so much wheat and barley that it had sprouted and looked like a grassy hill (197). At the end of the crusade, however, Louis IX's resources were depleted. He lacked enough money to pay 300 knights to go to Constantinople, as he had intended (199). In between, the crusade cost great sums. The king negotiated a ransom equivalent to 500,000 *livres* for his people held prisoner by the Turks (250). While Louis and his men were in captivity, his queen bought all of the food in Damietta for the sum of 360,000 *livres* (263). When the king asked for advice on how to get more knights, Joinville recommended higher pay: "Let the king spend some of his own resources in getting knights from Morea and other parts oversea. When they hear that he is paying well and generously, knights will come flocking in from everywhere." (270). And then Joinville himself held out for a royal payment in the amount of 200,000 *livres* to cover his own expenses and those of his knights if they were to be retained in the king's service (273).

Everything on crusade seemed to be expensive, from the price of oxen, sheep, pigs, eggs, and barrels of wine (237) to the cost of construction work. "I will not attempt to give you an accurate account of the huge sums the king spent in fortifying Jaffa," says Joinville, "for they are too great to be reckoned." Joinville may not tell us the total cost, but he and the papal legate certainly found the subject interesting. "To give you an idea of what the king spent on all this I will tell you that I asked the legate how much the gate and part of the wall had cost him. He asked me how much I thought, and I estimated that the gate must have cost a good five hundred *livres* and his part of the wall three hundred. He told me—as God is his witness— that wall and gate together had cost him full thirty-thousand *livres*" (305). And Louis had paid for walls, two gates, and 24 towers!

As money became the cement for many contractual relationships and a practical necessity to get many things done, the landed nobility was at a distinct disadvantage when compared to a king like Louis. Joinville had to mortgage most of his land to go on crusade, and even so, his knights complained that he needed to provide himself with more cash or they would leave him (192, 198). Louis worked on a larger scale and had many more resources he could tap, so long as he was careful. Reporting first about Louis's war with England, but then thinking more broadly about his reign as a whole, Joinville writes, "In the course of his recent campaign against the king of England and the barons, King Louis had made many generous gifts of money, as I was told by those who returned from this expedition. But neither on account of such gifts nor on account of expenses incurred in that campaign, nor in any others, either oversea or at home, did he ever demand or accept any monetary aid from his barons, his knights, his men, or any of his fine cities in such a way as to cause complaint" (190). The cities were the key. So long as they were growing, like Paris under Louis IX, and so long as trade was prospering, cities could afford the king's monetary aids and not begrudge them, as long as the king provided in return what the cities needed to make their business environment secure: peace, justice, law, and order. Paris and Saint Louis were by no means unique in their relationship: the same process was at work in transforming kingship elsewhere in the medieval West, in Spain, Portugal, England, and the empire, in ways that Louis the Pious could not have dreamed.

Bibliographical Note

The texts mentioned in this essay include Joinville's *Life of Saint Louis* in Jean de Joinville and Geoffroy de Villehardouin, *Chronicles of the Crusades*, trans. Margaret Shaw (Harmondsworth: Penguin Books, 1963); the Astronomer's *The Life of Louis the Pious*, most readily available in Thomas F.X. Noble's *Charlemagne and Louis the Pious: Lives by Einhard, Notker, Ermoldus, Thegan, and the Astronomer* (University Park: Penn State Press, 2009); Abbot Suger of Saint Denis, *The Deeds of Louis the Fat*, trans. John Moorhead and Richard Cusimano (Washington, DC: Catholic University of America Press, 1992); Galbert of Bruges, *The Murder of Charles the Good*, on which see Chapter 13 in this volume; William Fitz Stephen, *Norman London* (New York: Italica Press, 1990); *De expugnatione Lyxbonensi/The Conquest of Lisbon*, trans. Charles Wendell David, (New York: Columbia University Press, 1936); and Odo of Deuil, *On the Journey of Louis VII to the Orient*, on which see Chapter 14 above.

For a priceless close-up look at the workings of a medieval city, see Robert Brentano, *Rome before Avignon* (Berkeley: University of California Press, 1990). An outstanding source book of documents from an important urban center is Gene Brucker, *The Society of Renaissance Florence* (Toronto: University of Toronto Press, 1998). An old classic still well worth reading is Henri Pirenne, *Early Democracies in the Low Countries* (New York: Harper and Row, 1963). See also the more recent books of David Nicholas: *The Later Medieval City 1300–1500* (London: Longman, 1997) and *The Growth of the Medieval City: From Antiquity to the Early Fourteenth Century* (London: Longman, 1997). Finally, a pleasant introduction to the Paris of Saint Louis can be found in the chapter by that name in F. Roy Willis, *Western Civilization: An Urban Perspective*, 2nd ed., vol. 1 (Lexington, MA: D.C. Heath, 1981).

TWENTY-THREE

The Virgin and the King
Alfonso X's *Cantigas de Santa María*

Amy G. Remensnyder[1]

"**A**n uneducated king is like a crowned ass." This pungent declaration that a king needed to rule not only with his sword but also with his head was quoted by many Christian writers of the twelfth and thirteenth centuries as they reflected on political power.[2] In their efforts to promote learning as a royal virtue, these authors urged kings to model themselves on the biblical paragon of wise rule, King Solomon. Monarchs of the period took such admonishments to heart. Unlike earlier rulers such as Charlemagne, who never quite learned to write, Christian European kings of the thirteenth century were highly literate. Some even composed texts to instruct their heirs in the virtues of kingship, as King Louis IX of France did. But the slim text Louis wrote for his children pales in comparison to the flood of literary production presided over by his first cousin once-removed, Alfonso X. Ruler of the kingdoms of León and Castile from 1252 to 1284, so learned was Alfonso that he has been known for centuries as *Alfonso el Sabio,* Alfonso the Wise.

The graceful poem-songs of *Cantigas de Santa María* bear eloquent testimony to Alfonso's erudition. Yet these 400-odd poems in honor of the Virgin Mary and her miracles represent a mere fraction of the numerous texts of which this learned man was the patron. Chronicles, law codes, love

---

[1] I thank John V. Tolan for his comments on an earlier version of this chapter.

[2] Herbert Grundmann, "*Litteratus und illiteratus:* Der Wandel einer Bildungsnorm vom Altertum zum Mittelalter," *Archiv für Kulturgeschichte* 40 (1958): 50–52.

poetry, and treatises about subjects as diverse as astronomy, backgammon, chess, ethics, and magic poured forth from Alfonso's court. An active scholar who tirelessly promoted learning, this monarch even stipulated in his law code that kings should study as much as they could.

As Alfonso fashioned himself into the epitome of an educated king, he drew on the new ideas about monarchy emerging in the Christian kingdoms north of the Pyrenees. He also found models closer to home in the kingdom located just south of his own: Muslim Granada. For centuries, Muslim rulers had been poets and writers, avid bibliophiles who amassed vast libraries. It might seem odd that Alfonso would have been influenced by the Islamic tradition of learned rulership. After all, as the *Cantigas de Santa María* make abundantly clear, Muslims and Christians of the Iberian Peninsula were at war in the thirteenth century.

Raids, skirmishes, and even full-fledged military expeditions pitting Muslims and Christians against each other had been a fact of life in the Iberian Peninsula since 711, when an army largely composed of North Africans recently converted to Islam crossed the Straits of Gibraltar and conquered the Visigothic kingdom. For the next several centuries, the Muslims dominated the peninsula, overshadowing the tiny Christian kingdoms located in the far north and east. But beginning in the eleventh century, the Christian kingdoms began to gain ground. After the particularly spectacular victories of Alfonso's father and his father-in-law, Christians controlled most of the peninsula. Only an ever-thinner slice of land in the extreme south remained in Muslim hands: the kingdom of Granada, as brilliant in its cultural life as it was fractured in its politics.

As the *Cantigas* reveal, Alfonso did his best to conquer Granadan territory. The collection opens with a martial flourish, vaunting the king for his victories over the Muslims (Prologue A). The poems even articulate his dreams of winning for Castile not just the remainder of the Iberian Peninsula but also the shores of Muslim North Africa (169). Although Alfonso beseeched the Virgin to aid him in this grandiose project (360, 401, 406), at the time of his death Granada was still intact and Castilian expeditions to North Africa had brought only short-lived success.

This long history of warfare between Muslim and Christian kingdoms in medieval Iberia might seem to suggest that relations between Christians and Muslims were marked by implacable enmity. Indeed, in the twelfth century, the pope declared the Iberian Peninsula a theater for crusade. Accordingly, Christians in thirteenth-century Castile could draw on the same charged language of holy war that so inspired French crusading kings such as Louis VII and Louis IX. One of the *Cantigas,* for example, characterizes Alfonso as "a king who led a great army to honor the faith of Christ and destroy that of the Moors" (348).

Yet as the *Cantigas* hint, there was another side to Muslim-Christian relations in medieval Iberia. The history of diplomatic exchanges and military alliances between Muslim and Christian leaders was just as long as the history of hostility. Friendly relations could occur at the local level, uniting Christian and Muslim castellans (185). Cross-faith allegiances could appear too on the grander stage of royal politics. Toward the end of his reign, for example, Alfonso sought to quell the rebellion of his son Sancho by enlisting as his military ally the powerful North African Muslim leader, Abu Yusuf. In this bitter struggle, Sancho himself counted among his supporters Muhammad II, the Muslim ruler of Granada. Just a few years earlier, however, the court of Granada had expressed its loyalty to Alfonso by sending high-ranking representatives to the sumptuous ceremony he held annually to commemorate his father's death.[3] In those years, Abu Yusuf was Alfonso's avowed enemy, pillaging the Castilian countryside (323). Tracing relations between the Muslim and Christian states of medieval Iberia and North Africa is like looking into a kaleidoscope: one shake, and the patterns of alliances and enmities change.

More or less constant, however, was Christian admiration for the sophisticated culture fostered by Muslim rulers. Like his predecessors on the throne of Castile, Alfonso did not hesitate to borrow from these Muslim cultural traditions in order to showcase his own power. In his architectural projects, for example, he often appropriated the visual language that had been associated with power in the Iberian Peninsula for centuries, the vocabulary of Islamic forms. The king built an exquisite chapel in this style (known as Mudejar) in the conquered city of Cordoba, making sure that the new structure harmonized with the magnificence of its setting — the city's former mosque, functioning by then as a cathedral dedicated to the Virgin. For this enterprise, Alfonso probably engaged Muslim master architects, as he did for the construction of a church in El Puerto de Santa María (358). The verbal architecture of the *Cantigas* themselves betrays Alfonso's appreciation of Islamic culture. Most of the

---

[3] *Crónica de Alfonso X según el ms. II/2777 de la Biblioteca del Palacio Real (Madrid),* c. 9, ed. Antonio Carmona Ruiz (Murcia: Real Academia Alfonso X el Sabio, 1998), 27.

poems in the collection were written in a verse form derived from Arabic poetics, the *zajal*. Alfonso even sponsored translations of Arabic works into medieval Castilian, the ancestor of modern Spanish and the language the king favored over Latin.

Jews fluent in Arabic and Castilian helped Alfonso and his collaborators with the difficulties of translation. These men were respected members of Alfonso's court and enjoyed his favor despite laws prohibiting Jews from holding positions where they might exercise power over Christians. In fact, as the *Cantigas* show, living among the Christians in Alfonso's kingdom were large and thriving communities of Jews as well as those Muslims who, rather than emigrate to Granada, had chosen to stay on in the areas conquered by the Christians.

In its cultural and religious diversity, Alfonso's Castile resembled the kingdoms of Sicily and Hungary much more than it did the relatively monochromatic realms of Germany, France, or England. It is perhaps no accident that the only other thirteenth-century Christian king as celebrated as Alfonso for his learning ruled one of these vibrantly diverse kingdoms: Frederick II of Sicily. Even the thirteenth-century Franciscan chronicler Salimbene de Adam, who detested Frederick, had to admire him for his erudition and intellectual curiosity. Like Alfonso, if not more so, this ruler was profoundly influenced by the Muslim traditions that were so pronounced in his kingdom. Frederick even wrote works that in their sophistication rivaled some of those produced by Muslim rulers.

Whether or not Alfonso himself was the actual author of the works associated with his court, he wielded an active hand in shaping the dozens of books listed under his name in library catalogues today. He seems to have been intensely involved with the creation of the *Cantigas de Santa María*, a project on which he spent a princely sum. Two of the four extant manuscripts of the *Cantigas* are exquisite luxury objects. Made from the finest-quality parchment and boasting sumptuous full-page illuminations for each poem, these manuscripts are fit for a king — and for the Queen of Heaven, Mary.

So committed was the king to this Marian project that he wrote some, if not many, of the poems enshrined jewel-like in these manuscripts (Prologues A and B). The miniature accompanying Prologue B shows the king at work on the collection. Majestically seated in the center of the scene, Alfonso holds an open book and dictates to scribes. Meanwhile, musicians holding instruments practice their parts — like much poetry in this period, the *Cantigas* were meant to be sung.

It's hard to believe, however, that Alfonso composed each of these more than 400 poems in Mary's honor. After all, as king, he was busy with the tasks of governing, trying much like Louis IX of France and other thirteenth-century kings to consolidate his power as sovereign, to extend the boundaries of his kingdom through military conquest, and to control his rebellious aristocracy. The *Cantigas* themselves depict the king as preoccupied with such duties. Alfonso probably personally composed only the *cantigas* in which he speaks in the first person (169, 180, 200, 209, 279, 300, 360, 401). The others were doubtless written under his direction by the poets who flocked to his court, attracted by his well-deserved reputation for generosity. In any case, the king must have sat with his poets and told them about the miracles Mary had performed for him and his family—wondrous favors celebrated in at least 28 poems. So vividly present is the king in the *Cantigas* that we could read the collection as Alfonso's "poetic biography," perhaps even an autobiography revealing some of the king's most intimate hopes, fears, and memories.

If the *Cantigas* are an unusually immediate expression of royal personality, they are an equally spectacular declaration of royal piety. Alfonso was deeply devoted to the saint in whose honor the poems were written. Not only did he create the *Cantigas*, but he built churches for Mary; he commissioned beautifully dressed statues and richly decorated containers for her relics and fine ivory carvings depicting scenes from her life; and he had masses said in her honor for the spiritual welfare of his family. In his law code, he even commanded his Christian subjects to show her relics the greatest respect. Alfonso deserved the title he claimed for himself in numerous royal documents: this king was indeed the Virgin's faithful "servant."[4]

The Virgin had many other loyal devotees in thirteenth-century Christian Europe, an era when Marian devotion flowered. The first hints of budding veneration of the Virgin date from the late tenth century, although its blossoms opened only in the late eleventh or early twelfth century. By the time Alfonso was creating the *Cantigas*, Marian piety was in full bloom. So intense was high medieval devotion to the Virgin that she came to rival her son for first place within the hearts of many Christians. This increasingly Marian quality to Christianity visibly marked the landscape: by the thirteenth century, Europe was blanketed with churches ded-

---

[4] *Diplomatario andaluz de Alfonso X*, ed. Manuel González Jiménez (Seville: El Monte, Caja de Huelva y Sevilla, 1991), no. 80, 81 (also nos. 186, 211, 262, 451, 458; pp. 205, 232, 292, 475, 485).

icated to her. As the poems in the *Cantigas* indicate, many of these Marian churches attracted pilgrims. Just as people expressed devotion to local saints, such as the popular child-martyr Sainte Foy of Conques, by making pilgrimages to their shrines, so Christians began to flock to the Virgin's churches.

The earliest sites of Marian pilgrimage were in the kingdom of France. They included several shrines mentioned in the *Cantigas*, such as the famous cathedral of Chartres (117, 148, 362) and the equally celebrated church of Rocamadour (8, 22, 147, 153, 157, 158, 159, 214, 267, 331, 343). But by the time the *Cantigas* were composed, pilgrims seeking the Virgin's aid could choose from a large number of churches throughout western Christendom, including in Alfonso's own realm. The king was clearly proud of the many Marian shrines located in his cultural ambit. El Puerto de Santa María, Elche, Montserrat, Salas, Salamanca, Seville, Toledo, Tudia, Villasirga — these are only a few places in the wide web of Marian churches flung across Aragon, Castile, and Portugal that figure in the *Cantigas*.

In these churches, pilgrims pressed and pushed to get close to the shrine's devotional heart: its image of the Virgin, usually a statue according to the poems' illuminations. So popular were Marian images as devotional objects that thirteenth-century Europe was crowded with them. Kneeling before these representations of the Madonna, Christians prayed to her. The *Cantigas* allow us to eavesdrop on these intimate moments, as Mary's devotees implore her for miracles or make thanksgiving offerings for wonders she has already performed. A naughty little girl pleads with a statue of Mary for help in escaping her aunt's spanking hand, and a crippled mute regains the use of his tongue and limbs when he sheds penitent tears before a Marian image (303, 163). The *Cantigas* also reveal just how socially diverse were the people who bowed in veneration before statues of the Virgin. Powerful kings suffering from severe pain (209, 279), rich merchants lost at sea (267), blind knights (314), grieving poor women (315) — all begged for Mary's aid.

In response to this barrage of requests, the Virgin performed so many miracles that people felt the urgent need to write them down. Some authors of the Marian miracle collections that began to accumulate in thick books were clerics or monks affiliated with a particular shrine. To promote their own community's interests, they focused on the wonders performed by their Virgin. But by the time Alfonso presided over the creation of the *Cantigas*, another type of Marian miracle collection also circulated in Christian Europe. The authors of this newer form freed Mary's miraculous powers from the narrow constraints of the local, assigning her a far-flung realm embracing all of Christendom. And her wondrous powers now included not just the immediate past of the last hundred years or so, as was common in the local collections, but reached as far back as the origins of Christianity itself. Many of the miracles included in these collections therefore float indeterminately in time and space, bound by neither— like Mary herself, they become manifestations of the eternal truth that the high medieval Church claimed to embody.

The authors of these universalizing collections prized originality no more than most medieval writers did. Content to repeat the same stories, they created a standard miraculous repertoire for the Virgin. Alfonso and his collaborators borrowed freely from this common fund of Marian stories. Yet the *Cantigas* also have a distinctly local flavor, if by local we understand the Christian kingdoms of Iberia. The king obviously relished tales of the miracles Mary performed daily in his own world. The majority of the poems in fact recount such miracles, many of which occurred at shrines that Alfonso knew well and patronized. The form of the *Cantigas* is then hybrid, combining the universal and the local. The king and his poets evidently believed that while Mary's power knew no bounds, she favored Alfonso's own realm in particular.

The *Cantigas* help us understand why Alfonso and so many of his contemporaries distinctly preferred the Virgin to any other saint, including her own son: Mary's burgeoning popularity resulted in part from a softening of her persona. To be sure, these poems often present Mary as the imposing Queen of Heaven well-known to early medieval Christians. Alfonso's miniaturists graced her with a golden crown while his poets wrote of "glorious Queen Mary, lovely light of the saints" (40). Yet the *Cantigas* also portray the Virgin as a beautiful woman who arouses love in her devotees as easily as she does awe. Knights in these poems spurn ordinary women to take Mary, lovely beyond compare, as their lady love (16, 84).

The Madonna's new approachability signaled a shifting spiritual climate. In twelfth- and thirteenth-century western Europe, Christianity became increasingly affective, emphasizing the love humans should feel for God and his representatives. Often borrowing from the richly erotic language of the Song of Songs, clerics and monks wrote rapturously about the intimate love humans might have for figures such as the Virgin and Christ. Secular authors too increasingly were inspired to apply this affective vocabulary to the Virgin, as was Alfonso himself.

Passion for the Virgin — as intense as any lover's ardor for his beloved — filled the king's heart. The very language Alfonso chose for the *Cantigas* tells us so. These poems were written in the elegant cadences of Galician, an ancestor of modern Portuguese and the language preferred by medieval Castilian poets for their love songs. The *Cantigas* then are as much the sweet plaints of a lover addressing his beloved as they are the king's devotional offerings to the Mother of God. Alfonso's songs of Marian praise even draw explicitly on the vocabulary of love popularized by the troubadours in their lyric poems. Deeply influenced by Arabic poetic traditions, troubadour poetry emerged in southern France in the twelfth century and spread rapidly to other parts of Europe, including Castile. Its aristocratic authors, mostly male, sang in sensual words of impossible love between a young knight and an ultimately unattainable woman of higher social stature.

Alfonso clearly enjoyed troubadour verse. He even wrote some love poems himself. So when he decided to celebrate the lady of the highest possible rank, the most unattainable and best of all women, Mary, he naturally appropriated the vocabulary and conceits of this literary tradition. Alfonso's ardent declaration in the second prologue sets the amorous tone for the *Cantigas*: "I wish from this day forth to be [Mary's] troubadour and I wish that she will have me for her troubadour and accept my songs.... Hence from now on I choose to sing for no other lady."

Alfonso was hardly the Virgin's only troubadour in thirteenth-century Europe, although he was one of the most famous. By the time he began work on the *Cantigas*, the troubadours' lush language had fused with the emotionally charged imagery of love that ecclesiastical writers themselves increasingly used for the mother of God. Singing of their passion for the Virgin, the troubadours ornamented the celestial object of their affections with the same literary motifs they used for the earthly women whose charms aroused their pens — and thus they, like Alfonso, made Mary into the most desirable woman of all.

While the introduction of the Virgin into the exuberant discourse of love might seem like a radical exaltation of the feminine, even an enthronement of women over men, poetry is rarely a simple reflection of social realities. Singing Mary's praises did not school men to treat the women with whom they actually had relationships like heavenly queens. It is worth noting that Alfonso's considerable skills as Mary's troubadour did not lead him to deal particularly gently with his own wife, Violante. The royal couple fought bitterly at times, especially over the troubled matter of whom to designate as Alfonso's heir. Nor did Alfonso's professed steadfast love for the Virgin translate into marital fidelity. During his years with Violante, the king fathered several illegitimate children and wrote earthy poems to the famous courtesan, María Pérez Balteira.

In fact, the language of romantic love has not always brought benefits to women. Just as behind the seductive veil of the idealized love affairs in the medieval romances lay the harsh realities marriage often imposed on aristocratic women, so the poetic elevation of the Virgin as the ideal object of male heterosexual desire could mask a denigration of real women. Many Cantigas explicitly deliver the message that all women are hopelessly inferior to Mary, especially in the domain of love. Cantiga 130 is particularly pointed in this regard, jubilantly cataloguing the vices of ordinary women while exalting the Virgin's perfections as a lover. Once, Mary even inserts herself between a man and woman lying in bed (42). Not content with preventing the couple from consummating their love, the Virgin whisks the man off to heaven to be with her forever. No wonder that the author of Cantiga 10 writes that he has "consign[ed] to the devil all other loves" in favor of Mary. The accompanying illumination provides a disturbingly graphic representation of the gulf between the Virgin and other women: smiling serenely, Mary watches as a devil seizes a woman in his claws and drags her away.

Such poetic celebration of Mary as love object beyond compare thus contributed to the misogynist discourse that almost always formed one strand of medieval thought. It may also have created a situation of psychological tension for women. How could they possibly hope to imitate Mary, the paragon of feminine perfection? Mother yet virgin, she embodied an ideal unrealizable by any other woman and thus may have counted more men than women among her devotees.

Yet women and men alike crowd the folios of the Cantigas, beseeching the Virgin for her miraculous aid. Many high-medieval Christian women in fact felt as much faith in her as men did. And like their male counterparts, those women who prayed to Mary hoped to be enfolded in her gentle maternal love. As the Cantigas themselves suggest, if in the surge of affective piety in the High Middle Ages, the Virgin became the most beautiful of women, she also became the most tender of mothers, the very embodiment of compassion. By the time that Alfonso and his poets celebrated her maternal virtues, Christians believed that she offered unconditional love and mercy to her devotees, no matter how wayward they might

be. In bright paint and carved stone, artists captured the protective qualities of this love, depicting Mary enveloping men and women in the ample
womb-like folds of her cloak.

The Virgin's infinite maternal compassion served as a counterweight to
the austere powers her son commanded. Although in high-medieval texts
and images Christ often descended from his majestic throne to play as a
sweet child on Mary's lap, he nonetheless retained his awesome position as
the judge who meted out to individual Christians their eternal fate: heaven
or hell. It was to his merciful mother that men and women trembling in
fear for their souls could turn for help. "All sinners will praise Holy Mary,
for they have reason to praise her, for when Our Lord is most stern on
Judgment Day, He will pardon them for her Love, and the Christians will
not be lost" (240). These sober words are echoed by many other poems in
the collection. Merciful maternal intercession at Christ's celestial court,
the softening of the heavenly ruler's justice through his mother's tender
pleas — this is exactly what countless Christian women and men hoped for
from the Virgin.

Confident that she would always come to their aid, the Virgin's devotees
especially invoked her in moments of crisis and despair. So the hero of the
famous thirteenth-century Castilian epic, *The Poem of the Cid* (discussed
in Chapter 15 above), commended himself to Mary as he rode off into
exile and all its uncertainties (215–22). In the *Cantigas* themselves, the
Virgin repeatedly rescues people in danger of shipwreck or caught in other
dire situations. Alfonso's Marian collection as a whole might be read as testimony to the fervent declaration that the Virgin "does not abandon those
she loves, even though they err against her" (55). Mary was particularly
renowned for her loyalty to the most sinful of her devotees. Among the
more popular miracle stories of the High Middle Ages was, for example,
the tale of how she helped a pregnant abbess escape punishment for fla-
grant sexual sin (7).

Alfonso's own sins were perhaps more minor than those committed by
this abbess. Yet the king yearned for Mary's intercession. Composed in the
waning years of his reign, the final poems of the *Cantigas* poignantly articulate his need for her intervention. Alfonso is perhaps at his most plaintive
in *Cantiga* 401. Entitled "the petition the king made to Holy Mary," this
poem opens by imploring the Virgin to help the king obtain forgiveness
for his sins. It then turns into the bitter lament of an old man watching his
power fade and witnessing the failure of many of his political ambitions.

Behind Alfonso's complaint lay the crises that beset his final years: the rebellion of his nobles, aided and abetted by his son Sancho; his abandonment by his wife; and the invasion of Castile by Muslims from North Africa.

Like so many Christians of this period, then, as the end of his life drew near, Alfonso took refuge in the mercy of the saint who never failed her devotees. Indeed, the *Cantigas* represent a rich offering to Mary by a supplicant seeking to assure his eternal salvation. Alfonso suggests as much in his testament of 1284: he stipulated that after his death the manuscripts of the *Cantigas* should be kept in the church where his body lay.[5] It was his wish too that on every Marian feast day, the clerics who watched over his burial place should solemnly sing the *Cantigas*. Thus, this ruler tried to ensure that his poems became an eternal litany of Marian praise, a permanent posthumous offering to the Virgin.

We can read the *Cantigas* as both product and evidence of the great wave of Marian devotion in the High Middle Ages as embodied by one person. But we should remember that Alfonso wasn't just anyone; he was a king. As intensely personal as his devotion to Mary was, the *Cantigas*, like most displays of piety by medieval rulers, also possessed a distinctly political edge. These poems commemorate what Alfonso saw as the special relationship of reciprocal patronage between the monarchs of Castile and the Virgin. As the refrain of one *cantiga* bluntly states: "Holy Mary performs many miracles for kings whenever she so wills" (122). For Alfonso, she was so bound up with royal power that he even proclaimed her its source: "Kings and emperors [should] joyfully render [Mary] great praise, for because of her they are the lords of all the people" (409, 200).

In choosing the Virgin as a symbol of monarchy, Alfonso made shrewd use of her cult to serve his agenda of centralizing power. Maintaining control over Castile was no easy task given its fluid frontier with Granada and the necessity of somehow integrating newly conquered territories with the rest of the realm. As Alfonso sought to make his kingdom cohere, he capitalized on popular devotion to the Virgin. To attract Christian settlers to the vast reaches of his realm left underpopulated when Muslims were expelled by the Christian victors or emigrated to Granada, he promoted pilgrimage to strategically located Marian shrines. The new church dedicated to the Virgin that appears so often in the final poems of the *Cantigas*— El Puerto de Santa María—was central to Alfonso's ambitious plans for

---

[5] *Diplomatario andaluz*, no. 521, 557–64.

the colonization of the southern stretches of his realm. *Cantiga* 379 explicitly describes how the king and the Virgin of El Puerto worked in tandem to create a thriving Christian port in the former Muslim town.

If the promise of Mary's miraculous patronage could draw Christians to settle near her shrines, how did the Muslims and Jews who were among Alfonso's subjects figure in the king's Marian political calculations? The *Cantigas* are eloquent on this subject. They reveal, for example, that Castile was not immune to the viciously negative stereotyping of Jews increasingly common in the rest of western Europe. In the *Cantigas,* Jews are avaricious money-lenders (25) who amass fabulous treasures (348), wicked sinners (89) who tormented and killed Christ (12, 286, 419), implacable enemies of the Virgin and her son (4, 6, 286), and faithful allies of the devil (3). They often meet gruesome deaths, twisted in the agonies of bonfires or crushed by falling buildings (4, 6, 286). Alfonso's miniaturists painted spiritual perversity right onto the faces of adult male Jews, disfiguring them with grossly prominent chins and noses. It is sobering to realize that as vehement as is the stereotyping of Jews in the *Cantigas*, it pales in comparison to the vitriolic anti-Semitic rhetoric of many other thirteenth-century Marian texts, particularly those from France.

Muslims fare somewhat better than Jews. As one poem puts it, Mary may count both Muslims and Jews among her enemies, but she "hates" the Jews "worse than the Moors" (348). Alfonso's artists indulged in little visual stereotyping of Muslims. They did paint the worst Muslim malefactors as black, a color they also used to distinguish lower- from upper-class Muslims, but they gave Muslim rulers and aristocrats faces as white and even-featured as those of Christians.

The verbal portraits of Muslims, while not always flattering, likewise often show less religious animosity than the poems' depictions of Jews. In fact, Alfonso and his poets depicted Muslims as people who, like Christians, offered respect, even reverence, to Mary (165, 181, 183, 329). The authors of the *Cantigas* knew that Muslims regarded Mary as the virginal mother of a prophet—a woman chosen above all other women, in the words of the Qur'an. This knowledge, however, didn't prevent the king and his collaborators from sometimes describing Muslims as infidels (401) or associating them with the devil (264)—the language of holy war was just too tempting. But to portray Muslims as enemies, the *Cantigas* just as often had recourse to the imagery of rivalries played out in military and political terms. In particular, the poems cast the Muslims of Granada and North Africa as Alfonso's formidable adversaries.

Although the *Cantigas* shade their depiction of Jews and Muslims somewhat differently, the poems do assert that both groups have something in common: each is ripe for conversion to Christianity. Conversion is in fact the predominant theme of those poems figuring non-Christians. In these *cantigas*, Mary transforms herself into a missionary. Drawing on her considerable miraculous arsenal, she charms or coerces Muslims and Jews into the baptismal font.

These conversion stories do not indicate that Alfonso himself nurtured evangelical dreams—during his reign he gave only lukewarm support to missionary efforts. Yet these miracles do convey some powerful messages about how Jews and Muslims figured in his conception of his kingdom. Offering proof to their audience of Christianity's inherent superiority over Islam and Judaism, these poems suggest that Jews and Muslims themselves are inferior to Christians. In his laws, Alfonso codified this hierarchy, granting his Muslim and Jewish subjects religious freedom but mandating their social subordination to Christians.

The poems about Mary as evangelist also suggest how Alfonso crafted the Virgin of the *Cantigas* as a mirror of the sovereignty he claimed over all the peoples of Castile, regardless of their religion. Each of these conversion stories declares that Mary's domain of influence extended far beyond the boundaries of Christianity. Indeed, all Jews and Muslims in the *Cantigas*—whether or not they convert to Christianity—are subject to Mary's lordship. Tellingly, the Queen of Heaven wasn't the only royal figure in thirteenth-century Castile believed to wield power over Christians, Muslims, and Jews. Her loyal devotee, Alfonso X, also styled himself the ruler of the three faiths. So central was this concept to his political ideology that he even had the epitaph on his father's tomb written in not just Castilian and Latin, but Arabic and Hebrew as well.

This king of the three religions found a fitting final resting place—right next to the tomb bearing his polyglot tribute to his father, Ferdinand III. Ferdinand's tomb was part of a magnificent burial complex Alfonso constructed for his parents (292). As the site of this memorial, he chose the cathedral of a city dear to his father's heart and to his own, Seville, wrested by Ferdinand from the Muslims in one of his greatest military triumphs. This cathedral was unlike any that could be found in western Europe beyond the Iberian peninsula. It had been built not as a Christian church nor even by Christians, for it was Seville's main mosque. When Ferdinand conquered the city, he triumphantly appropriated the building for Christianity and dedicated it to the Virgin. In this Marian church that still looked like a mosque, Alfonso, the king of the three faiths and the educated monarch influenced by Islamic as well as Christian traditions of rulership, joined his parents after his death. Today most traces of the mosque are gone, obliterated when a Gothic cathedral was erected on the site in the fifteenth century, but Alfonso and his parents still lie in state in the royal chapel. And every now and then, the last wishes of the king who so loved the Virgin are honored, and the cathedral echoes with the elegant melodies of his poetic offering to her, the *Cantigas de Santa María*.

Bibliographic Note

The Centre for the Study of the *Cantigas de Santa María* of Oxford University hosts an online database that is an invaluable resource for the study of the text: http://csm.mml.ox.ac.uk. The site includes a regularly updated bibliography and critical edition of the *Cantigas*. For an English translation, from which I quote throughout, see Kathleen Kulp-Hill, *The Songs of Holy Mary by Alfonso X, the Wise: A Translation of the Cantigas de Santa María* (Tempe: Arizona Center for Medieval and Renaissance Studies, 2000).

There are countless studies of specific aspects of the *Cantigas*, Alfonso X's rule, and medieval Iberia. I acknowledge here my debt to the following scholars on whose insights I have drawn for this essay: Mercedes García Arenal, Dwayne E. Carpenter, Vikki Hatton, Manuel González Jiménez, A.J. Lappin, Peter Linehan, Angus MacKay, Walter Mettmann, Joseph O'Callaghan, Connie Scarborough, Joseph T. Snow, John V. Tolan, and Francisco Márquez Villanueva. For specific references to their work, see my own "Marian Monarchy in Thirteenth-Century Castile," in *The Experience of Power in Medieval Europe, 950–1350*, ed. Robert Berkhofer, Alan Cooper, and Adam Kosto (Aldershot: Ashgate Press, 2005), 247–264, and my forthcoming book on Mary, conquest, and conversion in medieval Iberia and colonial Mexico.

The medieval cult of the Virgin itself is only now beginning to receive the attention it deserves. In addition to my forthcoming book, see the very general, if still useful, study by Marina Warner, *Alone of All Her Sex: The Myth and Cult of the Virgin Mary* (New York: Knopf, 1983), which should be read in conjunction with Rachel Fulton, *From Passion to Judgment: Devotion to Christ and the Virgin Mary, 800–1200* (New York: Columbia University Press, 2002), and the recently published Miri Rubin, *Mother of God: A History of the Virgin Mary* (New Haven: Yale University Press, 2009).

TWENTY-FOUR

Moving the Masses
Cola di Rienzo, the *Anonimo Romano*, and the Roman Crowd

Jennifer A. Heindl

Cola di Rienzo (c. 1313–54) is one of the great characters of fourteenth-century Rome. So is his "biographer," the Anonimo Romano, author of a vernacular chronicle that is, along with letters by both Petrarch (1304–74) and Cola himself, the major contemporary source for those who would unravel a famously chaotic and bizarre period of Roman history. A grammarian and, like his author, a student of Livy (59 BC–17 AD), Cola can, we are told, read the ancient city, decipher its inscriptions, and declaim its ancient glory. He is as deeply immersed as his creator in the alternately vivid and moribund reality of Rome, a reality that, because it is Rome's, must always include the dreams and ruined monuments of the past. It may not be too much to say that the Anonimo's Cola is his creator's alter-ego, his bigger, gaudier—perhaps his more tragic? more classical? more Livian?—self. As the Anonimo's chronicle is framed by historical narratives (*exempla*, really) from the *Etymologies* of Isidore of Seville (c. 560–636) and the monumental history of Rome by Livy, so Cola spans history, reading, and interpreting ancient inscriptions while composing his own messages to the world in mysterious allegorical murals that, along with his oratorical skills, briefly make the city and its people his.

The city of Cola and the Anonimo was a Rome without popes. Beginning in 1305, the popes and the papal curia took up residence in Avignon in the south of France, where they would remain until 1377. In their absence—and with no central authority of which to speak—a number of noble families jostled for power within a city that grew increasingly violent and divided into neighborhoods that served more or less as camps for rival factions. Cola, a notary whose father was an innkeeper, stepped into this scene and, after having galvanized a group of supporters, led an insurrection that culminated, in 1347, with his adoption of the ancient title "Tribune of Rome." For a short time, he was celebrated as the ruler of the city, but within seven months he fled Rome and abdicated his rule. After several years of self-imposed exile, in 1354, with a small band of mercenaries and the sanction of a papal legate, he returned to the city where he was welcomed back by the populace as their "senator" and leader once again. But within a couple of months, his authority and his life would come to an end as he was killed by the very people to whom he had so appealed such a short time before.

Cola's is a remarkable story, but I should explain here that I am not particularly interested in the historical Cola or any other Cola — the Cola of the Italian poet Petrarch, with whom he corresponded, or the Cola we see in his own letters. Rather, I am interested in how one man, and surely, I think, an extraordinary man, chose to represent another extraordinary man. Shortly after Cola's death — probably in 1358 — the Anonimo composed in the dialect of Italian spoken and written in his Rome an account of events in the city over the course of the previous three decades, including but not exclusively focused on those concerning the charismatic figure of Cola.

Central to any understanding of the dynamic between character and author is the city of Rome and its volatile populace. I suggest in this chapter that the projects of the Anonimo and Cola — one historical, one political — are deeply complementary, and, more tentatively, I tease out some of the implications of this relationship for the authority of each figure and the ultimate success or failure of his endeavor. Both the Anonimo and his Cola present themselves as able, perhaps uniquely able, to understand and interpret Rome's past, to connect the present to the past, and, in the process, make the present, in a period of uncertainty and crisis, meaningful and comprehensible to their respective audiences.

In the Anonimo's text, Cola is over and again presented as the master interpreter of Rome and its history. He comes to power through the manipulation of memories and ruins scattered throughout the city. His reign is described in highly visual terms of remapping and reinscribing the city in an effort to recapture the past and to recreate the ancient glory described in the marble inscriptions that he had deciphered and dreamed over.

If Cola's material is the physical city, his audience is the Roman crowd. As presented by the Anonimo, Cola's rise to power (as well as his fall) is a series of vivid performances, complete with repeated costume changes. Cola decries the depredations of Rome's noble families through elaborate allegorical murals painted on the palace of the Capitol (at this time also the site of a major market) and at the church of San Angelo in Pescheria (*Cola* 33–35). He asserts his authority through the public display and translation of the ancient bronze tablet of the *Lex Regia* of Emperor Vespasian (*Cola* 35–36). It is perhaps notable that while Cola is described by the Anonimo as an orator of great skill, the reading audience hears surprisingly little of Cola's speech. More often we get the reactions of the crowd and a detailed description of Cola's spectacular ensemble.

Throughout the chronicle, the Anonimo's point of view is that of the Roman populace. He frequently places his readers directly into the presence of that visual experience upon which his account is based. We see what he saw; we see, he cannily suggests, just what was there. Long before Cola makes his appearance in the chronicle, in the first entry after the preface, which I will discuss presently, the Anonimo recalls, "like a dream," standing in the doorway of the church of Santa Maria in Publicolis in 1325 and watching a procession pass on its way to the Capitoline Hill: "The proud went forth in great numbers. There were many, well-horsed and well-armed. The last of these, if I remember rightly, was wearing a jacket of red sendal and a cap of yellow sendal on his head, a crop in his hand. They passed along the street on the right, along the place where the smithies live, by Paolo Iovinale's house. The procession was long. The bell was ringing. The people were arming themselves. I stayed in Santa Maria in Publicolis" (*Cronica* 8–9). The Anonimo quickly rejects this episode as a fitting beginning to his project. It lacks, he says, *aitezza* (loftiness or grandeur), and, besides, he was too young at the time to be a proper witness.

Nonetheless, it is in many ways a typical entry. The Anonimo is concerned with local events first and foremost. Actually, he is specifically concerned with the localness of events, and his view is generally from street level. Throughout his narrative he connects greater events to local streets. He maps the events with the specificity of one speaking of his own town (and as to an audience equally familiar with it), telling us whence the processions and mobs come and where they go, often as a means of implying something about their makeup and identity. In the penultimate scene in the chronicle, he describes the mob closing in on Cola's palace on the

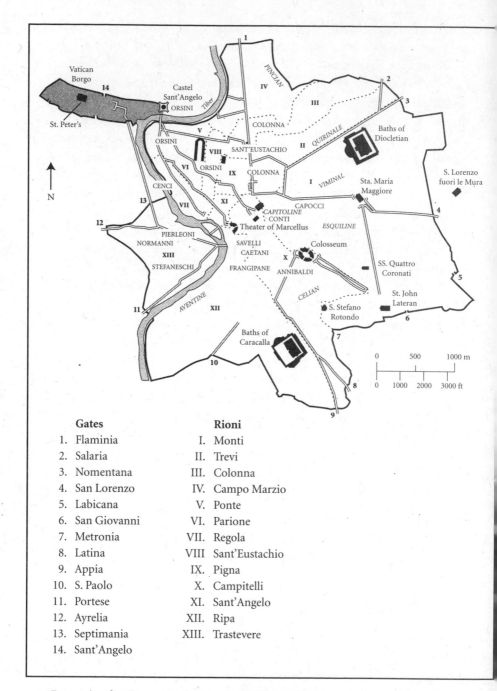

Gates
1. Flaminia
2. Salaria
3. Nomentana
4. San Lorenzo
5. Labicana
6. San Giovanni
7. Metronia
8. Latina
9. Appia
10. S. Paolo
11. Portese
12. Ayrelia
13. Septimania
14. Sant'Angelo

Rioni
I. Monti
II. Trevi
III. Colonna
IV. Campo Marzio
V. Ponte
VI. Parione
VII. Regola
VIII. Sant'Eustachio
IX. Pigna
X. Campitelli
XI. Sant'Angelo
XII. Ripa
XIII. Trastevere

Rome in the Fourteenth Century: Gates, *Rioni*, and Baronial Families.
Source: Map permission of Italica Press, New York.

Capitol as consisting exclusively of people from specific parts of the city. The first cry against Cola comes from the northeast; the author makes a point of mentioning specifically those crowds from the *rioni* (neighborhoods) of Colonna and Trevi, that is, neighborhoods associated with the Colonna, one of Rome's most powerful families and Cola's great rival. He further records that Cola's broken body is displayed at the church of San Marcello, in the heart of Colonna territory (*Cola* 151–52). The Anonimo thus suggests through location something about the agency of Cola's death.

Likewise, in the opening scene of the chronicle, the Anonimo gives us important information about what is going on and who is involved by disclosing the path and origin of the crowd on its way to the Capitoline Hill. At the sound of the bells of Santa Maria Aracoeli, armed men come from neighborhoods to the north of Santa Maria in Publicolis—neighborhoods controlled by the powerful Orsini and Colonna families—at the behest of Stefano Colonna and Poncello Orsini to encourage the departure of a leader of a rival faction (*Cronica* 10–11).

The Anonimo's focus is visual. Perhaps as a result of his medical training—just about the only personal fact he reveals to us in his chronicle—he excels at close observation (*Cronica* 89–90). Throughout the chronicle, he sets up his scenes with a sort of cinematic clarity—he practically storyboards them as he layers, arranges, and cuts from one view to another to construct a complete scene. He provides a specific point and angle of view. His switch in the above quotation from the past tense to the imperfect as if pulled back into the past by his memory—from recollection to experience itself—lends immediacy to his telling. The procession passes before the reader's eyes as it did before his. He presents the reader with what he saw as he saw it, complete with exclamations of amazement and exhortations to "pay attention." Over and over again in the Anonimo's chronicle the onlooking crowd and the reading audience share an identical perspective relative to the spectacle they observe, eliding not only the experience of reader and spectator but also the authority of the chronicler and the tribune.

The spaces of the city are the means by which both the Anonimo and his Cola can communicate with the Roman past and transmit that past to their respective audiences. The hills, ruins, and piazzas of Rome are the ever-present links between their city and that of the ancients they admire and emulate. The Anonimo sees nothing odd in comparing the 1354 attack on Cola in his palace on the Capitol with Livy's story of the Gaulish (or French, as the Anonimo says) attack on the same site in 390 BC (*Cola*

153–54): Roman history continues on the streets of his (and Cola's) own neighborhood. The reliefs Romans see on triumphal arches and the stories they read in Livy and Lucan (39 BC–65 AD)—the poet's *Pharsalia* tells the story of the civil war between Julius Caesar and Pompey the Great—are not just available to them, they are their entitlement as Romans. The procession the Anonimo watches from Santa Maria in Publicolis—although he ultimately rejects it for the grubby and rather insignificant coup it is—looks like history to him because it happens on Roman streets and recalls the monuments and texts that belong to him as a Roman (*Cola* 51–52).

The Anonimo's Cola is set as firmly in the physical fabric of his neighborhood as his author. Cola's first appearance in the chronicle occurs in a setting similar to that of the author, indeed physically nearby; the Anonimo records Cola's birth "on the street leading to the Regola, behind San Tommaso, below the Jew's temple." From this neighborhood, near the Capitol and the Forum, Cola emerges, reading ancient inscriptions, commenting on the events he sees from the street, and comparing them, as does his author, to the events of Rome's glorious past. Says the Anonimo, "Lord, how often he said, 'Where are those good Romans? Where is their high justice? If only I could live in their time.'" In this brief description, Cola resembles no one so much as his author, standing within the city, watching events swirl around him, and comparing them to the past as represented in the works of Livy and Valerius Maximus, as well as in the inscriptions and reliefs of surviving ruins (*Cola* 31). Both process and evaluate what they see on the streets, selecting and judging memory, personal and inscribed, according to its worthiness as history.

The historical associations of the setting and spectacle of Cola's fall enhance the Anonimo's narrative authority in much the same way as Cola's presentation of the *Lex Regia* enhances his political authority. Spectacle provides both the opportunity to connect present to past, linking their audiences' experience to that of their forebears and establishing their primacy as makers of meaning.

Both the Anonimo and his Cola are working on a project of shaping the past to address the needs of the present. Their respective projects have a particular urgency during a period in which Rome has been abandoned by the papacy and divided into barricaded camps by its noble families. Both author and character are looking for order and meaning in the physical city and its history to convey to their respective audiences. Cola's political project promises reconnection to Rome's classical past, and in this it both echoes and supports an historical endeavor equal to those of the ancient writers that the Anonimo admires and imitates.

The relationship between the Anonimo's and Cola's respective projects is suggested in the chronicle's prologue, where, rather than starting with the beginning of the world, the Anonimo starts with the beginning of writing. Borrowing from Isidore of Seville's *Etymologies,* he ascribes the creation of writing to Cadmus. Like Isidore, he suggests that letters serve to hold and preserve memory outside of any human physiological faculty. He alters and expands upon Isidore a good deal, however, and in a particularly telling way. He is typically concrete; he turns Isidore's passing detail into a narrative, relating it to Rome, to his visual experience of the city and his understanding of its history. He writes that before the invention of the alphabet memorials visually describing important events would be sculpted in stone and set up in the places where the events had taken place. The ancient Romans continued this practice, he says, "throughout Italy and in France and especially in Rome. That they might make their deeds known to their successors, they made triumphal arches with images of battles, armed men, horses and other things, like those found in [Perugia] and Rimini" (*Cola* 21). Before Cadmus, historical memory had been intimately tied to a specific place. Only with the creation of writing did mobile, disembodied memory become possible.

While the Romans made great use of monuments — of visual, nonverbal communications — they also wrote books, books to which the Anonimo compares his own work: "After Cadmus created letters, people began to write things down, because of the weakness of memory, especially eminent and magnificent deeds: thus Titus Livius made his book of the founding of Rome up to the time of Octavian, thus Lucan wrote the deeds of Caesar, thus Sallust and many other writers did not let die the memory of many past things about Rome. So how can I who, thanks to God, have seen so much in this world, let these things pass without writing about them" (*Cola* 21). Here, the Anonimo sees that Roman monuments and Roman books are parallel expressions — both exist together as a means of preserving memory outside the body. However, he also marks the development from a visual, non-verbal form of memorialization to one perhaps more permanent and effective. The Roman historians Sallust (86–34 BC) and Livy stand as improved memorials, providing clearer memories, less contingent on space and time, less subject to the weakness of human faculties. The author here sets up his own project as parallel to that of the ancients. Cola, it seems, will be his Caesar.

Within the Anonimo's text, Cola will, also like the Romans, create his own monuments, although they will prove less durable and less readable than the works of the ancients, despite or perhaps because of the way they often recycle or work in elements from the ancient city. They provoke gasps of amazement from his audience but also incite debate or meet with simple incomprehension. They and their message will not hold steady. Is this a problem? By allying himself and his project so closely with Cola, did the Anonimo not partake in Cola's ultimate failure? Was it for this reason that the failure of Cola's project to reinscribe Rome and his utter destruction at the hands of the Roman crowd marked the rather abrupt end of the Anonimo's own textual project? Perhaps not.

In categorizing his own work as a memorial, the Anonimo is clearly drawing—as he does for much of his prologue—on Livy's comments in the prologue of *Ab urbe condita*. Livy describes his own work as an *inlustris monumentum*, "a splendid memorial," and says, "The special and salutary benefit of the study of history is to behold evidence of every type of behavior set forth as on a splendid memorial; from it you may select for yourself and for your country what to emulate, from it what to avoid, whether basely begun or basely concluded."[1] Cola may be the only one in the city who can read and interpret the monuments of ancient Rome to the crowd, but the Anonimo, can, like Livy, make a monument, a transparent (another meaning of *inlustris*) and complete transmission of the past containing every kind of *exempla*. The Anonimo's text is not an interpretation of historical evidence but the thing itself—the monument, the embodiment and extension of the city. As such it has the authority and permanence that Cola's interpretive spectacles lack.

The Anonimo in the end, as at the beginning of his chronicle, allies himself with the crowd that Cola initially dazzles and then disappoints. It is a nice irony that Cola is destroyed by the crowd at the moment he seeks integration into it. He is captured by an angry mob while trying to escape the Capitol palace wearing a shepherd's cloak and speaking in a rustic accent. The Anonimo in his text, like the Roman crowd, ultimately turns

---

[1] Livy, *Ab urbe condita*, Preface; the translation is from *The Rise of Rome, Books 1–5*, ed. and trans. T.J. Luce (Oxford: Oxford University Press, 1998), 4.

away from Cola, whose mangled corpse was finally given to the Jews to burn until "not a speck was left" (*Cola* 152). He tells another story, the *exemplum* drawn from Livy about the sack of Rome by the Gauls and the noble behavior of the Roman elder Papiris, who faces death with stoic nobility, not, the Anonimo dryly notes, "with a coverlet on his head, the way Cola di Rienzi died" (*Cola* 154). Cola's saga is neatly turned into a very Livian *exemplum* — in fact, a mirror image of one of Livy's *exempla* — a warning of "what to avoid," just as Papiris's story tells us "what to emulate." Cola, his successes and failures, are thus neatly absorbed within the monument of the Anonimo's history, reinforcing for the audience the authority of the Anonimo's project through the failure of his own.

Bibliographic Note

In this chapter, I refer in two ways to the anonymous chronicle on which I focus. In most cases, I refer parenthetically to *Cola* with the pages for passages that have been excerpted from the chronicle and translated by John Wright as *The Life of Cola di Rienzo* (Toronto: Pontifical Institute of Medieval Studies, 1975). In those cases where I quote from or refer to those passages within the chronicle that do not appear in this translation, I cite the pages of the most recent edition of the entire chronicle: *Anonimo Romano: Cronica*, ed. Giuseppe Porta (Milan: Adelphi, 1979). Unfortunately, it has not been translated completely into English. Nor have all of Cola's letters, but his correspondence with Petrarch appears in *The Revolution of Cola di Rienzo*, trans. Mario Emilio Cosenza (New York: Italica Press, 1986).

While the life (or at least the legend) of Cola di Rienzo has provided fodder for all sorts of artists and writers, little serious scholarship was available in English until very recently. Two serious attempts at revealing the real Cola di Rienzo have appeared almost simultaneously: Ronald Musto, *Apocalypse in Rome: Cola di Rienzo and a New Age* (Berkeley: University of California Press, 2003), and Amanda Collins, *"Greater than Emperor": Cola di Rienzo and the World of Fourteenth-Century Rome* (Ann Arbor: University of Michigan Press, 2002). Otherwise, Richard Krautheimer, *Rome: Portrait of a City (312–1308)* (Princeton: Princeton University Press, 1980), and Robert Brentano, *Rome before Avignon: A Social History of Thirteenth-Century Rome* (Berkeley: University of California Press, 1990 [1974]), although addressing the thirteenth- more than the fourteenth-century city, are still the best and certainly the most beautiful introductions to the medieval city.

TWENTY-FIVE

Christine de Pizan on Gossip, Misogyny, and Possibility

Dallas G. Denery II

Born in Venice in 1365, Christine de Pizan moved to France when her father, Thomas de Pizan, accepted an invitation to become King Charles V's court astrologer and physician. It was there in the royal courts of Paris that she grew up and eventually married Étienne de Castel in 1380 — an arranged marriage, to be sure, but a happy one as it turned out. Unfortunately for Christine, Charles V died that same year and with his passing went much of the Pizan family fortune. Her father died sometime between 1385 and 1390. Her beloved Étienne died in 1390. Creditors and financial predators soon came pounding at Christine's door as she sought some means of supporting her three children, her mother, and a niece. Married at 15, a widowed mother of three at 25, Christine turned to writing out of necessity.

Even today writing is rarely a lucrative profession and probably not the safest career choice when times are tight and the rent is coming due. Before Christine it is not at all clear that there was even such a thing as a professional writer and certainly not a female professional writer. But this is the career she chose to support herself and her family, and success came fairly quickly. She completed her first set of lyrical poetry in 1493 and soon found eager patrons among the Burgundian nobility for whom she would write an astonishingly diverse assortment of treatises, handbooks, and poetry. During her own life she may well have been best known for her involvement in the *Querelle de la Rose,* a debate that pitted her and her friend and ally, Jean Gerson, Chancellor of the University of Paris, against the defenders of the *Romance of the Rose,* a work originally written during the first half of the thirteenth century by Guillaume de Lorris and then expanded to nearly five times its original length by Jean de Meun sometime around 1275. As popular as it was, and it was very popular, Christine found Jean de Meun's additions to the *Rose* to be deeply offensive, full of misogyny and slander, a poem in which women are depicted as universally hateful, deceitful, and utterly lacking in virtue. She wrote letters in defense of women and against de Meun's work, responded to the men who defended it, held her ground, and perhaps even won the debate. In 1405, in the aftermath of that controversy, she wrote the two works, both in French, for which she is best known today, *The Book of the City of Ladies* and *The Treasure of the City of Ladies.*

While *The City* and *The Treasure* can be, and usually are, read independently of each other, they clearly form an interconnected whole, both in terms of their narratives and themes. Christine herself signals the narrative connection at the very beginning of *The Treasure*, which opens with an explicit reference to the earlier book. "After I had built the City of Ladies," she writes, "with the help and by the commandment of the three Ladies of Virtue — Reason, Rectitude, and Justice — in the form and manner explained in the text of that book, and after I, more than anyone else, had worked so hard to finish the project and felt so exhausted by the long and continual exertion, I wanted only to rest and be idle for a while" (*Treasure* 3). Of course, rest is not to be hers. The three ladies reappear and tell her that she has only completed half of the job at hand, and so she begins to write *The Treasure.*

What is the job that connects these two books, that transforms them from two books written in succession into a single work? Here it is important to think broadly about the term "work." While Christine instructs us to read the two books as complementing and completing each other, as a single literary work, she also describes their creation as the result of a single lengthy and tiring endeavor, the accomplishment of a long day's work. The three ladies offer a somewhat cryptic explanation in *The Treasure* when they compare *The City* to a bird cage and Christine to a bird catcher: "We hope just as the wise bird catcher readies his cage before he may take his birds, so, after the shelter of honored ladies is made and prepared, devices and traps may be set with your help as before." The three virtues order Christine to lay out traps and snares "where ladies and generally all women pass and congregate, so that those who are wild and hard to tame can be grabbed, taken, and snared in our nets so that no one or very few who get caught can escape" (*Treasure* 4). One interpretation of this analogy is straightforward and useful, if not entirely sufficient. It may well seem that having built the City of Ladies, Christine is now charged with populating it. Although there is merit to this interpretation, what it means to populate a literary city constructed out of the biographies of famous women (and, therefore, I would imagine, already populated with those same women) requires some explanation. Something else requires explanation as well. *The Treasure* is a handbook of courtly conduct in which Christine instructs women of all ranks, from princesses to commoners, on how to maintain their honor and dignity in the face of trying circumstances. How does offering instruction and advice constitute trapping, snaring, and caging? We can also ask the same question from a different perspective, one that assumes her book is read, understood, and followed. What does it mean to claim that women who take Christine's advice will be trapped and installed in the City of Ladies?

To trap and to snare imply a degree of forethought and planning. Traps must be constructed and camouflaged, strategically placed, and carefully set. As a writer, Christine constructs her traps out of language, turns of phrase, juxtaposition, stories, and structure, in other words, out of the tools and materials of rhetoric. She signals both her knowledge of and the importance of rhetoric early in *The City*. While she ponders the often hyperbolic slurs that men write and say about women, Lady Reason cautions her that sometimes poets mean the opposite of what they say; that is, they employ *antiphrasis* (*City* 1.2.2). Knowledge of rhetoric, in other words, is necessary to understand what people do and say and write. Today, we often think of rhetoric in derogatory terms as empty speech or, taking a cue (whether we realize it or not) from the ancient Greek philosopher Socrates, as a tool of deception. The skilled rhetorician, because of his eloquence, his ability to obfuscate and enthrall with powerful and emotional language, makes the weaker argument seem like the stronger and in so doing sways and bends crowds to his own self-centered will. Certainly and at first glance, Christine's use of terms such as "snaring" and "trapping" speaks to this seemingly negative depiction of rhetoric.

Rhetoric had a much different connotation for Christine and her peers than it does for us. During much of the Middle Ages, rhetorical studies formed the very basis of education. Rhetoric, along with grammar and dialectic, constituted the *trivium*, the three building blocks upon which education into the liberal arts depended. Most of these educational ideas came from the Roman world of Cicero, Quintilian, and Seneca, whose speeches and rhetorical treatises were read and reread endlessly, copied and commented upon, excerpted and quoted. No doubt the Roman conception of the good orator as the ethically responsible man eased this assimilation of pagan cultural ideals into a Christian world. Cicero argued at length and in numerous places, for example, that the good orator, the man who knows how to behave, who knows what to say and when to say it, is by definition a good citizen and that there can never be a discrepancy between what is right and what is beneficial. In other words, it is always beneficial to do the ethically (and, therefore, rhetorically) proper thing. As a result, rhetorical ideas shaped the nature of medieval educational practice and seeped into religious and courtly literature of all sorts.

The Book of the City of Ladies begins with Christine in her study, exhausted from a long day of work, looking at her bookshelves for some "light poetry" with which to relax. She accidentally reaches for Matheolus's *Book of Lamentations,* a book a friend had given her. Soon, however, her mother calls her down for supper. Christine puts the book aside, forgetting about it until she returns to her study the next morning only to discover that it repeats the same lies about women that she had found in the *Rose,* the same lies she has repudiated in public debate. There in her study, she tells us, she begins to wonder why so many male philosophers, poets, and orators assert almost unanimously "that the behavior of women is inclined to and full of every vice." How could such learned authorities, "such solemn scholars," all be wrong? Such assertions she writes, "made me conclude that, although my intellect did not perceive my own great faults and, likewise, those of other women because of its simpleness and ignorance, it was however truly fitting that such was the case." And so, she adds, "relying on the judgments of men, a great unhappiness and sadness welled up in my heart, for I detested myself and the entire feminine sex, as though we were monstrosities in nature" (*City* 1.1.1).

Rhetorically, Christine's despair accomplishes a variety of things. First and foremost, it sets the stage and establishes the topic for the rest of *The City,* an eloquent defense of women against these slanderous lies. Implicitly, it points out the ubiquity of medieval misogyny, impossible to escape even behind the locked doors of a woman's reading room, forcing itself on her even when she is alone with her thoughts. Christine's despair is rhetorical in another sense as well, a sense more appropriate to the classical and medieval art of rhetoric. In order to do and say the right things, the good orator needs to know himself, needs to know his true character and nature, as well as the people with whom he interacts. "The universal rule in oratory, as in life," Cicero writes in *The Orator*, "is to consider propriety. This depends on the subject matter under discussion, and on the character of both the speaker and the audience."[1] It is precisely this self-understanding, this awareness of her own true character, that Christine seems to have lost in the opening pages of *The City*. She finds herself accepting slander and lies as truth. If so many men, respected and educated men, authorities one and all, unanimously assert the same horrible things about women, then mustn't there be some truth to their statements? The danger is both ethical and epistemological. Christine will not be able to lead a virtuous and ethical life if she does not know who she is and how she should act.

It is at this moment in her story that three crowned women suddenly appear before her, their faces shining with a splendor that illuminates her entire study. They have appeared in her room even though the doors are all shut fast, and Christine, "fearing that some phantom had come to tempt" her, is understandably terrified. But these women are not demons. They are incarnations of the virtues of Reason, Rectitude, and Justice, and they certainly are not interested in tempting her. Rather, they want to prove to her that men lie about women and that Christine has been duped, that she no longer knows who she is and, therefore, no longer knows how to behave. Lady Reason, who speaks first, makes this clear almost immediately. "You resemble the fool in the prank who was dressed in women's clothes while he slept," she tells Christine, "because those who were making fun of him repeatedly told him he was a woman, he believed their false testimony more readily than the certainty of his own identity" (*City* 1.2.2).

A similar situation sets the stage for *The Treasure*. Exhausted from constructing her literary City of Ladies, Christine (as we have seen) wants "only to rest and be idle for a while" (*Treasure* 3). The three ladies reappear, saying, "Do you now intend to take seriously the propaganda of Laziness, who, if you are inclined to believe it, will sing sweetly to you: 'You have done enough. It is time that you had a rest'" (*Treasure* 3). Perhaps Laziness avoids the misogynistic diatribes of the men with whom Christine contends in *The City*, but its suggestions and words are no less dangerous and

---

[1] Cicero, *The Orator*, trans. H.M. Hubbell (Cambridge, MA: Harvard University Press, 1939), 21.71, 357–58.

false. It urges her to think falsely about herself, to think that she has done enough and to give up before completing her work. "The knight who leaves the field of battle," the ladies remind her, "before the moment of victory is deeply shamed, for the laurel wreath belongs to those who persevere" (*Treasure* 3). Later, Christine makes the connection between the books even clearer. She imagines a princess, waking late one morning in her luxurious bed in her beautiful and well-appointed room, surrounded by ladies-in-waiting ready to satisfy her every command. A different kind of propaganda, Temptation, is ever ready to seduce her with its own false advice. "By Almighty God, is there in this world a greater lady than you or one with more authority? To whom should you defer," Temptation asks her, "for don't you take precedence over everyone else?" (*Treasure* 6). And so Temptation, rooted in pride, urges her on from bad actions to worse, tells her she has the right to do whatever she wants, to mistreat others while satisfying her every whim.

In both *The City* and *The Treasure,* Christine presents a world in which false and dangerous speech is everywhere—in the mouths of men and in the words they write, behind locked doors, and in the private thoughts of women who have heard nothing else since birth. Slander, gossip, and bad advice are ubiquitous, often hidden, presenting themselves under a façade of truth and well-intentioned concern. "It wouldn't be fitting," Temptation might say to the princess, "for you to do this, to deny yourself that." While the figures of Laziness and Temptation that frame the first examples of false speech in *The Treasure* are allegorical, Christine fills the rest of her book with examples of false and dangerous speech taken straight from the life of the medieval court—the gossip of the envious, the false praise of sycophants, the slanders of her equals, and even the lies and excuses of adulterous husbands. Temptation's silent urgings merely echo the self-serving conversations that resound throughout the court. In other words, despite their allegorical trappings, Christine sets both works in the real world, offering them as tools to provide women with the means of discriminating between true and false speech, between what is helpful and what is harmful. In *The City,* this takes the form of a dialogue between Christine and the three ladies. Christine poses a series of questions reflecting the pervasive claims of the misogynists, which the three ladies roundly reject with arguments and examples proving their vacuity. "Why do men say such terrible things about women?" Christine asks (*City* 1.8.3). Is it true that women are weak and cowardly (*City* 1.14.1), less intelligent than men (*City* 1.27.1), verbose gossips and nags who ruin whatever happiness could ever be found in marriage, love, and life (*City* 2.13.1)? The three ladies respond to each question patiently, offering example after example of women whose lives and deeds show up these misogynistic claims as nothing but empty slanders. In so doing, they offer true speech as a foil to false speech (*City* 2.3.3).

Christine's immediate goal is to correct the self-understanding of women. If acting well, if doing the right thing, requires that the orator know himself, she structures her books in such a way that they will allow women to see themselves as they truly are and not through the lies of men. Early in *The City*, Lady Reason invokes the popular metaphor of the mirror. "Since I serve to demonstrate clearly and to show both in thought and deed to each man and woman his or her own special qualities and faults," she says to Christine, "you see me holding a shiny mirror which I carry in my right hand in place of a scepter. I would have you know truly that no one can look into this mirror, no matter what kind of creature, without achieving clear self-knowledge" (*City* 1.3.2). In *The Treasure*, Christine links this self-knowledge explicitly to right action when the three ladies advise the use of discretion when choosing how to lead one's life. Discretion allows us to know who we are, what we are capable of, what skills we possess, and what skills we lack. "[A]nyone who fails to do any undertaking [with Discretion] will find that all the work comes to nothing and is of no effect," they advise, "because it is necessary to work by discretion" (*Treasure* 16).

Self-knowledge may well open the door to appropriate action, but the model of self-knowledge Christine offers stands in marked contrast to what the misogynists want women to think about themselves. The slanders of men like Matheolus and Jean de Meun depict all women as if they are identical. There was, naturally enough, some sort of allegedly theoretical underpinning for this monolithically conceived misogyny. Medieval medical ideas, derived in large part from the Greek physician Galen, asserted that women were imperfect versions of men, colder, weaker, less developed, and less intelligent.[2] Similarly, there was no shortage of priests and theologians to make a similar universalizing case against women by pointing especially to Eve's failure to resist the seductive words of the ser-

---

[2] Galen, *On the Usefulness of the Parts of the Body*, trans. Margaret Tallmadge May (Ithaca, NY: Cornell University Press, 1968), vol. 2, 620–54.

pent in the Garden of Eden. These ideas came together in hundreds of medieval religious and scientific treatises, most notoriously (and ludicrously) in *Women's Secrets,* a thirteenth-century book that Christine mentions in *The City* and that, among other things, suggests that women not infrequently place sharpened pieces of iron in their vaginas in order to sever and infect men's penises.[3]

Christine's response to this homogenizing medieval account of women is telling. Taking her lead from Scripture as opposed to Galen, she stresses God's power and perfection. God would never make something evil or imperfect, and those men who suggest that God created women as flawed versions of the human species demean Him and His goodness (*City* 1.10.1). Christine's argument is more nuanced than the one the misogynists put forth. On the one hand, her emphasis on God's power, goodness, and perfection undercuts the misogynist's belief that biology necessarily makes women evil. Both men and women are created perfectly and in accord with God's wishes. On the other hand, she does not counter one stereotyped depiction of all women as essentially evil with another portraying all women as essentially good. Given the wealth of examples of noble and virtuous women throughout *The City,* it is hardly surprising when Lady Rectitude asserts, "It is wrong to say that the majority of women are not good.... But what a surprise that all women are not good!" (*City* 2.53.2). There are good and evil men, just as there are good and evil women. It is not our sex that makes us saints or sinners, it is what we do, what we make of ourselves. "The man or woman in whom resides greater virtue is the higher," Reason tells Christine, "neither the loftiness nor the lowliness of a person lies in the body according to sex, but in the perfection of conduct and virtues" (*City* 1.9.3). It is a point Christine stresses throughout *The Treasure,* assuring her readers that both rich and poor can be saved if they act appropriately and that one should never confuse one's rank with one's real worth (*Treasure* 16–17).

Christine does not mean to suggest that there are no differences between men and women. When she asks why women do not appear in court as prosecutors, defenders, or judges, Lady Reason responds, "One could just as well ask why God did not ordain that men fulfill the offices of

---

[3] *Women's Secrets: A Translation of Pseudo-Albertus Magnus' De secretis mulierum with commentaries,* ed. and trans. Helen Rodite Lemay (Albany: State University of New York Press, 1992), 88.

women, and women the offices of men.... Just as a wise and well ordered lord organizes his domain so that one servant accomplishes one task and another servant another task, and that what the one does the other does not do, God has similarly ordained man and woman to serve Him in different offices" (*City* 1.11.1). Each person — each man and each woman — has a divinely ordained position, function, and role in society. Social and sexual hierarchies are not arbitrary. They are inscribed into the very nature of things, and part of this is, in fact, rooted in biology. Falling back on long-standing ideas rooted in Galenic medicine, Christine claims that men are warmer than women and therefore "more courageous and hot-headed," whereas women are cooler and "by nature more timid and also of a sweeter disposition" (*Treasure* 23–24). Christine is not at all interested in undoing sexual and economic inequality, in replacing the French monarchy with some sort of democracy. While she may not share modern notions of equal rights, she nonetheless passionately defends the dignity of each function and each member of society. Excellence and virtue are not the prerogative of the few — of the nobility, for example, or of the religious, or of men. Rather, everyone can achieve excellence and live lives of virtue so long as they act in ways that are appropriate to their sex, their station, and their character.

Despite Christine's belief that society has an essential ontological grounding and ordering in the divine will, hardly a surprising belief for someone living in the Middle Ages, her inclinations as a writer and thinker are always to move away from the demands of universal law and toward the demands of the moment. Practical necessity matters more than universal necessity. Lady Reason makes this clear when, soon after describing the divinely ordained structure of society, she distinguishes between what is normal and what is possible: "It would not be at all appropriate for [women] to go and appear so brazenly in court like men, for there are enough men who do so." It would be a mistake, however, to conclude from this statement that women are incapable of appearing in court, judging cases or even ruling countries. "If anyone maintained that women do not possess enough understanding to learn the laws, the opposite is obvious from the proof afforded by experience, which is manifest and has been manifest in many women." Natural and divine hierarchies matter, but they are not absolute, and in extraordinary circumstances women must act in extraordinary ways. Reason assures Christine that "a woman with a mind is fit for all tasks" (*City* 1.11.1). The bulk of *The City* bears out this claim with example after example of women who performed remarkable and virtuous actions when circumstances demanded it. Christine relates stories of empresses and queens who, suddenly finding themselves widowed and threatened on all sides, take control of their countries, rule them wisely, develop laws, defend them from attacking enemies, and conquer neighboring countries.

The difference between the epic lives recorded in *The City* and the lives of the women Christine counsels in *The Treasure* are not as different as they may at first appear. If there is one lesson to draw from both books, it is that circumstances are always trying for women. These trials may well have been woven into the very fabric of courtly society itself. Christine was far from the only medieval writer to describe the aristocratic court as a place of intrigue, gossip, and slander. Medieval romances, for example, are replete with stories that center around the dangerous hushed whispers of the royal circle. Even before Tristan, the most famous of all medieval literary courtiers, began his ill-fated romance with Iseut, his flawless service to King Mark had already incited the envy and backbiting of his comrades.[4] If things could be dangerous for the most perfect of courtiers, they were so much the worse for women. Often living far from her family, politically disenfranchised in her husband's court as part of an arranged marriage, surrounded by strangers hostile and otherwise, the princess, Christine makes it clear throughout *The Treasure*, will often have only herself to rely on. Her husband might begin an affair with another woman or may side with her enemies in some dispute. Her only defense will be her honor, which she must cultivate constantly. To do this, she must know how to behave at every moment, how to win over her in-laws (*Treasure* 41), the other members of the court, and the religious. She must even win the love of the common people so that their voices will cry out in support of her if she is ever wronged (*Treasure* 47).

All of which brings us back to the questions of what unites *The City* and *The Treasure*, what makes them a single work, and how we should read them. The image of a City of Ladies, of a castle whose foundations and walls and rooms are constructed out of the lives of brave and virtuous women, is a powerful one. It suggests an edifice strong enough to withstand the cruel and relentless assaults of its enemies. Christine intended

---

[4] Gottfried von Strassburg, *Tristan: With the Tristan of Thomas*, trans. A.T. Hatto (New York: Penguin Books, 1960).

this, and her image of women whose virtues are purified like gold as they endure the fiery slander of cruel and vicious men is one of the most memorable in all of medieval literature. On the other hand, the image of the fortress itself imposes an inert and static quality on *The City*. It suggests that *The City* is simply an argument in defense of women, while *The Treasure* exists as an independent treatise of practical advice. This interpretation sits uncomfortably with the content of the two books. *The City* is a book full of action, at the center of which is Christine's own transformation from ignorance to knowledge, a transformation made possible through stories about women whose dramatic actions reveal the misogynists' claims to be false. Christine's argument here is decidedly non-theoretical. It is empirical and topical, as specific examples of women behaving in novel ways reveal the truth about what women are and of what they are capable. Christine's despair at the beginning of *The City*, a despair that renders herself unintelligible to herself, incapable of acting properly and virtuously, slowly gives way to a self-knowledge that teaches her the range and nature of virtuous female action.

Significantly, membership in the City is not guaranteed through sex. If it were, there would be no concern that some women, having been snared like birds and placed in the cage of the City, might escape. Put differently, the City of Ladies is not a place or structure so much as it is a way of knowing and living, of seeing through the lies that surround women everywhere so that they can perceive themselves and others for what they really are and so that they can fit their words and actions to events as they unfold. A woman inhabits the City so long as she recognizes who she is and acts according to that self-knowledge. Of course, this is easier said than done, and even virtuous action can generate problems that require additional precautions, planning, and action. "The better and more virtuous a lady is," Prudence instructs Christine in *The Treasure*, "the greater the war Envy very much makes upon her. There is no man or woman so powerful (nor ever was, except God himself) who could avenge himself for every affront. Therefore, the wise princess, and similarly all those who wish to act prudently, will be aware of this problem and provide themselves with a remedy" (*Treasure* 44). Sometimes this remedy will violate what seem to be inviolable principles. Though Christine, for example, repeatedly expresses an absolute abhorrence for lies and hypocrisy, an abhorrence founded in universally accepted theological dogma that every lie (even one told to save another's life) is a sin, sometimes, when circumstances require it, this rule must be ignored. When dealing with her enemies or those who envy her position, sometimes virtue will require the princess to feign friendship for them, to deny knowing things she knows, and to lie about herself and others. "Thus the wise lady," Prudence adds, "will use this discreet pretence and prudent caution, which is not thought to be a vice, but is a great virtue when it is done in the cause of goodness and peace without injuring anyone in order to avoid a greater misfortune" (*Treasure* 45).

Trying times sometimes require extraordinary responses, and while both *The City* and *The Treasure* are deeply religious books, their religion is tempered by a rhetorician's sober vision of the world. Christine is clear that she intends *The Treasure* as a book to help women lead religious and virtuous lives while remaining active in the world. Unfortunately, it is a world full of difficult choices made all the more difficult because Misogyny, Envy, and Cruelty are everywhere, speaking their lies, spreading their propaganda, and whispering their gossip. In such a world, the range of virtuous acts becomes almost endlessly fluid, and actions that in some instances would be utterly unacceptable violations of the divine order of society become necessary. *The City*, for example, includes the biblical story of Judith who seduces and slays the oppressive ruler Holofernes (*City* 2.31.1), and in *The Treasure*, Christine advises women to occasionally make a hypocritical show of their religious devotion to impress the masses (*Treasure* 47–48). Everything depends upon knowing oneself, one's nature and status, one's abilities and limitations, and how they fit into this precise moment. Sometimes one should be forthright, sometimes not; sometimes it is best to lay snares and traps, to dissimulate and pretend. Fortune itself can be cruel. A happily married woman can suddenly find herself widowed without financial support. What should she do? It is a predicament in which Christine found herself in 1390, and it is difficult not to think that her own experiences shaped her conception of the City of Ladies and of how a single mother must make her way in the world. Christine de Pizan turned to writing not merely out of necessity but also possibility.

Bibliographic Note

For this essay, I have used Earl Jeffrey Richards' translation of *La Cité des Dames, The Book of the City of Ladies* (New York: Persea Books, 1982), and Sarah Lawson's translation of *Le Livre du Trésor de la Cité des Dames, The Treasure of the City of Ladies*, rev. ed. (London: Penguin Books, 2003). Christine McWebb's collection, *Debating the Roman de la Rose: A Critical*

Anthology (New York: Routledge, 2007), brings together most of Christine's contributions to the debates surrounding *The Romance of the Rose*, as well as those of her supporters and opponents.

Although there is still no critical edition of Christine's complete works, nor, for that matter, have all of her works been translated into English, she has been the subject of much academic interest for several decades now. Charity Cannon Willard, *Christine de Pizan: Her Life and Works* (New York: Persea Books, 1984), remains the best general introduction to Christine. Rosalind Brown-Gant, *Christine de Pizan and the Moral Defense of Women: Reading Beyond Gender* (Cambridge: Cambridge University Press, 1999), offers one of the most sustained and interesting analyses of Christine's critique of misogyny. See also the three very good collections of essays devoted to Christine's life and work: *Reinterpreting Christine de Pizan* eds. Earl Jeffrey Richards *et al.* (Athens: University of Georgia Press, 1992); *The City of Scholars: New Approaches to Christine de Pizan* eds. Margarete Zimmermann and Dina de Rentiis, (Berlin: Walter de Gruyter, 1994); and *Christine de Pizan: A Casebook* eds. Barbara K. Altmann and Deborah L. McGrady, (New York: Routledge, 2003).

Christine not only wrote her books, but she involved herself in all aspects of their production. James Laidlow, "Christine and the Manuscript Tradition," in *Christine de Pizan: A Casebook* (cited above), 231–49, describes how Christine worked with her copyists and illustrators.

TWENTY-SIX

Why Margery Kempe is Annoying and Why We Should Care

Clementine Oliver

This chapter is not about Margery Kempe. So many scholars have written so many important books and articles about her that any attempt to distill the meaning of her life down to a few pages would be ineffectual. Instead, this chapter is about how we, as students of the Middle Ages, react to this Englishwoman from the late fourteenth and early fifteenth centuries and what we can discover about her world from our own subjective responses to her actions and words. Her life and experiences, available to us in a book she dictated to a scribe, are unquestionably provocative. This is a woman who, after having borne 14 children, convinces her husband to live chastely, eroticizes Christ, travels to both Rome and Jerusalem, and once back in England is arrested and nearly burned at the stake for her unorthodox behavior.

It is important to consider the sort of things that we think and say about Margery's more outrageous moments if only because we might wonder how her contemporaries responded to her: did they feel about her as we do? What did her peers think of her white clothes, her constant weeping, and her refusal to eat meat? How did she manage to get away with such outlandish behavior? And did she get away unscathed? Such questions are departure points for a broader discussion about the complex social world of the later Middle Ages. One of the most common reactions of first-time readers is to ask, "What is wrong with this woman?" This question is inevitably followed by, "Why does she cry so much?" And the more outspoken reader might also wonder, "How does her husband put up with her?"

Such questions are implicit criticisms of Margery's behavior and therefore raise the concern that readers of this fifteenth-century text will be left with the impression that the end of the Middle Ages was brought on by bouts of hysteria that could only be quieted by the cooler heads of the Renaissance. And there is possibly something to this notion, for if one were to say anything definitive about Margery Kempe, it is that her book shows us that the Middle Ages did not just fade away, that the later Middle Ages were not a period of cultural decline. On the contrary, the later Middle Ages were punctuated with the same kind of emotional energy (if not exactly spiritual creativity) that we tend to displace onto the Renaissance and Reformation.

So how then might one think about such questions and criticisms of Margery from first-time readers? Perhaps by admitting that they are truthful. Margery is annoying; she does cry too much; and it is difficult to imagine, despite the rather touching negotiations between them (11), how her husband puts up with her. Such criticisms of Margery's behavior are important because they best approach the reaction of her peers and so provide readers an easy entry into her world. For example, we are offered a glimpse of her fellow pilgrims' frustration with her behavior. The text records that "they were most annoyed because she wept so much and spoke all the time about the love and goodness of our Lord, as much at table as in other places. And so they rebuked her shamefully and chided her harshly, and said they would not put up with her as her husband did when she was at home in England." (26) It is difficult to love Margery because it is far too easy to empathize with her companions, but we must also consider further the repercussions and implications of her relationship with her peers, for to do so permits us to see the complexity and the rich network of social relations at the end of the Middle Ages.

Conversely, to indulge our reactions to Margery's text precludes some of the traditional approaches to her book offered by scholars, such as the usually obligatory discussion of Margery as a woman or Margery as a part of a female spiritual tradition in the later Middle Ages. Despite the many attempts by scholars to prove otherwise, it is actually quite difficult to determine just how much we can learn about the lives of late medieval English women from Margery's book. This is because most of the characters that inhabit Margery's world are men, for she was an active participant in public and social spaces shaped primarily by men, as opposed to typically female domestic spaces or the reclusive space of the convent. In other

words, as Margery was not content to stay at home, she had frequent interactions with men. Indeed, during the course of her travels she seems to
encounter very few women from her own peer group and even fewer who
are not openly hostile to her — most treat her with scorn, as do the women
she encounters in Rome, who taunt her for switching her clothing from
white to black at her confessor's command (34). Certainly the predominantly male characters that populate the book reinforce some commonly
held assumptions regarding the status of gender relations in late medieval
England; because Margery did not assume the usual female roles of housewife or nun, her only alternatives were either to live alone or to live in a
world predominantly of men.

We should proceed with greater caution when drawing such a sharp
line between the worlds of women and men in this period. Some scholars
have documented nicely that economic necessity often dictated or over-
turned convention, for housewife and nun were not the only options for
women at this time. Women routinely engaged in a wide variety of economic activities both within and outside their homes to supplement their
family incomes. They baked bread and brewed beer on a large scale. They
worked on other people's land for wages. They spun thread to sell to
weavers. Some worked as servants in other households; many more were
in the business of loaning money. Even "housewives" were visible, important, and active participants in public life, particularly in the marketplace.
Thus, the use of the term "housewife" is itself misleading. We are better off
thinking of women as significant contributors to the household economy,
for the household was the center of economic production and consump-
tion for the vast majority of people in this period. Indeed, Margery herself
engages in many of these activities before she commits to her spiritual life.

Why then does the *Book of Margery Kempe* make such infrequent reference to other women? The answer lies with Margery herself, for it is
equally plausible that men populate Margery's book by choice. She herself
seems to have disliked secular women — they did little to help her achieve
the status she wanted and served only to remind her of what she was supposed to be — a devoted wife or mother — or to remind her of her failed
worldly ambitions, such as her attempt at operating a brewery (2). Instead,
her book focuses primarily on those holy women who kept company with
Christ, for she is preoccupied with these women to the exclusion of nearly
everyone and everything else, except Christ himself. In this sense Margery
is not unlike Anne Baxter's character of Eve Harrington in the cinematic

classic *All About Eve,* a woman whose obsession with stepping into the shoes of the great Broadway star Margo Channing (played by Bette Davis) obscures all rational processes. This seemingly unconventional comparison provides us a window on our own often emotionally charged responses to Margery's motivations and actions, for it suggests just how disruptive and destructive her behavior is perceived to be by those driven only by the mundane concerns of everyday life. For similar reasons, to consider her as part of a larger tradition of spiritual women serves to isolate her from the world at large, thereby isolating her from us and fixing her book as a fleeting historical moment. Instead, we ought to incorporate her into a survey of the history of the much broader world of writers and readers, for this is where she hoped to find a place for herself.

Let us think of Margery as a public figure, if for no other reason than because she excels at exposing the private to public scrutiny. Consider, for example, the passage in which she reveals to a highly respected widow that her deceased husband is languishing in purgatory for some unspecified sin, the implication being that neither the widow nor her husband was nearly as respectable as their neighbors had been led to believe (19). In another passage, she confronts a hostile monk with the information that she knows that he has sinned with wives. The monk is suitably chastened by this revelation and gives her both dinner and gold for her to pray for him (12). These encounters remind us that Margery is a conspicuous participant in both the secular and spiritual spheres. In each, she strives to expose the private lives of individuals to public scrutiny, thereby not only disrupting the social order but also gaining ground for herself in the process. By doing so, she helps us to see more clearly notions of public and private in the later Middle Ages, categories that were becoming charged with a new significance as they were exposed to the pressures of increasing social mobility and gentrification in the fifteenth century.

Margery was born around the year 1373, but most of the events in her book take place in the early decades of the fifteenth century, a period paradoxically characterized by both economic recession and rising expectations for upward social mobility within many segments of society. In conjunction with this, there is an insidious sort of social conservatism, to which Margery is subject, that comes along with such rising expectations that are too often overlooked by many historians of the Lancastrian era (the period ushered in by Henry IV's usurpation of the throne in 1399). During Margery's lifetime an abrupt shift occurred in the religious tolerance of England, marked by the first burning of a lollard, William Sautre, in 1401.

Lollards were initially nothing more than the followers of the radical intellectual Oxford theologian John Wyclif, who during the course of the late 1370s published several anti-clerical and reformist religious treatises that were eventually condemned by the Church. As these anti-clerical ideas spread over the course of the next two decades among the many non-academic factions in England discontented with the Church, the designation of lollard became a pejorative catchall for a wide range of heretical beliefs and practices. The threats made against Margery by those who call her a false lollard contained an element of physical danger that was not present in the late fourteenth century. No wonder her body trembled and quaked dreadfully (13).

The life contained in this book is, of course, significant in other ways. The *Book of Margery Kempe* is often said to be the earliest known autobiography written in English. This claim seems to have remained current, though as she makes clear in the proem, Margery herself could not read or write and had to go to great lengths to find someone to perform these tasks for her. So, while her book is not an autobiography in the strict sense of Augustine's *Confessions* or the memoirs of Guibert of Nogent, the term "autobiography" best captures the spirit of Margery's project, a testament to just how much a woman who was seemingly illiterate felt the need to have a book written about her life. There are several very specific reasons for her to feel this way, and we shall consider them momentarily, but here it is particularly important to point out that Margery's determination to record her experiences in a book occurs nearly 40 years before the technology of printing was introduced to England by William Caxton in 1476. It is almost as though she knew that with the advent of the printing press there would be an ever-growing readership out there that she must reach and that her book would give to her what even the ability to wear white clothes could not: it would recontextualize her. She would be like Saint Bridget, the fourteenth-century Swedish saint whose book recounting her visions of Christ was wildly popular in late medieval England. The book of Saint Bridget — "Saint Bride's" book — is one of the main reasons that Margery wanted her own story written down, but her desire to be part of a literate world transcends her simple emulation of Bridget, in part because Bridget was educated in a way that Margery was not. Despite that fact, or simply because Margery dictated her story, her voice is so direct that she cannot help but to expose her own desperate attempt to be part of a literate world, revealed by the lists of texts she mentions repeatedly but first in Chapter 17: "Saint Bride's book, Hilton's book, Bonaventura's *Stimulus Amoris, Incendium Amoris,* and others similar." I think her reference to these popular devotional texts is not only one of the most interesting things about Margery but also one of the most important, for they shape her vision of her place in the world to such an extent that even the cutting words of her companions do little to circumscribe her behavior.

Readers of Margery's book should consider this vernacular text not only as an important late medieval text but also as a bridge to the world born after the printing press. Certainly, Margery herself belongs to an historical tradition of medieval women writers and mystics, but pointing this out doesn't make it any easier to tolerate her, and furthermore it doesn't do her justice. Margery was ambitious in a way that someone like Bridget was not, and it is this combination of ambition, emotion, self-interest, and self-reflection that links her with the world of print. She has as much in common with someone like the great sixteenth-century essayist Michel de Montaigne as she does with the thirteenth-century beguine Marie of Oignies—a woman whose spiritual visions also made her weep uncontrollably—for Montaigne too is bent on exposing the private to public scrutiny and so reveals to his readers the supposed boundaries between the two just at the moment he is blurring them. Margery's greatest gift is to make us consider the prehistory of the print revolution, the immense and uncontainable energy of the vernacular world of literate and semi-literate individuals with rising expectations. These are individuals who wanted to use the vernacular and, more specifically, the written vernacular to recast their relationship with the commonality at large. They could not wait for the arrival of William Caxton and his printing press to begin this project. This is what the culture of the later Middle Ages is all about, and this is precisely why Margery's book is such a wonderful way to close out a course on the Middle Ages. She is as much about beginnings as about endings.

Having said this, it is necessary to return to the subject of lollards in the early fifteenth century, primarily because the accusations of lollardy against Margery were likely the greatest obstacle to her achieving the recognition she desired. Margery well knew that if she were successfully labeled a lollard, not only might she lose her life, but her story would not find its place among those devotional works she cites. Of course the most curious thing about these accusations is that that she clearly wasn't a lollard and in fact finds acceptance with one who knew all too well what it meant to be a lollard, Philip Repingdon (15). As a young man, Repingdon had been an early and active Wyclif supporter, but after suffering official condemnation in 1382 he fully recanted his defense of Wyclif and went on to enjoy a lengthy career of service in the Church, culminating in his election as bishop of Lincoln in 1405. It is, incidentally, during Margery's visit with Bishop Repingdon that we see the degree of calculation with which she approaches the idea of a book about her life, for when he counsels her to have her feelings written down, she replies that "it was not God's will that they should be written so soon." Though she is accepted by Repingdon and by the many others who examine her, nevertheless many of the people she encounters on her travels through the towns of Canterbury (13), London (16), Leicester (46–49), York (52), and Beverley (53) call her lollard, or "loller" as it appears in Middle English. Why? Is it because by appropriating this term, those who find her most annoying hope to be able to burn her?

One possible answer that has gained greater currency in recent scholarship is that the meaning of the word lollard or "loller" changed over the course of the late fourteenth and early fifteenth centuries, becoming a more flexible term that could be easily applied to someone like Margery. It no longer just referred to a follower of John Wyclif or even to a heretic. Rather, it had now come to encompass anyone who did not observe the sacraments and social rites that were so important to the average late-medieval Christian; it was particularly applied to someone like Margery who regarded her own spirituality as superior to others. In other words, a lollard now referred to someone whose spiritual practices and attitudes made them unpopular with their community at large.

Precisely because Margery could be accused of such unpopular behavior — because she was guilty of scoffing at her neighbors — she was painted a lollard. Margery repeatedly failed to observe the social rites of fifteenth-century England, and this is precisely the complaint of her companions who do not understand why she won't eat meat (26). She certainly was unpopular, and this is why she was called a lollard. Again, this is parallel with the varieties of criticism frequently offered by readers.

Indeed, in considering the changing meaning of the word "loller," we might think of the boisterous exchange between Geoffrey Chaucer's Harry Bailly and the Parson in the *Canterbury Tales*, the quintessential vernacular representation of late medieval community. Harry, the host of the

Canterbury pilgrims, accuses the Parson of being a "loller," but of course the Parson is not. What does Chaucer's Harry understand to be a "loller?" Perhaps for him, just as for Margery's companions who endured her cryings and disruptive behavior some two decades later, a "loller" was just an annoying person, someone who did not understand that religious discourse had its time and place, and this was certainly not at the dinner table. However, given this interpretation of Margery as an annoying and unpopular individual, should we then conclude that the threats to burn her were simply meant to be a lesson in manners?

It is difficult to know the answer to this question, but in the end, although many townspeople in England called her a lollard, she was not burned. The word does have something of a sticks-and-stones quality about it, but it is the power of threats, and ultimately the power of language, that drives Margery Kempe. Threats are exchanged on both sides: the threat to disrupt, the threat to expel. This is very much what Weronika Patena, an undergraduate at the California Institute of Technology in 2001, observed in a final exam on medieval European history: "Overall, Margery Kempe is a good example of what her society could bear, and what was considered crossing the limits." This is a remarkable statement because it is at once so astute and just a bit off. Margery always crossed the limits. And we can never be sure that society really could bear her, which is perhaps why she kept moving, and why she waited 20 years to fix her story in writing. Somehow, though, she made her contemporaries bear her. She successfully stretched the limits of society, just as I think her book successfully stretches the boundaries of the Middle Ages. And this is the very best reason to read her.

Bibliographic Note

The most accessible translation of *The Book of Margery* remains that of B.A. Windeatt (New York: Penguin Books, 1985). However, Lynn Staley's more recent translation (New York: Norton, 2001) contains indispensable excerpts from relevant primary sources, such as *The Book of Saint Bride* and *The Shewings of Julian of Norwich*, as well as essays from notable scholars. For Margery's life in the original Middle English prose, consult the TEAMS Middle English Text (Kalamazoo, MI: Medieval Institute Publications, 1996), edited by Lynn Staley.

Staley's own book, *Margery Kempe's Dissenting Fictions* (University Park: Pennsylvania State University Press, 1994), is a departure from all other approaches to the text and will leave one with a greater appreciation of the possibilities for interpreting late-medieval women's writing. For a discussion of how Margery operates in the late-medieval world at large, see Clarissa W. Atkinson, *The Book and the World of Margery Kempe* (Ithaca: Cornell University Press, 1983). There are many good essays on Margery, among them Nancy Partner, "Reading the Book of Margery Kempe," *Exemplaria* 3 (1991): 29–66. On the vast subject of late-medieval Christianity, begin with John Bossy, *Christianity in the West* (Oxford: Oxford University Press, 1985). To place Margery's life in an historical and social context, Barbara Hanawalt, *The Ties that Bound: Peasant Families in Medieval England* (Oxford: Oxford University Press, 1986), is useful. All current work on Wyclif and his lollard followers owes a debt of gratitude to Anne Hudson, *Premature Reformation: Wycliffite Texts and Lollard History* (Oxford: Oxford University Press, 1988). On the changing meaning of the word "loller," see Anne Middleton, "Acts of Vagrancy," in *Written Work: Langland, Labor, and Authorship*, ed. Steven Justice and Kathryn Kerby-Fulton (Philadelphia: University of Pennsylvania Press, 1997), 282–84.

Contributors

The contributors to this volume received their doctorates in medieval history at the University of California at Berkeley. Additional details follow.

Judith Beall wrote her dissertation, "Bede and Irish Monasticism," and received her Ph.D. in 1998. She is currently an Adjunct Assistant Professor of History and of Religious Studies at the University of Wisconsin, Milwaukee.

Kathleen Casey received her B.Sc. from the London School of Economics and Political Science. Now retired, she taught gender-based law at Sarah Lawrence College and at UCLA. She is author of "The Cheshire Cat: Reconstructing the Experience of Medieval Women" in B. Carroll, ed., *Liberating Women's History*, and "Women in Norman and Plantagenet England" in B. Kanner, ed., *The Women of England from Anglo-Saxon Times to the Present*.

Katherine Christensen is Associate Professor of History at Berea College, where she teaches medieval and early modern European history, historical methodology, the history of the British Isles, the history of Christianity, and calligraphy. Her own studies concentrate on the medieval church (especially in England), monasticism, and canon law.

Sam Collins received his Ph.D. in 2005. He is currently Assistant Professor of History at George Mason University and at work on a study of the meaning of holy places in the Carolingian world.

Dallas G. Denery II is Associate Professor of History at Bowdoin College. He is the author of *Seeing and Being Seen in the Later Medieval World:*

Optics, Theology and Religious Life (2005) and various essays on medieval religion and philosophy. He is currently writing a history of lying.

Kathleen Stewart Fung completed her Ph.D. in 2006. Her research focuses on the cult of the Virgin Mary in southern France and Iberia. She currently teaches at Virginia Tech and Foothill College.

Jason Glenn is Associate Professor in the Department of History at the University of Southern California. He published *Politics and History in the Tenth Century: The Work and World of Richer of Reims* (2004) and is currently working on its sequel, a study of Frankish kingship and community in the tenth and eleventh centuries.

Jennifer A. Heindl received both her Ph.D. and J.D. from the University of California at Berkeley. She currently works for the federal government in Washington, DC.

Adnan Husain is Associate Professor in Medieval Mediterranean and Islamic World History at Queen's University in Kingston, Ontario. He co-edited (with K.E. Fleming) *A Faithful Sea: Religious Cultures of the Mediterranean (1200–1700)* for a series he edits, "Islam and the West: Influences, Interactions, Intersections," and is author of *Identity Polemics: Encounters with Islam in the Medieval Mediterranean World* (forthcoming).

Lawrence R. Jannuzzi received his J.D. degree from Boalt Hall School of Law in 1987 and his doctorate in 2004. He has been practicing law in San Francisco since 1987, specializing in charitable, nonprofit, and religious organizations. His current research interest is fourteenth-century monastic responses to dominium theory and ecclesiastical disendowment.

Rudi Paul Lindner is Professor of History at the University of Michigan. He teaches comparative medieval history and the history of astrophysics. He recently published *Explorations in Ottoman Prehistory.*

John M. McCulloh is Professor of History at Kansas State University. His scholarship focuses on medieval saints and their cults. He has published several editions and numerous studies of medieval martyrologies, as well as articles on the cult of relics in the transition from Antiquity to the Middle Ages and on the *Life of Saint William of Norwich.*

Susan P. Millinger received her B.A. from Wellesley College in 1964 and her Ph.D. a decade later. She taught briefly at Lakehead University and then for more than 30 years at Roanoke College until her retirement in 2007.

Victoria M. Morse has held a postdoctoral appointment with the History of Cartography Project at the University of Wisconsin, Madison, and a Rome Prize at the American Academy in Rome. She is currently Associate Professor at Carleton College, where she teaches later medieval and Renaissance history. Her research interests include Italian religious history and the history of cartography.

Helen Nader has focused her research on the intellectual, economic, and gender history of Castile from 1350 to 1650, as well as on Christopher Columbus. Her most recent monograph, *Liberty in Absolutist Spain,* won the Gershoy Prize of the American Historical Association for the best book in modern European History. She has taught at the state universities of Hawaii, Indiana, and Arizona and retired from the latter in 2006.

William North is Associate Professor of History at Carleton College. He has published articles on aspects of the Gregorian reform and Ottonian cultural history, as well as intellectual life in eleventh-century Normandy. He is currently at work on several translations for publication, an edition of the exegetical works of Abbot Richard of Préaux, and a study of the relationship between exegesis and institutional reform in the eleventh and early twelfth centuries.

Clementine Oliver is Associate Professor of History at California State University, Northridge. Her research centers on the political culture of late medieval England, with a particular focus on political pamphlets before the printing press and the emergence of the public sphere in the later fourteenth century. She has published *Parliament and Pamphleteering, in Fourteenth-century England* and a number of articles.

Nancy Partner is Professor of History at McGill University. Her most recent publications in medieval history include an edited book, *Writing Medieval History,* and "Christina of Markyate and Theodora of Huntingdon: Narrative Careers" in Robert Stein and Sandra Pierson Prior, eds., *Reading Medieval Culture.* She is working on the *Handbook of Historical Theory* with co-editor Sarah Foot.

Amy G. Remensnyder is Associate Professor of History at Brown University. The author of a book about medieval monasteries in southern France, she is currently finishing a study of the Virgin Mary as symbol of conquest and conversion in medieval Spain and colonial Mexico.

Jay Rubenstein is Associate Professor of History at the University of Tennessee in Knoxville. He is author of the book *Guibert of Nogent, Portrait of a Medieval Mind* and co-editor (with Sally N. Vaughn) of a collection of essays entitled *Teaching and Learning in Northern Europe: 1000–1200.* Currently he is completing a book on the interpretation and impact of the First Crusade in the twelfth century.

Carole Straw is Professor of History at Mount Holyoke College. Her publications include *Gregory the Great: Perfection in Imperfection, Gregory the Great,* and (edited with Richard Lim) *The Past before Us: The New Historiographies of Late Antiquity*; she has also published articles on topics in early church history and is presently completing a book on martyrdom from the early church through the crusades.

John Tuthill received his Ph.D. in 1982 and has taught for many years at the University of Guam. He was a Fulbright Lecturer at the Ukrainian Catholic University in Lviv. Formerly Vice President of the College of the Marshall Islands, he is now Vice President for Academic Affairs and Student Services at Truckee Meadows Community College in Reno, Nevada.

Index